DATE DUE

DEC – 5 1994			
MAY 2 4 1995			
DEC – 6 1995			
MAR 1 0 1997			
FEB 1 3 2001			
MAR 4 2001			
MAR 1 9 2002			

DEMCO 38-297

Human Resource Planning

McGraw Hill Series in Management

Keith Davis and Fred Luthans, *Consulting Editors*

Allen: Management and Organization
Allen: The Management Profession
Argyris: Management and Organizational Development: The Path from XA to YB
Beckett: Management Dynamics: The New Synthesis
Benton: Supervision and Management
Brown: Judgment in Administration
Buchele: The Management of Business and Public Organizations
Campbell, Dunnette, Lawler, and Weick: Managerial Behavior, Performance, and Effectiveness
Cleland and King: Management: A Systems Approach
Cleland and King: Systems Analysis and Project Management
Cleland and King: Systems, Organizations, Analysis, Management: A Book of Readings
Dale: Management: Theory and Practice
Dale: Readings in Management: Landmarks and New Frontiers
Davis: Human Behavior at Work: Organizational Behavior
Davis: Organizational Behavior: A Book of Readings
Davis, Frederick, and Blomstrom: Business and Society: Concepts and Policy Issues
DeGreene: Systems Psychology
Dunn and Rachel: Wage and Salary Administration: Total Compensation Systems
Edmunds and Letey: Environmental Administration
Fiedler: A Theory of Leadership Effectiveness
Finch, Jones, and Litterer: Managing for Organizational Effectiveness: An Experiential Approach
Flippo: Personnel Management
Glueck: Business Policy and Strategic Management
Glueck: Readings in Business Policy from *Business Week*
Hampton: Contemporary Management
Hicks and Gullett: The Management of Organizations
Hicks and Gullett: Modern Business Management: A Systems and Environmental Approach
Hicks and Gullett: Organizations: Theory and Behavior
Johnson, Kast, and Rosenzweig: The Theory and Management of Systems
Kast and Rosenzweig: Experiential Exercises and Cases in Management
Kast and Rosenzweig: Organization and Management: A Systems and Contingency Approach
Knudson, Woodworth, and Bell: Management: An Experiential Approach
Koontz: Toward a Unified Theory of Management
Koontz and O'Donnell: Essentials of Management

Human Resource Planning

James W. Walker
Towers, Perrin, Forster & Crosby

McGraw-Hill Book Company

New York St. Louis San Francisco Auckland Bogotá Hamburg
Johannesburg London Madrid Mexico Montreal New Delhi
Panama Paris São Paulo Singapore Sydney Tokyo Toronto

This book was set in Times Roman by Black Dot, Inc. (ECU).
The editors were John F. Carleo and James R. Belser.
The production supervisor was Richard A. Ausburn.
The drawings were done by Danmark & Michaels, Inc.
The cover was designed by Scott Chelius.
Fairfield Graphics was printer and binder.

HUMAN RESOURCE PLANNING

Copyright © 1980 by McGraw-Hill, Inc. All rights reserved. Printed in the United States
of America. No part of this publication may be reproduced, stored in a retrieval system, or
transmitted, in any form or by any means, electronic, mechanical, photocopying,
recording, or otherwise, without the prior written permission of the publisher.

3 4 5 6 7 8 9 0 FGRFGR 8 9 8 7 6 5 4 3 2

Library of Congress Cataloging in Publication Data

Walker, James W.   date
    Human resource planning.

    Bibliography: p.
    Includes index.
    1. Personnel management.   2. Manpower planning.
I. Title.
HF5549.W3116   658.3   79-21956
ISBN 0-07-067840-5

Contents

2

NEEDS FORECASTING

3

PERFORMANCE MANAGEMENT

4

CAREER MANAGEMENT

5
CONCLUSION

Preface

There are many books on human resource management (personnel administration, industrial relations, etc.), but few on *planning* for human resource management. Concepts, research, theories, and techniques are abundant in the literature and are valuable to both the manager and the academician. However, the plethora of changes occurring in the legal, economic, social, and organizational environments calls for special attention to the analysis of human resource requirements of organizations and the related needs for management policies, programs, and resources to satisfy these requirements. Human resource planning represents this process.

This text discusses many basic aspects of human resource management, but from the unique perspective of *change*. The planning dimension permits the manager (and the reader) to reconsider existing assumptions and practices and to chart new courses of action to meet future demands. In some areas, of course, new waters are uncharted, such as future demands of age discrimination and equal employment opportunity laws, or of continuing rampant inflation for a decade or more in the future. Yet human resource planning equips the management of an organization to assess the likely future conditions that will affect its human resource practices, and to act to anticipate and prepare for them.

There are four areas of human resource planning covered in this book, and each comprises a set of related chapters. First, Part One examines these dynamic forces just mentioned in relation to management concerns and human resource staff roles. Following is Part Two on needs forecasting. Long considered the essence of "manpower" or "personnel" planning, the analysis and forecasting of demands for talent and the availability of talent provide a basic set of planning tools. Part Three examines the issues and approaches concerning performance management, including organizational performance (or productivity), individual performance, and compensation. Finally, Part Four details issues, practices, and opportunities concerning career planning, career development, and manage- ment succession.

The book is intended for use both in advanced courses in personnel and human resource management and as a guide for the human resource planning professional. It is pragmatic in orientation, without being a "how to" book. It is a reference to the literature relevant to human resource planning, but it is not an exhaustive research review. Having moved from teaching (Indiana University and San Diego State University) to management consulting (TPF&C) and again to teaching (Arizona State University) and back to consulting, I believe that a textbook on this subject must be relevant to both classroom and "real world" needs. It is a difficult balance to strike, but an aim of this book.

I am indebted to many professional colleagues for their assistance, ideas, guidance, and encouragement in my discovery of what human resource planning is all about. Particular appreciation is due Robert Armes, my coworker at TPF&C, for his vigorous help in wrestling with so many of the difficult issues discussed in this book. Thanks are due to our numerous clients, who gave us the opportunity to help develop approaches to resolving human resource issues that had become important in their organizations. And I am indebted to my many other colleagues at TPF&C for their interest and support as this dimension of TPF&C's services has grown. The views presented in this book, however, must be considered my own, and do not necessarily represent those of the firm. I also assume responsibility for any errors of fact, judgment, or opinion. I am quite sure there are errors of omission in this first broad-scopework, and for these I apologize.

In writing this book I have recognized the profound impact that my mentors have had on my professional interests and opportunities to pursue them. I am deeply indebted to them for their inspiration, guidance, and assistance: Glen R. Smith and Warren A. Sappington (Millikin University); George C. Hoyt, Henry Albers, and Max S. Wortman, Jr. (formerly at the University of Iowa); Bill Reed and Thomas B. Porter (American Oil Company); and David R. Hampton (San Diego State University).

Finally, I would like to thank Harriet for her help and Molly for sleeping quietly under my desk.

James W. Walker

Human Resource Planning

Part One

Introduction

Chapter 1

Managerial Concerns and Practices

KEY POINTS

- Human resource issues are of substantial and increasing importance in the management of large organizations.
- Human resource planning is the process of identifying and responding to these issues, and charting new policies, systems, and programs that will assure effective human resource management under changing conditions.
- While certain professional staff roles have evolved in human resource planning, the process remains largely a line management activity, linked to ongoing business planning.
- Forecasting human resource needs is a central aspect of the process and involves anticipation of changing staffing and organizational requirements.
- Performance management involves the planning and implementing of programs for improving overall productivity through organization of work activities, appraisal and development of individual competencies, performance planning and appraisal, and compensation practices.
- Career management provides a coordinated process of recruitment, selection and placement, promotion and transfer, training and development, and other actions influencing individual career plans and development. An important focus is on the development of careers of high-talent managerial employees.

The management of human resources is an increasingly important concern in large organizations. Issues include the availability of talent needed to staff planned business growth, the quality of managerial talent, and the control of tremendous costs now associated with managing a large high-talent work force. Specific concerns that have become senior management concerns include:

Shortages of specialized technical talent needed to staff specific programs for business expansion (for example, petroleum engineers).

Shortages of broadly experienced and tested managers, both to manage new and expanding operations with large capital investment and to progress to senior executive responsibilities.

The substantial costs of implementing reductions in force or layoffs, of relocating employees great distances, of recruiting talent at high salary levels (with associated search fees), and other human resource management actions. Personnel costs are critical.

Demands imposed on management practices by external forces such as affirmative action program requirements, and the threat of substantial costs associated with settlements in discrimination suits.

Improvement of productivity, particularly at the professional and managerial levels. Control over the work being performed and over performance itself is considered a necessary objective if a business is to remain competitive and vigorous.

Providing career opportunities and a working environment that will attract, motivate, and retain the quality of talent needed.

Such concerns have given rise to new human resource management practices, as well as bringing a new dimension to the work of the personnel function in many organizations. For example, the human resources department in one corporation has swelled fourfold in recent years, to provide new functions mandated by a flood of governmental regulations, more complex personnel administration tasks, and the development and implementation of a planning system linking human resource programs with corporate strategies. The chief executive officer and the senior operating officers look to the department for assistance in anticipating needs and implementing programs that will meet these needs. "Management realizes that its important assets are not simply financial resources but having the people on hand at the right time and in the right place to make a thing go," observed a human resource staff director.

The attention being given human resource planning represents a broadening of the dimensions of the personnel function and the involvement of operating managers in personnel matters. New programs and systems are being developed and installed by staffs, in response to evolving organizational needs, and the roles played by personnel staff professionals are changing, becoming more heavily directed to consulting and problem-solving roles. But the major change is taking place among operating executives and middle-level managers, in the form of an increased awareness of and interest in human resource planning issues: forecasting future needs, career management, and performance management.

ABOUT THIS BOOK

This book provides a definition of the issues concerning management and of the techniques that may be applied to resolve these issues effectively. *Human resource planning* is viewed as a management process, not as merely a piece of the personnel staff function. It is, in essence, the process of *analyzing an organization's human resource needs under changing conditions and developing the activities necessary to satisfy these needs.* As will be discussed, certain professional roles and functions in human resource planning have emerged in organizations, but the thrust of this book is the definition of the work involved in the human resource planning process itself and not so much the differentiation of staff and line functions in implementing the process.

The book has a practical emphasis and contains many illustrations of techniques and applications. There is less consideration of research or theory than might be found in some textbooks, and more attention to the ways human resource planning can actually be implemented in organizations. For this reason, the book will be useful as a reference handbook to managers and human resource planning professionals.

In this first chapter, the origins and evolution of human resource planning practices are examined. This provides a historical perspective of current practices and concerns and also points the way toward future directions in human resource planning in the decades ahead. The purpose of the chapter is to address the question "Why human resource planning?" and to provide an initial definition of the elements of the process.

ORIGINS AND EVOLUTION

Human resource planning has been a function of management since the origins of modern industrial organization. Economist Alfred Marshall observed in 1890 that "the head of a business must assure himself that his managers, clerks, and foremen are the right men for their work and are doing their work well." Division of labor, specialization, organization of management into levels, work simplification, and application of standards for selecting employees and measuring their performance were all principles applied early in industrial management. They were also applied in large nonindustrial organizations, including religious, governmental, and military organizations.

Planning for the staffing of work to be done is not a recent notion. The relatively sophisticated techniques available to management today are the outcome of a long period of evolution in practices, beginning decades ago with simple, pragmatic, short-term planning. As shown in Exhibit 1-1, the techniques used by management tended to fit contemporary conditions and events. During

Exhibit 1-1   The Evolution of Human Resource Planning

Periods and emphasis	Conditions and events	Techniques introduced or emphasized
1900–1940 Work engineering Hourly personnel	Search for efficiency in production Labor intensive, unskilled Modern work organization, division of labor, professional management Union movement Depression years	Task measurement/simplification Output-related incentive pay Testing for employee selection Skills training Payroll budgeting and control Manning tables for workloads Labor relations Welfare programs
1940–1960 Productivity and continuity Hourly/managerial	Talent shortage due to war Emphasis on productivity for wartime and postwar demand Increased mechanization, automation Job satisfaction/productivity studies	Organization charting Management backup charting for replacements University executive development programs Work group effectiveness and leadership style changes Workload forecasting using ratios and regression analysis Attitude surveys, human relations programs
1960s Balancing supply and demand Managerial, professional, and technical employees	Sputnik-stimulated demand for high-talent personnel Age 30 to 40 gap; shortage of scientists and engineers Rapid organizational expansion and diversification Multinational expansion Rapid technological change, risking obsolescence Civil Rights Act Student/youth activisim Vietnam war	Intense college recruitment Fast-track programs; career ladders Skills inventories Matrix organizations Assessment centers Disadvantaged/hard core programs Formalized forecasting activity Experiments with mathematical models Job enrichment projects Performance goal-setting
1970s Affirmative action Salaried employees, particularly the protected classes	Court- and government-imposed goals and timetables New legislation (OSHA, age discrimination, ERISA, privacy, etc.) Slowing of business expansion Concern for retention, utilization of present staff; cost control Women's liberation movement "Discovery" of midlife crisis Energy crisis	Models used in setting AA goals Computer-based information systems Human resource planning functions established Human resource analysis related to business planning and budgeting Assessment of human resource costs and benefits Early retirement and outplacement Quality of work life and productivity programs "Zero-base" budgeting Broadening of managerial development (multifunctional) Job posting/bidding systems

Exhibit 1-1   The Evolution of Human Resource Planning *(continued)*

Periods and emphasis	Conditions and events	Techniques introduced or emphasized
1980s	Consolidation of federal law governing personnel practices and administration	Job-related criteria for personnel decisions (hires, promotions, pay, terminations, etc.)
Work and career management	Aging of the work force Competition among young managers for responsibility	Individual career planning Work analysis a tool for designing jobs, forecasting needs, organization, etc.
All employees	Accelerated unionization of professionals and managers Expansion of adult education Stronger pressures for egalitarian practices in pay and employment Participation in management more commonplace Increased pressures on human resources for cost control and profit contribution	Flexible work schedules Direct use of computer systems; development of flexible models Clarification of management commitments in human resource management; policy changes
1990s and beyond 2000 Individual autonomy within large-scale work organizations All employees	Energy, food, other resource shortages Limited work available; increased leisure time Stress on family, privacy, personal independence Extended life expectancy, improved health Legislation governing pensions, health insurance, and lifetime income security Political/social challenge to large institutions; drive for individual freedom, autonomy, and recognition	Reshaping of work environments and customs Work sharing; reduced work week Extended vacations, sabbaticals Job matching/career guidance by government and employers New careers in emerging fields of communications, health, energy sciences, etc. Measurement and auditing of human resource changes as part of management accounting

the first part of this century, for example, the focus in manpower planning was upon the hourly production worker. The aim of improving efficiency through work engineering and early industrial psychology applications was consistent with the need to improve productivity and introduce greater objectivity to personnel practices (Ling, 1965; Merrill, 1959; Yoder, 1952).

During World War II and the post-war years the focus intensified on employee productivity. Concern also was great regarding the availability of competent managerial personnel, as there was a talent shortage in combination with significant demand for goods and services. New technologies and interest in behavioral aspects of work also added complexities to the manpower planning task.

1960s

Expanded demand for high-talent personnel resulted in the 1960s from high-technology programs (the space race) and rapid corporate expansion and diversification. In response, manpower planning practices were focused on balancing supply with demand, particularly demand for managerial, profession-al, and technical personnel. The demographic shortage of men aged 30 to 40 and shortages of specific engineering and scientific skills were noteworthy during this period. Textbooks which were written during the latter part of the decade document well these conditions and concerns; manpower planning was viewed as a system linking the organization with its environment (Patten, 1969; Vetter, 1967).

The prevailing view of manpower planning at that time, which has dominated the literature ever since, was that "companies forecast their needs for manpower into the future, forecast their internal labor supply for meeting these needs, and identify the gaps between what will be needed and what will be available." Manpower planners develop plans for recruiting, selecting, and placing new employees; provide for training and development; and anticipate necessary promotions and transfers (Buráck and Walker, 1972; Geisler, 1967; Heneman and Seltzer, 1968; Wikstrom, 1971).

At TRW manpower planning was considered a necessary process for allocation of scarce resources.

> Manpower planning has as its prime objective the effective utilization of scarce or abundant talent in the interest of the individual employee and the company. In its broadest sense, it is a matter of anticipating the future business environment and pattern of organization, and then relating manpower requirements to these conditions. They are first stated grossly and then further defined in terms of disciplines, skills, and qualifications, all of which are related to time. Realistic plans for recruitment and development of the manpower resource are made after consideration of the external and internal factors affecting the manpower objectives of each organizational unit. I think that if we are going to anticipate future conditions in terms of business environment or organization or the skills we need and then try to do something constructive about it, we have indeed a number of problems to which we can address ourselves (White, 1967).

1970s

With new legislation, court decisions, and governmental regulations, manage-ment attention turned in the 1970s to affirmative action planning and other aspects of compliance. While many companies adopted the techniques that had been introduced by leading companies during the previous decades, others experimented with such new tools as career planning, activity analysis, and reshaping of work.

Most companies, however, were concerned primarily about compliance with the significant new regulations governing discrimination, safety, and pensions. Attention was also directed toward the updating and refinement of salary administration practices to ensure competitive and motivational compensation in an era of rapid inflation. Generally, it was an unsettled decade, during which managers coped with the energy crisis, uncertain costs and profits, the slowing of business expansion, and heightened employee anxieties about women's liberation, reverse discrimination, and the "midlife crisis."

However, during these years, "manpower" planning—now broadly termed "human resource" planning—became widely established as a staff activity in major business and governmental organizations. The term "human resource planning" implied a scope broader than merely supply-demand balancing or quantitative forecasting. The new term shifted attention from these parts of the process, although recognizing their importance, to the more comprehensive view of the process encompassing both needs forecasting and program planning. Also, the term "human resource" gained favor as a way to minimize the sexist implication of *man*power and to emphasize the positive view of personnel as a basic corporate *resource*.

State of the Art

In the 1980s there may be less new legislation, but administration and enforcement of laws will likely be strengthened and diverse regulations affecting company human resource practices will be consolidated. At the same time, employee desires for participation in decisions that affect their work and careers will become stronger, as will management desires for improved control over costs and profitability. As a result, companies will adopt work and career management practices of the type reflected in innovations under affirmative action programs. Needs forecasting, work/job analysis, and career planning will become commonplace.

Beyond 1990 and the turn of the century, practices considered radical today will likely become conventional. For example, job sharing, reduced working hours, and significant reshaping of work and work customs (such as not going to an office) are all projected. It is possible that the government will have more direct involvement in matching individuals with jobs, both across organizations and within organizations under "equal opportunity" objectives. The conditions anticipated by futurists indicate continued work force expansion, limited availability of work, and strong desires for individual autonomy within large and complex work organizations (Dunnette, 1973).

Techniques and practices have therefore been developed and applied to satisfy needs resulting from managerial concerns and, indirectly, from economic, social, and technological changes in the environment. The state-of-the-art practices applied in a few leading organizations indicate emerging needs and priorities that may ultimately affect many organizations (Churchill and Shank, 1976; Grinold and Marshall, 1976). For example, Sears, Bank of America, AT&T, and General Motors have led the way in developing advanced career management techniques, in part because of their EEO and affirmative action commitments. Many other organizations, including retailers, banks, utilities, and large manufacturers, have not felt the same degree of pressure to move so boldly into broad new programs. It takes time for the majority of organizations to catch up to the leading edge of practice, as they come to feel the pressures felt earlier by others (Walker, 1974).

THE CONTEMPORARY APPROACH

Effective human resource planning is a process of analyzing an organization's human resource needs under changing conditions and developing the activities necessary to satisfy these needs. It is essentially a two-step process, as shown in Exhibit 1-2. The emphasis is on responsiveness to needs emerging within and outside the organization, and not on techniques or systems to be applied. The forecasting of needs allows the determining of priorities and allocating of resources where they can do the most good.

Analysis of needs leads to the planning of programs to be conducted. While the activities and programs may run the gamut of human resource management, the emphasis of new programs tends to be on areas relating directly to current issues. During the seventies and eighties, three basic areas appear to be of primary concern to management. These concerns reflect issues identified in the above discussion of changing conditions and events:

Needs forecasting: improved planning and control over staffing and organizational requirements, based on analysis of conditions

Performance management: improving the performance of individuals and of the organization as a whole

Career management: activities to select, assign, develop, and otherwise manage individual careers in an organization

In focusing on these areas, the contemporary approach to human resource planning establishes a link between the broad range of external and organizational factors, on the one hand, and specific personnel programs on the other. The planning approach defines human resource needs in the context of the organization's overall needs and defines a strategy by which they will be satisfied. In this way, individual development, recruitment, compensation, and other activities become integral parts of a dynamic process. Training programs, for example, are no longer warranted if they are not shown to be pertinent to prevailing skill or knowledge needs. College recruitment is tailored to satisfy specific forecasted needs.

Effective Human Resource Planning

Many techniques are used in human resource planning, and refinements have been made through years of applications and research. But the crux of human resource planning is neither a particular set of techniques nor their relative sophistication, but the capacity to help managers anticipate and meet changing needs relating to the acquisition, deployment, and utilization of people.

Exhibit 1-2   The Human Resource Planning Process

1. Needs Forecasting

Analysis of external conditions
- Economic, social, political
    factors
- Government and legislation
- Population and work force
- Markets and competition
- Technologies

Future human resource requirements
- Organization and job design
- Plans and budgets
- Management policies and philosophy
- Technologies and systems
- Affirmative action/EEO goals and plans

Future human resource availability
- Current inventory of talent
- Forecasted attrition
- Forecasted movement and development
- Effects of past human resource
    programs

Forecast of human resource needs
- Immediate and longer term
- External hiring needs
- Reductions and reallocations
- Improved utilization
- Development

2. Program Planning

Performance management
- Organization
    Activities
    Relationships
    Responsibilities
    Standards
    Quality of work life
    (climate)

- Performance appraisal
    Performance plans
      and goals
    Coaching
    Evaluation
- Reward structures
    Compensation
    Benefits

Career management
- Policies and systems
    Recruitment
    Selection and placement
    Promotion and transfer
    Development and training
    Termination or retirement

- Management succession
    Individual assessment
    Position requirements
    Replacement charting
    Succession planning
    Tracking career progress
- Career opportunities
    Job requirements
    Career paths
    Career communications
- Individual career planning
    Self-analysis
    Personal career plans
    Development action plans

For example, a study of manpower planning practices in 775 local and state governments observed that some organizations designed and implemented manpower planning systems in an effort to provide initiative in management.

> Actually, these systems are combinations of new tools which, when properly coordinated and combined with manpower information, may be used to evaluate current issues, anticipate future circumstances, and design relevant program alternatives. Such "systems" facilitate the hiring, development, and efficient utilization of the right number of people, with the required skills and skill levels (District of Columbia, 1973).

Effectivenness of human resource planning largely depends on how *relevant* it is to *practical* managerial concerns and practices and, in turn, to the demands prevailing upon an organization. Professor Larry Moore observes,

> Benefits associated with effective manpower (human resource) planning and management include, for example, the identification of sources of manpower which are likely to provide sufficient numbers of employees having the appropriate levels of training and appropriate patterns of work attitudes, the development of a system for providing a suitable worker-job "fit", and the capability of integrating important elements of manpower planning into the overall corporate planning system in the organization. As a concept, manpower planning rests on two notions—integration and analysis (Moore, 1975).

An Integrative Process

Decisions in different parts of an organization or in different functional areas are brought into the same planning framework. Termination of employees for poor performance cannot logically follow sizable bonus awards or salary increases for these individuals. Laying off employees in one quarter while recruiting comparable employees in another would also be avoided. All programs are measured against affirmative action plans and against the other tests of necessity.

The contemporary approach also features a strong link between individual goals and plans and those of the organization. Historically, programs have been designed to meet organizational needs. But in the years ahead, it will be increasingly important to balance organizational needs with needs of employees and society in general. Employee career interests, relocation preferences, and development plans will be weighed in needs forecasting. Societal pressures for disclosure of company policies and practices for hiring of minorities, job sharing, more flexible work schedules, and other new programs will also be evaluated. In the future, what is considered good for individuals may be what is considered good for the company as well.

Above all, human resource planning is pragmatic. Each program is evaluated on the basis of needs, costs, and expected benefits. In many instances, the needs, costs, and benefits are not directly measurable, but they must be considered, nevertheless. Human resource management is clearly not an isolated staff function, nor human resource planning a staff exercise. Line managers and staff share the responsibility of accurate assessment of needs and for the effective planning and implementation of programs to meet these needs.

Chapters 2 and 3 in this book examine the external environmental factors and the internal organizational factors that both impel and constrain effective human resource planning. The former identifies the various legal, social, demographic, technological, and economic factors impacting the management of an organization. Additionally, the chapter provides a logical structure for studying changes in environmental conditions affecting human resource planning. The latter chapter considers the obstacles often encountered in bringing about changes in human resource practices in a company and provides guidelines for the gradual introduction of change and the roles of an effective human resource function in relation to management.

NEEDS FORECASTING

Few executives today are not concerned about controlling personnel costs. In an era of continuing inflation, rapidly rising costs, and increased competitive pressures on profits, personnel costs are a big concern. In many businesses, personnel costs rank near the top among all costs. In banks, total personnel expenditures rank second only to expenditures for cost of capital. In many manufacturing firms, labor costs have risen more rapidly than any cost except energy. Considerable interest in improved forecasting and control of staffing extends into all ranks, particularly professional and managerial.

The common approach to the problem of staffing is the planning and budgeting process, involving participation by successive levels of management. Properly conducted planning and budgeting yield estimates of future demand, supply, and net human resource needs accepted as valid by managers. In the past, forecasting has been enhanced by:

Including human resource forecasting in the budgeting cycle, requiring submission of plans along with financial budgets

Requiring estimates of needs from each organizational unit (bottom up), so that unit managers are committed to them

Analyzing supply through computerized models (forecasting flows of employees in, up, across, and out of the organization)

Careful reviews of facts and forecast assumptions by senior executives, in authorizing future staffing levels

Advance Planning

To improve the objectivity of staffing plans, companies are also including human resource planning at an earlier stage in the planning cycle. It is not enough, many executives argue, for staffing plans to be budgeted. Human resource needs must be considered in the context of longer-range, strategic planning. A number of firms have found themselves short of talent when they were all set to implement broad capital expansion programs. Others have found themselves heavily overstaffed with employees whose talents no longer fit the company's changing needs, and thus in the uncomfortable position of having to terminate many individuals or force them to retire early. In the years ahead, increased lead time will be provided to allow advance planning for staffing and related career development and organizational changes (Bell, 1974; Walker, 1977a).

Work Analysis

More emphasis is also being placed on the qualitative aspects of human resource needs. In many cases improved control of staffing is being achieved through closer attention to the actual nature of the work. Analysis and planning of work activities, organizational changes, and specific job requirements is an increasingly important part of needs forecasting. In an effort to manage the "work" as well as the "people," companies are giving studies of work activities high priority in planning. Numbers alone simply do not tell the whole story; for example, an agency in Washington reviews its staffing levels and utilization each year using information on activities and output indicators provided by job incumbents. The analysis yields guidelines used in controlling staffing through the budget process and also points out specific areas deserving in-depth study and reorganization of the work.

Improved Human Resource Information

Computers are also being used more extensively as reliable personnel data are maintained. Introduced early in the seventies in many companies, personnel data systems are just now starting to be used for analysis and planning purposes. Companies are now providing computer-generated analyses of personnel complement, attrition, movement, and projected requirements. The use of mathematical models, largely experimental in the seventies, will become more common in the years ahead. An impelling force for the use of models has been the need for projecting career opportunities in affirmative action planning. To date, most models have focused on the forecasting of talent supply. In the future, models will be used extensively for forecasting staffing needs in relation to both changing demand and changing supply. To achieve this, data on changing work activities, work-load demands, and organizational patterns will be necessary elements in the data systems. In large, complex organizations (such as the military services), large-scale modeling is relied upon to assure optimal staffing and organization to meet planned objectives.

Overall, improved forecasting of needs precedes other substantial changes in organizations. The analysis of current and projected personnel supply provides a chart management can follow in adapting job designs and organization structures to changing requirements, adjusting business plans where talent clearly is unavailable, and planning the kinds of activity programs needed to develop and maintain the work force needed for achieving the organization's objectives.

Four chapters in Part Two of this book examine needs forecasting concepts, issues, techniques, and applications. Chapter 4 examines three levels of human resource planning in relation to business planning and illustrates ways to link these parallel processes. Chapter 5 reviews the methods available for forecasting human resource needs and provides a framework for selecting and applying applicable methods. Chapter 6 is devoted to the subject of computer-based modeling techniques, with emphasis on their practical applications. Chapter 7 examines alternative methods of work analysis and job classification, important in establishing models for forecasting talent flows, developing career paths, defining job requirements, setting performance standards, and managing career movement.

PERFORMANCE MANAGEMENT

Many executives are convinced that company productivity can be increased through better management of employee performance. Individual employee motivation is seen as a key factor, but other factors such as the structure of jobs, individual competencies, and appropriateness of performance goals and standards of measurement are considered important and are more directly controllable. The results of efforts to directly motivate employees to improve performance have, by and large, been disappointing. And so companies are trying alternative approaches for obtaining closer control over the factors influencing behavior and end results.

For many years, managers have relied on job descriptions and performance appraisals as basic tools in managing performance. But job descriptions are commonly out of date and are not really descriptive of the actual duties on the jobs. Appraisals are often too general and not specifically related to the work being done. As a result, the approach has shifted in recent years to appraisal of performance in terms of results achieved. Implicit in management by results (or by objectives) are:

Agreement on performance objectives or standards and the activities necessary for their achievement
Review of achievements, with measures or indicators of results

Although participation by the individual employee in the planning of work and the review of results has been considered an important principle, in practice it has not always worked. All too often, performance planning and review has been an exercise which has not significantly influenced productivity. Among the reasons often cited are the following:

Paperwork tends to become a bureaucratic routine.
Supervisors/managers are not accustomed to discussing goals and results with employees.
Many jobs are in flux, and performance standards or objectives are elusive.
Rewards are not adequately tied to results achieved.
Aspects of many jobs overlap, making individual performance difficult to identify.

Performance is often constrained by skill or knowledge gaps, or by organization or staffing problems.

To overcome these obstacles, companies are strengthening vital supervisory skills, equipping employees to manage their own work better, and modifying the structure and environment of work in ways that promote performance improvement.

Improved Systems

To strengthen managerial practices in this area, companies are modifying their performance planning and appraisal systems, making them simpler and easier to use, and tailoring them to overcome difficulties experienced in the past. Training and coaching for appraisers have been stepped up in many companies to help managers carry out their part of the process. In some large companies, for example, workshops help appraisers conduct the most difficult part of appraisal: actually discussing performance and future plans with the individual employee.

Additionally, employees are being brought more actively into the process, and are being asked to prepare their own plans and past performance reviews in advance of discussions with their managers. Management policies and statements of philosophy are being liberalized to encourage open and constructive discussions of performance plans and results. Too often, goal-setting systems were forced into organizational settings that simply were not prepared to make them work.

An understanding of the work to be performed is viewed as a critical element in good performance. Many companies are supplementing their job descriptions with additional tools for analysis of the actual work requirements. Time sheets, activity reporting, special studies, and supplemental job analysis questionnaires are being used to build a broader picture of the activities *actually performed* and those *desired* on a job. Such activity/work analysis is becoming more common in part as a response to requirements for improved job relatedness of employee selection, promotion, pay, termination, and other personnel decisions under EEO regulations.

Changing Work Life

Finally, companies are making noteworthy changes in working conditions. Experiments to improve the "quality of work life" have pointed the way toward flexible job design, flexible working hours, flexible benefits and compensation, more open communications, open posting/bidding for job assignments, and other innovations. Many companies are working to build rewards into the design of jobs, and to make compensation incentives more meaningful to employees.

Overall, practices in managing performance are changing significantly as companies feel pressures to improve their productivity through improved management of people. Such traditional practices as performance appraisal and job description are being reexamined and given new vitality through new approaches. As an important management concern, human resource planning focuses on improving performance.

Part Three of this book examines the several components of effective performance management. Chapter 8 provides an analysis of the meaning of productivity and the ways performance-related aspects of human resource planning may contribute to improved organizational effectiveness. The chapter provides a framework for examining productivity in an organization and for planning activities directed toward its improvement. Chapter 9 focuses on the need for individual performance appraisals, for purposes of individual development and performance planning. Chapter 10 examines compensation policies, systems, and practices from the perspective of human resource planning. Appraisal and compensation systems are commonplace in business organizations, but rarely achieve fully the purpose for which they were designed. Performance management can achieve results by providing a better-planned approach for the design and use of such tools.

CAREER MANAGEMENT

Companies are also giving more attention to employee careers. With high turnover, a limited supply of competent talent, and changing requirements, career development has become an important focus of human resource planning. Retention and improved utilization of talent are receiving greater emphasis in many organizations than external recruitment. This means greater attention to selection, appraisal, individual counseling, career planning, and innovative training and development programs.

Another factor prompting heightened interest in career management has been increased governmental intervention through EEO and affirmative action programs. To achieve EEO/AA objectives, companies have developed new job-matching/career progression systems, explicit career paths and job requirements, more objective ways to identify and evaluate prospective candidates for promotions and transfers, and expanded employee development programs. To achieve specific targets for utilization of protected classes, procedures are being adopted in recruitment, selection, placement, and development.

Recruiting and selection practices are focused on job criteria. What are the skills, knowledge, and experience really needed on a job? Can these requirements be demonstrated to be job-related? Executives are increasingly concerned with the quality, not only the quantity, of talent employed, and their concern goes beyond the initial candidate selection and progresses through each assignment.

Management Development

An important focus of career management efforts is the planning of managerial succession and management development. Management development has long been a personnel concern, but the emphasis is shifting toward developing new managerial capabilities and new ways of doing so through job assignments. Competition, rapid organizational and technological change, financial pressures, and the many other strains on management have heightened a need for more broadly experienced, rigorously tested, and seasoned managers. "It would take a lifetime to give a manager all the experience he needs to become a top notch group vice president," observed one executive. "Our challenge is to give him that experience before he reaches age 45."

In the past, the common question was merely, "Do we have backups for our key positions?" The right answer was ensured through one of several alternate techniques. In many companies, the "cream" was assumed to rise naturally; if high-talent individuals are recruited, they will develop themselves. In others, backup charting techniques have been used to spot the "comers" and help management plan promotions and transfers to ensure that individuals will get the necessary experience. In still other companies, committees or staff officers have maintained files of data on key management candidates and advised management on developmental moves.

A Talent Pool

The primary concern today, however, is to develop broadly experienced and seasoned managers in a way that is simple, practical, meaningful, and fair. Companies are focusing on a talent pool, rather than on individual backups for key positions. This allows greater flexibility in planning developmental assignments across organizational/functional lines.

Planning for management development begins today with clarification of job requirements: Exactly what do the management positions require? And requirements are changing as the business changes. Rarely do executives feel that their successors will closely "fit their own image." Rather, new skills, knowledge, and types of experience will be called for. A number of companies develop position profiles, or behavioral job descriptions, for key positions based on inputs from the incumbents and senior management.

Job-Related Assessment

Assessment information on candidates is also changing. The trend is toward more specific job-related appraisals rather than global assessment of managerial qualities. The search continues for the basic qualities sought of "every effective manager," and assessment programs and appraisals are focused on the qualities currently felt to be important. But the emphasis is turning toward the specific skills, knowledge, and experience that candidates may obtain through career development. Less weight is given to ratings of "potential" or "promotability" than to specific job-related development needs and plans.

Also, there is greater consideration of individual goals, interests, and preferences in management development. Many companies have acknowledged that they have little "hold" on high-talent individuals. To keep them in the organization and keep them motivated, executives are listening to individual desires regarding career paths, location, and other factors. Young managers are particularly vocal about their personal career goals and plans, and they are being heard.

Individual Career Planning

For many individual employees, the point of human resource planning is personal career development. Each individual has a contribution to make to an organization and the challenge is to develop each person's talents fully and to match them with opportunities that best fit the organization's needs. The organization helps by providing developmental resources for job-matching vehicles, but responsibility for career development rests largely with the employees themselves (Hall, 1977).

Some companies have provided their employees with tools for individual career planning—workbooks, workshops, counseling, and career information. The focus of career planning is upon self-analysis and development planning. It normally includes examination of personal goals, interests, and values; capabilities and limitations (assets); career options and how they relate to personal goals, values, and assets; current job performance, so that development may begin immediately and not wait for a different job; and specific development action plans (Walker and Gutteridge, 1979).

Companies are expanding the resources available in support of individual career planning and development. Training programs are being redesigned and expanded to meet identified needs. Tuition aid programs are being used more extensively to meet both company and individual needs. More job rotation and special assignments are allowing mutual assessment of individuals as candidates for different kinds of jobs. Data systems are being used to provide practical inventories of available job candidates, often as supplements to open job posting or bidding systems. And appraisal programs are being expanded (or sometimes split into dual programs) to give improved consideration of individual development progress and plans.

Career development programs have been expanded. Formerly, special programs have focused on needs of women and minorities to acquire career planning skills and development assistance necessary for equal footing. But the trend is toward broad-based programs open to all employees. Even "fast-track" management development programs, popular in the 1960s to move young managers into executive ranks, have waned as the supply has become greater and the lead time for development planning has extended.

Careers and Retirement

But companies are turning attention to the needs of one new minority group—older workers. Careers of employees approaching retirement were never considered an issue until the Age Discrimination in Employment Act started having an effect. Performance appraisals are now essential in terminating employees over 40 if there is any chance of age discrimination charges. Also companies are providing special counseling and more flexible work/retirement options to employees facing retirement or career changes. Career planning is a natural way of life in many companies, and is likely to become commonplace in the future.

Overall, companies are adopting more formal and more objective systems for appraising individual capabilities and potential, identifying candidates for position vacancies, and guiding individual career development. While managing careers still is primarily on the shoulders of employees themselves, the trend is toward providing resources to aid their planning.

Part Four of this book provides guidelines for career management. Chapter 11 suggests how often-fragmented policies and systems such as employee selection, placement, training, promotion and transfer, and retirement or termination may be more closely coordinated as a planned process of career management. Chapter 12 examines the process of developing managerial talent, including the identification of managerial candidates, the planning of managerial succession and developmental actions, and the tracking of career progress of candidates. The emphasis is on the special needs of diversified, decentralized organizations where developing managers with broad experience is a special challenge. Chapter 13 describes techniques for defining and communicating information to employees regarding career opportunities, and Chapter 14 suggests ways to help these employees conduct their own self-analysis and career planning.

GETTING STARTED

Where does an organization begin its human resource planning? There are so many aspects to this process that a company could start doing things which are wholly inappropriate and a waste of time and resources. The varied needs for human resource planning come both from the internal organizational sources and from external pressures. The first step, therefore, is to weigh the various needs and determine their relative priorities for management attention. It would be an extraordinary organization that could do everything at once. Few organizations ever try to respond to all their human resource concerns simultaneously any more than they try to satisfy all their marketing or other needs all at once.

Chapter 15, the final chapter of this book, provides a guide to conducting an audit of human resource practices and policies, with the purpose of identifying the most pressing needs for attention. An audit provides a periodic checkup on directions and emphases for human resource planning. It also permits a periodic assessment of the results attained and the effectiveness of management practices in managing human resources.

External Forces

Some forces are compelling, such as affirmative action commitments, lawsuits, and union demands. But labor shortages, economic pressures to reduce staff, technological changes, and changing social attitudes strongly affect companies. One organization may experience more difficulty than others in recruiting high-talent employees; another may have difficulty recruiting but not consider it a noteworthy problem. Those companies that are "in the crunch" respond with action; others direct attention to other concerns.

Even the pressure of competitive employment practices is unevenly felt.

Some companies, and some industries in particular, are more sensitive to competition than others. For example, the shortage of petroleum engineers, particularly females, is a concern of only a few companies that are aggressively competing to attract them. Retention and motivation of clerical employees tends to be a problem in urban areas and locations with a concentration of businesses.

Internal Factors

Some companies have levels of profitability that allow them to implement human resource programs whether or not they are demonstrated to be essential. Utilities, oil companies, and other capital-intensive businesses allocate staff and money to human resource programs because personnel expenses are low relative to other costs. Smaller, rapidly growing companies also tend to support innovative human resource programs under the philosophy that continued growth requires extraordinary attention to the development of required talent. In the first instances, human resource needs and costs are not felt to be particularly significant in the realm of business operations; in the latter instances, human resources are felt to be potentially key factors affecting future growth and profitability.

In many companies, the concerns, attitudes, values, and personal managerial styles of key senior executives tend to set the priorities among human resource needs. In these cases, changing internal organizational conditions affect planning far more than any changes in external conditions. Preserving the status quo is often a number one priority in the mind of conservative executives. Only when external factors or changing internal conditions result in mounting pressures do human resource policies and programs begin to change.

Subjective Weighting

Naturally, executives have primary responsibility for identifying, sorting, and initiating action upon human resource needs. But it is important that their judgment be based on objective analysis of conditions and not upon their personal biases or assumptions. In many cases, priorities for human resource planning are selected on the basis of:

> Minimum costs and lowest risk of upsetting existing practices
> Previous personal experiences (for example, practices of a previous employer)
> Practices and concerns of other companies (for example, industry leaders)
> Consultant advice (for example, what the consultants advocate or have done in other companies)
> Package approaches readily available on the market

These factors are commonly considered in human resource planning, but should never obscure current needs. Goals and priorities should be determined by business plans, obstacles, and changing external demands on the organization.

The key to effective human resource planning is the analysis of the factors representing change—change that potentially affects the survival, growth, profitability, or efficiency of the business.

Staff Responsibilities

In most organizations, the responsibility for needs analysis and needs forecasting rests with staff professionals in human resource planning. Typically a manpower/human resource planning manager or analyst reports to the personnel executive and has responsibility for maintaining the information and the systems necessary for human resource planning. The role was aptly described by Walton Burdick, an IBM personnel executive:

> Probably the major challenge to personnel is anticipating, and adjusting to, change. But I don't think that personnel should be the department or the individual that leads the corporation to change; it should not be the change agent. I would think that what a personnel professional ought to do is anticipate what's likely to occur and make certain that his or her company gets headed in the right direction in the way that will best serve their business needs. A good example would be anticipating developments in legislation (Burdick, 1976).

Formalization of human resource planning as a staff function ensures that this anticipating and adjusting to change get accomplished. So much of ongoing staff activities is concerned with maintenance and day-to-day problem solving that someone needs to be assigned responsibility to carry the ball for longer-range analysis and planning (Foulkes and Morgan, 1977).

The number of professionals engaged in human resource planning has grown in recent years to the extent that an association tailored to their interests has been formed. The Human Resource Planning Society holds an annual conference of members, publishes a quarterly journal, and sponsors professional development and research activities. Members include human resource planners from both public and private organizations (*Human Resource Planning*, 1978).

Conclusion

Today, human resource planning is viewed as the way management comes to grips with ill-defined and tough-to-solve human resource problems facing an organization. The tools used in the process as well as the importance of the process depend on the problems being confronted by management. And the nature of the problems relates to broader external changes and issues inherent in corporate strategies and plans. This chapter has examined the evolution of human resource planning over the past decades and has identified the basic concerns of management which are the context for contemporary human resource planning.

Chapter 2

The Environment of Human Resource Planning

KEY POINTS

- In the next two decades we will have a gradually aging work force, reflecting the aging of the "bulge" of population resulting from the "baby boom" following World War II and an increasing longevity of older people.
- Our work force has expanded dramatically with the absorption of younger workers and a greatly increased participation in the work force by women.
- Work opportunities are shifting toward the higher-skilled "knowledge worker" jobs; lower-skilled occupations are diminishing in employment, both relatively and absolutely.
- Gains in economic productivity have slowed, in large part due to a slower rate of technological advancement in basic industries. There are other factors, however, which are addressed through human resource planning.
- Legal and regulatory factors represent significant constraints on management practices in human resource management—employment discrimination laws being of foremost concern in most organizations.
- Changing employee attitudes toward work and careers are causing management to modify human resource policies and practices. Dual careers, resistance to mobility, and career aspirations are growing concerns.

Human resource planning cannot be performed in a vacuum. The objectives, strategies, and circumstances of an organization are critical determinants of human resource requirements and management priorities. However, these are influenced by social, economic, and technological changes occurring outside an organization. To understand the forces impelling human resource planning, we must look beyond the organization to the broader environment.

Somewhat like weather forecasting, the assessment of changing environmental conditions is a difficult and uncertain task in human resource planning. We may survey the clouds, the winds, and weather conditions prevailing elsewhere as we develop forecasts of conditions to come. But we cannot always predict the future weather accurately and we certainly cannot change it. Nevertheless, the information is vital in our efforts to anticipate and prepare for it.

This chapter surveys five environmental factors which impact human resource planning. Each represents an area of significant change that calls for responsive management actions. The factors include changes in the makeup of our population and our work force (demographic changes), economic changes, technological changes, governmental regulations, and changing attitudes toward work and careers.

DEMOGRAPHIC CHANGES

First, we should recognize that significant shifts are taking place in the composition of our population and, consequently, in our labor force. The ability of an organization to meet its staffing requirements depends on the availability of talent. Because everyone in the total work force for the next twenty years has already been born, it is instructive to analyze demographic information. Such information is provided by the Bureau of Labor Statistics, based on census data and periodic labor supply studies.

Population

In the 1970s we experienced a relative shortage of people in the age group 35 to 45, due to a low birthrate during the Depression. At the same time, an extraordinarily large proportion of the population was under age 18, straining schools and then expanding universities and colleges.

As shown in Exhibit 2-1, these young people are changing from "postwar babies" and students to workers. The age group 25 to 34 will expand by 43 percent from 1970 to 1980 and will stay at that level through replacements. By the year 2000 this group will swell the age 50 and over segment of our population, placing burdens on the younger age groups to provide their economic support in retirement.

Our population is slowly growing older, on the average. The median age was 28 in 1970 and 30 in 1980, and it will rise to 35 by the year 2000.

These shifts are due to three drastic variations in birth rates during the past half century. The first was the "birth dearth" of the Depression years, when births dropped to about 2.5 million from a previous average of about 3 million

Exhibit 2-1   Total Population of the United States*

Age group	1970	1980	1990	2000
Under age 18	68.8	63.2	67.7	71.1
18–24	24.7	29.4	25.2	26.3
25–34	25.3	36.2	41.1	34.5
35–44	23.1	25.7	36.5	41.3
45–54	23.3	22.6	25.2	35.7
55–64	18.7	21.0	20.5	22.9
65 and older	20.1	24.5	28.9	30.6

*In millions; includes armed forces abroad.
Source: U.S. Bureau of the Census, Current Population Reports, Series P-25. Projections based on 1974 data.

per year. The next variation was the "baby boom" following World War II and which continued into the early 1960s. In the mid-1950s the number of births each year surged past the 4 million mark, representing 3.8 births per women (fertility rate) from a Depression low of 2.1. The third shift was a steep decline in the fertility rate in the 1970s, to a low of 1.76 in 1976. The effects of these marked shifts in births have strained hospitals, schools, and now employers.

Future population changes depend, of course, on future birth patterns, It was thought that the fertility rate might stay low as more and more women opted for careers rather than families. But a countertrend is appearing; women are simply deferring having children to an older age. In fact, a new "baby boom" may be in the making in the decades ahead.

Also, longevity is an important factor. Life expectancy is increasing thanks to improved health and advanced health sciences. If people in their thirties today live well beyond 100 years of age, the demands placed on younger working people will increase. And such longevity is a real possibility in the view of many scientists (Rosenfeld, 1976).

An Expanding Labor Force

The impact of the "baby boom" on the labor market began to be felt in the late 1960s when people born after World War II started to enter the labor market. Strains were not severe, as many persons stayed in school, expanding college enrollments, and others were involved in the Vietnam war. But by the 1970s, rising unemployment figures brought the issue into focus.

Our economy must create jobs for increasing numbers of younger workers. We must produce jobs that will absorb available workers into the economic system. Otherwise we will have unemployment—either among the younger workers or among displaced older workers. As shown in Exhibit 2-2, the age group 20 to 24 expanded markedly from 1960 to 1970 and to 1980. After 1980, however, this young group will not show significant expansion, portending possible future shortages of talent to meet needs, or to support growing numbers of older, retired workers.

The age group 25 to 34 expanded by 72 percent from 1970 to 1980. This

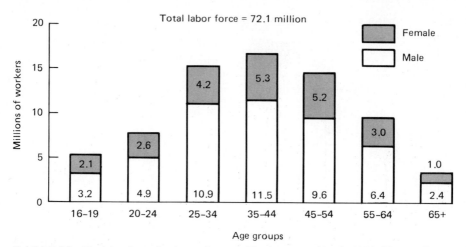

Exhibit 2-2A   The labor force: its size and composition by age and sex in 1960. (*Source:* Bureau of Labor Statistics, Special Labor Force Report, 1976.)

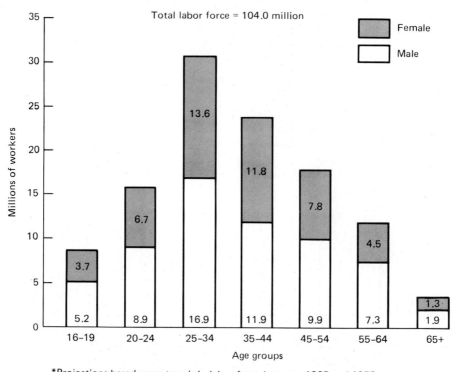

*Projections based upon trends in labor force between 1965 and 1975.

Exhibit 2-2C   The labor force: its size and composition by age and sex in 1980. (*Source:* Bureau of Labor Statistics, Special Labor Force Report, 1976.)

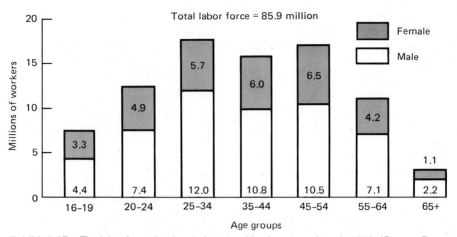

Exhibit 2-2B The labor force: its size and composition by age and sex in 1970. (*Source:* Bureau of Labor Statistics, Special Labor Force Report, 1976.)

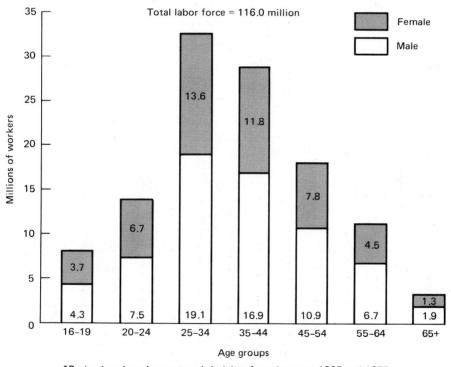

*Projections based upon trends in labor force between 1965 and 1975.

Exhibit 2-2D The labor force: its size and composition by age and sex in 1990. (*Source:* Bureau of Labor Statistics, Special Labor Force Report, 1976.)

tremendous increase places demands on management for meaningful careers, training and development, and challenging job assignments. And the pressures may be felt more severely in the 1980s as frustrations and expectations build up. Our ability to utilize these people effectively will depend on economic growth—the creation of jobs—and on the number of vacancies created through retirements and other attrition. In many companies, the shortage of "Depression babies," now aged 40 to 55, may result in a dipping into the younger category of individuals where we actually may have an abundance of talented individuals competing aggressively for career opportunities.

We will also gradually have more and more older employees and, as they elect to retire, retirees. When they retire, benefits costs and competition for second careers or continued work may rise. When they opt to continue working, career paths may be blocked for younger employees.

Finally, it is noteworthy that due to a lower birth rate in the 1970s we will have somewhat fewer teenagers available for work in the decade ahead. This may mean increased payroll costs to attract people to relatively menial jobs. It may also impel more liberal governmental policies toward employment of aliens who are willing to do the work.

Just from a numbers viewpoint alone, it will be a challenge to keep everyone working, let alone on jobs that are sufficiently challenging and satisfying.

Women in the Labor Force

The expansion of the labor supply is not due solely to population patterns. As shown in Exhibit 2-3, an increasing proportion of the labor force, particularly in younger age groups, is due to entry of females in the labor force.

In 1960, 37.1 percent of all females aged 16 and over were in the labor force, either employed or seeking employment. By 1978 the rate passed the 50 percent mark. Employment of females in the 25 to 34 age group, the most employable age group, reflects even higher percentages, as shown in Exhibit 2-3. The participation rate is estimated to be near 60 percent in 1980 and will rise to 66 percent by 1990. At the same time, remember that the number of available females in this age group is expanding significantly. The net result is a tripling of

Exhibit 2-3   Labor Force Participation by Females*

Year	Age 25–34		All ages	
	Participation rate	Number (millions)	Participation rate	Number (millions)
1960	35.8%	4.2	37.1%	23.2
1970	44.8	5.7	42.8	31.6
1980*	58.4	10.6	47.9	41.8
1990*	66.0	13.6	51.4	49.3

*Projections.
Source: U.S. Bureau of Labor Statistics, Special Labor Force Reports, 1975.

female workers in this age group alone and a doubling of its share of the total work force (from 5.8 percent in 1960 to 11.7 percent in 1990). The entry of females into the labor force in large numbers puts considerable strain on our ability to create jobs and careers.

At the same time the labor force participation by men is actually declining. In 1960, 82.4 percent of all men age 16 and over were employed or were seeking employment (including armed forces). This percentage fell to 79.2 percent by 1970 and will decline to 76.7 percent by 1990. So while more women are working, fewer men are working. The primary reason for this decline is a continuing trend toward early retirement. Other reasons include decisions to stay in school longer before entering the work force, ill health, and disability. Some men have opted for responsibilities at home, the traditional reason women were not in the work force.

Higher Knowledge Levels

At the same time, the caliber of our work force is rising. Many men and women have higher educational levels than their counterparts of decades ago. With this education come different outlooks toward social and work values and greater work expectations.

For example, in 1964 only 6,000 graduate business administration degrees were awarded. By 1976 the number was 30,000 and by 1985 it is estimated to hit 60,000. Managerial, professional, and technical jobs are increasing in number far more rapidly than clerical, service, or blue-collar jobs (Mandt, 1978). Direct production workers such as machinists, bricklayers, and farmers are a steadily declining portion of the work force. The fastest growing groups are knowledge workers including accountants, engineers, nurses, computer experts of all kinds, researchers, and most of all, managers.

Yet, observes Peter Drucker, ". . . the knowledge worker tends to be disgruntled, or at least not fully satisfied. He is being paid extremely well. He does interesting work and work that does not break the body as so much of yesterday's work did. And yet the 'alienation' of which we hear so much today . . . is not primarily to be found in the working class. It is above all a phenomenon of the educated middle class of employed knowledge workers" (Drucker, 1975).

If we are unable to respond to the needs of our growing numbers of knowledge workers, we will likely see increased interest in union organization efforts at professional and technical levels, led by equally young, vigorous, and educated union leaders. We face a challenge to modify the bureaucratic qualities of our organizations to satisfy the growing demands for "quality of work life" of our young, talented workers.

ECONOMIC CHANGES

It should be no surprise that economic conditions affect human resource management. Inflation, recently a fact of life, plays havoc with personnel costs. Recession economics places strains on management practices, strains that are often wrenching. In both conditions, productivity is a nagging concern for management. Calling personnel a "human resource" bears the burden of managing personnel as an economic resource, with each expenditure viewed as an investment.

As costs of interviewing, recruiting, relocating, training, and compensating employees rise, we are impelled to do a better job of planning. The costs associated with recruiting and orienting new professional and managerial employees are often astounding when the rates of attrition during the first two years are taken into account. One company estimated that the net total investment per professional remaining after two years exceeded $100,000. For some companies, this estimate is probably low.

Relocations of employees often entail costs of $25,000 or more per move. It is necessary to make relocations attractive and to minimize the personal and family disruptions involved. Particularly with inflation in housing costs, employees want to keep themselves "whole" and hopefully come out a bit ahead. Payments are often made by employers for all realty costs, carrying costs for homes unsold (or provision of home transfer services), no-interest "bridge" loans between mortgages, no-interest or low-interest mortgage loans on new housing, lump-sum payments for draperies and new home expenses, and liberal relocation visits and travel expenses. And these costs do not address the central issue of housing costs. New home prices are going up 13 percent and more each year. In 1978 mortgage interest rates passed the 10 percent mark, complicating the challenge of obtaining comparable housing in a new area at comparable costs. Average new home prices are well above $60,000 and rising. Housing in southern California is considered "out of sight" by many prospective recruits and transferees.

Housing costs, as a result, are taking up an increasing share of the personal household budget. The old rule of thumb of 20 to 25 percent of pay going for housing has given way in many families to 35 or 40 percent. Dual incomes may alleviate strains on budgets in some families, but the pressure is on salaries, nevertheless. Salary costs inevitably rise as costs of living rise.

One central point of pressure is at the starting level for professional employees. Some top MBA graduates are starting their careers at $25,000 and more. Rising starting salaries place us in a salary compression box. If we do not pay the going rates we find ourselves unable to hire and keep talent. If we pay the rates and move our whole pay scale upward, our costs soar. If we allow compression to build up, we create inequities that lead to turnover and dissatisfaction.

Productivity

The flip side of cost control is productivity improvement. For two decades following World War II, productivity in the United States sprinted up the growth charts untiringly. Spurred by a labor force anxious to get back to peaceful industrial employment and by a string of technological breakthroughs that gave the United States a commanding lead in many product markets around the world, our economy seemed unfailing and unstoppable. But the rise slackened in the 1960s and 1970s. Productivity gains slowed to 1.6 percent, half of the golden-growth years.

Without strong productivity improvement and economic growth, it is difficult to control inflation and it is difficult to compete effectively in world markets. Further, the effect is erosion of the standard of living of workers and a shrinking of the value of real wealth. "America's economic survival will depend on its ability to increase its rate of productivity advance to former levels," observed General Motors Corporation Chairman Thomas Murphy in an interview. "That is no exaggeration" (Graham, 1978).

Productivity means different things to different people. To some it means hard work and efficiency. To others it means automation and new technologies. Basically it represents a measurement of outputs divided by inputs, computed quarterly by the Bureau of Labor Statistics. The productivity rate is the economic benefit relative to the economic costs associated with them.

Numerous factors affect productivity, including changes in technology, changes in the quality of the labor force, changes in the rate and type of capital investment, the impact of short-term business cycles and market demand, and changes in the composition of industrial activity, employment, and outputs. Changes in the age and sex composition of the labor force may have affected overall productivity, along with associated changes in attitudes toward work itself, toward employers, and toward society. However, shifts in the growth of our economy, from production of goods toward services and slower technological innovations to enhance production, may have a lot to do with a slowed productivity growth. We have seen a slowdown of growth in the capital to labor ratios and a maturation of technology in many industries. Also, some economists attribute slower growth to the diversion of investment capital from production, research, and development to pollution-abatement expenditures.

The reasons for our productivity dilemma are undoubtedly complex. Employee productivity alone is not a sufficient explanation any more than any other single factor. However, in human resource planning, we need to be alert to the patterns of productivity change as they relate to economic conditions and to the causes that we may influence through organizational practices and programs (Kutscher, Mark, and Norsworthy, 1977).

TECHNOLOGICAL CHANGE

The development and application of new technologies have been significant forces in shaping organizations and management practices. The advent of advanced technologies in production and transportation systems, communications, computers, energy, medicine, and the life sciences, and the use of materials and natural resources have brought major changes in the way organizations function. Future technological change will undoubtedly pose challenges for further adaptation, particularly in areas concerning human resource planning.

Recent decades have seen technological advances in virtually every aspect of business. Automation became reality in every management function and revolutionized production and materials usage, transportation and communications, information processing, and problem solving. The development of jet freight transportation, "piggy-back rail," containerized shipping, pipelines, and supertankers have changed the movement of raw materials and goods. New power tools, assembly equipment, lift trucks, conveyors, automated material management systems, lasers, new alloys and other materials, and growth of "management sciences" are among advances that have virtually revolutionized production and distribution (Bright, 1963; Dunlop, 1962).

The rapid development of the computer, however, deserves credit for the most dramatic advances in management. From technical applications to the processing of information on everything from costs to airline reservations, computers have found roles in every aspect of an organization's functioning. Computers acquire, sort, manipulate, interpret, store, and display selected data. Processing of information and solution of complex scientific, engineering, and business problems are possible in instances that would have been unfeasible only a few years ago. The flow of information stimulated by this capacity has resulted in an "information explosion" that has impelled advances in the entire field of communications, as well. Television, advanced use of radio transmission, the use of microwave and satellite transmission, advances in the technology of preparing the printed word (for example, photocomposition and transmission); and miniaturization (for example, microfilm and microfiche), as well as direct computer storage and access, have changed the fundamental patterns of communications in business, technology, and government (Sirbu, 1978).

A synopsis of technological advances would not be complete, either, without recognition of recent breakthroughs in the physical and life sciences, impelled to a considerable degree by the space program and by nationally supported programs for health research. Medicine, agriculture, environmental controls, preservation of goods (freezing, dehydration, irradiation, chemical treatment, etc.), and synthetics are among the fields that have experienced major changes in recent decades. Life itself is being extended through the application of results attained in these areas (Rosenfeld, 1977).

Looking Ahead

While the rate of technological change may slow somewhat and the number of major breakthroughs in science may be fewer in the decades ahead, there will certainly be advances that will represent further factors of change. In energy research, we are still nearing the threshold of a revolution. Solar energy, nuclear energy, or perhaps some wholly unanticipated development will force new thinking and major modifications in every sector of industry. Indeed, the need for a breakthrough in energy development promises to change personal lives as well. Transportation, residential construction and design, and patterns of work and leisure may all be directly affected by the availability of energy and the way it is generated.

Second only to energy technology as a future dramatic factor of change will be the rapid adoption and further development of the computer microprocessor or "chip." This minute piece of silicon, the size of an oat flake, contains miniature circuitry with about the capability of a room-sized computer only a few years back. Miniaturized circuitry promises to inject computer power into almost everything imaginable, from ovens to watches to cars. Mechanical equipment, instruments, virtually any tool that we use may involve computer technology in the future. And management tools are no exception; pocket calculators are only the beginning of a revolution in information processing and problem analysis for management.

The developing capacity to reduce time, space, and complexity through computer applications will further contribute to a shrinking of the business world. Problems inherent in international business, for example, become trivial when communications and information-processing obstacles are knocked down. Organizations may function effectively as massive, complex enterprises through new technology; roles of managers and technical personnel shift to take advantage of the technologies introduced. Longer-range planning and control of business strategies may at last become practical realities. Improved forecasting, planning, and control generally will come of age.

With technological change also may come alienation among employees, obsolescence of skills and knowledge, and resistance to organizational adaptation to new processes. These problems are not new, and have accompanied technological progress for generations. As people accept change as a way of life, the dysfunctional aspects may wane. The challenge in human resource planning is to facilitate this process (Burack and McNichols, 1973; Hodges and Kelly, 1970).

LEGAL AND REGULATORY CONDITIONS

Human resource management practices are increasingly influenced by laws. Employment discrimination laws pose very apparent and direct constraints and demands on human resource planning. Additionally, federal tax laws, labor laws, safety and health laws, privacy laws, and a plethora of executive orders and agency regulations all serve to guide management practices in the human resource area. Further laws at state and local levels compound the complexity by providing a patchwork of regulations in such areas of employment practices as age discrimination, hours of work, compensation, and recently, discrimination based on sexual preference (homosexuality).

Employment Discrimination

Federal employment discrimination laws and associated court decisions interpreting these laws have had profound impact on employer practices during the past two decades. Exhibit 2-4 identifies the principal federal laws regulating employment practices with regard to equal employment opportunity. The Equal Pay Act and Title VII of the Civil Rights Act set the stage for broad intervention

Exhibit 2-4   Federal Employment Discrimination Laws

Law or executive order	Purpose and implications	Coverage
Equal Pay Act of 1963, Amended in 1972	Requires all employers subject to Fair Employment Standards Act to provide equal pay for men and women performing "substantially" equal work. Jobs do not have to be identical to be considered equal. The law deals specifically and directly with the issue of equal pay.	Originally only nonexempts; extended in 1972 to cover executive, administrative, and professional employees.
Title VII of the Civil Rights Act of 1964, Amended in 1972	Prohibits discrimination because of race, color, religion, sex, or national origin, in all employment practices, including hiring, firing, promotion, compensation, benefits and all other terms, privileges, and conditions of employment. The EEOC receives and investigates job discrimination complaints and when charges are found justified, efforts are made to reach an agreement eliminating all aspects of discrimination revealed. Suits may be filed by organizations on behalf of aggrieved individuals as well as by employees and job applicants themselves.	All private employers of 15 or more persons, labor unions, state and local governments, educational institutions, employment agencies.
Executive Order 11246, 1965; amended by EO 11375 to include sex	Prohibits federal contractors and subcontractors from discrimination in employment because of race, color, religion, sex or national origin. Further, it requires employers to take affirmative action to ensure equal employment opportunity. If contractors do not comply, their contracts may be canceled, terminated, or suspended. They are also subject to court action brought by the government.	Employers with federal contracts or subcontracts in excess of $10,000 (affects about 250,000 contractors employing a third of the nation's work force.)
Revised Order No. 4	"Results-oriented" programs are required; written affirmative action programs for each location are required within 120 days after commencing a new contract. Among other aspects, a utilization analysis is required, indicating areas where the contractor underutilizes women and minorities, and goals and timetables for correction, to-	Contractors and subcontractors with contracts over $50,000 and 50 or more employees.

Exhibit 2-4 *(continued)*

Law or executive order	Purpose and implications	Coverage
	gether with the procedures for implementation. "Good faith efforts" are judged.	
Revised Order No. 14	Sets forth a standardized evaluation procedure for compliance agencies in conducting reviews of contractors required to develop affirmative action programs: desk audit, on-site review, and off-site analysis.	See above.
Title VI of the Civil Rights Act of 1964; revised guidelines, 1973	Prohibits discrimination based on race, color, or national origin in all programs or activities which receive federal financial aid.	Apprenticeship, work study, training or similar programs; any federally funded project or program.
Civil Rights Acts of 1866 and 1870; Equal Protection Clause of 14th Amendment	Employment discrimination has been ruled by courts to be prohibited by these laws. Action under these laws on behalf of individuals or groups may be taken.	Any employer.
Age Discrimination Act of 1967; amended in 1978	Prohibits discrimination in the terms, conditions, and privileges of employment based on age. Forced discharge or mandatory retirement is prohibited for protected individuals; hiring is also covered by age ban. Exemptions cover "highly paid" executives, positions for which age is a bona fide qualification, and tenured college professors (until 7/1/82).	Employees and job applicants ages 40 through 69; all private employers of 20 or more persons, state and local governments, employment agencies and labor unions with 25 or more members. Federal employees are covered from age 40 with no upper age limit.
Vocational Rehabilitation Act of 1973; Vietnam Veterans Readjustment Act of 1974	Requires affirmative action to employ and promote qualified handicapped individuals and qualified disabled veterans and Vietnam veterans. Training, job modification, and other reasonable accommodation to limitations are required.	Employers with federal contracts or subcontracts in excess of $2,500. Operationally, contractors of $50,000 and 50 or more employees must file an affirmative action plan for each of their facilities.
Section 11 of the National Labor Relations Act	It may be unlawful for employers to participate with unions in the commission of any discriminatory practices on the basis of race, religion, or national origin. Discrimination may give rise to racial or other divisions among employees to the detriment of organized union activity; or unions may exclude individuals discriminatorily from membership, etc.	Union-management relationships.

by the government in human resource practices of employers. Confusion over the legal requirements was gradually clarified through federal court decisions—which bear the ultimate burden of interpreting and applying the various nondiscrimination laws. The courts have applied broad penalties and controls on employers who have not acted voluntarily to comply with laws and end discrimination. Nondiscrimination is clearly the law.

Courts have ruled that compliance means far more than merely avoiding overt discrimination against protected individuals, or even the impartial use of personnel policies and procedures. The end result of employer action, not the intention, determines compliance. It is illegal to use practices, policies, or standards that result in a *disparate impact* on the employment status or opportunities of protected employees, unless the employer can show that such a discriminatory effect is essential to the safe and efficient operation of the business. Proving business necessity is tough, and is narrowly interpreted by the courts (Higgins, 1976; Freiburg, 1977).

Under application of the various executive orders, noted in Exhibit 2-4, employers are also required to provide *affirmative action.* That is, they must seek out and employ qualified members of all protected groups that are represented in the available labor force for jobs in all parts and levels of the organization where they are underrepresented. Employers must correct and avoid perpetuating unnecessary adverse impacts resulting from past discrimination, especially among present employees (Schlei and Grossman, 1976; Schaeffer, 1973, 1975).

The effect of court judgments in suits brought under equal employment laws has been financially as well as morally suasive. Exhibit 2-5 lists some of the actions pressed against employers for employment discrimination in recent years and the dollar settlements involved. Increasingly the progress of equal employment programs in this country has been guided by the courts' interpretations of the requirements imposed on employers and by imposition of substantial penalties for failure to comply.

The attention has also shifted over the years from an initial focus on blacks and other racial minorities to women, religious minorities, older employees, and the handicapped. The Age Discrimination in Employment Act, passed in 1967 and amended in 1978, protects employees aged 40 through 60 from discrimination in hiring, employment terms and conditions, and in terminations or retirement. Implications for retirement policies and practices are discussed in Chapter 11 (Walker and Lazer, 1978).

While no affirmative action programs are required under age discrimination laws, they are required under laws protecting veterans and handicapped employees. Regulated employers (about 3 million, or half of all businesses in America) are required to take affirmative action to hire handicapped people; to make "reasonable accommodations" in jobs and working conditions; and to make available job assignments, promotions, training, transfers, and other employment opportunities. Not every handicapped person is eligible. A person must be "qualified" or capable of performing a particular job, with reasonable accommodation to the handicapping condition if needed (Decker and Peed, 1976; U.S. Civil Service Commission, 1973).

Exhibit 2-5

Dollar amount	Number of people affected	Employer	Issue(s)	Action pressed by	Comments
24,100,000	1,800	Northwest Airlines	Sex—stewardess pay	Private suit	
10,000,000/year	*	Bank of America	Sex—hiring, promotion	Private suit	Plus $3,750,000 training fund
375,000	210	Rutgers University	Sex	EEOC	
210,000	172	Iowa State University	Sex	Department of Labor	
1,186	1	Boeing Company	Sex—weight lifting	Washington State Human Rights Commission	
2,000	2	Snelling & Snelling	Sex—referral practices	Washington State Human Rights Commission	
9,000	1	Avco Financial	Sex—"girl" reference	New York State Human Rights Commission	
600,000	*	Corning Glass	Sex—day-night shifts	Department of Labor/Women's groups	Decided by United States Supreme Court 60% to women
30,000,000	*	AT&T	Equal pay—management personnel	*	
30,900,000	40,048	9 Steel Companies	Race—job assignments	EEOC, Department of Labor	$250.00 to $3,000.00 per employee
43,000	79	Carborundum Company	Equal pay	Department of Labor	
10,000	1	City of Chicago	Pregnancy leave*	Private suit	
22,000	1	Ford Motor Company	Race—job assignment	Private suit	Paid to male
2,500	1	Western Electric Company	Sex—pregnancy	Missouri Commission on Human Rights	
2,750,000	160	Standard Oil of California	Age	*	
21,000	1	Newsweek Magazine	Race	*	$50,000 to one individual Includes $20,000 legal fees
350,000	137	Eastex, Inc.	Sex—race	Justice Department	
87,000	2	Malden (Mass.) School Committee	Sex—pregnancy	Massachusetts Commission against Discrimination	
55,000	13	Boston Redevelopment Agency	Sex	Massachusetts Commission against Discrimination	
6,400	1	Rutgers University	Sex	New Jersey Division of Civil Rights	
319,000	*	Jersey Central Power & Light	*	EEOC	
26,264	1	U.S. Steel	*	Private suit	

Exhibit 2-5 *(continued)*

Dollar amount	Number of people affected	Employer	Issue(s)	Action pressed by	Comments
37,000	1	Continental Trailways (a division of)	Race	Private suit	Includes $30,000 legal fees
50,000	1	Ford Motor Company	Sex—reverse discrimination	Private suit	
62,500	*	Union Electric	Sex—maternity leave	EEOC	
2,100,000	360	Georgia Power	Race—back pay	Justice Department	
157,686	96	Loveman's Department Store	Sex—equal pay	Department of Labor	Payment range $3 to $1,300
88,000	*	University of Montana	Sex—equal pay	H.E.W.	
23,000	2	University of Arkansas	Sex—equal pay	H.E.W.	
100,000	750	Weyerhaeuser Lumber Company	Sex—reverse discrimination	EEOC, Union	Back pay for men
350,000	276	General Electric (Philadelphia)	Race	EEOC	Put in escrow re: 1969 complaint
175,000	100	East Texas Motor Freight	Race—seniority	Justice Department	
250,000	29	Pan American Airways	Age	Department of Labor	
275,000	98	Uniroyal (Chemicals Division)	Race	EEOC	
4,000,000/year	476	Quaker Oats	Race	P.U.S.H.	Commitment re: new minority jobs
45,000,000	*	AT&T	*	EEOC, Justice Department	First year payment re: earlier settlement
450,000	140	El Paso Natural Gas	Sex	EEOC	Includes pay increases, back, pay, training
31,862	18	J. M. Fields Stores	Sex	Department of Labor	Includes 8 years back pay
45,000	1	Cambridge Housing Authority	Sex	Massachusetts Commission against Discrimination	
102,100	70	New York Telephone	Sex	Private suit	
40,000	1	Friendly Ice Cream	Age	Department of Labor	
100,000	*	Texaco	Sex	*	
48,000	39	Container Corporation of America	Sex	EEOC	

*Information not immediately available

Source: Towers, Perrin, Forster & Crosby.

Predating federal employment discrimination laws were various state laws. Exhibit 2-6 indicates the personal characteristics now protected by state laws. State laws apply whenever they are as stringent as or more stringent than federal law, which sets a minimum standard in terms of protecting employees' rights. The Civil Rights Act of 1964 and other federal EEO laws do not preempt this area.

EEO law has profound implications for human resource planning because it directly influences employer practices in hiring, assigning, transferring, promoting, training, and terminating employees. While attention in the past decades has focused largely on hiring decisions of employers, emphasis is quickly broadening to include participation in training programs, compensation job evaluation, and career development actions. Thus the human resource planning process will join the employment process as a primary target of EEO efforts (Ginzberg, 1978).

Privacy Legislation

An area of emerging significance in human resource planning is the legal right of employees to privacy in their employment relationships. The first major legislation in the information privacy area was the Fair Credit Reporting Act of 1970. The act regulates consumer-credit reporting practices by imposing certain requirements on the accuracy of information and by limiting the uses of information. It also guaranteed the right of individuals to have access to and to contest information pertaining to themselves. This law may have increased the public's awareness of the need for protection of data privacy and for access to personal information in public and employer files.

A Health, Education and Welfare committee studied the issues and set forth principles that should govern handling of information, with particular attention to policies and procedures of federal agencies. This report led to the enactment of the Privacy Act of 1974, which essentially prohibits an agency from disclosing any records about individuals except those required under the Freedom of Information Act (FOIA). This law did not cover private sector employers, but it did set up a Privacy Protection Study Commission to look into the needs for further legal protection (Bushkin and Schaen, 1976; Privacy Protection Study Commission, 1977).

Legislation governing public information has continued, impelling a trend toward regulation of private employer information practices. Amendments to the FOIA and enactment of the Family Educational Rights and Privacy Act of 1974 follow guidelines set forth in the HEW report with regard to public records and educational records. Several states have also enacted laws governing aspects of data disclosure and privacy.

A California statute that became effective in 1976 is the first major state law setting forth requirements for employee privacy. It states:

Every employer shall, at reasonable times upon the request of an employee, permit that employee to inspect such personnel files which are used or have been used to

Exhibit 2-6 Types of Discrimination by Private Employers Prohibited by State EEO Laws

This chart illustrates the personal characteristics protected by various state laws. In other words, a private employer may not make any adverse employment decisions based on these characteristics.

State	Age	Marital status	National origin	Physical handicap	Pregnancy[1]	Race	Religion	Sex	Number of employees[2]
Alabama			No EEO statute						
Alaska[3,4]	X(18 and over)[5]	X	X	X	X	X	X	X	1
Arizona			X			X	X	X	15
Arkansas			No EEO statute						
California[6]	X[7]	X	X	X	X	X	X	X	5
Colorado	X(18–60)[8]		X	X	O	X	X	X	1
Connecticut	X[7]	X	X	X[9]	X	X	X	X	3
Delaware	X(40–65)[10]		X			X	X	X	4
District of Columbia[4]	X(18–65)[10]	X	X	X	O	X	X	X	1
Florida	X[11]	X	X	X		X	X	X	15
Georgia	No comprehensive EEO statute; exception: Age (40–65)[10]								
Hawaii[12]	X(18 and over)[10]	X	X	X			X	X	1
Idaho	X(18–60)[10]		X			X	X	X	10
Illinois[13]	X(45 and over)[10]		X	X[9]	X	X	X	X	15
Indiana	X(40–65)[10]		X	X[9]		X	X	X	6
Iowa	X(18 and over)[10]		X	X[9]	X	X	X	X	1
Kansas			X		O	X	X	X	4
Kentucky	X(40–65)[10]		X	X	O	X	X	X	8
Louisiana	No comprehensive EEO statute; exception: Age (40–70)[10]								20
Maine	X(18 and over)[10]		X	X[9]	X	X	X	X	1
Maryland	X(18 and over)[10]	X	X	X[9]	X	X	X	X	15
Massachusetts[4]	X(40–65)		X	X	X	X	X	X	6
Michigan	X(18 and over)[10]		X	X	X[9]	X	X	X	4
Minnesota[15]	X[16]	X	X	X[9]	X	X	X	X	1
Mississippi			No EEO statute						
Missouri				X[9]	O	X	X	X	6
Montana	X(18 and over)[5]	X	X	X[9]	X	X	X	X	1
Nebraska	X(40–65)[10]	X	X	X[9]		X	X	X	15
Nevada	X(18 and over)[10]		X	X		X	X	X	15
New Hampshire	X(19–65)	X	X	X[9]	O	X	X	X	6

State	Age statute									No.
New Jersey[17]	X(18 and over)[10]	X		X[9]	X[9]			X	X	1
New Mexico	X(18–65)[10]	X		X[9]	X[9]			X	X	4
New York	X(18–65)[10]	X	X	X[9]	X			X	X	4
North Carolina[18]	X(18 and over)[5]	X		X				X	X	15
North Dakota	X(40–65)[10]	X		X				X	X	15
Ohio	X(40–65)[19]	X		X				X	X	4
Oklahoma		X			O			X	X	15
Oregon	X(18–65)[10]	X		X[9]	X[9]			X	X	1
Pennsylvania	X(40–62)[10]	X		X[9]	X[9]			X	X	4
Rhode Island	X(45–65)[10]	X		X	X			X	X	4
South Carolina	X[11]	X		X	X	O		X	X	15
South Dakota		X			O			X	X	1
Tennessee		X		X	X			X	X	8
Texas	No comprehensive EEO statute; exception: physical handicap									1
Utah	X(40 and over)[10]	X	X	X[9]	X[9]			X	X	25
Vermont		X		X	X			X	X	1
Virginia[20]	No comprehensive EEO statute; exception: physical handicap									1
Washington	X(40–65)[10]	X	X	X[9]	O			X	X	8
West Virginia[21]	X(40–65)[10]	X		X	X			X	X	12
Wisconsin	X(40–65)[10]	X		X[9]	X			X	X	1
Wyoming		X		X				X	X	2

[1] "O" denotes prohibition in guidelines issued by agency responsible for enforcing state's EEO law.
[2] Employers with fewer employees than the indicated number in a particular state are not subject to the law.
[3] Alaska also prohibits discrimination on the basis of changes in marital status or parenthood.
[4] State law also prohibits discrimination on the basis of sexual preference.
[5] State law could be interpreted to prohibit mandatory retirement at any age.
[6] California also prohibits discrimination on basis of medical condition.
[7] State law prohibits mandatory retirement at any age, except for "executives."
[8] Prohibition only against discharge on basis of age.
[9] These states also prohibit discrimination on basis of mental handicap.
[10] Exemption for retirement under pension or retirement plan.
[11] State law prohibits mandatory retirement prior to age 70, except for "executives."
[12] Hawaii also prohibits discrimination on basis of arrest and court records.
[13] Illinois also prohibits discrimination on basis of unfavorable military discharge.
[14] Massachusetts also prohibits discrimination on basis of arrest and conviction (misdemeanor) records.
[15] Minnesota also prohibits discrimination on basis of status with regard to public assistance.
[16] State law will prohibit mandatory retirement prior to age 70, except for "executives."
[17] New Jersey also prohibits discrimination on basis of liability for service in the U.S. Armed Forces.
[18] North Carolina also prohibits discrimination on basis of a person's possessing sickle cell trait or hemoglobin C trait.
[19] Prohibition only against discharge or refusal to interview applicants on basis of age.
[20] Virginia also prohibits discrimination on the basis of arrest records.
[21] West Virginia also prohibits discrimination on the basis of blindness.
Source: Towers, Perrin, Forster, & Crosby, May 1979.

determine that employee's qualifications for employment, promotion, additional compensation, or termination or other disciplinary action.

The act, although sweeping, excludes letters of reference and records relating to the investigation of an employee's possible criminal offense.

There are hundreds of bills pending at federal and state levels which will likely increase the requirements for data privacy and disclosure among employers, toward the California example. As well as personnel records, the proposals cover information in medical and health status records and also cover the "invasion of privacy" created by the use of the polygraph (lie detector) for certain employment purposes (Ewing, 1977; Linowes, 1978; Murg and Maledon, 1977).

Other Pertinent Laws

To round out the legal picture, it is important to note additional federal laws affecting human resource management. The Comprehensive Employment and Training Act (CETA) provides federal sponsorship and funding for programs to train disadvantaged individuals through private employers. The programs expand the supply of available labor for an employer and at the same time serve to aid the disadvantaged.

The Occupational Safety and Health Act (OSHA) imposes a wide range of requirements on employers relating to working conditions and operating practices, but also imposes demands on staffing and on training practices of employers. OSHA may also cause changes in the design of jobs, leading to shifts in staffing and training requirements.

The Employee Retirement Income Security Act (ERISA) establishes certain standards for employer-sponsored benefit programs. Under ERISA, personnel policies and practices regarding termination, retirement, and reemployment may be regulated and thus have an influence on human resource planning. Also ERISA requirements impose burdens on personnel-related costs and upon informational records and reporting relating to employees.

Finally, there is an extensive body of labor law which directly affects the determination and administration of employment terms for covered employees. As professional and technical (white-collar) employees are represented by labor unions, this body of federal law, regulations, and administrative rulings of the National Labor Relations Board (NLRB) all directly affect employment practices. Human resource planning needs to take into consideration the potential implications of legal requirements under collective bargaining and contract administration.

CHANGING ATTITUDES TOWARD WORK AND CAREERS

Changes in the demographic composition of our work force and changes in economic, technological, and legal environmental conditions are accompanied by changing worker attitudes. In fact, much of the legislation affecting human resources is attributable to changing social attitudes toward work, management, and governmental intervention. Also, the growth of the work force due to entry of women reflects changing attitudes toward work and sex roles.

Changing employee attitudes are discussed in various sections of this book, but it is useful to highlight here three primary changes that are occurring. The increased participation by women in work and the changes in management practices necessitated by dual careers, particularly, are important points to consider. Changing employee attitudes toward relocations and transfers are creating new patterns of worker mobility in our society. Third, changes in individual work values and career attitudes are bringing strong pressures to bear on the work ethic and on management efforts to improve productivity and work satisfaction.

Working Women and Dual Careers

As pointed out earlier in this chapter, an increasing proportion of adult females in our society are opting to work rather than function as housewives, mothers, and dependents. More women are working, particularly younger women. Nearly one of every two women now works. And in the prime working age classification (25 to 45), the absolute number of working women will more than triple from 1960 to 1980, due to the aging pattern of the population and the "post-war baby" bulge that is moving into the work force.

Women who work tend to be higher-educated and to come from higher-income families than women who do not work. And nearly 60 percent of all working women are married and have a working spouse. As a result, statistics show that of all families in the United States with incomes of $22,200 or more, representing the top 20 percent of all families, more than half (54 percent) have dual careers (Kronholz, 1978; Malabre, 1978).

Of mothers with children enrolled in school, 58 percent are employed. Of mothers with children too young for school, 41 percent work. The constraints traditionally perceived as restricting employment among young mothers have been struck down by strong motivations to work. Among these motivations are certainly career aspirations and desires for self-development and self-fulfillment. But a more pervasive motive relates to the economic conditions described earlier, a desire to increase family income as a way to improve or maintain a desired standard of living in the face of inflation. Family constraints on work, inflexible working conditions, occupational barriers, and sex stereotyping of job roles all have been obstacles to female employment and career advancement, but all are relenting (Bailyn, 1973; Blaxall and Reagan, 1976; Schonberger, 1972; Schreiber, 1977; Theodore, 1971; Young, 1976).

In low-income families, both spouses often work to make financial ends meet. Personal career fulfillment may have little to do with the decision to work. For more affluent couples, women typically seek satisfying professional or managerial careers, and while income certainly may be a motivating factor, it is not the primary factor. Disturbing tensions arise between wives who work because of strict financial need and those who work because they want the

status, satisfaction, and adventure of carving a niche in the labor market
(Ignatius, 1978). According to one report, it is increasingly common to hear
lower-income wives express resentment at the competition, social as well as
economic, they face from middle- and upper-income women who, they feel, do
not have to work. Yet the types of work and the motives for doing it differ
widely.

Any dual-career family must cope with common problems centering on
conflicting goals and conflicting roles. Career-based tensions can be a factor
prompting marital strife and divorce. Indeed the divorce rate nationally has
increased as dual-career prevalence has increased. But by and large, open
communications, careful planning, and resolution of conflicts as they develop
can smooth dual-career relationships. For employers, too, dual careers create
needs: for empathy, certainly, but also for flexible personnel policies concerning
employment (and nepotism), vacation and work scheduling, maternity leaves
(and even paternity leaves), and employee benefits. Such actions are discussed
in applicable chapters in this book (Hall and Hall, 1978; Holstrom, 1973;
Rapaport and Rapaport, 1969).

Mobility Patterns

One effect of dual careers is an increased reluctance of such couples to consider
transfers or promotions involving relocations. A relocation for an individual
usually means uprooting both careers, a generally unwelcome disruption. As a
result, we may find in the future an increased career rigidity among dual-career
employees. Aspiration levels may be suppressed by the desire to maintain the
dual-career situation. Career path blockages and possible performance problems
may thus occur and would need to be addressed by management. Similarly,
employers may need to offer special inducements to dual-career couples to
relocate, including identification or creation of a suitable job opportunity for the
adversely affected spouse.

Moving is becoming less popular for all employees, however, not merely
dual-career employees. Getting people to relocate is an increasingly difficult
task. In the 1960s, mobility was perceived as the goal for many career-minded
employees, who believed that if "you're moving, you're a fast track supermobile" (Jennings, 1967, 1970, 1972).

But today, mobility is not always seen as critical to career development and
to personal work satisfaction. A major factor is the leveling of career goals.
More and more employees are setting sights on desirable jobs rather than a rapid
sequence of jobs leading to "somewhere in the executive suite." Goals are more
realistic. And so are economic assessments of individuals who recognize the high
costs entailed in frequent relocations. The difficulties of obtaining desired
housing in different parts of the country at comparable costs and financing alone
discourage many relocation decisions. Even if the employer foots all the related
expense bills and gives time off for the move, the dislocations created by the
move are often considered to outweigh the benefits of the relocation. When
professional and managerial employees do agree to move, the tab is high for the
employers, impelling them also to weigh each move's merits.

A Changing Work Attitude

Underlying this shift is the possibility that many Americans no longer flatly subscribe to the work ethic and choose instead to trade income and opportunities for a recasting of life values and activities. Work gives way to leisure, study, volunteer activities, and family activity. Nonwork activities are increasingly important for many workers. Sociologist Amitai Etzioni observed in a *Psychology Today* editorial,

> They increasingly feel that what used to be called nonproductive pursuits are quite legitimate patterns of living. That having more time for leisure, each other, sex, education, culture, politics, is as good as working 10 more years, or better. That you can't take it with you, and hence, you might as well spend your savings now, enjoy your life now, even if this may mean that you will have less to spend later or may run out of money one day (Etzioni, 1977).

Some authors have called for changes in our economic system to enhance participation and satisfaction of individuals in their careers. They cite research on employee attitudes indicating employees find work tedious, boring, and stifling. The solutions called for involve enrichment of jobs and sweeping modifications of organizational and management practices governing work (Gooding, 1972; Levitan and Johnston, 1973; Myers, 1970; Sheppard and Herrick, 1972). Recent attention to the quality of work life, discussed in Chapter 9, has provided a focus for studies and employer applications.

Some authorities call for an interspersing of earning and learning of a living, for interweaving employment and self-renewal, as a condition for effective careers. Education and work need not, they argue, be two separate phases in life, but can be two roles between which individuals move freely (Wirtz, 1975).

Employee Aspirations

Aspirations and expectations of individuals entering business organizations to become managers focus on the meaning of work and careers. Studies by Procter and Gamble revealed four key job qualities sought by men and women today:

1　To get a feeling of achievement from their work
2　To see long-range opportunities for advancement
3　To feel they are in the kind of work where their abilities are used best
4　To know their ideas are welcomed

Cold cash has not lost its appeal, but companies such as Procter and Gamble have considered these demands noteworthy and have reacted to them with organizational changes (Ewell, 1977).

Competition for such meaningful working situations and for scarce promotional opportunities is heightened by the fact that there are so many younger people in the work force. The swell of younger workers is an important factor contributing to changing work and career attitudes. Arnold Weber, of Carnegie-Mellon University, noted:

Clearly you're going to have a lot more mid-career disappointment because of that hump in the 24 to 44 year olds. There will be a greater sense of personal frustration and a lot more competition as more women and minorities come looking for jobs (*Business Week,* 1978).

The glut of talent is beneficial to the employers, such as P&G, as they can screen out the best talent for the jobs available. But employee reactions cannot be expected to remain hopeful and achievement-oriented. Weber observed:

Their aspirations eroded by the extreme competition, their opportunities crimped by what they judge to be unfair advantages given to some groups at the expense of others, their economic gains dampened by their great availability and their feelings of injustice heightened by the need to contribute to programs of income mainte- nance for others, these individuals are likely to view collective action as necessary to stake their claim in the labor market.

This collective action may take the form of increased interest in labor unions, efforts to push out older workers through early retirement, or an overt backlash against programs for affirmative action. Most likely, however, it will result in a redirection of career interests and a lowering of career aspirations to fit the realities of actual job opportunities available (Flint, 1978).

The changes in career attitudes are sweeping, having roots in economic, technological, and demographic changes, and reflecting fundamental shifts in values regarding work and leisure. Heightened public awareness of careers may have had something to do with deteriorating aspirations. Concerns about life adjustment and passage through critical life stages (or crises) have heightened as people realize that life is short and there is much to do. Working alone is not all there is, and when the going gets rough perhaps it is not the strategy but the goal that needs revision.

Chapter 3

Implementing Human Resource Planning: Staff Roles

KEY POINTS

- The emergence of human resource planning reflects a broadening of the mission of the personnel function.
- New full-time staff roles have been established in many companies to provide support and guidance to managerial practices in human resource planning.
- HRP professionals fulfill various roles, depending on the tasks and organizational priorities. Seven basic categories of activities represent core roles found common in a study of human resource planning positions.
- A checklist of activities involved in human resource planning provides a basis for defining roles to be performed.
- Consulting roles and skills are vital in effective implementation of changes called for in human resource planning.

The value of human resource planning depends on effective implementation. Neither the importance of implementation nor its difficulty is a new insight. In fact, the critical issue confronting human resource planning professionals today is highlighted in comments made by Niccolo Macciavelli, the Italian political observer, in 1514:

47

> It should be borne in mind that there is nothing more difficult to arrange, more doubtful of success, and more dangerous to carry through than initiating changes. . . . The innovator makes enemies of all those who prospered under the old order, and only lukewarm support is forthcoming from those who would prosper under the new. Their support is lukewarm partly from fear of their adversaries, who have the existing laws on their side, and partly because men are generally incredulous, never really trusting new things unless they have tested them by experience.

Great is the challenge, and seemingly small is the reward for anyone attempting to introduce new ways of managing in an organization.

Yet, as has been explained in the previous chapters, changes in organizations are not wished, but are rather necessitated by external developments. The needs for human resource planning are often apparent, but the means of implementing the necessary processes are often elusive. This chapter addresses the crucial issue: How do we get on with the tasks of human resource planning?

Human resource planning is not a staff function, per se. It is fundamentally a management responsibility, and an aspect of the general management process. However, to achieve results, this responsibility is assigned. The buck stops somewhere, and in this case it is typically passed to the personnel/human resources staff. Occasionally human resource planning is performed solely within operating units or in other staff functions, such as business planning, accounting, or finance. Typically, systematic efforts to forecast and respond to changing human resource needs fall on the shoulders of staff professionals somewhere.

To a considerable extent, human resource planning has been viewed as a logical extension of traditional human resource/personnel staff functions. Accordingly, we will examine in this chapter the evolving scope and structure of the overall function in large organizations, with specific attention to human resource planning activities performed.

With a view toward continuing recognition of human resource planning as an important process, we also profile the activities considered pertinent to this function. Based on a study of the work of professionals in human resource planning, a role model is presented describing roles and activities performed.

Associated with roles and component activities are competencies. Certainly the ability to help managers understand and apply the techniques and systems of human resource planning is central to the implementation problem. Unless managers and human resource professionals alike have the understanding, the skills, and the resources to take practical actions, changes are not likely to occur. Too often human resource programs are conceived and proposed, then languish for lack of effective implementation support. And there is a natural resistance to change in organizations, as Machiavelli noted—even to change in relatively innocuous personnel systems.

Development of effective strategies for overcoming resistance to new management practices is, then, another key in human resource planning. Inherent in the roles of the professional is a need for effective consulting skills, along with specialist and managerial skills. This chapter considers the behavioral implications of the human resource planning process and offers guidelines for effective implementation strategies.

AN EMERGING STAFF FUNCTION

In many companies, human resource (personnel) concerns have commanded increasing amounts of attention from managers and increasing allocations of resources for programs and staff support. As companies deal with changing social and individual values, come face-to-face with the application of employment-related laws, and experience human resource constraints in achieving business plans and objectives, human resource management takes on increased significance.

Managing human resources, like other resources (financial, physical, natural, etc.), is primarily a line management responsibility. But the demands have grown in this area, as in other resource management areas, and staff functions have emerged and expanded to aid management. Top management continues to provide companywide policy and philosophy relating to human resource matters and participates in decisions and negotiations having broad, long-range impact on the direction of the company's human resource management. Operating management (intermediate level in an organization) has primary responsibility for implementing policy. Programs and varied compliance and reporting requirements consume increasing amounts of the time of managers at this level. And it is often difficult to convince operating managers that human resource matters are, in fact, critical in their profit performance. To help them, many have been given broader authority and greater staff and budgets to deal with human resource problems. And corporate-level human resource staffs have expanded to provide needed expertise, guidance, and support.

IBM's vice president of Personnel, Walton E. Burdick, described the role of his staff in this way: "Our major objectives are to: educate line management, particularly to potential change; prepare them to address this change, by developing the right policies; and help them to communicate these policies to their people." Where does the line fall between line and staff responsibility? Burdick observed: "We must keep our personnel professionals from attempting to manage the business. Maybe this is terribly elementary, but it has been my experience that when the personnel people fail in their task they do so primarily for two reasons: either they do not get involved sufficiently to *influence* management or they overstep their staff role and attempt to usurp management's role" (Burdick, 1976).

The human resource (personnel) staff function has expanded in the number, variety, and scale of its activities. It has also changed in the nature of the roles performed and the emphasis of its activities. Naturally, human resource planning is a direct reflection of the changes that have evolved over recent decades.

New Emphases

Human resource staff functions have long been charged with administration of company policies and programs in such bread-and-butter activity areas as labor relations, recruitment and employment, benefits, compensation, communications, and training. Responsibility for basic personnel functions continues to grow as the scale of these activities grows. And the sophistication of practices and techniques in these areas has increased as well.

The principal change in the human resource function is in the emergence of new activities. Staff have been added to develop and administer affirmative action programs and look after EEO compliance and reporting requirements. OSHA has prompted addition of specialists in safety and health programs and compliance requirements. Thanks to ERISA, increasingly complex IRS regulations, and EEO regulations, all affecting employee compensation and benefits practices, staff attention has also swelled in this changing area. All compliance requirements have impelled the introduction of comprehensive computer-based employee information systems, in turn requiring additional specialized staff to build and operate the systems.

Increased emphasis on the development of the organization and individual employee competencies has resulted in new staff activities in training and development, organizational development, planning, and research. More sophisticated employee inventory systems and internal placement systems and procedures are the result of increased staff attention.

The specific growth in these areas is represented by the data in Exhibit 3-1, drawn from the results of a Conference Board survey of 673 companies in 1975 (Janger, 1977). Other studies confirm the trends in the human resource staff function (Burack and Miller, 1976; Foulkes, 1975; Meyer, 1976).

Most important, the human resource function is providing a planning thrust for human resource management in an organization. "A major focus has been on integrating the company's personnel plans with the business plans of the divisions and the company as a whole," reported the Conference Board study (Janger, 1977). The staff is dealing with longer-term issues regarding laws, values, and the future effectiveness of the organization. Above all, changing emphases have called for strengthened practices in planning and control, as a basis for more effective and more comprehensive management of people as resources.

The president of Cummins Engine Company, James A. Henderson, was asked what he expected of his company's human resource function. In his reply he said:

> The job ahead for both top management and the personnel department can be summed up very simply as: fewer people, better people, and leadership. That is, fewer people to do a given amount of work, thereby increasing productivity and ultimately cash flow. Better people, in order to cope successfully with a less favorable environment and find new ways to do the job, and leadership, in order to make major changes in the way we do business (Henderson, 1977).

Exhibit 3-1   Personnel Activities Emerging as Important Since 1965 in 673 Companies

	Percentage of companies	
Activity	Corporate level	Intermediate level
Equal Employment Opportunity	66%	26%
Occupational safety and health	47	21
Safety	18	9
Medical programs	12	5
Industrial hygiene	15	8
Monitoring compliance	42	20
Benefits	36	6
Compensation	37	6
Of managers	24	4
Of nonsupervisory employees	13	4
Of sales representatives	7	3
Training and development	35	7
Of managers, professionals and supervisors	29	6
Of nonsupervisory employees	12	4
Of disadvantaged groups	13	6
Labor force forecasting and planning	28	6
Organization development	25	4
Planning and research	20	3
Labor relations	21	6
Recruitment, selection, and placement	18	4

Source: Excerpted from Allen R. Janger, *The Personnel Function: Changing Objectives and Organization,* The Conference Board, New York, 1977, Table 4-4, p. 40.

This kind of expectation involves a requirement for needs analysis, information gathering and analysis, integrative forecasting and control, all basic human resource planning functions.

Staff Roles

The emergence of new activities has been accompanied by the emergence of new patterns of staff involvement in the human resource management process. The human resource professional is far more than an administrator or mere clerk. The function involves identification of forces affecting management practices and advising managers on suitable responses. The staff function is not so much to initiate change as to help lend perspective to changes facing the organization. "With so much potential for change facing us," observed IBM's Burdick, "we have to be very selective. We must anticipate it and get there far enough in advance so that our companies can be foresighted and progressive, yet not subject to short-term changes that probably won't exist two or three years from now."

The human resource staff professional is, at least in part, a consultant to management. A far more popular role, consulting implies fact gathering, diagnosis, prescription, and objective assistance and guidance on human resource problems facing managers. Yet there is a shortcoming in assuming the consulting mantle; not all managers may readily want or even accept consulting assistance, particularly from a personnel staff heretofore administratively attuned.

Similarly, trends indicate a continuing need to specialize, with the result that personnel professionals are now compensation specialists, benefits specialists and actuaries, counselors, trainers, EDP specialists, and "human resource planners." Specialization continues to be necessary in the face of complexity, but not at the expense of the breadth necessary to be attuned to business needs.

The various activities being performed in the human resource staff functions of large organizations have had an effect, too, upon the staff professionals. Certainly the increased resources and top management recognition have upgraded the caliber and image of personnel managers (Meyer, 1976; Murray, 1975). And yet, at the same time, the multiplicity of functions, the lack of training in many of the new disciplines required, and the frequent absence of clearly defined roles and authority limits drive some human resource professionals wild (Berkwitt, 1972). A personnel officer in Wells Fargo Bank observed that many personnel people by training and temperament have developed a truncated view of their role in the organization. Personal development through the lower levels of the function, as in any function, is segmented and specialized. This early experience leaves an indelible imprint on perceptual faculties, with the result that many look at their position as a collection of specialties which are to be practiced separately and in a passive or reactive manner (*Personnel Journal*, 1973).

The emerging human resource function comprises individual professionals who are able to keep up with the external changes and the technology applicable and who can effectively manage the tensions inherent in a staff function. The identity crisis of personnel staff is giving way as the function matures and gains strength within organizations (Hoffman, 1978; Kmetz, 1973; Ritzer and Trice, 1969; Trice and Ritzer, 1972).

Staff Responsibilities

The activities associated with human resource planning (that is, forecasting, succession planning, career development, and productivity improvement) have been scattered among the traditional personnel functions. Training staff determined training needs and looked after career management. Recruitment and employment forecasted staffing needs and specified job requirements. Job design and performance standards were considered as job descriptions were written or updated for salary administration purposes. Surveys of personnel practices found that most companies claimed they performed "manpower planning" activities (Janger, 1965; TPF&C, 1971). However, the activities were not always regular nor were they performed by a separate unit or staff member. Janger found 240 to 249 companies said they had manpower planning, but this work was assigned to "management development, organization planning, compensation, recruiting, or personnel research units because much of the normal work of these units necessarily involves manpower planning." In some cases, it was performed as a part-time responsibility of the personnel executive (Janger, 1965).

A survey by IBM researcher Ed Geisler found that "manpower planning" was conducted by various organizational functions, including financial, planning, operations, and personnel units. In the early 1970s the placement of the function was unsettled. Enthusiastic efforts of staff personnel frequently overlapped and resulted in duplication, confusion, and general inefficiency (Geisler, 1967, 1968).

In the 1970s, however, manpower planning, reborn as human resource planning, emerged as a separate unit of the human resource staff in many large organizations. Clearly "personnel" was the place for the function to be; and to achieve results, full-time staff committtment is necessary. The shakeout of human resource planning accompanied a reevaluation of the entire personnel function in many organizations, resulting in redirection of activities and reorganization. Human resource planning was identified as an important theme for companies concerned with issues of policy formulation, policy implementation, innovation, and audit and control (Foulkes and Morgan, 1977; *Personnel,* 1978).

Some companies found that traditional personnel specialists had difficulty accommodating these new processes. Here the personnel function was effectively split in two parts: one concerned with traditional personnel "maintenance" functions such as employment, records, payroll, benefits, salary administration, and labor relations and the other concerned with human resource planning and development, including forecasting, management development and succession, EEO and affirmative action, and organization development (see Sokolik, 1969, for a discussion of this split function concept).

Decentralization

At the same time there was the question whether human resource planning should be centralized at the corporate staff level or decentralized to the operating departments and divisions. In many companies duplicative functions emerged, in part due to lack of effectiveness of those that existed. The need for staff support and guidance was clearly recognized by many managers, and these managers responded by establishing functions that could serve these needs, regardless of staff assignments elsewhere in the organization. As a rule, if the divisions act first, corporate management finds it difficult to add corporate staff later. Yet a small corporate staff unit can rarely make a substantial impact in a large diverse organization.

Staff functions should be performed at the corporate level wherever any of the following conditions prevail:

Interests conflict among the profit centers or divisions.
Corporatewide consistency is desired.
Corporate negotiation with external parties is necessary.
Economies are achieved by performing the work centrally.

Functions should be performed at the profit center or divisional level wherever any of the following conditions prevail:

> The work is unique to that profit center.
> Ongoing close coordination with divisional operations is necessary.
> The work is within the competence of the local staff.
> There is little or no benefit to be gained by corporate scope.

Of course, close cooperation among corporate and decentralized staff units is vital for their respective functions to be performed effectively.

Through the past two decades staff functions have developed to perform activities in human resource planning. Beginning as extensions of traditional activities, they took root wherever the soil was fertile, that is, where management needs existed. Government-mandated programs have resulted in more extensive staffing, but human resource planning has nevertheless emerged as a staff function. By 1979, more than half of the *Fortune* 500 companies, and an even greater share of banks and insurance companies, had full-time, human resource planning staff professionals. The trend is toward recognition of the function as a necessary specialization in human resource management (Foulkes, 1977; *Business Week,* 1979).

Within the past five years, many companies have established staff positions to deal with emerging human resource programs and management concerns. New position titles have emerged, such as the following:

> Director, human resource utilization
> Director, management resources
> Director, management resources planning
> Director, personnel planning and development
> Director, organization and management planning
> Director, human resources
> Manager, human resource planning
> Manager, human resource planning and development
> Manager, human resource planning and staffing
> Manager, organization and management resources
> Manager, personnel resources planning
> Manager, staff planning and career development

These titles represent the introduction of new staff positions charged with anticipating future personnel requirements and planning program, policy, and organizational changes that will satisfy these requirements. These positions have been established because corporate executives believe that human resource management activities require the same future-oriented perspective and direction that guide financial, marketing, and other management activities.

Organization of Human Resource Planning Staff

How are human resource planning activities translated into professional staff positions and organizational structures? Many variations in practice are reported by the study respondents. However, the organizational pattern illustrated in Exhibit 3-2 represents a structure common to many of the respondents.

The human resource planning activity is typically headed by a manager or director of human resource planning and development who reports directly to the senior personnel or human resource officer of the company. Whether the title is director or manager is a moot point, depending on a particular organization's nomenclature and salary administration practices.

The human resource planning function typically includes a combination of two or more of the following functional areas:

• Manager, human resource planning—Concerned with forecasting and planning activities and the collection and analysis of pertinent human resource information. The position may involve supervision of a personnel information center, maintenance of personnel policies and standards, and services relating to affirmative action planning (for example, labor market analysis or flows analysis).

• Manager, management or executive development—Concerned with senior-level management succession planning (including charting and replacement planning where practiced), arranging for executive transfers and promotions, arranging for external management development program participation (for example, Harvard), and assessment of management candidates (whether systematically or merely personal judgment). The position may also involve coordinating external searches for executive candidates, supervision of assess-

Exhibit 3-2   Generic Organization of the HRP Staff Function

Vice president, human resources

Manager or director, human resource planning and development

Human resource planning	Management development	Training and development	Recruitment and staffing
• Forecasting	• Succession planning	• Training programs	• College relations
• Planning			• Professional staffing
	• Executive development	• Career programs	
• Information systems			• Internal placement
	• Executive search	• Organization development	
• Policies and standards			• Clerical staffing
	• Executive assessment		
• EEO/AA support			
	• Management organization charts and consulting		

ment centers or other assessment programs, consulting on organizational changes and executive position description, and maintenance of management level organization charts.

• Manager, training and development—Concerned with determining training needs, developing or obtaining programs to satisfy these needs, and administering in-house programs. The position often includes programs in career planning and development and projects or programs aimed at organizational development (for example, team building, job design, survey feedback).

• Manager, recruitment and staffing—Concerned with the various dimensions of recruitment of personnel from outside the organization. College relations and professional (experienced hire) staffing are usual concerns. Internal placement (including job posting) and nonexempt staffing are also sometimes part of the job.

In the full-blown function, equal employment opportunity and affirmative action planning, personnel research, and various employee relations responsibilities (for example, relocation, employee counseling, outplacement services, community relations) may be included.

The scope of activities, the position titles, and the extent of staff resources are all variable. However, most positions characterized by the respondents may be described within the context of this generic organization structure. An important finding is the prevalence of the broad "umbrella" functional responsibility characterizing the managerial position in human resource planning. Sometimes simply titled director of human resources, the position represents a recognition of the developmental and planning elements of the personnel function. Counterparts to the position typically include managers of compensation and benefits, labor relations, and any functions such as training and development, staffing (employment) that are not included under the HRP "umbrella." When training and development are not included, for example, the HRP manager's title is often manager of human resource planning and staffing.

Also, the reporting relationships of the generic positions may shift: The forecasting and planning function may report to the recruitment and staffing manager or one of the others. Management development is sometimes a part of a broader training and development (or "human resource development") function. In a few companies the difference is marked by the existence of two entirely separate human resource functions, each headed by a corporate officer. One is concerned with traditional maintenance activities and services, the other with planning and development activities and services. Nevertheless, there is a relatively new thrust in human resource management which is reflected in the emergence of these new positions and activities. We may expect human resource planning to become an increasingly common part of the human resource staff function as management looks for guidance and support of activities in this area.

Roles in Human Resource Planning

Exhibit 3-4 illustrates eight categories of activities commonly performed in human resource planning. These categories represent roles of human resource

Exhibit 3-3   Excerpts from HRP Position Descriptions

Manager, employee development and planning

Accountable for identifying, developing, implementing, and evaluating policies, practices, and programs which assist management to (1) optimize the return on its investment in employees, (2) select and develop highly effective members of management, and (3) assist employees in developing the knowledge and skills for increased productivity and performance.

Reports to the vice president for employee relations along with the directors of compensation; benefits and employment; employee relations services; health and safety; program review, communications, and compliance; and administrative projects and information systems. Eight professional staff positions in the unit are assigned to the following program areas: employee development, employee planning, executive development, management/supervisory development, management/supervisory selection, and program design and development (including training programs and appraisal programs).

Manager, personnel resources planning

Develops, installs, and administers a program of personnel resources planning for all levels of professional and managerial positions, worldwide, based on coordination of strategic business plans and inventory of current availability. Identifies shortfalls and coordinates development of candidates for future needs with other units of the management resources department, with the corporate planning department, and with the appropriate operating executives.

Reviews group, division, and departmental strategic plans to identify those specific plans or strategies that require additional professional or managerial personnel within the next five years. Consolidates data into a total corporate needs review, and communicates the information gathered to the appropriate managers to ensure coordination.

Director, organization and management resources

Coordinates an integrated human resources management plan that responds to the organizational needs reflected in annual and long-range business plans. Directs organizational design and development support for facilitating organizational restructuring, staffing, team building, and other organization development strategies. Designs and executes programs for early identification, development, and guidance of high-potential employees for executive positions. Establishes career planning and counseling programs for professional, technical, and clerical employees to improve staff utilization and growth. Analyzes human resources data to provide management with information about trends as an aid in identifying problems and making sound staffing decisions. Directs corporate recruitment of candidates for management positions.

Director, human resource utilization

Directs human resource planning activities in all appropriate components and levels of the corporation. Ensures that all departments and divisions have effective performance appraisal systems that are in compliance with corporate procedures. Directs the design and functioning of career-planning systems. Provides mechanisms to identify and act on high-potential employees, substandard achievers, and requests for voluntary transfers. Provides rosters of candidates to fill management position openings. Negotiates difficult interdepartment/interdivision transfers. Identifies and promotes candidates for developmental programs and assignments. Directs data gathering, analysis, and reporting of human resource flows into/through/out of the corporation. Participates in defining opportunities and means to im-

Exhibit 3-3   Excerpts from HRP Position Descriptions (Continued)

prove productivity and the quality of work. Analyzes corporate recruiting needs; provides upper level recruiting services; and gives guidance to the corporation in recruiting, selecting, and placing qualified employees. Provides programs, activities, and assignments to ensure development and maintenance of effective staff.

Manager, human resources planning

Contributes to the corporation by analyzing and recommending policies and procedures and developing systems and models which contribute to the effective hiring, development, and utilization of human resources. Analyzes and recommends revisions to policies, regulations, and procedures (for example, candidate search and selection, performance evaluation, career pathing, promotions and transfers). Develops and applies systems and models for human resource planning, including forecasting future requirements, defining logical career paths, inventorying human resources, and projecting future time periods, identifying future hiring needs by skill type, level, and location, identifying future voids and imbalances, and performing analyses of human resource situations to identify opportunities for improvement (e.g., EEO and AA objectives, turnover, organizational profiles, job tenure).

Exhibit 3-4   Eight roles of human resource planning professionals.

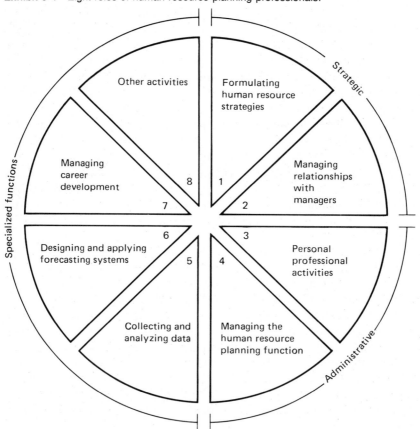

planning professionals identified through a study of activities actually performed (Walker and Wolfe, 1978). The eight role categories are not necessarily found in every human resource planning professional's work, and they certainly are not evenly weighted in time allocation or importance, as might be suggested by the geometric figure. In fact, many combinations of roles are possible, with different emphases based on organizational circumstances.

Two roles are weighted quite heavily relative to all others: *formulating strategies* and *managing relationships with managers.* The activities in these areas are uniquely important in human resource planning because of the implicit purposes of anticipating and effecting change in organizations, of leading and integrating human resource management functions. The *strategic* roles are crucial to the human resource planning professional's effectiveness. However, the skills for these sets of activities are unfamiliar to many people and are often more difficult to develop than technical or administrative skills.

The *administrative* aspects of the work are represented in managing the staff function of human resource planning and in managing personal professional activities. These aspects are often seen as supplementary to other aspects and as expanding inordinately in the attention they demand. Neglect of these roles, however, is often the downfall of human resource planning professionals, as they are necessary maintenance roles.

The four remaining roles identified represent *specialized functions* performed. Primary attention is given one or a combination of three categories of activities: collecting and analyzing data, designing and applying forecasting systems, and managing career development (especially managerial careers). These activity areas are somewhat new to the human resource function in many companies and are also closely linked with the mission of anticipating and managing human resource change. Accordingly, they are viewed as central roles of human resource planning professionals. Additionally, other activities are sometimes performed by the professionals, including recruiting, training, individual employee assessment, or employee counseling. But these other activities are rarely substantial relative to the primary roles.

Changing Roles

The mix of roles changes as demands on human resource planning processes shift within organizations. Certainly there are differences as an organization gains experience in human resource planning (Walker, 1974). And with greater demand and greater staff resources available, increased specialization is possible. Some professionals in large companies today are solely concerned with certain roles such as management succession planning (one aspect of career development), managing personnel information systems, or forecasting and modeling of future staffing needs. A few companies have individuals solely concerned with external labor market analysis, in support of human resource planning and affirmative action planning. At least one corporation has full-time staff devoted to long-range forecasting of conditions affecting strategic plans of the business.

Naturally, not all professionals in human resource planning do the same things. Each HRP professional performs those activities that fit the requirements of the particular job situation. Involvement in particular roles and performance of particular human resource planning activities depend on numerous factors, including the organizational level of the clients served, the availability of other professionals to share the tasks to be performed, the stage of development of the organization's human resource planning process, and the individual's own interests and professional competencies.

Three Role Patterns

We may consider three primary role models to guide our thinking about the activities that might be performed. These models are generalizations regarding the combinations of roles actually filled by human resource staff members. They are: specialist, consultant, and manager.

The primary "doer" in human resource planning is the specialist. Serving as the primary technical expert, this professional acts as a task specialist—a clinician, engineer, analyst, or practitioner. Typically this is the entry position in a large human resource staff, but it may be the only position in a newly established or emerging human resource planning function. The function involves a heavy involvement in developing and applying systems and techniques in such areas as forecasting and data analysis, job and career path analysis and definition, and training design and evaluation. To a considerable extent, the specialist performs tasks that could be performed by operating managers or delegated by managers to other employees. But for economy and for technical proficiency, the work is performed as staff work. Of course, specialist positions need not be in the human resource function itself, but may report (and often do) to divisional managers or to other staff managers (for example, finance, engineering, project management).

The consultant is a role model concerned with the analysis of needs and formulating of human resource strategies. This type of position is that of a change agent, a facilitator of the human resource planning process, and a diagnostician. The primary task is to induce action and effect change in the organization. Specialist roles are performed, but the emphasis is on interaction with managers as clients, to help them identify changes calling for action and to equip them with the necessary tools. In some organizations, human resource planning is primarily viewed as consultative; specialized support is not provided by staff. The function is thus one of catalyst only, and if anything is to be *done* operating management must get it done.

In organizations with formalized human resource planning processes and numerous professionals, the managerial role model appears. Particular emphasis is given to the internal management and administration of the human resource planning function itself: budgeting, staffing, organization, work assignments and scheduling, coaching and counseling, and reviewing the work performed. Monitoring and supervising are important functions. Also, managers negotiate for resources needed and run "interference" for staff in establishing and maintaining working relationships with managers in other units of the organization. The managerial function necessarily is more important in larger, more complex organizations and in organizations with a high level of "politics."

Roles Vary with Level

As shown in Exhibit 3-5, the functions served by these role models vary with the organizational level served. Any professional in human resource planning typically adopts a configuration of roles based on the activities actually performed and tends to focus on a particular organizational level. These factors may be consciously determined in the structuring of the function.

This provides the professional with an array of opportunities for professional growth. A specialist may pursue a specialist career track, building on personal competencies considered to be strengths—analysis, research, reporting, and program implementation support. Alternatively, the specialist may shift to another role model, getting more involved in consulting and managerial roles, first at the same organizational level and then at higher levels.

It is important to note that each role model is important and potentially satisfying professionally. Individual competencies and interests should be considered in the development or adoption of the functions to be filled. Typically, salary administration systems allot greater recognition to consultative

Exhibit 3-5   How Professional Activities Vary with Organizational Level

Organizational level of clients served	Professional role models		
	Staff manager	Staff consultant	Staff specialist
Top management/ board of directors	Obtains and allocates resources: accounts for overall human resource planning process, including costs and benefits	Educates: clarifies goals and influences strategies and structures	Informs: provides requested information
Middle management/ departmental or divisional management	Collaborates: acts as liaison between clients and staff, and among clients	Prescribes: changes in policy, systems, and practices	Diagnoses: identifies multiple alternative solutions to solve problems or satisfy needs
Supervisory management/ technical and professional contributors	Supervises: specialized functional activities	Influences: acceptance and use of systems and practices adopted by management	Provides: training and support; help as well as know-how

Source: Adapted from a figure in James A. Cannon, "Introducing Manpower Plans: Problems and Some Possible Strategies," *Personnel Review,* Spring 1973, pp. 28–36.

and managerial functions and to higher organizational levels. However, people committed to the specialist role model may expand their salary opportunities by moving to organizations that pay more for such jobs.

HUMAN RESOURCE PLANNING ACTIVITIES

Each of the roles described above represents a group of specific activities performed by human resource planning professionals. A survey of eighty-three members of the Human Resource Planning Society identified the activities in Exhibit 3-6 as pertinent to the function. Weights as to the extent each is a part of the job are indicated. The data in this table provide a snapshot of practices that can help fix images of human resource planning, at least for a moment, and provide a useful perspective for structuring one's own job priorities.

Eighty-two different activities are listed in Exhibit 3-6, grouped into eight broad categories, or roles. The role categories were developed through factor analysis of all responses for activities which were reported to have an average weighting score of 1.5 or greater (see the scale in Exhibit 3-6). Seven role categories emerged as distinct. The eighth was added to provide for other activities which commonly round out the work of a human resource planning professional (Walker and Wolfe, 1978).

Interpreting the Activity Listing

Before you study the responses of others, reported at the right side of the activities, go through the entire table and weight the importance and frequency of occurrence of each activity for your own human resource planning function. Follow the instructions provided at the top of the table, which are the same as those used in the original study questionnaire. Once you have put down a number weighting by each activity (0, 1, 2, or 3), you will have a basis for contrasting your activities with those of the study respondents.

Both your answers and the other responses given reflect activities actually performed. It may be that the function should be structured differently, however, and this is quite appropriate. Once you know where you stand now, you have a basis for planning which activities you will give greater or lesser emphasis in the future.

There are other activities that might appropriately be part of the human resource planning function. For example, the list does not explicitly include activities linking human resource planning with business planning. Several respondents mentioned that they:

> Analyze business plans and budgets regarding human resource needs
> Assist in formulating human resource strategies in business plans
> Coordinate with corporate planning and development on strategic human resource issues

Additionally, the work may include organizational analysis, control over

Exhibit 3-6   Human Resource Planning Activities

Below is a list of human resource planning activities which provides a profile of the job of the HRP professional. Consider the extent each activity is an appropriate part of your job and indicate a weight in the margin at the left. Consider both the importance and the frequency of occurrence of each activity and mark the answer that best describes what your job involves:

0   Does not apply, is not a part of my work
1   A small part of my work, occurs occasionally
2   A substantial part of my work (either frequent but not necessarily important or infrequent but highly important)
3   A most significant part of my work (both highly frequent and important)

At the right of each activity is reported the arithmetic mean response of the human resource planning professionals surveyed.

1. Formulating human resource strategies

_____ Propose objectives and goals for human resource planning.	2.31
_____ Propose approaches or strategies.	2.13
_____ Obtain approval and support for strategies.	2.06
_____ Determine resource and related implementation requirements.	1.94
_____ Determine priorities.	1.93

2. Managing relationships with managers

_____ Establish and maintain good working relationships with managers as clients.	2.53
_____ Make formal presentations to obtain management support for specific projects and programs.	2.11
_____ Explain recommendations to gain acceptance for them.	2.07
_____ Consult with managers on human resource planning methods and applications.	1.93
_____ Consult with managers on organizational and human resource problems.	2.06
_____ Prepare (annual) presentation on the organization's human resource conditions and future plans.	1.69
_____ Participate in committees or task forces relating to human resources.	1.46
_____ Train and coach others on human resource planning.	1.40
_____ Interact with governmental, academic, and other human resource planning professionals.	1.40
_____ Effect organizational and job design changes.	1.05

3. Personal professional activities

_____ Organize your work and activities.	2.33
_____ Keep managers/supervisors informed of activities and results.	2.01
_____ Read published materials on human resource planning concepts, theory, and approaches.	1.86
_____ Attend external programs and meetings on human resource planning.	1.68
_____ Write memos or announcements.	1.64
_____ Keep abreast of human resource planning in other organizations.	1.55
_____ Participate as a speaker in external meetings or programs.	1.10
_____ Conduct HRP research to advance the available technology.	0.89
_____ Write articles, papers, or books on HRP.	0.45

Exhibit 3-6   Human Resource Planning Activities (Continued)

4. Manage the human resource planning function

_____ Supervise the work of members.	1.88
_____ Staff and organize the function.	1.83
_____ Set schedules and priorities for work assignments.	1.76
_____ Prepare budgets and plans for human resource activities.	1.68
_____ Allocate resources to activities (funds, computer time, people).	1.48
_____ Obtain (contract with) consultants and vendors.	1.43
_____ Supervise the work of consultants and vendors.	1.43
_____ Write proposals for programs or budgets.	1.41
_____ Interpret statistics and data on results and costs.	1.40
_____ Maintain information on program costs and progress.	1.33

5. Collecting and analyzing data

_____ Design and develop data systems and inventories.	1.68
_____ Identify needs through group discussions or meetings.	1.63
_____ Collect and prepare data.	1.63
_____ Store, analyze, and retrieve data.	1.61
_____ Evaluate past results attained.	1.57
_____ Conduct needs analysis interviews.	1.36
_____ Identify implications of other personnel programs (for example, layoffs, affirmative action programs).	1.36
_____ Identify needs through questionnaire surveys (for example, attitude surveys).	0.93
_____ Maintain organizational charts and manuals.	0.76
_____ Evaluate the human resource condition of prospective acquisitions and vendors.	0.35

6. Designing and using forecasting systems

_____ Design and develop human resource planning systems and techniques.	2.22
_____ Design forecasting systems.	1.64
_____ Forecast recruitment/staffing needs.	1.54
_____ Prepare reports for management (for example, consolidated forecasts).	1.48
_____ Analyze and forecast turnover, mobility.	1.31
_____ Conduct staffing analysis (optimal staffing, productivity).	1.11
_____ Forecast effects of human resource changes on business plans or needs.	1.10
_____ Forecast EEO/affirmative action impact.	0.90
_____ Analyze and forecast labor supply and demand in relevant external labor markets.	0.65

7. Managing career development

_____ Analyze individual development and management succession plans to identify program needs.	1.81
_____ Design and develop systems for management succession planning.	1.71
_____ Design and develop systems for career management/tracking.	1.64
_____ Design and develop systems for internal transfer and promotion.	1.72
_____ Design and develop training and development programs.	1.49
_____ Design and develop systems for appraisal and performance management.	1.46
_____ Conduct or maintain appraisal/assessment data.	1.30

Exhibit 3-6 Human Resource Planning Activities (Continued)

_____ Maintain succession plans.	1.30
_____ Identify job candidates.	1.27
_____ Design and develop management assessment systems.	1.21
_____ Coach/counsel individual employees.	1.07
_____ Monitor achievement of individual development plans.	1.00
_____ Maintain job requirements, career paths.	0.95
_____ Administer cost-reduction programs (for example, layoffs, outplacement).	0.43

8. Other activities

_____ Recruitment/employment	1.28
_____ Individual assessment	1.28
_____ Organization development/team building	1.23
_____ Personnel policies	1.19
_____ Counseling employees	1.12
_____ Conducting training	1.08
_____ Personnel research	1.00
_____ EEO/AA compliance	0.97
_____ Other personnel activities	0.82
_____ Salary administration	0.49
_____ External consulting	0.47
_____ Other nonpersonnel activities (for example, administration, marketing, facilities)	0.41
_____ Employee benefits	0.31
_____ Labor relations	0.31
_____ Health and safety	0.28

Source: Reprinted with permission from _Human Resource Planning,_ vol. I, no. 4, 1978. Copyright 1979 by the Human Resource Planning Society, pp. 192–194.

organizational and positional nomenclature, community and professional relations, employee relocations, and special projects. In some instances, the work might involve serving on a human resource committee composed of senior management.

The checklist presented in Exhibit 3-6 is intended to serve as a profile of the job of the professional in human resource planning, as it is perceived by a sample of such professionals in large organizations. It serves also as a starting point in designing or reviewing the content and structure of such positions, through a consideration of major roles performed.

OVERCOMING OBSTACLES TO CHANGE

At the heart of the human resource planning process is the anticipation and management of change. The professional working in this field, then, must be alert to the many factors impeding organizational responses to change and must be equipped to overcome them. In this section certain critical obstacles commonly encountered by the professional in planning human resources are identified. Some obstacles arise from organizational circumstances while others are personally imposed obstacles.

Management Obstacles

One basic problem often is apathy on the part of operating managers. Managers have traditionally been concerned more with material and financial resources than with human resources. Even top management may give merely lip service to human resource issues confronting the organization. However, where human resource issues are real, the obstacle is a lack of managerial sensitivity. A key function of staff, then, should be to facilitate planning of changes by bringing relevant issues and problems to the attention of managers on different organizational levels at appropriate times. Staff members should advise managers of areas in which they are not taking needed actions. Sensitivity is promoted through awareness and understanding, and these can occur with exposure to the subjects, both through dialogue and through other media, including business and trade journals, professional contacts, and interactions among managers.

Managers are typically concerned with short-term profitability and related business results. Human resource issues often involve long-term benefits with short-term costs. Further, human resource expenditures are often viewed as overhead expenses, not as investments with future returns. A risk of integrating human resource plans with operating business plans is that the latter may tend to focus on short-term costs and results and thus deemphasize the importance of human resource actions. It is incumbent on staff to demonstrate the likely effects of short-range planning and of failure to take necessary human resource actions on future results.

The fact that human resource actions rarely have concrete measures or indices of accomplishment also impedes human resource planning. Buildings and equipment depreciate over time, measured each period by accepted accounting practices. People appreciate over time, come and go from an organization, and have never been measured except as a source of periodic operating expense. Managers must be helped to recognize that human resource variables, while elusive and sometimes abstract, are nevertheless actionable. They must learn to be tolerant of this ambiguity and do their best to assess effectiveness in this area without precise, objective measures. The obvious available measures such as turnover, payroll costs, cost averages, and rates of participation in programs merely scratch the surface of human resource management and should not be overemphasized (Bennett, 1972; Cannon, 1973).

Business complexity, expanded scope, and rapid change experienced by managers today in large corporations also confound human resource planning efforts. In fact, resistance to human resource planning, or planning in any area, is sometimes a defensive reaction to the seemingly threatening characteristics of today's organizational circumstances. Managers tend to resist changes and may avoid admitting needs for changes. The more organizations grow and change, the greater the centripetal force toward the status quo. Thus human resource planning staff face the challenge of introducing additional complexities and constraints in the form of human resource policies, practices, and systems, while at the same time allaying managerial concerns and anxieties about their bureaucratic implications. An important function is to help managers grow as their organizations grow, so that management capabilities (and systems) will be suitably matched with the organizations' changing needs.

Personally Imposed Obstacles

Staff, too, set up barriers to effective human resource management. A common pitfall is excessive zeal: Too much is attempted, too quickly, and with too little resources. Hastily conceived changes in human resource practices are often rushed into implementation without laying adequate groundwork. As a result, new appraisal systems are introduced periodically, none with adequate depth of development and care of implementation. When one fails, another is soon adopted to "correct" previous deficiencies, without an overall strategy for management change. Staff often assume that time and resources are not available and that quick results must be obtained where longer-term efforts are more suitable.

Staff often are too concerned with the sophistication of their systems. Overspecialization, concern for precision and accuracy, and passion for advanced state-of-the-art systems and approaches create problems for the professionals attempting to win management support for changes. Staff often overburden managers with data and with unnecessarily elaborate forms, procedures, and manuals. There is a tendency to concentrate on the design of systems whenever the going seems rough in directly effecting changes in management practices. With this, there is also the risk that staff will turn to professional peers for acknowledgment when managers fail to provide desired responses. And so staff become more concerned about how wonderful their techniques are and about the opinions of their professional colleagues than about the pressing management problems they are supposed to solve.

It is also possible that some staff professionals get bogged down in detail and in organizational politics. In seeking to gain the favor and support of operating managers, many human resource planners tackle minor day-to-day problems while failing to address broader issues. They may settle for impact that falls short of the needs, but which is acceptable to the managers, often meaning the actions do not "rock the boat." Line-staff relationships may be excellent, but at the high price of addressing difficult human resource issues (Austin, 1975; Hills, 1978).

THE CONSULTING PROCESS

In the face of such obstacles and the pressing needs for effecting change in organizations, effective staff-line relationships are critically important. As noted previously, consulting is an important staff role. While consulting has different meanings to different people, it is a process that can be defined, planned, and applied. This final section of this chapter examines the consulting process, its purposes, pitfalls, and techniques.

Purposes

There are dual purposes implicit in consulting, whether it is performed by internal staff of an organization or by external consultants. One purpose is to *induce action*—to get the clients (the managers) to begin a program of change and to continue on this program. The other purpose is to *effect change,* that is, to help clients sustain the momentum of change and bring about lasting improvements in the way the organization functions.

Inducing action is the starting point in human resource planning. Through fact finding, analysis of organizational problems and needs, diagnosis of existing systems and practices, and direct negotiations with managers, the human resource planning professional focuses management attention on key issues requiring attention. Formal audits or problem-oriented study projects follow systematic procedures leading to recommendations for management action. Often as effective, however, are more informal diagnostic and prescriptive efforts of staff as consultants (Schein, 1969).

Many people view this aspect of the process as the essential purpose of consulting. As independent and usually technically expert advisers, consultants consider an organization's particular needs and circumstances and propose a plan of action which the clients may take or leave, as they wish. The consultant is seen as having little or no responsibility for the decisions adopted or for the subsequent implementation of the programs planned.

However, it is the hard work of implementing changes, usually in how people go about doing their jobs, that results in the actual improvements. An important second purpose of consulting, then, is substantive assistance to managers in applying the recommended changes. After recommendations are offered, refined, and adopted, new consulting skills are called for—focusing on the preparation of detailed implementation plans, working closely with people in the client organization, and providing tangible support in the implementation phases (Baker and Schaffer, 1969; Walker, 1970).

Consulting Roles

Consultants are often thought of as providers of information, expertise, or services. The buyer, the client manager, has some specified need—something to be accomplished, information needed, or a problem to be solved. The client who feels his or her own personnel and resources are inadequate to satisfy the need turns to staff or outside resources for consulting assistance. To be retained as a consultant in this situation, the provider must offer some special capability or expertise.

At the same time, many people believe the consultant's proper role is not to impart knowledge and provide assistance, but rather to facilitate change. If the purpose of consulting is, at least in part, inducing action, then the consultant needs to be heavily involved in the defining of needs and the diagnosing of the problems to be solved. This is sometimes compared to the doctor-patient relationship (Edgar H. Schein, 1969). Process consultation emphasizes helping clients solve their own problems. The basic techniques are facilitating the

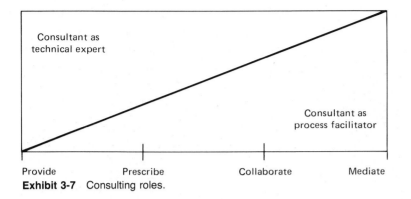

Exhibit 3-7 Consulting roles.

gathering and analysis of information, considering alternative solutions, and making collaborative decisions regarding a course of action. The consultant's own technical expertise and opinions are of less importance than the group's consensus.

These two primary role models are illustrated in Exhibit 3-4. As the technical expert role yields to process facilitation, the consultant assumes less and less leadership, and responsibility for actions rests with the clients. Four points are identified on this continuum representing consulting approaches:

Provide: principally unilaterial provision of ideas, opinions, technical information and designs, with specific recommendations for action. The consultant is objective, detached, and task-oriented, generally short-term; may stay on in implementation phases.

Prescribe: collecting of information and ideas from the clients, used as inputs in defining the client's needs and solutions. The consultant recommends actions with a presumption that the client may assume responsibility for implementation; expertise is still important.

Collaborate: jointly defining the needs and considering the alternative solutions. The consultant offers technical counsel and provides ideas and suggestions, but the ball is clearly in the client's court.

Mediate: principally facilitating the client's own identification and solution of the problems. The consultant is not involved to provide technical expertise, but rather to help the clients reach a satisfactory plan of action on their own. The consultant aids the problem-solving process on a personal, long-term basis.

Which role is best suited for consulting depends on a number of factors, including how well defined the needs are in the first place, what kind of help the client managers want and are comfortable with, and the clients' desire for involvement in the problem-solving process (versus purchasing a solution), the nature of the needs (they may be people-process problems in themselves), and the capabilities of the client personnel to generate pertinent information and develop appropriate solutions (Edgar H. Schein, 1969).

The consulting roles adopted by human resource planning professionals are "all over the map." Some feel their mission is to apply their know-how in the direct solving of problems, such as development of forecasts, succession plans, and development programs. In other instances, they feel they should only facilitate discovery by operating managers of the needs in such areas and help them gain the know-how to meet their own needs. The choice of role may vary from situation to situation within an organization, adapting to the circumstances.

Sometimes human resource planning efforts fail, however, because the responsible staff adopted the inappropriate consulting role. When clients are looking for specific, tangible assistance of a technical nature (for example, determining areas for overhead cost reduction), the last thing managers want is nonspecific, nondirective "facilitation." Similarly, in other situations, managers may be technically competent and feel they can implement whatever actions are required, but may desire assistance in sorting out the problems and alternatives. The human resource planner must be able to shift gears and respond to client needs in the appropriate role pattern (Nord and Durand, 1978).

Guidelines for Consulting Practice

Whatever role is adopted in a given situation, effective consulting is pragmatic. Experience indicates that client managers are *induced to act* and actually *effect change* when the actions of consultants are down-to-earth and realistic. Four guidelines are outlined below as basic qualities of effective consulting (Baker and Schaffer, 1969).

First, *involve the clients* in the problem-solving process. People are more receptive and commit themselves more readily to a change that they have had a hand in formulating. Understanding of why the change is needed, what it will accomplish, and how they should behave under it is greatly increased if they participate in solving the problem. Solicit the client's thinking on the problem. Expose the client to new facts (or old facts presented in a more meaningful format). Have managers participate in thinking through alternative solutions and their likely impact. And remember that nothing cements involvement like public commitment. If you can get client managers to speak out publicly regarding the problem, they will take a more active interest in the solution. But clients also need to be reassured as the process evolves; they need help in understanding the consulting strategy, what is to come, and what results are expected.

Second, the consulting should *begin where the clients are ready to begin*. If the work is beyond what the managers are ready to take on, or if recommended changes entail too great a risk, failure and frustration are likely. A key to effective consulting is to verify managerial *readiness* for change. The adjustment in recommended actions may not be in the scope or direction, but merely in the timing of implementation.

Third, the consultant should *develop workable recommendations*. It is better to concentrate on two or three key recommendations than on a laundry list of proposals that may end up being ignored. An initial sense of accomplishment and success is important in winning the confidence and support of client managers. Workable recommendations have clearly discernible advantages, feasibility, and acceptable risk. Above all, the path for implementing the recommendations should be clearly conveyed, and potential roadblocks should be identified and removed. It is a common error in consulting to try to accomplish too much, too quickly, with too few resources and too little support.

Finally, it is important to *transfer knowledge, ownership, and control* of the planned changes over to management. Once management has approved a plan of action, it is often tempting for the consultants or staff to move right on proudly into implementation. After all, they developed the proposals and know what they entail. The risk is that the results become the responsibility of the consultants, not the decision-making managers. And managers feel quite comfortable in delegating responsibility to others, disassociating themselves from the problems, and then later pointing a finger at the consultants for any resulting failures.

It is essential to get the client managers' full understanding of what must change and the roles they must play in bringing about the change. Action programs must be management programs, not staff programs, and this attitude must be conveyed to other influential managers, or they may drag their feet. The planning of the changes should be jointly conducted to ensure deep involvement by those who will be affected. An administrative mechanism should also be built into the process for managing and monitoring the process.

Managers often use their own "busyness" as a reason for not getting involved in planning of human resources. As a result, they are slow to understand the issues and techniques involved and are reluctant to support human resource programs when the going gets rough. Staff consultants often accept the excuse and assume that their job is to "supplement" management. But the successful implementation of new management practices depends on line managers' understanding and appreciation. It is important to induce action and obtain management approval of actions, but it is more important to make human resource planning a *management activity* that can bring about lasting change.

IBM's Walt Burdick observed:

> The future will require the further professionalization of the personnel function—the right people, the right training, a complete understanding of corporate principles and business objectives and a thorough understanding of the role of personnel in the organization. The last quarter of this century is going to be one of primary emphasis on human resource management. The time is right for professional personnel people to make the most significant contributions of their careers (Burdick, 1976).

Because the leading edge of human resource management is defined through the planning process, it is incumbent on professionals to lead this change. Effective implementation of planning requires a set of professional roles and competencies that are not quite matched by any other personnel function. It is a new and varied set of responsibilities calling for intense consulting competence. This chapter has reviewed the roles performed in human resource planning and the skills necessary for effective performance.

Part Two

Needs Forecasting

Chapter 4

Linking Human Resource Planning with Strategic Planning

KEY POINTS

- Human resource issues should be considered in the formulation of business plans.
- Human resource issues are particularly important in strategic planning—long-range business planning which is aimed at achieving a major change in an organization's direction or emphasis.
- Linkages between human resource planning and business planning differ at three levels or time frames of planning: strategic, middle-range, and annual.
- The common approach for considering human resource plans in the context of strategic planning involves addressing a series of pertinent questions as part of the planning process.
- The approaches for planning may be informal and highly subjective or they may be formal, structured, and systematic.
- Responsibility for planning lies with operating management, but the analysis work is usually performed with assistance from business planning staff and human resource staff.

Planning is generally accepted as vital to effective management in most large organizations today. During the past several decades, companies have adopted systematic processes for deciding on objectives, resources needed, and manner of operations. In many instances, this planning is *strategic* in nature.

That is, the planning addresses prospective changes in business objectives and the forces affecting the business. Drucker notes that it is necessary in strategic planning to ask: "What is the business?" "What will it be?" and "What should it be?" With respect to the last question, the usual assumption is that the business will be different (Drucker, 1974).

Natural resources, technological capacities, patents and products, market share and position, and financial capital are all given close consideration in strategic planning. However, human resources are rarely given attention. Consideration of human resource needs is usually limited to annual budgeting and planning, or to analysis and planning conducted by personnel specialists in planning programs such as training and recruiting. Often, human resource planning is viewed as a necessary, but subordinate, process of ensuring that adequate numbers and types of people are available to staff planned operations. Published discussions of planning practices indicate that human resource needs are determined by business programs and strategies, but generally ignore the possibility that human resources may affect business plans (Burack, 1972; Ettelstein, 1970; Keys et al., 1971; G. A. Steiner, 1969; Vetter, 1967).

This chapter presents the concepts and techniques necessary to link human resource planning with business planning. The planning process is first described by drawing distinctions among strategic long-range, middle-range, and short-term or annual planning and budgeting. The issues of human resource management in relation to business planning are identified to suggest the potential impact of human resource issues on business achievements. The balance of the chapter examines specific approaches and techniques used in companies to implement strategy-linked human resource planning.

THE IMPORTANCE OF PLANNING

Companies often give lip service to the importance of human resources in achievement of business objectives, but rarely is detailed, thoughtful analysis performed. Executives are confident that necessary personnel can always be recruited in the marketplace to meet future needs, should the internal supply prove inadequate. Business planners tend to focus on financial and marketing aspects of planning, often the functional specializations in which they were primarily educated. Personnel professionals, even human resource planning specialists, often are not well informed regarding business planning processes (and rarely have any direct contact with business planners) and are thus ill-equipped to introduce linkages between human resource planning and business strategic planning.

Yet the risks of neglecting this important link are great. In its plans to consolidate product lines, a consumer products company assumed that the same sales personnel could represent all lines. The assumptions turned out to be wrong, and previously profitable lines turned sour and were ultimately divested. As another example, a chemicals company rapidly added new production facilities and expanded existing plants to meet demand without planning for the grooming of necessary managers. As a result, start-ups were sometimes delayed and problems were encountered due to inadequate experience and training of key personnel.

On the positive side, a major lumber and paper products company anticipated its requirements for new mill managers and senior technical personnel and systematically rotated prospective candidates among mills and pertinent headquarters and regional staff positions to satisfy the projected needs. As another example, a bank staffs its offices to satisfy work-load demands as projected in its business plans and develops banking office managers according to plans for long-range banking expansion. Positions are authorized in the offices (branches) to support specific business plans such as a new business "call" program desired as part of a specific marketing program.

Objectives and Benefits

Companies commonly prepare annual forecasts of staffing needs as a basis for external recruitment, personnel reassignments and promotions, and annual training program planning. But the one-year planning horizon fails to take into consideration longer-range business plans and needs, such as new facilities, new products, retrenchment, expansion, or gradually changing talent requirements of a qualitative nature. Effective human resource planning involves longer-range *career* development of talent and longer-range planning for utilization and control of human resources in an organization.

The need for a strategic perspective in human resource planning was stated in a manufacturing company as follows: "As the company grows larger and more complex, we recognize a need to plan more systematically for the people needed to staff the business. A lack of adequate talent may be the single major constraint in our ability to sustain future company growth. This (process) is a practical step toward more comprehensive employee planning and development."

In this same company, the benefits anticipated from longer-range human resource planning include the following:

1 An improved understanding of the human resource implications of business strategies
2 Recruiting experienced talent well in advance of needs, both from campuses and from the market
3 Improved planning of assignments and other employee developmental actions such as lateral moves to permit longer-range broadening of managerial perspective
4 Improved analysis and control of personnel-related costs, by providing more objective criteria concerning payroll, turnover, relocation, training, and other costs

These benefits were perceived from shorter-range planning. The link with strategic planning was seen as the logical next step in human resource planning in this company.

WHAT IS STRATEGIC PLANNING?

Strategic planning is the process of setting organizational objectives and deciding on comprehensive programs of action which will achieve these objectives. In a major oil company, strategic planning includes:

- Formulating corporate and regional company objectives and operating charters (statements of identity or purpose)
- Choosing the mix of business which will make up the operating entity and will reflect that entity's objectives and its concepts of its own identity
- Determining the organization structure, processes, and interrelationships appropriate for managing a chosen mix of businesses
- Developing appropriate strategies for carrying out the objectives and directing the evolution of the chosen mix of businesses within the organizational structures thus established
- Devising the programs which are the vehicle for implementing the strategies

Strategic planning should not be confused with shorter-range operational or tactical planning. Strategic planning is concerned with those decisions aimed at achieving a major change in direction or velocity of growth. For example, a company may review its various product lines or component businesses and conclude that one or more should be discontinued because they no longer fit the company's overall objectives and plan. New business may be sought, new investments made, or new management approaches adopted (Ackoff, 1970; Ansoff, 1965; Drucker, 1974; Lorange and Vancil, 1976). Operational or tactical planning deals with the normal ongoing growth of current operations or with specific problems, generated either internally or externally, which knock the pace of normal growth temporarily off the track.

Strategic planning decisions involve major commitments of resources, resulting in either a quantum jump in the business along the path it is traveling or a change in the fundamental direction itself. Because assumptions must be made about an unpredictable future (and the resources committed could be lost), strategic planning involves a significant amount of risk. As a result, strategic planning is more complex, more conceptual, and less precise than shorter-range operational planning. Typically, it involves consideration of not just one but several possible scenarios about the future business environment and consideration of several alternative courses of action for the enterprise.

Operational planning, on the other hand, generally assumes a fairly constant business environment and considers changes concerning only such factors as immediate tactics; production efficiency; fine tuning of ongoing systems and practices; adjustment of levels of business activity; responses to customer or other demands; and modification of products, advertising, services, or other business processes. The central difference is the degree of change resulting from the planning—hence the degree of impact on human resource planning.

Steps

New directions in management do not come about easily. Strategic planning, therefore, involves a series of steps, each of which may involve considerable data collection, analysis, and iterative management reviews. The important elements of strategic planning and their potential effects on human resource planning are as follows:

1 *Define the corporate philosophy.* As a first step, fundamental questions regarding the nature of the corporation are addressed, including: "Why does the business exist? What is the unique contribution it makes or can make? What are the underlying motives or values of the owners or key managers?" In a large electronic equipment manufacturing firm, for example, providing employment and promotional opportunities for employees is held to be an important purpose of being in business and therefore an important guide for future growth and change. The dependence of the community on the company is an overriding factor in the minds of the key executives.

2 *Scan the environmental conditions.* The question here is, "What economic, social, technological, and political changes are occurring which represent opportunities or threats?" Labor supply, increasing legal demands governing human resource policies and practices, and rapidly changing technology may, for example, have significant impact on a business. Additionally, the question is asked: "What are the competitors' strengths, strategies, etc.?" Even human resource strategies of other companies may affect the future direction of a business (for example, the ability of a DuPont to attract and retain the best available talent).

3 *Evaluate the corporation's strengths and weaknesses.* Next it must be asked, "What factors may enhance/limit the choice of future courses of action?" Human resource factors such as an aging work force, overspecialization (immobility) of key managers, a lack of promotable "high-potential" talent, and past failure to develop broadly experienced general management talent are common problems that may constrain strategic planning.

4 *Develop objectives and goals.* Other important questions are, "What are the sales, profit, and return on investment objectives? What specific time-based points of measurement are to be met in achieving these objectives?" Too often, the organization structure and the styles of management applied in a company are not supportive of specific objectives and goals. Where commitment is difficult to attain, strategies suffer. Also, important qualitative goals give way to more easily defined and measured quantitative objectives even though strategic objectives frequently involve commitment to changes in quality of service, quality of management, quality of research and development, etc.

5 *Develop strategies.* Last it is important to find answers to these questions: "What courses of action should the corporation follow to achieve its objectives, while meeting specific operational goals along the way? What types of action programs are required in the pursuit of these strategies? What changes in organization structure, management processes, and personnel are required?" Here the focus is sharply on human resource planning and the acquisition, assignment, development, utilization, and (frequently) termination of employees to properly staff the organization. It is at this point that human resource planning most directly links to the strategic planning process.

THREE LEVELS OF PLANNING

The different levels of planning suggested in the above discussion are illustrated in Exhibit 4-1. As shown, strategic planning deals with a long-range perspective and flows into operational planning. This level of planning has a midterm perspective and is concerned with the specific programs planned, the kinds and amounts of resources required, the organizational structure, and management succession and development, as well as specific plans for implementing the strategic plans. Finally, an annual budgeting process provides specific time-tables, assignments, allocations of resources, and standards for implementation of actions. Simply, the detail in planning moves into sharper focus as the time frame telescopes into the shorter term.

   Human resource planning logically parallels the business planning process. Some companies hold that the annual budget is all they need, particularly for human resource planning. In practice, their "strategic planning" is really vague operational planning. "Any people we need we can hire when the time comes from outside," they state. And in some instances, such as construction, retailing, or project-oriented engineering (or aerospace) firms, the lead time for planning is necessarily short. But even in these kinds of organizations, engineering talent, managerial talent, and specialized skills required in support of strategic objectives may not be readily available on the market and may require lead time for recruitment or development.

   College recruitment plans, for example, are not always reliable if they are

Exhibit 4-1   Links between Business Planning and Human Resource Planning

	Strategic planning: ___ long-range perspective	Operational planning: ___ middle-range perspective	Budgeting: annual perspective
Business Planning Process	Corporate philosophy Environmental scan Strengths and constraints Objectives and goals Strategies	Planned programs Resources required Organizational strategies Plans for entry into new businesses, acquisitions, divestitures	Budgets Unit, individual performance goals Program scheduling and assignment Monitoring and control of results
	Issues analysis —	Forecasting requirements —	Action plans
Human Resource Planning Process	Business needs External factors Internal supply analysis Management implications	Staffing levels Staffing mix (qualitative) Organization and job design Available/projected resources Net requirements	Staffing authorizations Recruitment Promotions and transfers Organizational changes Training and develop- ment Compensation and benefits Labor relations

developed solely on an annual basis. Rather, they are more accurate when based on a rolling plan involving a multiple-year forecast of needs as part of operational planning which, in turn, is based on strategic planning. Similarly, training and development activities are often budgeted and scheduled on a short-term basis without a long-range context defining the needs that are to be satisfied. As a result, training programs often represent a smorgasbord for employees with little assurance of either cost-effectiveness for the business or career relevance for the employees.

Linking human resource planning with strategic planning involves focusing on major changes planned in the business—critical issues: "What are the implications of the proposed business strategies? What are the possible external constraints and requirements? What are the implications for management practices, organization, development, and succession? What can be done in the short term to prepare for longer-term needs?"

THE IMPACT OF HUMAN RESOURCES

The capacity of an organization to achieve its strategic objectives is influenced by human resources in three fundamental ways:

- Cost economics
- Capacity to operate effectively
- Capacity to undertake new enterprises and change operations

The factors contributing to these three impact areas are listed in Exhibit 4-2. The factors identified are useful as a basis for helping business planners and executives think about the relevance of human resource planning. They also serve as the basic elements comprising the approaches commonly used to bridge the two planning processes.

Personnel costs are significant in many organizations, frequently ranking below the cost of financial capital or the cost of goods and materials. Costs of capital, equipment, and materials are increasingly difficult to control due to their scarcity and to inflation. Accordingly, control over staffing levels, compensation and benefits, and staffing mix are important focal points of management attention. In one instance, a midwestern manufacturing firm established a plant in Europe as a step toward increasing its penetration of that market. But when the plant was operating, it was found that local managers with the necessary expertise could not be found, or at least corporate management back home felt more comfortable having individuals personally known to them managing the foreign operations. As a result, the costs of maintaining the United States expatriates were extremely high, and yet the individuals were not as effective as they needed to be because they did not adequately understand the market, language, or customs. After five years, the plant was sold to a European company, with management problems cited as a principal factor.

This suggests the importance of the second group of factors—the positive benefits human resources may have on business plans. The talents and efforts of

Exhibit 4-2   The Strategic Impact of Human Resources Factors

Sales and net earnings per employee

Compensation and benefits costs as a percentage of total costs and expenses

Employee replacement costs including recruitment, training

Legal and regulatory expense vulnerability (for example, EEO, OSHA)

Labor relations vulnerability for cost increases

Other

Technical complexity, specialization required

Stability and motivation of work force employed

Employee competencies relative to job requirements

Organizational effectiveness

Managerial style and philosophy

Other

Untapped/undeveloped potential of human resources

Depth of management resources

Adaptability/receptiveness to change

Competitiveness for talent

Other

Cost economics

Capacity to operate effectively

Capacity to undertake new enterprises and to change operations

Capacity to achieve strategic objectives

employees can have tangible effects on productivity, organizational effectiveness, management competencies, organizational stability, external relations, adaptivity to changes, and other changes supportive of a company's strategic objectives. Such effects are often taken for granted, but companies that fail to grow and change are frequently characterized by an absence of such positive support by their employees. An electronics company holds that its phenomenal record of growth and technological innovations is due in large part to the quality and motivation of its employees.

The assumption of positive "people impact" is used in an oil company as a way to stimulate management thinking about human resource issues in relation to business plans. In this company, oriented toward technology, capital, and natural resources, the impact of human resources was identified through "zero-base analysis." "We assume there is no impact at all in any area of human resource management, and then through the strategic planning process examine each potential cost and benefit factor on its actual merits. If human resource planning is found to have no relevance to strategic planning, we won't require any further attention to the subject." This null hypothesis worked well in getting the attention of the managers, and now a procedure of considering human resource needs is an integral aspect of the company's strategic planning.

APPROACHES FOR IMPLEMENTATION

What specific techniques may be used to do this kind of analysis and planning? How have companies implemented the planning approach to link with strategic planning? Few companies have had very much experience in this area. Most companies limit their human resource planning to short-term forecasting (discussed in Chapters 5 and 6). But the feasibility of longer-range strategic planning focused on human resource issues has been clearly demonstrated by major corporations.

The approaches usually involve strong staff support to management in the analysis of business plans and objectives and in the examination of pertinent human resource information (forecasting of turnover, retirements, transfers, and promotions, etc.). But the primary responsibility for identifying emerging trends and changes in business requirements relating to business strategies rests with the operating managers. In some instances corporate planning staff professionals also get into the act and assist in the human resource planning efforts.

The efforts are typically modest at the start, but attract management interest and attention. In successive years, greater depth is achieved in the analysis and planning as managers perceive the benefit of such planning and become comfortable with the planning process. It has taken many companies years to become proficient in financial planning and budgeting, capital allocation, and other functional planning processes. Adoption of new approaches for "people planning" is also slow. As one executive observed, "It is the first time we have put down on paper our thinking about the long-range needs in this area. Our managers are simply not accustomed to answering questions like these and I think they did a pretty good job for a first time effort."

Application of an Approach

A chemicals and plastics manufacturing company guided its division managers through an analysis of human resource issues through the use of a simple printed guidebook. Exhibit 4-4 presents the essential pages of this guidebook consisting of a series of questions regarding human resource factors relating to strategic plans. The information presented in the exhibit in response to the questions is a synthesis of actual responses and is provided for illustrative purposes only.

The approach called for each division's management to analyze and plan its future human resource needs, organizational changes, and other programs and actions. Assistance was provided both by business planning staff assigned to work with the divisions and the corporate human resource planning staff.

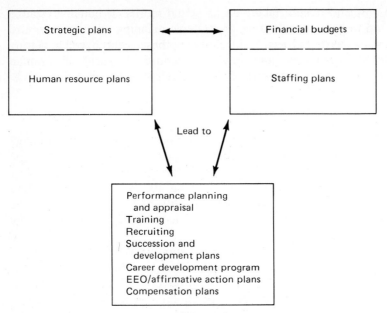

Exhibit 4-3   A human resource planning process.

Responsibility for the process was given to the division managers for several reasons:

- Corporate management did not want the process to be viewed as a staff exercise.
- The division managers are most familiar with their own units' strategic plans and related human resource circumstances, and therefore they were the best source of reliable information.
- This approach focused the attention of line managers on important human resource issues, increasing their appreciation for them and potentially influencing their judgment in business planning.
- The process focused attention on the need for employee development as an ongoing process and not merely a once-a-year appraisal exercise.

Also, the process was viewed as a way to present to managers the full gamut of human resource functions as a single, unified system. As illustrated in Exhibit 4-4, the company's various personnel programs and the process of human resource planning fit together logically with the ongoing business and financial planning cycles.

Each section of the human resource planning guide in Exhibit 4-4 lists a series of questions relating to issues affecting business strategies. The four sections are:

A   Business needs—the human resource implications of planned expansion, contraction, or other changes indicated in the strategic plans

B External factors—the business impact of governmental regulations, union activity, and human resource availability

C Internal analysis—the implications of professional turnover, employee mix, and performance patterns

D Management implications—the changing managerial staffing needs and management skills required

Finally, a format for forecasting exempt staffing needs is included on the last page. This calls for a projection of staffing levels planned for a five-year period, by year, for departmental and functional groups. This rough long-range forecast reflects the general parameters suggested by strategic and operational plans. The first two years of the forecast serve as a basis for planning specific requirements in the annual budget.

The managers are asked to consider each question and briefly note pertinent factors, observations, or assumptions. Questions that are not considered pertinent are deleted, and additional questions may be added where appropriate. The guidebook is intended to be a workbook to direct and stimulate management thinking, and not a rigid procedure.

The second column lists possible responses to stimulate thinking about the human resource implications of each question. Other possible actions may be considered practical under the circumstances as known to the managers. The third and fourth columns call for a translation of the long-range strategy-related needs into specific near-term needs and planned actions. The interpretation of strategic issues into near-term objectives and programs for human resource management is an important step in making the whole human resource planning effort worthwhile.

The guidebook is disseminated to the operating divisions as part of the overall strategic planning guidelines and instructions. In this way the two planning processes are conducted concurrently. The resulting responses indicate to management the important human resource issues that need to be considered in the future.

Alternative Approaches

In a major oil company, the manpower planning staff provided a summary analysis of the previous year's strategic plan, highlighting the pertinent facts and issues for each division. These summaries, together with tabulations of present employment, past and projected attrition (due to turnover, retirements, etc.), and appraisal statistics provided "substantive starters" to the divisions for use considering pertinent human resource issues. The analysis of strategic issues was termed a "situational analysis," as a first step in the company's manpower planning cycle. Questions similar to those presented in Exhibit 4-4 were posed in four areas:

- Impact of people on the growth or profitability of the business
- Personnel-related costs having a substantial impact on the profitability of the business

Identify below those strategic plans having *human resource implications.*	Possible areas for action. What *could* be done?

A. BUSINESS NEEDS

1. Expansion of existing business activities?

☐ Recruitment
☐ Training/development
☐ Organization changes
☐

2. Addition of new capacity (new plants, distribution facilities, etc.)?

☐ Recruitment
☐ Training/development
☐ Organization changes
☐

3. Deemphasis or discontinuance of any business activities?

☐ Reassignments
☐ Terminations
☐ Retraining
☐

4. Ventures, acquisitions, or divestitures?

☐ Management reassignments
☐ Recruitment
☐ Organization/position changes
☐ Training/development
☐

5. New products or services?

☐ Training/development
☐ Recruitment
☐ Organization/position changes
☐

6. New technologies or applications?

☐ Training/development
☐ Recruitment
☐ New specializations
☐ Organization/position changes
☐

7. Changes in operating methods or productivity improvements?

☐ Organization/position changes
☐ Training/development
☐ Reassignments
☐

8. Changes in administrative, information, or control systems?

☐ Orientation/training
☐ Organization/position changes
☐ Staffing changes
☐

Exhibit 4-4 Human resource planning guide.

Objectives: what will be *accomplished* in the year ahead?	What specific *programs or actions* are planned?

Identify below those strategic plans having *human resource implications.*	Possible areas for action. What *could* be done?
9. Changes in management or organizational structure (matrix management)?	☐ Reassignments ☐ Communications/training ☐ Staffing changes ☐ Recruitment ☐ Terminations ☐ Reassignments ☐
10. Other:	☐ ☐

B. EXTERNAL FACTORS

1. Are qualified (competent) recruits available in the market?	☐ Modify recruitment approach ☐ Modify staffing requirements ☐ Develop more talent from within ☐
2. Are you able to recruit competitively the desired talent?	☐ Modify compensation/job evaluation ☐ Modify recruitment approach ☐ Modify job requirements ☐
3. Are there changes in the personnel relations climate?	☐ Employee communications ☐ Management orientation/training ☐ Fact finding ☐
4. Are there new EEO/affirmative action requirements?	☐ Modify recruitment ☐ Training/development ☐ Modify job requirements ☐ Performance appraisals ☐
5. Are there new OSHA or other regulatory requirements affecting human resources?	☐ Management orientation/training ☐ New systems/procedures ☐ Additional staffing ☐ Fact finding ☐
6. Are there new international business demands?	☐ Management orientation/training ☐ Recruitment ☐ Adapt managment systems ☐ Fact finding ☐
7. Other:	☐ ☐

Objectives: what will be *accomplished* in the year ahead?	What specific *programs or actions* are planned?

Identify below the *human resource issues* pertinent to the strategic plans.	Possible areas for action. What *could* be done?
C. INTERNAL ANALYSIS	
1. Do we have excessive turnover in any group?	☐ Modify recruitment/selection ☐ Accelerate career advancement ☐ Organization/position changes ☐ Reassignment/lateral moves ☐
2. Is there too little turnover or mobility in any group?	☐ Terminations ☐ Reassignment of work ☐ Organization/position changes ☐ Improved employee appraisals ☐
3. Are age patterns imbalanced in any group, suggesting high future attrition or career path blockage?	☐ Modify recruitment/selection ☐ Reassignments ☐ Accelerate career advancement ☐ Terminations ☐
4. Is there a proper balance (employee mix) of managerial, professional/technical, and supporting personnel in each group?	☐ Organization/position changes ☐ Reassignment of work ☐ Modify recruitment/selection ☐
5. Are there noteworthy performance problems in any group (or appraisal results signaling significant problems)?	☐ Organization/position changes ☐ Reassignments ☐ Improved employee appraisals ☐ Modify job requirements ☐
6. In what areas are levels of technical competency potential shortcomings?	☐ Modify recruitment/selection ☐ Reassignments ☐ Career counseling ☐ Training/development ☐
7. Is the employee mix desired for EEO/AA being achieved? (women and minorities)	☐ Modify recruitment/selection ☐ Modify job requirements ☐ Career counseling ☐ Training/development ☐
8. Other:	☐ ☐

Objectives: what will be *accomplished* in the year ahead?	What specific *programs* or *actions* are planned?

Identify below the *human resource issues* pertinent to the strategic plans.	Possible areas for action. What *could* be done?

D. MANAGEMENT IMPLICATIONS

1. Are there enough employees who could become general managers? (pool of successors)

   ☐ Modify recruitment/selection
   ☐ Improved employee evaluation
   ☐ Special career development plans
   ☐ Organization changes for future
   ☐

2. Do the present managers have adequate technical competence in the face of changing demands?

   ☐ Training/development
   ☐ Reassignments
   ☐ Specialized recruitment
   ☐ Specialization
   ☐ Career counseling
   ☐

3. Do they have adequate managerial skills to meet the changing demands of a growing company? (leading, planning, decision making, etc.)

   ☐ Training/development
   ☐ Organization/position changes
   ☐ Reassignments
   ☐ Recruitment of managerial talent
   ☐

4. Do key managers and successors have adequate management experience (multiple function exposure)?

   ☐ Training/development programs
   ☐ Job rotation among functions
   ☐ Recruitment of management talent
   ☐ Evaluation of successors
   ☐

5. Is the management structure and staffing appropriate for the achievement of our business objectives?

   ☐ Organization/position changes
   ☐ Reduce/increase staffing levels
   ☐ Accelerate management development
   ☐ Study of strategy implications
   ☐

6. Other:

   ☐
   ☐

Objectives: what will be *accomplished* in the year ahead?	What specific *programs or actions* are planned?

SUMMARY FORECAST OF EXEMPT STAFFING NEEDS
AS OF

	CURRENT	9/79	9/80	9/81	9/82	9/83	9/84
DEPARTMENTS							
TOTALS							
FUNCTIONS							
TOTALS							

- Avoidable people-related problems that require inordinate time and attention by management
- Management values requiring emphasis on certain human resource programs

In this case, employee relations staff in the divisions performed much of the necessary analysis and completed the planning submissions. The quality of the responses varied, therefore, with the experience, skills, and time availability of these staff, and with their access to the line executives in their divisions for purposes of discussing the human resource analyses.

In a packaging company, guidelines were included as a section in the annual one- to three-year planning process. The initial request for information was minimal, the response was positive, and "the seed was planted from which a full-size human resource planning process can grow." Each division in this company was able to pinpoint issues that were important and that needed attention which had not been explicitly considered before.

Subsequent cycles yielded more comprehensive plans regarding the human resource issues. Submissions were reviewed and synthesized as a corporation-wide plan by the human resource staff; highlights and issues of corporatewide concern were brought to the attention of senior management in a formal presentation. This corporatewide plan also provided the basis for targeting of objectives, priorities, and resource requirements for corporate programs and staff activities. Exhibit 4-5 presents excerpts from one year's corporate human resource plan.

The link between human resource planning and business strategic planning is vital if personnel programs and systems are to be attuned to the changing needs of an organization. This chapter has examined the qualities of such an effective linkage and its practical importance. Approaches were described for implementing the link, using a formal process of questioning business managers, usually as part of the normal business planning process. In some organizations, where the process has been applied for several annual cycles, human resource issues are now routinely addressed as a component of business planning.

In other organizations, human resource issues are studied solely by staff personnel, who present their findings to management or to the business planning staff as inputs to strategic or operational planning. In several instances, committees or task forces have been appointed to consider long-range human resource issues and needs, usually on a one-time basis. Particularly in the task of scanning the environment to identify emerging legal, competitive, labor supply, and other constraints, such a study group has proven a useful tool. Of course, some companies rely on consultants or outside experts to advise on trends, issues, and needs warranting company attention.

Perhaps the most common approach applied, however, is the informal planning process. While not always thorough or systematic, informal management thinking about business strategies often leads to recognition of human resource issues. Planning for the management of corporate resources, including

Exhibit 4-5   Excerpts from a Corporate Human Resource Plan Presentation

The human resource plan is presented against a background of significant changes in the corporation. Fundamental to these changes is an earnings goal of 10% growth per year. Growth will be achieved by expansion of existing businesses that are sound, reshaping of lower-potential businesses, and acquisitions. Major capital investments will occur in some business areas. International markets will account for an increasing share of our earnings goal achievement.

The plan, therefore, represents a synthesis of issues and activities aimed at supporting the objectives of the businesses as well as a guide for the respective human resource activities in the businesses. Activities must fit business unit needs, but must also be responsive to corporate, legal, and societal needs.

Focus of major strategies

Strategic actions planned	Representative programs or activities

I The demands for managerial and professional talent resulting from changing business strategies require improved management quality and improved salaried employee productivity.

A Terminate low performers	Train managers in more effective appraisals. Extend emphasis of termination program to marginally satisfactory performers.
B Motivate top performers	Establish program to make sure outstanding performers are being rewarded proportionately under the incentive compensation program. Develop a long-term incentive program.
C Upgrade managerial capabilities	Establish coordinated program for executive-level search/recruitment and placement. Extend management program (training) to 700 managers and supervisors.
D Influence retirement plans	Conduct management-level retirement preparation program. Provide appraisal guidelines to managers regarding age discrimination risks and appraisal of low performers and the use of termination versus early retirement.

II Control rapidly rising human resource costs.

A Hourly labor costs	Reduce certain job security provisions. Negotiate staffing reductions, productivity improvements. Establish uniform data base for planning negotiations. Establish uniform benefits for nonunion employees across businesses. Reduce accident ratios by 10%, thus reducing lost time and accident costs.
B Salaried pay and benefit costs	Introduce variable benefits program on a pilot basis (to provide cost-control mechanism against future escalation).

Exhibit 4-5 *(continued)*

Strategic actions planned	Representative programs or activities
	Consolidate insurance carriers for administrative savings. Reorganize corporate compensation function to provide better services to business human resource staffs. Develop a corporate compensation philosophy. Implement a manpower control reporting system to track staffing changes. Implement controls over use of search firms. Establish central relocation procedure and service. Expand attitude survey programs and follow-up communications programs (to detect and allay concerns in units with high risk of unionization).

III Manage the impact of external legal factors.

A Manage ongoing legal compliance	Establish training program for field management to improve handling of arbitration cases and on-site EEO audits. Implement toxic substances control program in XYZ divisions. Conduct comprehensive noise-abatement cost and feasibility evaluation study.
B Affirmative action plans	Establish an improved reporting system for surveillance of female/minority progress. Negotiate a combined compliance plan covering handicapped, veterans, females, and minorities to reduce administrative costs. Step up women-in-management program to advance female into management positions
C Upgrade legislative surveillance	Direct attention of legal staff and public affairs staff to emerging governmental initiatives and to address them.

IV Improve organizational effectiveness.

A Upgrade personnel data system	Complete implementation of phase I and design for phase II.
B Upgrade business organization effectiveness	Restructure businesses undergoing major growth or contraction. Assign new managers to key functions where called for; utilize assignments as corporate management development moves.
C Upgrade human resource staff effectiveness	Corporate staff provide more functional leadership to business staff counterparts. Conduct quarterly reviews of all programs, emerging demands, and budget compliance.

human resources, is a process inherent in the role of a manager. And few managers would admit that they do not consider human resource issues in strategic or operational planning.

However, the process is more likely to be effective if it is systematic, rational, organized, and based on knowledge, not merely assumptions. As Drucker observes, "The systematic organization of the planning job and the supply of knowledge to it strengthen the manager's judgment, leadership, and vision" (Drucker, 1974, p. 129).

Chapter 5

Forecasting Human Resource Needs

KEY POINTS

- Forecasting is a necessary step in any realistic planning of future human resource management actions.
- While many sophisticated techniques are available, forecasting in practice often is informal, highly judgmental, and subjective. It is often an applied art, not a science.
- The precision of forecasting improves with the reduced length of the time frame of planning; short-term forecasts tend to be more precise and accurate.
- Forecasting of available talent supply begins with an inventory of currently available talent. This requires the use of an information system, the classification of employee data, and the generation of suitable reports and analyses.
- Forecasting of talent supply also requires estimation of likely attrition, mobility, and skills utilization in the future.
- Forecasting of future requirements requires analysis of current staffing requirements and projecting, either based on subjective judgments or through reliance on prediction techniques (and thus predictive variable relationships).
- The matching of forecasts of supply and demand for human resources provides a picture of talent surpluses or deficits which must be satisfied through action programs.

To plan effectively for its human resource needs, a company ought to have a clear idea of what its needs actually are and what they will be in the future. It should be aware of how its employees are currently deployed, how well their talents are being applied, and how the available talent supply matches up with projected future requirements. This understanding requires an appreciation of changing conditions and anticipated future events affecting both the supply of talent and the demands for talent imposed by business plans.

Forecasting human resource needs is a central aspect of the human resource planning process, as it yields the advance estimates or calculations of staffing required to achieve the organization's stated objectives. For some human resource planners, analysis and forecasting is the *whole* of the process. The analysis of current staffing patterns, the projection of future requirements, and the matching of the two sets of results can easily be a preoccupation. The future, being uncertain, provides considerable challenge to those concerned with anticipating conditions requiring management action.

Yet it is the process of forecasting itself, as part of the planning process, and not the resulting *numbers* or the *plan per se,* that matters. "The techniques are basically simple and easy to describe," observed Walter Wikstrom of the Conference Board, "but applying them successfully may be enormously complex and difficult. And once the projection has been made, it may prove to be most useful when it proves itself to be least accurate as a vision of the future" (Wikstrom, 1971).

This chapter examines these techniques for forecasting human resource needs, the applications of the results, and the potential pitfalls to be avoided. Forecasting is viewed as essentially a process of estimating available supply of and demand for talent based on the best available information, generally provided by the managers responsible for operations in each unit of the organization. Mathematical and computer-based techniques are available, and are discussed in Chapter 6; but these are supplements to, rather than substitutes for, management-based judgments regarding future needs.

THE FORECASTING PROCESS

Forecasting human resource needs is an imprecise art, depending heavily on the judgment of those involved in the process. There is no generally recognized procedure or set of techniques that fits all circumstances and guarantees the desired results. Rather, the manager must construct a process which will ensure that the right numbers and kinds of people will be at the right places, at the right times, to meet the organization's requirements (Vetter, 1967; Walker, 1970).

Too frequently, human resource planning activities are fragmented and unintegrated. One finds managers performing one or several aspects of forecasting while neglecting other important aspects. This is often due to a desire to do *something*—to get started. But overall results are not often attained when efforts are concentrated on, say, the analysis of the mobility of employees within an organization, or on turnover analysis.

There are six essential components of an integrated forecasting process.

These are illustrated in Exhibit 5-1. While emphasis may be given particular aspects due to managerial priorities, all aspects are necessary in the development of a suitable foundation for the planning of human resource action programs attuned to organizational needs.

Forecasting logically begins with the development of an understanding of the environmental and organizational conditions affecting future requirements. The necessary analysis may result from the planning occurring as part of the strategic planning cycle, as discussed in the previous chapter. Alternatively, it may require independent review and analysis, and perhaps in-depth studies. Large companies commonly conduct or commission studies of changing conditions affecting human resource needs, such as causes and patterns of employee turnover, organizational structuring and job design changes, available labor supply (including availability of minorities and women in the applicable work force), legal and regulatory constraints and pending legislation, and technological changes affecting staffing requirements. At a very minimum, these various conditions are subjectively considered, as a first step in the forecasting process.

The second step in the process involves taking *inventory* of the talent available in an organization. Some companies maintain "perpetual" inventories; thus this step involves merely examination of readily available information on current staffing, individual qualifications and appraisals, expressed employee career interests, and targeted development plans (targeted assignments, planned training and development). In other companies, the step requires collection of these kinds of data from the employees and their managers. A computer-based payroll administration system or broader-scope "human resource information system" provides valuable data-storage and reporting capabilities.

Through analysis of the current supply of talent (inventory), past patterns of change in this supply (such as mobility and attrition), and logical assumptions regarding future changes, managers can project the future available supply of talent in an organization. It is difficult, if not impossible, to predict precisely the future promotions, transfers, terminations, retirements, deaths, and other changes that affect the available supply of talent in an organization. But through this forecasting step, sufficiently reliable estimates may be derived for the purposes of human resource planning. As will be discussed later, the techniques for analyzing and projecting changes in the supply of talent in an organization are varied, and many are quite sophisticated mathematically. There are more techniques readily available for use than are ever used today in most business organizations.

Our capabilities are also strong in the analysis of current human resource requirements: the fourth step of the process. Staffing is usually controlled in business organizations through control over organization structure, job definition, and the number of authorized positions, controlled through a budgeting process. An organization may not be *optimally* staffed currently, but an examination of demand, as it is currently defined, is the place to start in planning future needs.

Projection of current staffing (or ideal current staffing) to the future

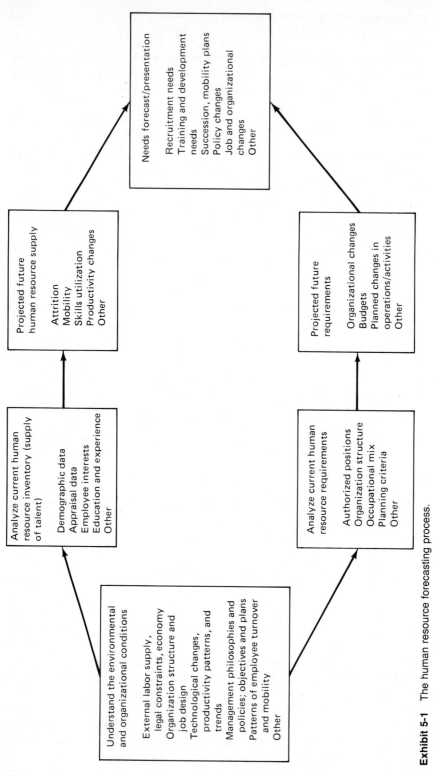

The following boxes appear in the diagram:

Needs forecast/presentation

Recruitment needs
Training and development needs
Succession, mobility plans
Policy changes
Job and organizational changes
Other

Projected future human resource supply

Attrition
Mobility
Skills utilization
Productivity changes
Other

Analyze current human resource inventory (supply of talent)

Demographic data
Appraisal data
Employee interests
Education and experience
Other

Understand the environmental and organizational conditions

External labor supply, legal constraints, economy
Organization structure and job design
Technological changes, productivity patterns, and trends
Management philosophies and policies; objectives and plans
Patterns of employee turnover and mobility
Other

Analyze current human resource requirements

Authorized positions
Organization structure
Occupational mix
Planning criteria
Other

Projected future requirements

Organizational changes
Budgets
Planned changes in operations/activities
Other

Exhibit 5-1   The human resource forecasting process.

involves application of planning criteria or assumptions. Ratios or regression relationships between staffing and work-load indicators are a commonly applied basis for projecting future requirements. As for projecting availability of talent, various mathematical techniques are available which are not commonly applied, but subjective managerial judgments are influential in actual demand forecasts.

Finally, the sixth step of the process calls for a matching or balancing of the net projections: future supply and future demand. The results represent needs for human resources indicating necessary actions, including recruitment needs, training and development needs, succession or job reassignment needs, and organizational adjustments. Specified needs, then, provide the link between identified issues relating to changing management conditions with the program planning aspects of the human resource planning process: performance management, career management, and management succession, as discussed in Chapter 1.

Why Forecast?

Forecasting of needs provides a foundation for other human resource planning activities. It translates broad needs, as identified through the planning process outlined in Chapter 4, into more specific quantitative and qualitative requirements. Accordingly, forecasts are not an end in and of themselves. Rather, they determine the recruitment, training, development, promotions and transfers, job design changes, and organizational changes necessary for achievement of the business objectives established. Forecasting helps management focus attention and allocate resources to areas most likely to have payoffs.

Specific types of questions that may be answered through forecasting are:

Are we properly staffed? Overstaffed? Understaffed?
Could we function efficiently with fewer people?
What will be our needs resulting from expansion and business changes?
What will our recruitment needs be next year? After that?
What staff will we have available during the future planning period (after attrition, promotions, etc.)?
Are we likely to be caught short in any skills area?
Are we achieving our EEO affirmative action objectives?
How can we better utilize our employees?

The questions concerning management logically flow from the broad analysis of business and environmental issues.

The benefits of effective forecasting represent better-informed management: knowing what is required to adequately staff the organization. Effective forecasting allows management to manage (balance) fluctuations in staffing requirements, plan ahead for recruiting adequate new talent, allocate available talent to best satisfy needs, and maintain control over costs. Less directly, forecasting enables management to improve productivity of employees, attract and retain desired employees, and motivate employees toward organizational careers. The very act of forecasting indicates a degree of predictability and stability—a forward-looking management process.

The value of forecasting human resource needs is greater under circumstances of rapid change and in larger organizations relying upon managerial, professional, and technical talent. Where new technologies or operating processes are being introduced, effects fall heavily on human resources. Similarly, rapidly expanding enterprises and situations of new management directions and priorities create a high need for adequate staffing. Because of tight labor markets, planning for high-talent personnel is important; companies cannot easily recruit the talent needed on the spur of the moment. Of course, larger organizations also face the difficult task of allocating talent to diverse business activities, often shifting personnel among locations and divisions to meet changing requirements and to develop individuals' full potential. The complexity of planning for effective staffing and for development and utilization of staff is greatly increased under these conditions, and the value of forecasting is great.

Time Periods for Forecasting

In evaluating applicable techniques for forecasting human resource needs, it is helpful to spell out the demand and supply aspects appropriate to each of three planning periods—that is, short-range, intermediate-range, and long-range. These are presented in Exhibit 5-2.

Short-range forecasts are a matter of course in most companies. This is

Exhibit 5-2   Three Ranges of Manpower Forecasting

	Short range	Intermediate range	Long range
Demand	Authorized employ-ment (including growth, changes, and turnover)	Operating needs from budgets and plans	In some organizations the same as intermediate range In others, an increased awareness of changes in environment and technology —essentially judgmental
Supply	Employee census less expected losses plus expected pro-motions from subordinate groups	Manpower vacancies expected from individual promotability data derived from develop-ment plans	Management expectations of changing characteristics of employees and future available manpower
Net needs	Numbers and kinds of employees needed	Numbers, kinds, dates, and levels of needs	Management expectations of future conditions affecting immediate decisions

understandable because few projections or assumptions are necessary for a period of less than one year. Short-range forecasts only indicate managers' best estimates of the numbers and characteristics of individuals that must be recruited from outside the organization to fill its *immediate* needs. Short-range and immediate may mean different things in different companies, but the net effect is the same. In an oil or steel company short-range may mean two years, while in a construction company or a contract aerospace-engineering firm six months may be a more realistic planning horizon (Walker, 1969).

Intermediate-range forecasting involves projection of available talent supply and changing demands under less certain planning conditions. It requires more detailed data and greater reliance on assumptions regarding changes that will affect supply and demand. Judgments are therefore required of managers both regarding the future development and potential of people and regarding the changing operating needs of the enterprise. This period is typically one to three years and as great as one to five years. Forecasts are refined, of course, by adjusting them each year on a rolling basis (year four of the forecast becomes year three).

Management's tasks in long-range forecasting, to maintain an awareness of environmental and technological change and to gradually modify its human resource requirements, are widely taken for granted or disregarded. Long-range forecasting, in a period extending five to ten or more years in the future, is admittedly difficult. Developing expectations about vague or uncertain future conditions is always a highly judgmental process, one that depends on personal executive skills and therefore one best carried out by individual study and special staff studies (using the Delphi technique, for example). Several large companies, such as General Electric, have devoted staff and management resources to this aspect of forecasting, with the view that it provides a more enlightened context for intermediate and short-term human resource planning (Wilkstrom, 1971).

Segmentation

Organizational segmentation helps simplify the task of forecasting by eliminating the need for a single, overall forecasting model. Even where the organization is not naturally segmented by distinct levels or units, projections may be improved by focusing on segments of the work force. More realistic parameters and the most suitable techniques may be applied, and thus greater specificity in projections may be possible.

For example, in large companies where human resource activities such as recruiting, development, and job assignments are all decentralized, there may be no need for total forecasts. An executive of a brewing company observed,

> Within our company we use one approach for marketing, a different one for production, a third for industrial engineering, a fourth for plant purchasing, financing, and public relations. They all differ. The planning model is directed at the needs of that operation.

Also, in any organization there are bound to be levels at which human resource information must be pulled together to be fully useful. As represented in Exhibit 5-3, analysis and forecasting at the executive management level involves a relatively small population (50 to 500 in many companies, or 10 percent of the salaried exempt employment as a rule of thumb). Other salaried professional, managerial, and technical employees (generally the exempt salaried employee group) compose a proportionately large and highly important focal group for human resource planning, and thus for forecasting of needs. Nonexempt salaried and hourly staffing is generally handled in local divisions and locations and is not as great a concern in forecasting and planning.

As represented in the figure, also, the human resource planning of a particular organizational division includes attention at all levels. Yet forecasting and planning for professional, technical, and managerial employee groups is naturally a multidivisional or corporatewide concern. Hence there is an overlapping (and hopefully never conflicting) segmentation by functional division or units and by level (Tucker, 1974).

In adopting a forecasting process, it is appropriate to consider which segments of the organization's work force are the prime subjects for attention. A common strategy is to begin with the executive group by adopting some form of judgmental forecasting and follow-up succession planning programs. This activity may then be modified and cascaded, with management support to other levels, perhaps concentrating on functions or units where the opportunities or needs for human resource planning are greatest. Alternatively, some planners focus on target units or groups of employees (for example, engineers or sales representatives) in the salaried levels which represent pressing problems relating

Exhibit 5-3   Levels in human resource planning.

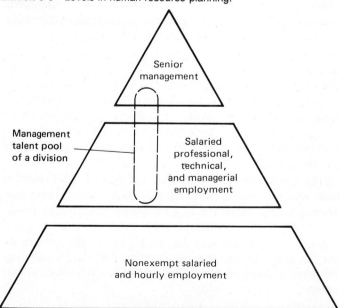

to recruitment or retention difficulties, rapid corporate expansion, etc. These efforts then provide a "showcase" to demonstrate the techniques and merits of forecasting and program planning activities as they may be applied to other groups.

Art or Science?

Forecasting human resource needs is an imprecise art, as noted earlier. At the same time there are many aspects of scientific method which may be applied in the process. The issue, then, is how much managerial judgment and how much mathematical rigor and scientific method are to be applied.

The techniques of forecasting human resource needs range from the highly subjective and rudimentary to the highly abstract, complex, and sophisticated. While simple models involving managerial estimates or guesses of staffing changes may be quite adequate (and surprisingly accurate) in some instances, the highly advanced techniques are equally necessary, adequate, and accurate in others (for example, work-load scheduling, military staffing, or airline staff scheduling).

Those techniques should be used which are best suited to an organization's circumstances, requirements, data availability, and managerial style. In a pragmatic view, the way a company forecasts its talent requirements may evolve in complexity and rigor over time and with the maturing of other management processes. Exhibit 5-4 highlights characteristics of four possible stages of such an evolution (Walker, 1974).

Conceptually, every organization could have a totally integrated, complete, and highly functional forecasting model. Some planners would not only say "could" but also "should." To ensure effective utilization of staff, including mobility among the "segments" defined and to optimize the total recruitment and development requirements of the organization, only a comprehensive forecasting approach would serve. The state of the forecasting practices, if not the state of the art, suggests that this ideal is far from attainment. Models for segments are the immediate practical concern, not syntheses of segment forecasts.

INVENTORYING AVAILABLE TALENT

A prerequisite to forecasting future talent supply and demand is the analysis of the talent available in the organization. Most managers feel they already have a pretty good idea of the talent they have and what they can do. But this knowledge is not always current and complete. Neither is the information in a form that can be assembled and used as a basis for forecasting future needs.

An inventory is necessary to provide a snapshot, both quantitatively and qualitatively, of the human resources in an organization. It provides a benchmark for planning future requirements, surfaces potential problems and issues relating to future staffing, and suggests reasonable assumptions regarding future attrition and mobility (Foltman, 1973).

Many employers have developed computerized information systems as tools

Exhibit 5-4   Forecasting: The Way We Anticipate Future Talent Requirements and Human Resource Management Needs

"Traditional" I	"State of Practice" II	"State of the Art" III	"Futuristic" IV
Managers discuss goals, plans, and thus types and numbers of people needed in the short-term.	Annual planning and budgeting process includes manpower needs.	Using computer-generated analyses, examine causes of problems and future trends regarding supply and demand (the flow of talent).	On-line modeling and simulation of talent needs, flows, and costs to aid in a continuing process of updating projecting of needs, staffing plans, career opportunities, and thus program plans.
Highly informal and subjective.	Specify quantity and quality of talent needs as far out in time as possible.	Use computer to relieve managers of routine forecasting tasks (such as vacancies or turnover).	Provide best possible current information for managerial decisions.
	Identify problems requiring action: individual or general.	Analyze career paths and career progress using computer data files.	Exchange data with other companies and with government (such as economic, employment, and social data).
	Analyze management succession and readiness of successors.		

for human resource management. Most applications are principally in areas of payroll processing, employment processing, benefits administration, and governmental reporting. Systems are typically justified on the basis of reduced administrative costs associated with traditional record keeping and reporting. However, the systems readily provide the resources necessary for human resource planning.

This section examines the data necessary for a human resource inventory, the basic reports that are generated, relationships of these data and reports to EEO and affirmative action planning and reporting, and characteristics of the information systems used.

Data Elements

Data necessary for human resource planning include individual data (work history, skills, appraisals, etc.) and organizational data (job structure, possible career paths, etc.). Emphasis is placed on data about people, but the organizational data are necessary to develop useful classifications of employee data for reporting and planning purposes.

Individual data usually include

Age (birth date)
Sex
Citizenship
Race (EEO classifications in the United States)
Educational attainment (highest level)

Company employment data on individuals usually include

Date of hire
Hire source
Employment status (full time, permanent, etc.)
Positions held in the company and service dates
Recent appraisal data

For analysis of career progression and pay practices, the following additional data elements are usually included:

Salary grade or job evaluation points
Position in salary grade or range
Rate and amount of last adjustment (may be annualized)

Career development data often include

Specific skills (technical training, functions, or specialties)
Interests (skills, functions, or target positions)
Recent training experiences
Educational degrees attained and specializations

Target positions for future career progression
Ratings of promotability, potential, or readiness

In some companies additional details are maintained on

Precompany work experience
Schools or development programs attended
Licenses and certifications
Outside hobbies and activities
Committees or professional memberships
Geographic relocation preferences

There are obviously trade-offs in the amount of detail to be maintained that would be useful in human resource planning versus the cost of obtaining, storing, and updating these data. One example is the "skills inventory," highly popular in the 1960s. A comprehensive skills inventory offers each individual a lengthy and detailed directory of skills (often literally thousands of items) applicable to the work in the company. The individual then checks off all those skills applicable from his or her personal experience. In some instances the skills are subjectively rated in terms of level of competency and how recently they were last applied. Even though the skills were typically coded in the information system, the mass of data was great and many companies ultimately reduced the size of the inventory to a smaller list considered useful, or abandoned the concept entirely.

If skills data are often unreliable, and educational and demographic variables such as age and sex are considered discriminatory, what is left as useful for human resource planning? Past work experience, performance evaluations, and certain skills data (objective skills such as languages and technical competencies) are used in identifying and evaluating prospective candidates for transfers and promotions.

Appraisals of individual promotability and potential have historically reflected managerial estimates of individual capacity to assume broader or greater responsibilities. Promotability implies capacity to handle more demanding positions ("up the ladder"). Potential is a longer-range assessment of capacity to become an executive or a senior specialist, or otherwise to attain a higher level at some point in the person's career. Although these assessments are largely subjective, companies have adopted more intensive (multirater, multicriteria) assessment programs and have used these data as a tool in forecasting future promotions and transfers in the organization. The results may be included in a computer-based information system.

In many companies, however, emphasis has shifted away from prediction and toward shorter-term career development targets. Each employee may then have a next step: promotion to one or two alternate positions, a geographic move, or even retirement. With today's interest in career planning and development (see Chapters 11 to 14), it is important to be realistic in assessing an individual's career options, to be specific in defining the development actions required, and to be able to disclose these data to the individuals. The use of target positions avoids many of the pitfalls of general assessments and provides a basis for specific short-term human resource planning.

For this approach to work, organizational data are required to define clearly a structure covering the various jobs and "career possibilities" in a company. This makes the use of target positions a practical development and planning tool. Positions are already classified and coded in most companies in terms of salary level or grade, organizational placement, functional groupings, and location. Further classification of jobs is needed for human resource planning based on job content (the work activities performed) and the skills, knowledge, and experience requirements. Techniques for analyzing job requirements and career paths are discussed in Chapters 7 and 14, respectively. An illustrative classification structure, developed at Dow Corning Corporation, is presented in Exhibit 5-5.

At a minimum, the organization structure and the various salary levels (or merely organization levels) provide a grid useful in classifying positions and analyzing personnel flows. Such a grid is also an effective starting point in identifying possible career paths across organizational units and within units.

The total array of data elements used in human resource planning and development are frequently displayed in a single output document, a career profile such as represented in Exhibit 5-6. This profile does not present the many data elements pertaining to employee benefits administration, safety, absentee-ism, or personnel actions (change of status, pay changes, etc.). Rather, it is a summary of data on file pertinent to each individual's career development. In addition to being a useful résumé for use by managers, it allows employees to know what data are on file and to update their qualifications and interests. For our purposes, it provides a summary of the data elements necessary in forecasting human resource needs.

Basic Reports and Analyses

It is relatively easy to amass a large amount of such data, manually or in a computer system. It is another task to *retrieve* these data in a format that makes sense to management.

Human resource planning begins with basic reports on the available inventory of talent. These are simply reports on present employment character-istics ("got shots") and reports on past personnel movement ("flow shows"). The "got shots" may include these items.

1 Employee rosters: listings of employees by name, with position, service, age, sex, organizational unit, and other data

2 Current and authorized staffing: a numerical tabulation of positions in each unit, by level or grade (or position title) and the actual current staffing (the net gap being vacancies).

3 Employment distributions: tabulations by sex, age, nationality, race, length of service, or other desired factors

4 Performance appraisals: tabulations of ratings by appraisers, annual-

Exhibit 5-5 Classfication Structure: Dow Corning Corp.

I. Type	II. Category	III. Activity	IV. Function
0 Management	To be coded by corporate salary administration	A Accounting and finance	1 RDE&S
1 Supervision		B Management information center	
2 Professional		C Research	2 Sales/marketing
3 New professional/non-exempt supervision	1 Grade I	D Development	
	2 Grade II	E Engineering	3 Manufacturing
	3 Grade III	F Distribution	
4 Technical	4 Grade IV	G Sales	4 Administrative
	5 Grade V	H Marketing	
5 Office	6 Grade VI	I TS&D	5 Technical service and development
6 Service	7 Grade VII	J Industrial relations	
	8 Full-time summer/temporary	K Production	
Exempt	9 Part time	L Maintenance	
		M Legal and patent	
7 Production—direct labor	1 "A" operator	N Planning/economic evaluation	
	2 "B" operator	P Quality assurance	
	3 "C" operator	Q Materials flow	
	4 Line packager	R Services	
	5 "E" operator	S General and administrative	
	6 Full-time summer/temporary	T Utilities/waste control	
Nonexempt	9 Part time		
8 Production—support	A Tradesman		
	B Apprentice tradesman		
	C Semiskilled maintenance		
	D Utilities operator		
	E General service		
	F Warehouseman		
	G Shipping packager		
	H Clerk		
	J Laboratory tester		
	Y Full-time summer/temporary		
Production and maintenance	Z Part time		

Source: Reprinted by permission from Kent Granat, "After Personnel System Installation, Then What?" *Personnel Journal*, November 1971, p. 869.

ized percentage of last increases, salary level or grade, listing of top performers, or employees receiving the largest percentage of increases

    5   Position tenure: recently staffed positions and long-service positions, indicating possibly hard-to-staff and blocked positions

    6   Open positions: current vacancies

The "flow shows" continue the list of basic reports by examining changes in staffing patterns.

    7   New hires: a roster, as above, for recent hires

    8   Attrition: retirements, voluntary and involuntary terminations, leaves of absence, etc.

    9   Reassignments: moves within organizational unit

    10   Job changes: listing of positions which have been redefined or reclassified (for example, new titles, new salary grades)

Exhibit 5-7 presents a list of inventory reports provided to division managers in a large commercial bank. The particular tables provide information most commonly requested by the managers. This is presented for illustrative purposes only (also see Traum, 1973).

Affirmative Action Planning: Linkages

Naturally, many of these same kinds of reports are prepared for purposes of affirmative action program planning and reporting. While the focus of affirmative action is upon sex and racial representation in the various job categories, the information generated for this purpose can be useful to human resource planning. And affirmative action is essentially one important subset of a complete, overall human resource planning process.

A unique feature in equal employment reporting and affirmative action planning is the use of defined job categories (EEO1 categories, so called because they are required in the basic federal report format with that number):

Officials and managers
Foremen
Professionals
Technicians
Sales workers
Office and clerical workers
Crafts (skilled) workers
Operatives (semiskilled)
Laborers (unskilled)
Service workers

Many companies have further elaborated these categories, either to provide greater specificity for their own planning, or in response to compliance agency requests. Such groupings are useful as an additional organizational classification system—a way of grouping positions for planning purposes. The categories are

NAME _____   PROFILE DATE _____

CAREER DEVELOPMENT PROFILE

PERSONAL DATA
Birth Date _____ Sex _____ EEO Code _____ Citizenship _____ Company _____ Officer Title _____ Hire Date _____

Social Security Number _____

CURRENT POSITION
Effective Date _____ Status _____ Department/Division _____ Location _____ Grade _____ Current Salary _____

Job Title _____

JOB HISTORY
_____

PREVIOUS EMPLOYMENT
From _____ To _____ Company/Industry _____ Description _____ Year _____

Job Title/Primary Duties _____

TRAINING PROGRAMS
_____

EDUCATION
Subject/Major _____ School _____ Year _____

Level/Degree _____

SPECIALIZED EXPERIENCE, SKILLS, KNOWLEDGE, AND CAREER INTERESTS

DEVELOPMENT TARGET POSITIONS

Description	Timing	Appraiser	Summary

PERFORMANCE APPRAISALS

Comment	Date	Appraiser

Exhibit 5-6 Career development profile.

Exhibit 5-7   Illustrative Table of Contents: Inventory

1 Grades
   a Full-time personnel
   b Full-time new hires
   c Full-time separations
   d Full-time personnel, by sex
2 Salaries
   a Average monthly salary (full time by grades)
   b Full-time nongraded personnel by $1000 salary grouping
   c Monthly salary ranges and nongraded equivalents
3 Job families
   a Job family listing
   b Full-time personnel by job families
   c Catagories by job families
   d Nongraded personnel by job families
   e College graduates by job families
   f Full-time personnel grades by job families
4 Education
   a Full-time personnel by education level
   b Full-time new hires by education level
   c Full-time separations of recent hires by education level
5 Organizational tabulations
   a Listing of organizational units and codes
   b Full-time personnel by units
   c Prime shift full-time personnel by units
   d Hourly personnel by units
   e Full-time new hires by units
   f Full-time nongraded personnel by units
6 EEO categories
   a Category totals
   b New hires by category
   c Categories by organizational units, counts
7 Other information
   a Full-time personnel age distribution
   b Full-time personnel (exempt or nonexempt)
   c Time since last promotion (sex by grade)

imprecise, however, and the task of sorting positions itself, particularly into more refined groupings, is a difficult analytical task.

A company's affirmative action plans and governmental reports are an excellent place to begin the development of a human resource inventory. The data already collected may be supplemented to examine all employee groups. The analysis and reporting procedures used in affirmative action planning may be used or adapted to meet the needs of human resource planning (Brookmire and Burton, 1978; Froehlich and Hawver, 1974; Grauer, 1976).

Human Resource Information Systems

A word is appropriate concerning the information systems used in human resource planning. Only a few hundred companies in the United States have full-blown, comprehensive human resource information systems which serve multiple management applications. Such broad-based systems are ideally suited for human resource planning, as they have all the data elements needed plus ready accessibility through retrieval and reporting systems (Tetz, 1974).

For those companies that do not have comprehensive systems, several alternatives are possible. Most firms have a computer-based payroll administration system, or at a minimum use a time-sharing or computer service firm for this function. Such a system includes many basic employee data elements and may be expanded to include other data elements necessary for human resource planning. Alternatively, a separate, supplemental system could be established and interfaced with the payroll system to provide the additional data elements required. This could be a step toward a modular approach to building a comprehensive human resource information system (HRIS). A third alternative is the establishment of a wholly separate information system for human resource planning purposes only.

The trend is clearly toward establishment of comprehensive systems. For example, B. F. Goodrich has a comprehensive information system used by management to store, change, and report personnel information. It is a centralized information source in a company that is diverse in its organization, products, and geography. Reports generated are used in merit budget control, compensation and benefits administration, job candidate searches, EEO reporting, forecasting staffing needs, and budget control. One feature of the system is the use of tables (indexed sequential access method) to store information common to a number of individual records, such as division name and job titles. Use of the tables provides the capability of updating a number of individual records by entering a single change to an element on a table. Because most data elements are coded in this way, reports for human resource forecasting are easily generated.

At Mobil Oil, the independent inventory system alternative is applied. Two automated data files are used for manpower planning applications. The data sources provide problem-oriented reports, formatted information, and statistical matrices using two general-purpose retrieval systems, Mark IV and Crosstabs, in addition to the original program developed by Mobil to search the inventory file. Standard formats, such as those outlined above, are used to inform managers on the status of available human resources.

PROJECTING FUTURE TALENT SUPPLY

With an inventory of current staffing and information on past hires, movement, and attrition, the next step in human resource forecasting is to project future inventory changes. This entails adjusting the current staffing tables to reflect estimated future staffing changes:

Temporary employees (or part-time employees) made permanent
Permanent employees made temporary, part time, or granted special status
(for example, leaves of absence, special assignments)
Reassignments (promotions, transfers, demotions) within unit

Movement into and out of the unit
Terminations and retirements

These estimated changes may be applied to current staffing to create a reasonably accurate one-year forecast of available supply. The same estimates may be projected two, three, or more years into the future, but the results are less reliable because conditions are less certain. The basic approach of adjusting current staffing data by applying enlightened estimates is pragmatic and commonly practiced. When combined with estimated adjustments in staffing requirements (demand), as shown in Exhibit 5-8, the projections provide a simple forecast of overall human resource needs.

More refined forecasting methods are available, focusing more specifically on projected changes in particular job classifications, locations, organizational units, employee classifications (age, length of service, etc.), or levels. Estimates may also be refined by use of statistical techniques; flows of talent in, up, over, and out of an organization may be examined as a total, integrated system using modeling techniques.

Projecting Turnover

The primary reason for change in the supply of talent in an organization is attrition. Employees leave for various reasons: retirement, voluntary termina-

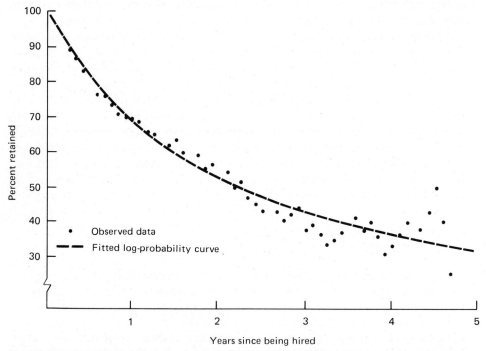

Exhibit 5-8 Retention of employee cohorts. (*Source:* United States Civil Service Commission, 1977.)

tion (to take other jobs, to return to school, etc.), and involuntary termination (because of poor performance, discipline, etc.). Turnover is normally reported as a ratio of the number of separations during a period to the average number of employees on the payroll during the period, expressed as a percentage. It includes all permanent separations, whether voluntary or involuntary, but does not usually include employees placed on temporary or indefinite layoff or granted leaves of absence.

Overall turnover rates reported by 516 companies surveyed in 1977 ranged from 0.0 to 32.9 percent in a given month (Bureau of National Affairs, 1977). The reported rates for May 1977 were as follows for all companies:

	May 1977	Annualized
High	32.9%	394.8%
Third quartile	3.3	39.6
Median	1.9	22.8
First quartile	0.8	9.6
Low	0.0	0.0

Turnover rates vary, of course, with occupational and job category, with length of service, and other characteristics. To control turnover it is necessary to identify the factors associated with high turnover rates and correct them (Cawsey and Richardson, 1975; Flowers and Hughes, 1973; Frantzreb, 1977).

Losses from death, disability, and retirements have long been considered actuarial-type losses because tables for estimating them have been available for years. These tables are based on past experience and serve as the basis for funding pension plans and determining insured risks. These are simple "annual loss probability" tables based on employee age and sex (although sex is not used as a differentiating variable where "unisex" tables are applied).

There are no tables to guide estimates of other forms of turnover, whether voluntary or involuntary. Additionally, as laws prohibit mandatory retirement based on age, the predictability of retirement timing may also change. Accordingly, tools are needed to help planners forecast turnover. One tool is simply previous turnover rates, subjectively adjusted to reflect knowledge of changing conditions such as pay rates and economic conditions. Trends in turnover rates may be examined for particular locations or occupational groups/job categories to project turnover (*Company Manpower Planning,* 1968).

Another tool, developed through years of research by the Civil Service Commission, assumes that turnover in any given group of hires fits a common curve, a "log probability nomography." The research found that "in any given group of hires, from two-thirds to three-fourths of all the quits that will ever occur prior to retirement age will have already occurred by the end of the first three years of service. And of these, more than half will have occurred by the end of the first year alone." The time scale on the curve may vary, from months to years, but repeated studies suggest that the log-probability curve is a useful characterization of attrition in a group of hires, or a cohort group. Thus by obtaining data on a given group of hires (what percentage are still on board one year after the date of original hire, two years after, etc.) points may be plotted and a curve fitted. This curve may then be used to project future attrition up to seven years. This calculation may be performed manually, but is aided by a computer program. The approach is explained in detail, complete with the required programs in a Civil Service publication (U.S. Civil Service Commission, 1977).

Mobility

Internal turnover also needs to be examined in forecasting changes in human resource availability. As illustrated in Exhibit 5-9, employees move in, over, up, and out of an organization. When segmented by levels, occupational groupings, or organizational units, it is possible to examine this flow and project future flows, or mobility.

One way to forecast mobility is to analyze the development plans for each employee. If each employee has a "target development position" and a rating of readiness to assume that position (or rating of promotability; for example, ready now, ready within two years, ready within five years), then these data may be processed to provide a projected availability of talent for the array of positions denoted. This type of forecast assumes that ratings are valid and that promotions targeted could, in fact, occur. An oil company analyzes its promotability ratings using its personnel data system. The forecast permits a view of manpower supply in all parts of the organization in each projected period of time. The staffing of the organization may be simulated and the shortfalls and surpluses made quite apparent by the analysis (Walker, 1970).

This individual approach is essentially a succession planning process involving appraisals on each individual employee. Succession planning techniques are discussed in Chapter 12.

A second approach to forecasting internal mobility is to ask each unit manager to estimate transfers and promotions into, out of, and within the unit. These estimates may be aggregate, and may merely reflect subjective probabilities of movement based on previous experience. Yet total figures of this type

Exhibit 5-9   Personnel mobility in an organization.

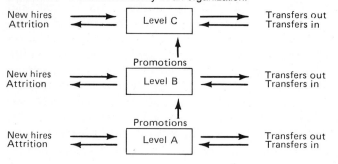

may be sufficiently accurate for purposes of forecasting future recruitment and development needs.

A third approach utilizes past movement data to project future movement through statistical analysis. As will be explained in the next chapter, models of personnel flows forecast the numbers of employees that will remain in an organizational classification based on past transition rates or probabilities. Other models rely on analysis of movement among levels created by vacancies, representing a "renewal" or pull effect.

Skills and Time Utilization

The number of people on the payroll may not directly reflect the capabilities being applied to achievement of organizational objectives. With personnel costs soaring and with employees seeking more challenging work assignments, we need to examine ways we can utilize staff capabilities more fully. Three questions may be asked to consider this aspect of forecasting available supply of talent:

1   Are people spending their time appropriately?
    Could the work be reallocated to provide a more effective use of skills?
    Could jobs be restructured?
2   Are productivity rates changing?
    Are we properly staffed now to achieve the desired outputs?
    Is our staff growth exceeding our expansion of outputs?
3   Are we staffed with the right kinds of skills?
    Skills not being applied?
    Skills missing

These broad questions are addressed through analysis of activities performed—the utilization of time by the various groups of employees. Data may be collected and analyzed on actual on-the-job activities: what people really do and how they spend their time. The techniques for work analysis are discussed in Chapter 7.

Once data are collected and tabulated, areas of "organizational slack" may be identified—time and skills that are not being appropriately applied for achievement of objectives. Such slack may represent up to 40 percent in some employee groups (Anderson, 1976; Neuman, 1975). Typically, overhead activities (staff work, coordination and administration activites, personnel work, accounting research, and planning) are common target areas. From an organizational viewpoint, the aggregate time allocations required to perform necessary tasks may result in fewer overall positions required; the available supply of talent may be more effectively allocated to the work required and thus reduce the overall demand for employees. For example, a group of engineers may allocate 20 percent of the time to clerical, drafting, and other support activities which could be reassigned to clerical positions. This would free up time for higher-skill engineering work and reduce the pressure for recruitment of scarce engineering talent.

Skills mix can also be analyzed, assuming job requirements are defined in terms of experience, skills, knowledge, and educational needs. In any group, there may be employees who are overqualified or underqualified in relation to the actual job requirements. If we can match more precisely the skills of the people with the skills required, we may utilize the higher-talent individuals better on more demanding jobs, motivate employees by challenging them more fully, and thus reduce the overall demand for talent and related payroll costs. Of course, there is the question whether an employee is underutilized in a position or whether the employee is overqualified for the position. And should employees be promoted before they are fully qualified for a position (stretching them and allowing mastery of a job once on the job), or should they be advanced only after becoming fully qualified through training preparation? The utilization of skills is an important variable influencing the availability of talent and thus forecasted requirements.

FORECASTING STAFFING REQUIREMENTS

If we do not know the staffing required, it does not really help much to know the available staffing. We implicitly assume in human resource planning that staffing demands will be the same in the future as at present, or at least differ only in predictable ways. This is reasonable, particularly in the short term (one to three years). But in the longer range or under rapidly changing conditions such as rapid company growth, forecasting techniques are needed.

To forecast the demand for talent and to match this demand with supply we need:

Knowledge of our objectives for the future and what various business indicators will be (revenues, outputs, volumes, etc.)
An organization plan
Knowledge of work activities and requirements
Appreciation of technological and productivity changes

Because we do not know precisely what future business requirements, organizational changes, economic conditions, productivity, and technological changes will be, forecasts are not often on the mark. And they are not expected to be. We are less concerned with the need for accurate forecasts of needs than with the need for enlightened thinking as a basis for management actions.

Analyzing Current Requirements

The most common approach to forecasting is to begin with an analysis of *current* staffing requirements. The organization structure and definitions of jobs (as presented in job descriptions) provide a logical place to begin the analysis of staffing requirements.

Many organizations use a vacancy allocation and control procedure to regulate additions to staff and modifications in jobs and organization structure. Here, an executive or a committee is responsible for reviewing recommended new positions or organizational changes, including expansion of staff. Whenever a position becomes vacant, the position may be reviewed to consider whether it is really necessary and whether it is properly structured. This approach, assuming a "zero change" strategy in planning for human resource needs, calls for justification by unit managers proposing new positions or replacements of staff.

A similar but somewhat less restrictive procedure involves a necessary approval or authorization of new positions, organization changes, and hires. An HRIS can provide an automatic indication of whether positions were included in budgetary plans and thus authorized.

Rather than controlling staffing by organization units, some organizations consider occupational groupings. Ratios of clerical and support staff positions to professional and managerial positions may serve as a guide for staffing. Authorizations for employment of engineers or other specialists may depend on the current availability of employees, organizationwide, in these occupational groupings (Grosskopf, 1978).

Simple budgetary procedures usually define precisely the positions authorized currently and for the near-term future, plus the related costs. If personnel costs are budgeted only in gross dollar terms, without detailed staffing, supplementary information may be required which does provide this detail, position by position. Many organizations control staffing very strictly by assigning a position number or code to each position. These must be authorized under the budgeting process for personnel to be added. The procedure also minimizes the staffing variability caused by use of temporary hires, "double-occupancy staffing" (essentially two people in the same job while one is in training, awaiting transfer, etc.), and "upward drift" in the grading of positions each time they are filled. Budgetary authorizations may specify exactly what staffing is needed and how it differs from previous staffing requirements.

Judgmental Forecasting

To estimate future requirements, someone must make a decision. Mathematical analysis and massive data may be useful, but ultimately, the determination of "how should we be staffed" is a human decision.

Accordingly, the basic approach commonly followed is a "bottom-up" estimation process, usually linked to a budget and position control procedure such as described above. In many instances these "enlightened guesses" are not formal plans, but are represented in actual authorizations for new positions, changes in job titles or content, recruitment and hiring, and by positions left unfilled.

The manager in a local unit is the best-informed person to make judgments regarding staffing requirements necessary to achieve that unit's objectives. The quality of judgments depends on the manager's estimates, but it is enhanced by the use of:

Rules of thumb for staffing
Comparisons with other units
Ratios or standard staffing guidelines for particular types of positions or operations
Information on actual work content, based on job analysis

The "ask and find out" method of forecasting is often adequate for an organization's needs, particularly where operations are stable and staffing requirements are not variable. It involves the gathering of judgmental estimates from unit managers and aggregating them into an overall forecast. Adjustments may then be made based on successive management reviews and analysis as the aggregate forecast is prepared. Once completed and approved, the forecast is disaggregated (broken back apart) and returned to the managers as authorized staffing plans.

This approach represents a formal, systematic planning process, but one which still relies heavily on the subjective judgment and knowledge of the unit managers. The "asking" in the forecast should include estimates of:

New positions needed
Positions to be dropped or left unfilled
Changes in existing positions
Double occupancies
Overtime expected
Slack expected (due to orientation of new employees or lag periods between projects, etc.)
Fluctuations in work load during the planning period
Budgetary impact (costs) of changes
Changes, if any, in overhead, contracted labor, and supervision

These adjustments are applied to the current staffing table, yielding a forecast of future staffing for each unit. This table provides a forecast and a benchmark for future planning by level and type of job within the unit (Ettelstein, 1970).

Organization charts may be used as an alternative way to forecast staffing changes, particularly in smaller organizations. These are simply charts of the organization structure showing the various positions and their reporting relationships, on which projected staffing changes are noted (W. E. Bright, 1976).

A final technique in the judgmental category is noteworthy: the Delphi technique. This is a technique used for long-range forecasts that is useful where inputs from a number of managers or experts are desired. It involves:

Obtaining judgments through a questionnaire or structured interviews from a panel of "experts"

Feeding the various inputs in a summary form back to all the panelists, for their review and reconsideration

Repeating this cycle until general agreement is reached on the projections (whether organization structures or changes in staffing requirements)

The technique was developed originally by Rand Corporation in the late 1940s as a set of procedures designed to obtain the most reliable consensus of opinion among a group of experts (Milkovich, Annoni, and Mahon, 1971).

Of course, judgments may be exercised by corporate management as well as by unit managers or groups of managers. A company that wishes to reduce staffing, reduce overhead costs, improve productivity in specific areas, or achieve affirmative action objectives, for example, may influence staffing plans from the *top down* rather than solely from the *bottom up*. And the analysis of productivity and achievable targets in productivity improvement or affirmative action requires different forecasting tools (Bell, 1974; Bramham, 1975).

The complexity of the forecasting methods used depends on a number of factors: the complexity of the organization, the availability of business or operating plans and indicators of future activities, the sophistication of top management, and the data available. Various quantitative analysis and forecasting methods are available to supplement intuitive forecasting. These are identified here and discussed in the next chapter.

Predictor Variables

The basis of most forecasting is what has happened in the past. This is even true of intuitive judgments by managers, as their estimates reflect their experience and training. Past experience is quantitatively represented by indicators of outputs by means of a ratio or regression (correlation) relationship.

Productivity is the ratio of output per labor input (hours of work or persons). To figure out such ratios, we thus need to have data on outputs—work-load indicators that represent the results of activities. We also need to be able to isolate the labor input that relates to the outputs—the time and effort spent to obtain the results identified. These are not easy tasks, but are important building blocks in forecasting staffing needs. Work study measurements may help define what these ratios have been and suggest what they might be (as staffing standards). However, simple ratios are more often applicable at operative and clerical positions than on managerial, professional, and technical (exempt salaried) positions.

Useful indicators include:

Organizational products: what is produced
  Revenues

Physical outputs
Units or volumes sold
Projects completed
Transactions, volumes processed
Benefits to other organizations
Services (frequency, duration, volume)
Quality of services
Customer relationships (size, longevity, quality)
Goodwill created
Benefits to society
Creation of ideas and innovations
Community services rendered

To be useful, predictor variables need to be directly related to the essential nature of the business, so that the same variables are used in the business and operational planning (for example, widgets produced, accounts opened or served, miles flown). Sales (in dollars) may not be a useful predictor variable if the figures reflect price changes (inflation), foreign exchange rates, and other indirect factors.

Also, some allowance needs to be made for possible productivity gains as volumes increase. Production of 30 percent more widgets may not necessarily require 30 more personnel. Thus estimates or targets for improvement in productivity need to be included as variables in forecasting staffing requirements.

Some companies have found that "value added" is a useful focus in defining work-load demands in forecasting staffing requirements. Value added is the market value of the goods and services after subtracting purchases for intermediate goods and services. Sales revenues would thus be reduced by the purchase costs of the materials, supplies, and services used in the production process. The net amount represents the "real" output created by the labor contribution at the last step. Of course, determining the value added involves estimations, but it has appeal as a direct indicator of staffing requirements (Vetter, 1967).

Determining Relationships

Various methods are available for determining the relationships between human resource requirements and indicator variables. Simple ratios and trends are useful in short-term planning periods and in circumstances where operations are static, change is slow, activities are "normal," and past ratios tend to have a strong influence over future staffing.

Correlation is the attempt to identify relationships among variables. Regression analysis is a widely used family of techniques for measuring the degree of correlation. Simple regression examines the relationship between two variables. Multiple regression has the capacity of identifying patterns among many variables simultaneously.

Without defining relationships among variables, mathematical equations may be derived as useful models for forecasting staffing requirements. Balancing equations, linear programming, nonlinear programming, and goal programming represent advanced techniques available for forecasting. These techniques are discussed in the next chapter.

The End Result

The point of forecasting is to create a logical forecast that is understandable and useful to managers. While many forecasting endeavors may result in reams of tables and printouts, and voluminous reports, the single end result desired is a table of projected staffing requirements.

An example of a forecast that integrates supply and demand projections is presented in Exhibit 5-10. In this example, the scope of the forecast is constrained by the premise that internal promotions would involve only individuals who are appraised as ready now and performing at an excellent or superior level. This represents, therefore, a specific scenario useful to guide management planning. This is a hypothetical case developed at Weyerhaeuser Company.

Presented in Exhibit 5-11 is a format developed and used at Vetco Offshore, Inc., a drilling equipment company. The format concisely summarizes (1) manpower requirements, (2) key ratios and indicators, and (3) planned staffing sources. It is a general structure for presenting the results of the forecasting effort, whether anchored in intuitive management judgments or in quantitative analysis.

Exhibit 5-10   Illustration: Human Resources Planning and Analysis

Mobility Criteria:	Promote individuals who are ready now and who are performing at an excellent or superior level.						
Demand	1974	1975	1976	1977	1978	1979	1980
Beginning in position	142	148	154	160	166	173	180
Increases (decreases)	6	6	6	6	7	7	7
Total demand (year end)	148	154	160	166	173	180	187
Supply (during year)							
Beginning in position	142	148	154	160	166	173	180
Less promotions	(19)	(21)	(21)	(23)	(23)	(23)	(25)
Less terminations	(8)	(8)	(9)	(9)	(9)	(10)	(10)
Less retirements	(4)	(4)	(4)	(4)	(4)	(5)	(5)
Less transfers	(3)	(3)	(3)	(3)	(4)	(4)	(4)
Subtotal	108	112	117	121	126	131	136
Plus promotions in	12	12	12	12	12	14	14
Total supply (year end)	120	124	129	133	138	145	150
Excess/deficit (year end)	(28)	(30)	(31)	(33)	35)	(35)	(37)

A. MANPOWER REQUIREMENTS

Covering Period _____ to _____

Prepared by _____

Date _____

Major Job Categories and Classifications	1 Current Manpower A/O ___	2 Planned Manpower A/O ___	3 Net Change ±	Anticipated Losses to Each Job Category						10 Total Needs for This Period
				4 Transfers	5 Promotions	6 Resignations	7 Retirements	8 Discharge	9 Other	
1. Executives and Managers										
2. First Level Supervisors										
3.										
4.										
5.										
6.										
7.										
8.										
9.										
Total Employees										

B. KEY RATIOS AND INDICATORS

	Current	Planned
Revenue/Employee		
Net Income/Employee		
Direct Labor/Indirect Labor		
Management/Employees		
Total Payroll Cost		
Average Salary		
Other Key Indicators (Specify)		

C. PLANNED STAFFING SOURCES

	Total Needs from Col. 10 Above	Promotion of Current Employees of This Organiz.	Promotion of Current Employees of Other Organiz.	Employees To Be Hired and Trained Prior to Promotion	Employees To Be Hired for Immediate Assignment
1. Executives and Managers					
2. First Level Supervisors					
3.					
4.					
5.					
6.					
7.					
8.					
9.					
Total Employees					

Exhibit 5-11 Manpower summary and forecast.

Chapter 6

Forecasting Models and Applications

KEY POINTS

- Mathematical techniques facilitate the analysis of complex patterns of personnel flows and changing personnel requirements in an organization.
- Models may be descriptive, representing current or past patterns, or they may be normative, presenting possible future patterns. Models are useful to managers in examining the implications of alternative policies and organizational conditions.
- Simple forecasting models rely on subjective judgments and extension of past staffing patterns into the future. They are useful in planning under stable conditions.
- Organizational change models examine the movement of personnel in a system as a basis for planning changes desired.
- Optimization models identify the actions required to achieve desired staffing objectives, within defined constraints.
- The ultimate model provides an integrated simulation of the patterns of change in a total entity, linked with business planning.

Models do not forecast, people do. But analytical models using mathematical techniques and computer processing can be a big help to people trying to forecast future staffing requirements. This chapter examines several types of models useful in forecasting human resource needs and discusses the opportunities and constraints in applying models.

A model is merely a representation of something else: a model train, a model airplane, an architect's model, etc. Models re-create the essential features of the original item, and they can be manipulated to act in a fashion similar to that of the original item. Of course, there are many different kinds of models, including physical, abstract, mechanical, mental, logical, verbal, and mathematical models. Mathematical models, while not physical or tangible, have the features of all models as noted above (Patillo and Secunza, 1971). They represent aspects of the "real world" and the structure of the "real world" in quantitative terms (Carruthers, 1966; Rivett and Ackoff, 1963).

MODELS

Models may be descriptive, representing what *is,* or normative, representing what *should be.* Descriptive models help to make sense out of masses of seemingly complex and often contradictory empirical data on staffing and personnel flows or movements. Data on past and current staffing patterns are manipulated by mathematical techniques. The result is typically a simplified and abstract view of the levels and flows of personnel throughout an organizational system. Forecasts of future personnel flows, surpluses and shortages of personnel relative to needs, and future needs themselves may be developed through operation of models. However, the future is determined by applying past patterns in projections (by use of probabilities and correlations) or by making certain assumptions about future flows and desired staffing objectives. Thus *normative* models of "proper" future staffing are less objective and thus less reliable as a basis for management decision making.

At this point, models serve primarily a descriptive and "reality-testing" function for managers in human resource planning. In one major company, for example, modeling efforts provided managers with "best estimates" of future demand and supply of talent for a number of years. Now, however, the models are used primarily to generate several alternative "scenarios" among which managers may select the forecasts they consider most realistic and practical for their planning needs.

Purpose of Modeling

Various mathematical techniques have been applied in exploring, to varying depths, various aspects of human resource flows and needs through models. Techniques such as regression analysis, Markov analysis, and linear programming permit manipulation of important historical data for variables managers consider to be significant. Additionally, assumptions or parameters underlying system behavior may be modified in models. Simulation techniques make it possible to evaluate the relative importance of the many factors that influence an organization's human resource needs and availability. Modeling enables managers to explore aspects of systems that cannot be observed directly, such as the patterns of movement of employees among different sets of jobs in an organization over time and reactions of internal manpower supply to changes in management policies and employment decisions.

Through modeling, managers may examine the implications of past policies and organizational conditions affecting the supply and demand of talent. Further, the effects of future policies, staffing and development actions, and organizational changes may be examined and considered in formulating human resource plans. Modeling, then, represents a powerful tool and a valuable source of feedback in this difficult management task.

In the longer view, models may be sufficiently expanded and refined so that they will incorporate objective measures, realistic parameters, and analytic techniques. Models may be combined to operate as a complex entity simulation, even a comprehensive corporatewide forecasting model. By matching the requirements of complex tasks, the need for subjective managerial judgment in this area may be reduced. Similar models with this degree of sophistication have already been developed in production and inventory control, operations planning, navigation, and other fields. Although the human resource area is at present less well defined and predictable, it is likely that greater sophistication is possible through modeling.

Types of Models

Various authors have reviewed the different techniques available for use in model building and have suggested classifications of models into types (Bryant, Maggard, and Taylor, 1973; Grinold and Marshall, 1977; Milkovich and Mahoney, 1978; Weber and Hofman, 1975). For the purposes of this book, four types of models are identified, representing a classification of techniques by their sophistication. Each type of model successively has greater scope, technical complexity, and added functions. As shown in Exhibit 6-1, these types are:

Simple forecasting, as discussed in Chapter 5

Organizational change models, which examine past changes and forecast future changes in human resource flows and requirements

Optimization models, which identify staffing requirements (including recruitment, flows, and vacancies) to achieve designated target objectives as defined by costs, staffing mix, etc.

Integrated models, which provide a total analytic view and synthesis of the patterns and requirements in a complex organizational structure

The forecasting techniques described in the previous chapter essentially represent models, as defined here. While simple, they provide a representation of projected future staffing conditions and, by adjusting the variables and assumptions, may be manipulated to achieve alternate results. These simple forecasting models are often integrated as aspects of more complex mathematical models, as discussed in this chapter.

Exhibit 6-1   Basic Types of Models and Applications

Type of model	Techniques	Applications
Simple forecasting models	Judgmental forecasts Rules of thumb Staffing standards Ratio-trend analysis Time series	Rudimentary forecasts of available supply and demand under stable conditions
	Delphi technique	Long-range forecasting
Organizational change models	Succession analysis	Replacement analysis and block-ages
	Markov/stochastic processes Renewal models	Probability-based flow forecasts
	Regression analysis	Correlations to project changes
Optimization models	Linear programming Nonlinear programming Dynamic programming	Future needs defined by constraints
	Goal programming	Future needs identified to achieve defined objectives
	Assignment models	Matching individuals with anticipated vacancies
Integrated simulation models	Corporate models: combined techniques	Total entity simulation linked with corporate planning

CHANGE MODELS

Whereas simple forecasting models provide judgmental estimates of needs and availability of talent in a given planning period, a change model provides a forecast covering two or more successive planning periods. Typically a model is designed to show how an organization will look under certain assumptions about the future. These assumptions may be based on past experience, such as probabilities of transitions among organizational levels and units based on past movements, or they may be proposed by the model designer. You can change some of the assumptions or policies, and you can add or drop variables to provide a somewhat different perspective of prospective changes. Where assumptions and variables are modified, the models are called "simulations."

This section briefly describes three techniques for modeling change in an organization: analysis of succession plans and patterns, probabilistic analysis of personnel movement in an organization, and regression analysis to project demand. Additionally, an example of a simulation model used for affirmative action planning is described.

Succession Analysis

There are only five possible shifts in a personnel system: in, up, over, out, and changes in individual capabilities, or behavior and potential (Haire, 1968). Tracing these flows makes it possible to plan effective actions that will result in improved human resource management.

In many organizations, succession plans are drawn for key positions and levels. These plans, often in the form of "replacement charts" (see Chapter 11) present various data pertaining to prospective personnel changes: organization structure and job relationships, age and promotability of position incumbents, identified backup candidates or successors (with age and appraised readiness or timing for promotion).

Through a manual process of projecting retirements, transfers, and promotions using these charts, a planner may analyze the movement of personnel and the related organizational changes. Charts may be drawn for future points in time, say three years and five years out. Assumptions regarding attrition and retirements may be based on subjective judgments about likely individual behavior or may be applied on a class basis in terms of projected loss rates. The results of such a manually operated modeling activity may include:

Projection of total attrition, or the number of additional persons needed to be added to the pool

Projection of blocked progression lines due to immobile incumbents

Identification of "problem positions" lacking available backup candidates

Identification of surpluses of talent in particular categories, calling for redirection of career plans

This analysis may alternatively be performed in a computerized model. A large company with succession plans covering 1,200 positions, for example, found manual analysis cumbersome. A computer model reduces the calculation tasks to manageable terms, permitting focus on trends, patterns, and implications of the present supply of talent in relation to projected changes. The model also has the capacity to analyze the effects of "second and third choices" of individuals regarding future promotions or assignments. A capable successor may be able to fill any of several assignments, and these alternatives may be considered in the model to help balance available supply with projected needs. The computerized model provides listings of incumbents and their targeted mobility as well as the flip side of the analysis: identification of the prospective candidates for succeeding position incumbents, and the projected timing.

Exhibit 6-2 presents a format used by an oil company for forecasting movement among certain job categories. The estimated numbers of employees moving to other job categories or leaving (attrition) may be derived from specific succession plans or may be estimated on a group basis. This is a useful way to summarize the results of a succession analysis by job category. The primary value of the work sheet is to target proposed transfers in or out, college hires, and experienced hires (section VI on the work sheet).

Probabilistic Models

While a succession analysis examines individual data to forecast changes in staffing supply and demand, a probabilistic model examines data on employees as groups. Movement of employees among different classifications (or states) in a model may be forecasted based on past movement. Classifications typically

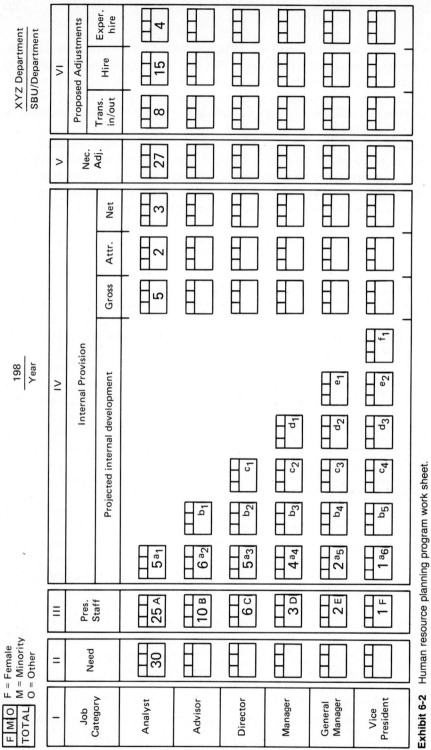

Exhibit 6-2 Human resource planning program work sheet.

involve organizational units and levels, but they could also represent locations, salary classes, functional responsibilities, job categories, length of service, educational levels, or even specific jobs.

If we look at the probabilities of employees moving from one classification to another or out of the organization altogether, we will have generated a matrix or table of "transitional probabilities." This gives us the dynamics of flow in the system from one time to another, the basis for a probabilistic or "stochastic" model (Bartholomew, 1973; Haire, 1968; Mahoney and Milkovich, 1971). The stochastic process tells us whether employees will remain in a given state or move to each of other possible states at some future time.

Data are typically gathered from one year or from several years averaged to determine probabilities. In most stochastic models it is assumed that these transition probabilities are stable among consecutive periods. Stability, in reality, depends on the definition of the states and the length of time intervals involved. If you adjust the probabilities based on managerial judgment of how movement will change, you are moving from a stochastic model toward more flexible simulation. Here projections are based on assumptions instead of past system behavior.

Exhibit 6-3 illustrates the basic technique of stochastic modeling. In this example, movement among four types of jobs (A, B, C, and D) is examined for 1970–1980 and projected to 1981. In this example, 80 percent of job A employees stayed on the same job during the year. One in ten transferred to job type B and another one in ten left the organization. Thus simple arithmetic

Exhibit 6-3 Markov analysis of personnel flows.

Initial staffing levels (end of 1978)*

A (250)	B 220	C 150	D 600		Net staffing (end of 1979)
.8 (200)	.1 (22)			A 222	
.1 (25)	.7 (154)			B 179	
		.6 (90)		C 90	
		.1 (15)	.9 (540)	D 555	
.1 (25)	.2 (44)	.3 (45)	.1 (60)	OUT (174)	

Levels (end of 1980)**

A 240	B 220	C 180	D 700
.8 (192)	.1 (22)		
.1 (24)	.7 (154)		
		.6 (108)	
		.1 (18)	.9 (630)

Forecasted levels (end of 1981)

214
174
108
648

*1978–1979 period used to determine transition probabilities.

**Staffing changes since 1979 due to recruitment, expansion, cuts.

calculation yields the probabilities of movement shown. These may be multiplied by the employment levels at the end of a year to forecast movement and staffing levels in each job category. Repetition of the calculation produces forecasts for succeeding periods.

This specific technique is called Markov analysis and the sequences of transitions are called "Markov chains." A true Markov process contains certain mathematical properties such as strict independence of the states (job categories), constant transition probabilities, and an infinite (or at least large) number of forecasting cycles. Because most human resource planning applications are for a few periods and the classifications may be somewhat arbitrarily drawn, it is more accurate to refer to such models as merely probabilistic or stochastic. Planners may wish to adjust the probabilities to take into account anticipated changes, such as a change in retirement timing (Blakely, 1970; Rowland and Sovereign, 1969).

Stochastic analysis helps analyze career movements within an organization. Such movement patterns of managers in a large manufacturing organization were examined in a study by Vroom and MacCrimmon. Turnover, promotions, demotions, and interfunctional mobility were examined to reveal mobility patterns. Projections yielded forecasts of additional personnel required in each position from outside in each year for a five-year period, availability of talent for higher-level positions, expected years in each position, and probabilities that new employees would reach third-level positions within five years (Vroom and MacCrimmon, 1968). Many subsequent applications have been reported by companies and governmental organizations (Merck and Hall, 1971; McNamar, 1972; Nielson and Young, 1973).

Mahoney and Milkovich have developed a computer simulation based on a stochastic process. The Minnesota Manpower Management Simulation (MMMS) is based on a model which represents as realistically as possible the important personnel decisions, the consequences for manpower performance measures, and achievement of corporate results. The model is based on the circumstances of a hypothetical casualty insurance company (Mahoney and Milkovich, 1975). Similarly, Elbert and Kehoe, also professors, have developed and demonstrated the practical utility of stochastic techniques in examining human resource needs. The emphasis of their model is upon (1) projecting the number of employees needed after normal attrition, (2) tracing career paths of employee movement in an organization, and (3) focusing on individual mobility (Elbert and Kehoe, 1976).

Another type of stochastic model is the "renewal model." Here, flows of personnel are viewed as triggered by vacancies. These vacancies, when filled from lower levels of the organization, *pull* personnel through the system (Cox, 1962). For example, when promotions are made only to fill jobs that become vacant and recruitment is constant, the movement of people responds directly to vacancies created. Of course, there is a chain effect as a person moves to fill a vacancy, creating a vacancy at another level. Renewal models have not been as widely applied as Markov-type models, but they are a potentially useful technique. For example, Harrison White developed a series of such models for analyzing mobility and measuring vacancy chains. His application of the models to a 50-year history of mobility of clergy in three national churches demonstrated that individual careers are not independent of the careers of others in an organization (White, 1970a, 1970b).

Regression Models

A correlation is a relationship among variables. The technique for measuring the degree of correlation is regression analysis. This technique is widely used in human resource forecasting where it is believed that future staffing requirements are correlated with some measurable indicators of output, revenues, etc. When we can quantify the relationship between staffing and other factors, we have a basis for accurate forecasting.

A manufacturing company explored possible relationships between employment and planned production levels. Among the results of the regression runs performed were the following:

Factory employment = 1143 + 0.0696 engine shipments
  Correlation coefficient = .989
  Standard error of estimate = 188
Office employment = 263 + 0.0163 engine shipments
  Correlation coefficient = .987
  Standard error of estimate = 48
Exempt employment = −59 + 0.177 parts sales
  Correlation coefficient = .920
  Standard error of estimate = 86

These regression equations do not necessarily represent *desired* or optimal future staffing levels. Rather, they represent levels which are based on historical policies and actions.

Regression models are most applicable where staffing needs vary directly with other measurable factors such as production, sales, and unit costs. Simple relationships are often difficult to isolate, however, and many planners have searched in vain for staffing determinants (Gascoigne, 1968; Drui, 1963). Complex, multivariate relationships may be handled by multiple regression analysis, although this technique has not been widely applied in human resource planning.

It is difficult to find correlates for staffing forecasts. General factors such as overall sales, volumes, or transactions simply are too broad to permit forecasts of the specificity necessary to define staffing needs by employee or job category. At the same time, correlates are not always available to use for particular employee groups. It may be feasible to forecast clerical and support staff requirements based on number of salesmen or engineers, for example, but even here the relationships may not be strictly linear.

Like trend-ratio analysis or time-series analysis, regression analysis provides a useful supplementary base of information to aid in making managerial judgments about future needs. Its real value may be in its usefulness in identifying alternative staffing levels as possible staffing objectives rather than in the precision of its quantitative forecasts. Regression analysis may alert management to the human resource implications of production, sales, and other operating plans.

OPTIMIZATION MODELS

Some models do more than manipulate data to forecast future staffing patterns. Some forecast, not what is likely to happen, but rather what is necessary to happen if certain objectives are to be achieved. The optimal (or "best") future staffing patterns might mean minimized costs, minimized turnover among employees, targeted proportions of women and minorities in certain groups, achievement of a specified talent mix, or other objectives. The tools described above are often incorporated in optimization models, but such techniques as linear programming are also used.

Linear Programming

This technique provides a specific solution which is "best" according to measurable criteria. It is useful for considering staffing needs at a particular point in time and within given constraints. Deviations from the plan can be examined through the model in terms of their impact on the actual end results. Essentially an LP model determines the level of staffing required to meet organizational objectives when a number of specified constraints are defined.

A model developed by Alan Patz examines the effects of personnel policy combinations on the flow of people into, through, and out of an organization (1970). Other linear programming models have been applied to the problem of recruiting and assigning people in organizations (Lawrence, 1971; Lilien and Rao, 1975).

Linear programming is a mathematical technique for determining the optimum solution under a set of given constraints, represented as mathematical expressions. It is applicable when expressions are proportional to the measure of the activities and all relationships are in the form of linear inequalities. However, relationships are not always linear, and hence *nonlinear programming* may be applied. This may involve convex, concave, or quadratic programming. Another variation on the technique is *dynamic programming,* which is similar, but which involves a series of optimization decisions or solutions, one at every stage of a multistage problem. At any one stage, several decisions may appear to be of equal merit; only when the effect of all stages on the overall goal is determined is the optimal solution reached.

Goal Programming

A refinement of a linear programming model is a goal programming model. This approach uses Markov analysis and linear programming in combination. It is applicable where several constraints affect staffing (for example, budgetary and promotion policies) and where the problem extends over several time periods (Charnes, Cooper, and Niehaus, 1972; Lee, 1972; Price and Piskor, 1972).

Goal programming as a "manpower planning" technique was pioneered by a group of researchers under the auspices of the Office of Civilian Personnel in the Navy Department (Charnes, Cooper, Niehaus, and Sholtz, 1968; Charnes, Cooper, Niehaus, and Stadig, 1969). A series of studies has provided models useful in planning recruitment, promotions and transfers, and affirmative action planning. A series of research reports has been published describing these models. An excellent summary paper in this series was written by Niehaus (Niehaus, 1977).

Goal programming models permit more comprehensive analysis of the behavior of human resource systems. Additionally they permit the development of goals that are realistic and attainable. The modeling tests alternative goals by examining the discrepancies between forecasted results and identified targets and thereby suggests optimum goals that are attainable. For this reason goal programming represents a powerful advancement in modeling technology for human resource planning as well as for planning equal employment opportunities and affirmative action. Included in such a system can be such factors as external availability of talent, personnel movement, and budgetary and other policy constraints—for example, required time on a job (Niehaus, 1979).

While most goal programming applications have been in governmental and military organizations, a few company applications have been reported (Clough, 1974; Grinold and Marshall, 1977; Kahalis, 1976). Applications to affirmative action planning have been reported in numerous organizations (Churchill and Shank, 1976; Flast, 1977; Miller and Haive, 1970).

Assignment Models

Most models examine personnel movement and staffing needs in terms of aggregates. Markov analysis, for example, requires approximately fifty persons in each category for useful results. A personnel assignment model, however, processes individual data, assigning individuals to job vacancies simultaneously. The purpose is to optimize the overall utilization of talent and to forecast, with the greatest possible degree of precision, the specific shortfalls and surpluses of talent anticipated. Essentially the model "assigns" each person, one at a time, to a suitable job (based on preferences, time, seniority, or other selected data) and simulates the entire organizational changes for a period all at once. Dynamic models of this type, covering multiple periods, are feasible, as are models that bridge multiple organizational units (Larson et al., 1973; Meusch, 1973).

Obviously, assignment models, goal programming, and even linear programming models are extremely complex. Their technical development at this time outstrips their actual use in industry, but the capacity (thanks to computers) to operate them clearly exists.

INTEGRATED SIMULATION MODELS

Computer-based simulation models are useful when parameters of future change are not known (for example, transition rates, correlations) and when managers wish to test alternative views of future conditions. When multiple problems are addressed by a simulation model (for example, recruitment, assignment, costs analysis) and when multiple employee groups or classifications are considered, a model may be said to be integrated.

It is somewhat idealistic, or perhaps hopeful, to believe that trends in human resource planning are pointing toward development and use of such integrated models. A company, for example, wishes to integrate its job evaluation system with its organizational planning activity to assure equitable pay for work performed. Another wishes to define competencies required of employees and to use these factors as a basis for massive assignment models, integrated further with job evaluation and other systems. Affirmative action planning models may logically be broadened in application to represent total entity simulations aimed at optimizing staffing in various units and at various levels. Progress to date suggests that integrated models are technically feasible and potentially practical for management use.

As evidenced in the abundant literature cited, the military has advanced the state of the art considerably and applied it to the large-scale human resource planning needs. Other models have also been developed which suggest promise. General Electric Company developed a forecasting and scheduling model which represents a pragmatic tool (Bassett, 1973). A division of GE uses a computer simulation model to determine the future effects of business, production, and economic variables on divisional human resource needs. This comprehensive model projects total staff required, cost of salaries and benefits, and turnover and replacement needs in fifty-eight discrete categories, spanning the entire exempt, nonexempt, and hourly levels. The categories can be grouped to reflect any current or projected organization pattern, by function, or by location (Sobkowiak, 1976). Bank of America developed a model to determine recruiting, training, and assignment needs among the bank's officers and support staff personnel. The model takes into account desired planning horizons, growth rates, and targets (Ceriello and Frantzreb, 1975). A model developed by Weber takes into account a variety of individual behavior and organizational structure, management decisions, and aspects of the organization's environment to represent the human resource system of an organization. Individual factors are captured along with the totality of the system's behavior in this complex simulation (Weber, 1971).

The value of advanced simulation models is not merely to forecast human resource needs, but to evaluate the effects of various sets of variables upon needs and vice versa. They help evaluate personnel policies and guide managers toward plans and objectives that are both realistic and optimal given the circumstances.

Mathematical models are particularly useful when integrated with "bottom-up" judgmental forecasts. An approach of TRW's Systems Group, for example, used marketing projections and project plans to determine staffing needs from the top down. At the same time, estimates by the managers on the various projects planned and underway were obtained. For each unit, direct labor, overhead (utilities, materials, services, etc.), and staffing needs were determined. These data were integrated, resulting in a dynamic plan for overall staffing levels and mix, recruitment, assignment, and development (B. H. White, 1972).

In an operating company of AT&T, an annual forecast is made based on "bottom-up" departmental forecasts by titles and pay grades. These data, in the form of desired year-end populations for the next six years, are then applied to a corporate model which forecasts all types of work force activity. From this model are determined actions necessary to reach desired populations. Embedded in the model is a stochastic process, using an "interaction flow simulator" software package developed by AT&T for the use of its companies. The actions are translated into assessment, promotions, development, and other necessary program plans. In this approach, the forecast by managers is the starting point, not the analysis of data through the model. The model itself involves hundreds of assumptions regarding future personnel movement and company needs; these are improved in quality through the integration of judgmental forecasts.

APPLYING FORECASTING MODELS

Forecasting is very difficult, especially if it's about the future. Presumably, a powerful enough model can accomplish any forecasting task, providing a detailed and reasonably accurate analysis of any number of variables. However, the costs might be rather great in relation to the value. To be practical in forecasting, you must recognize that sometimes the answer just is not worth the cost involved.

The trade-off between precision and cost has another side. If the question being asked is important enough, then the resources necessary to provide the answer should be adequate. Too often, human resource staff are asked seemingly impossible questions (for example, "How many engineering graduates will we need to hire three years from now?"). If the question has a significant business payoff and is relevant to the business plans and strategies, then adequate staff time, computer resources, management time for inputs and reviews, and other necessary resources should be provided. A model can be built in a day, but most problems require more carefully and extensively developed techniques.

And this brings us to the point of modeling purposes. The point of modeling is not to create a neat model for its own sake, or to do personnel "research." Rather, the purpose is to solve management problems. Hence the type of model should be selected which best fits the immediate need. A comprehensive, integrated model with bells and whistles may be just what is *not* called for by prevailing management concerns and planning issues.

Go Where the Action Is

In constructing and applying models, attention should focus on the principal problems—the areas where the leverage of possible beneficial action is greatest. Accordingly, modeling is most useful when focused on job classifications with the largest number of incumbents or the greatest turnover, or other problems. As a rule, 80 percent of the salaried employees will hold only 20 percent of the position titles; the balance will have virtually unique position titles. By focusing on the 80 percent, at least as an initial effort, the potential benefits are greater. Managerial, professional, and technical positions, usually including many unique titles, are less fruitful for aggregate modeling because apples and oranges are grouped together.

Similarly, models need not be all-encompassing, but may be tailored to the needs and system characteristics of a particular division, department, or location. The accuracy of projections lost due to smaller numbers is more than compensated for by constructing the model to fit the precise dimensions of the problem.

Start Small

Modeling efforts often fail, too, because they strive for accuracy of prediction. "The moment you forecast you know you're going to be wrong," says an economics folk principle, "you just don't know when and in which direction." To promise accuracy is a dangerous pitfall. Similarly, to assume that the solution derived suggests an optimal future staffing pattern is also dangerous. Conditions change too rapidly for forecasts to be "predictions." If the scope of the modeling effort is kept small and the time horizons of forecasting short-term, the results are more likely to be regarded as reliable and the risk of being completely out of line is reduced.

It is advisable to build upon subjective management judgments rather than to introduce a wholly new framework of thinking. The "black box" approach to finding solutions is alien to judgmental processes; the model should be positioned as a supplement to managerial planning. Human nature calls for mathematical solutions to problems to be suspect, if not rejected out of hand. Small steps toward rigorous analysis and forecasting are preferable to unsteady large ones.

It is also important to come out with results and conclusions for management to consider. Too often modelers become fascinated with the computer and the intricacies of model building and functioning. "Analysis paralysis" is a fatal syndrome. More than several companies have supported the formation of staff units or task teams to develop forecasting and planning models such as described here only to disband them months or years later. Small successes are far preferable to large failures.

Data, Not Reality

Finally, it is noteworthy that any forecasting technique merely provides more data. No technique known to humanity can provide a *plan* or a *prediction* of what will happen in the future. Yet the data provided by the techniques available are valuable for their increased objectivity. They provide an interpretation of available factual data for consideration by management. Nothing more and nothing less.

Chapter 7

Work Analysis: A Basis for Planning

KEY POINTS

- Objective human resource planning requires an objective understanding of what people actually do on their jobs. Accordingly, more powerful tools are becoming necessary for the analysis of managerial, professional, and technical work.
- There are at least seven different possible perspectives of a job, representing alternative levels of work analysis. It is important to strive toward an understanding of reality, and not merely plans, norms, or perceptions of the work.
- Work analysis results can serve multiple applications, including job evaluation, employee selection, performance evaluation, and organization design.
- Various aspects of work can be analyzed, depending on the particular applications desired: work outputs, activities or tasks performed, competencies required, and reward structure.
- Alternative techniques are available, which should be selected to fit the applications desired and cost constraints: descriptions, observation or self-reporting, functional analysis, or questionnaires.

Work analysis is a process of gathering and examining information on the principal work activities in a position and the qualifications (skills, knowledge, abilities, and other individual attributes) necessary to perform these activities. It may be variously referred to as job analysis, activity analysis, task analysis, or work study (although each of these terms may have a specific meaning in its use).

Various techniques have been developed and applied for the analysis of job content and job requirements. These techniques range from broad descriptions of job duties to highly detailed, weighted task definitions. The degree of detail and the nature of the content, and therefore the techniques applied, have varied with the purposes of the analyses performed. In some cases work analysis provides broad descriptions of job duties for purposes of job evaluation in salary administration procedures. In other cases detailed information on job tasks is required to establish precise standards of performance and opportunities for improved efficiency in job performance. Applications of work-analysis data have also included manpower planning, organization design, identification of training needs, setting of performance objectives, and determining employee selection and promotion criteria.

Any work-analysis approach has the aim of providing management with an in-depth understanding of the content and requirements of a position. In many organizations, needs forecasting has focused primarily on the supply and flow of *employees*. Planning has concentrated on recruiting, selecting, assigning, transferring, appraising, assessing, training, and developing people. But attention has broadened to consider the work performed as well as the people, as an important aspect of human resource planning.

Two forces are drawing attention to the analysis of work performed. One is the increasing pressure on management to assure equal employment opportunity and to provide affirmative action programs for protected employees. The other is the mounting pressure to improve utilization and development of talent in the face of increasingly significant personnel-related costs. Management concern for productivity and improved utilization of talent has been an impetus for more objective pay structures, in-depth analysis of what people actually do, and the linking of staffing plans with business plans and objectives. Additionally, recent federal legislation and court decisions have spurred work analysis as a basis for hiring, upgrading, termination, and "equal pay" actions.

No single approach developed to date has adequately demonstrated the capacity to satisfy all these needs. As a result, different techniques are being used for different purposes by management. A job description may provide a general outline of the responsibilities of a job, while job specifications indicate the qualifications and experience sought to perform the job. Organization changes and creation of new jobs may represent a third form of analysis, and individual performance appraisal and the standards of performance for the objectives by which performance are measured may provide another perspective of the work required.

No single method has clearly been accepted as applicable to *managerial, professional, and technical positions,* where daily activities are diverse and where the "person makes the job." Contrasted with the more routine, repetitive, and fixed work of many clerical and operative positions, these positions have received little attention until recently. Yet it is through the higher-level, generally higher-skilled salaried positions that opportunities are the greatest for management to influence work content and, thereby, contribute to organizational effectiveness. Work analysis at the managerial, professional, and technical levels has often been neglected as a element of human resource planning because it is time consuming, imprecise, and difficult, and because reliable techniques are not yet available.

This chapter reviews the principal approaches for work analysis, with primary emphasis on managerial, professional, and technical work. The origins of work analysis are examined, and alternative methods are described and contrasted. Various applications for the results of work analysis and criteria by which alternative methods should be selected for particular applications are discussed. Finally, new directions are discussed with attention to the practical problems experienced by companies.

ORIGINS OF WORK ANALYSIS

Analysis of work at the operative and clerical levels originated in the "scientific management" programs initiated in the early 1900s. Refinements have been introduced through work measurement, costs and standards, productivity improvement, and other industrial engineering procedures. Most of these efforts focus upon the psychomotor and physical proficiency aspects of work. Such approaches have been applied widely in virtually all types of organizations in our economy (McCormick, 1976).

A parallel, but not always related, process of work analysis has evolved for purposes of salary administration. In this context, work analysis is used to develop a description of the functional duties or responsibilities assigned to each position—a position description. Typically the position is then evaluated on the basis of the perceived importance of its content by some evaluation system adapted by the organization, and incumbents are compensated at a level that reflects the relative value of the position in the organization and the marketplace. Most job evaluation methods require scoring on a number of predetermined dimensions, assigning points or values to each position as a means of ordering positions within a structured system (see Chapter 11).

At the professional, managerial, and technical levels, job evaluation methods usually place emphasis upon position accountabilities, difficulty of tasks performed, and overall responsibility for assets, revenues, or budgets. Even innovative methods for evaluating such positions, such as that developed by Elliot Jaques (1961), call for evaluation on predetermined dimensions. Under this approach, the time frame or planning horizon of management decisions and the resource commitment potential of the job holder are weighted in determining job value.

Levels of Work Analysis

In analyzing work, it is not always easy to find out exactly what people *really do*. Definition of work activities and requirements must be based on data, and data have to be provided by people. Even the people who are doing the work on a given job may not have a complete or true understanding of the activities, time allocations, or requirements involved in their work. Managers, peers, and other individuals likely have an even less accurate understanding of the work *actually* performed.

As shown in Exhibit 7-1, four levels of work analysis are possible. The most common deals with perceptions—what individuals think they do on their jobs, or what managers think these individuals do. Perceptions, of course, are influenced by individual feelings, goals, attitudes, and ability to remember work performed. It may be that perceptions of work are an adequate basis for many applications, but they are, nevertheless, subjective descriptions of the work. As a result, the definitions of activities and requirements may not be entirely accurate or realistic.

Reality versus Perceptions

It is extremely difficult to find out what individuals actually do. Even direct observation may be influenced by the subjective perceptions of the observer. Time logs and reporting by the incumbent inevitably involve a summarizing of work activities, subject to perceptual influence. Some work-analysis techniques, of course, get at reality more effectively than others. As a rule, finding out what individuals *actually do* is more time consuming and costly than finding out what individuals and managers *think they do*. And as far as most organizations are concerned, what people perceive is acceptable as a statement of reality. In most methodologies, emphasis is given to data collection directly from the incumbents on jobs. The incumbent is assumed to have the best understanding of the work activities, and hence to be in the best position to provide realistic information.

Exhibit 7-1   Levels of Work Analysis

	Source of data	
Levels	Incumbents	Managers
Reality	What individuals actually do	
Perceptions	What individuals think they do	What managers think these individuals do
Norms	What individuals think they should do	What managers would like them to do
Plans	What individuals plan to do	What managers think they are going to do

Norms or Plans

In some applications, it is appropriate to seek to find out what individuals think they *should* do and what managers *would like* these individuals to do. This is applicable in the establishment of performance standards or objectives. Discussions between managers and position incumbents often serve as a means of negotiating mutually accepted definitions of the work to be performed (see Chapters 9 and 10). As a source of data for human resource planning, however, desires are the weakest level of work analysis.

A fourth level of work analysis focuses upon work plans. Here it is intended to find out what individuals *plan to do* and what managers think these individuals *are going to do*. Plans are not necessarily the same as desires, reality, or perceptions of work. And, of course, even the best-laid plans may not necessarily be achieved. But plans imply commitment to future activities, timetables, identified resource requirements, and measures of achievement. In the performance planning process, individuals and their managers normally identify with what they think the work involves now, identify what they feel they should be doing, and finally lay out plans for *future* work.

Therefore there are seven clearly different possible definitions of the work performed by an individual on a single job. It is important to identify which of these definitions is desired for a given application of work analysis. As a rule, job-related descriptions of work are focused upon reality—not perceptions, desires, or plans. What individuals *actually do* is considered an acceptable basis for job requirements, selection, appraisal, compensation, job design, and other applications. The difficulty of getting at reality forces work-analysis efforts toward perceptions or desires.

APPLICATIONS

Well-conceived, well-designed, and well-implemented work analysis potentially provides an information base that can serve not just one purpose, but many purposes. The increased cost of obtaining work data for multiple purposes is justified through the multiplied value received through applications. Eight primary areas of human resource management to which work-analysis results may be applied are illustrated in Exhibit 7-2.

This multiple use of work analysis is a newly emerging tool for human resource planning at the managerial, professional, and technical levels. Employers have considered such positions to be "soft," "unique," or "in a state of flux." They have generally provided descriptions of the work on an ad hoc basis to serve specific immediate needs. Now this practice appears to be changing, as new, more powerful work-analysis methods are being developed and applied (Ingraham and Lutz, 1974, McCormick, 1974; Roter, 1973).

Staffing Analysis

In analyzing an organization's staffing requirements, managers are seeking information on the work action being performed and not just how many people are needed. It is important to know how the work is distributed among the

Exhibit 7-2 Work-analysis applications.

positions in an organization in order to determine additional staffing requirements, opportunities for staffing reduction, or opportunities for reallocation of
work for improved staff utilization. As a rule, organizations will accept slack
(activities that do not directly contribute to organizational objectives) if it is
recognized and felt to be necessary or tolerable. It is difficult to reduce an
organization's staffing significantly (10 percent or more) without significantly
reallocating the work, thus creating organizational changes.

Zero-base budgeting, the process of examining different possible levels of
organizational activity and associated resource requirements, has impelled more
detailed analysis of the work being performed in organizational units. Zero-base
staffing calls for a justification of each position based upon the work that would
be performed and the outputs resulting from that work.

Much staffing analysis and planning deal only with gross numbers; actually
time-allocation data relating to specific types of work activities provide
substance vital to meaningful planning of staffing levels and mix requirements.
For example, a commercial bank obtained information on the allocation of time
to various types of activities relating to each of a number of products and
services in branches. The time spent on each product or service was correlated
with quantitative indicators of the business outputs, and thus guidelines could be
provided for improved allocation of staffing to achieve business results and to
identify areas where additional staff should be authorized. The process therefore
involved an analysis of both base staffing and incremental adjustments to
authorize staffing.

Organization Design

This same type of analysis is often applied in the design or redesign of specific
jobs and other relationships among jobs—organization planning. It is not
adequate simply to rearrange job titles, levels, and relationships, if significant

changes in organizational behavior are desired. It is necessary to analyze the specific elements of each position and to restructure each position within the organization in a way that will make the best use of talent (Ingraham and Lutz, 1974). Studies concerned with job enrichment usually include work analysis as a first step in identifying opportunities for job redesign. Understanding current activities provides a basis for restructuring jobs and redesigning related management systems (see Chapter 9).

Performance Planning and Review

In setting objectives or standards, information on work activities (whether perceived, actual, or desired) is a vital starting point. Work analysis provides a more objective, job-related basis for planning and review of individual performance. It complements a goal-setting approach to management, providing a realistic basis for setting specific performance objectives or criteria for subsequent performance evaluation. Performance planning must consider both the activities performed on a job and the end results or accomplishments resulting from those activities. Often performance planning or goal-setting programs suffer from an inadequate or unbalanced attention to these two key aspects of work. Focusing on activities alone risks purposeless behavior; emphasis on measurement risks losing control over the way time and talents are spent. In performance planning and review it is generally considered essential that the employee participate in the definition of the job and of the planned activities and accomplishments—to provide a clear direction and commitment for the work.

Some companies are also moving into a type of performance management process based on "behaviorally anchored scales." This is a technique which defines the specific types of behavior desired of an incumbent in a position based upon weighted examples (desired versus undesired behaviors). Usually the examples of behavior are provided by incumbents and managers, and are fully discussed in a vigorous sorting process to result in the final scales. Again, work-analysis methods are essential in providing the data for development of such performance evaluation dimensions.

Management Succession

Work analysis is also frequently applied in management succession planning. In one large company, for example, each of the key management positions was analyzed in detail through a process of interviews and discussions. A position profile was developed which identified the major activity areas, qualifications requirements, and accountabilities for each executive. This profile serves as criteria for assessing alternate candidates for each position and for identifying training and development needs (gaps) for the favorite candidates.

In many companies management succession programs cover several hundred managers and potential executives, as a talent pool for a smaller number of key positions. In these cases, profiles seek to identify the desired activities and qualifications, looking ahead toward the future successor to the positions. In developing this information, however, work analysis may begin with a definition of what incumbents think they do in the positions; this information is then modified through management discussions to provide the necessary management development criteria (see Chapter 12).

At the management level, individuals shape the job—so there is a need to reconsider the job content and requirements in planning for successors. It is often felt that the *worst* person to select a succession or backup is the incumbent, as the criteria used would tend to be the actual current work activities and requirements, not what would be necessary in the future.

Training and Development

Work analysis is often used to identify training and development needs for employees at all levels of an organization, on a far broader basis at the nonmanagerial level. Training programs may thus be tailored to needs identified for groups of employees—for example, understanding of financial concepts and techniques. Supervisory development programs may be tailored to focus upon specific skills and knowledge requirements found lacking through a work-analysis effort (De Cotiis and Morano, 1977).

Job requirements may be defined in skill and knowledge terms, based upon work activities actually performed on the job (or perceived as integral to the job). These data may then be used as a basis for pointing out gaps for individual development activities. For example, a retailing organization analyzed the various jobs in each of its stores and supporting staff operations to find the key requirements of each type of position, to be used as criteria for assessing individual training and development requirements for the employees. Programs were then developed to meet the needs identified as being the most pressing. The advantage of using job requirements for training needs analysis is that it enables an organization to provide building blocks for development, not just merely ad hoc programs. It has the potential of identifying the sequences of experiences necessary to equip an individual for assignment to specified types of positions.

Career Paths

Having information available on job requirements enables meaningful career planning by employees. Career paths are explicit descriptions of the possible alternative sequences of jobs that an individual may hold in an organizational career. Many companies have adopted programs of workshops, counseling, individual self-analysis and career planning, and other types of programs aimed at helping individuals assess their own objectives, career development needs, and plans. Work-analysis results provide vital information on the realistic opportunities available to individuals in an organization. It has the potential of making individual career expectations *realistic* and not idealistic (Walker, 1976). (See Chapter 14.)

Selection Criteria

Work-analysis results also provide a basis for employee selection, both at initial recruitment and for subsequent promotion or reassignment decisions. Current

EEO guidelines require job-related criteria for such decisions, and this means empirical study of the work actually performed. The aim is to get away from age, sex, race, or national origin—variables which are usually not bona fide work requirements. It is also important to avoid other requirements which might be related to these factors—education or work experience which may not be directly required to perform the work effectively (Rouleau and Krain, 1975; Spencer, 1974).

While there are many ways of defining job requirements as part of valid selection systems, interest is growing in content-oriented select tools (Guion, 1977). Predictive validity studies, which involve correlating selection criteria with subsequent measures of performance or success on the job, require time, rigorous analysis, and measures that may not be available. Also they inherently exclude individuals who are not hired under the criteria, and hence may be self-fulfilling in terms of validation. Current guidelines call for some form of direct observation or data collection regarding the activities and tasks peformed on the jobs. This means that *actual* activities are the desired focus of work analysis. However, perceptual data or desired work activities are often used as the basis for developing job-related selection criteria.

Job Evaluation

Finally, work analysis provides description of the work in a way that enables evaluation of job worth as part of a salary administration system. Most methods for job evaluation require information on job content, responsibilities, account-abilities, reporting relationships, and other factors which are weighted in the determination of pay levels. It is important, therefore, that accurate information be obtained with regard to jobs. Also, recent legislation (for example, the Equal Pay Act and the Age Discrimination in Employment Act) requires a basis for compensation which does not discriminate on the basis of sex or age. Equal pay for equal work remains an objective in virtually all salary administration systems, and thus accurate information about the work performed is important (Wendt, 1976).

WHAT ABOUT WORK CAN BE ANALYZED?

To serve these multiple applications, work analysis may provide information on several aspects of work. These are identified in Exhibit 7-3 and are discussed briefly below.

Work Outputs

Measures of work outputs are important in designing jobs, determining staffing requirements, setting performance standards and objectives, and evaluating job worth. As a rule, specific work outputs are more easily identified and measured on operative jobs where individual tasks lead to observable results. Examples are production jobs, sales positions, computer programming jobs, and adminis-trative and clerical positions. Here, engineering of the work requires a study of

Directly Measurable	Indirectly Measurable or Identifiable		Estimable
Work outputs			
Specific outputs produced	Work measures, cost/benefit indicators	Level of effort assessed per standards	Organizational products (individual contributions to the whole)
Activities/tasks performed			
Actual behavior	Perceived behavior	Normative behavior	Planned behavior
Competencies			
Job tenure, company tenure, age*	Educational attainments	Experience reference checks	Skills, knowledge, and abilities
Reward structure			
Reporting relationships, number of subordinates, assets controlled, etc.		Problem solving, difficulty in job	
Directly Measurable	Indirectly Measurable or Identifiable		Estimable

*Age as allowed under employment discrimination law.

Exhibit 7-3 Aspects of work that can be analyzed.

the outputs in relation to larger work systems, equipment, flows of work and materials, time and motion patterns, etc.

On managerial, professional, and technical jobs, specific outputs are much more difficult to identify, and measures become more subjective. Attention turns to effort expended rather than results, and individual contributions to products and services become entwined with the work of others. On these jobs, to focus on specific output measures may result in a narrow view of the job. The more subjective types of output indicators are necessary to get an accurate and complete view of the work.

ACTIVITIES/TASKS PERFORMED

How a person performs a job (the means) is often as important as what is achieved (the ends). Knowing the activities or tasks that compose a job is valuable for purposes of designing jobs and organization structures, defining job requirements and career paths, identifying training and development needs, defining management succession needs, and planning and reviewing performance.

As outlined earlier in this chapter, four levels of analysis of work activities are possible. On higher-level managerial, professional, and technical jobs, analysis typically focuses on reported activities, which are perceived behavior. It is extremely difficult to study actual behavior, because any sample is just that—a sample—and the data-collection procedure requires someone's perceptions of actual behavior. Analyzing work as it should be performed or is planned to be performed in an organization may be a practical approach, but the quality of the necessary subjective judgments is improved by concentrating first on actual behaviors. Job descriptions that say what a person should do typically are meaningless unless they represent reasonably accurately the work currently being performed. Most work-analysis techniques focus on reported activities— essentially perceived behaviors—as a foundation for further definition of desired (normative) future behavior or planned future activities.

Competencies

It is frequently necessary to know what skills, abilities, and knowledge are required to perform a job effectively. This information on competencies is used in defining job requirements for selection and placement, defining career paths, planning organization design, identifying training needs, and sometimes making job evaluations.

Often companies concentrate on obvious, directly observable factors such as age, length of service, time served on the current job (to indicate job mastery), and even sex, race, and religious preference. While all these factors are discrete and easily measured, they are not necessarily relevant to individual competencies. Under state and federal laws, discrimination is illegal on the basis of sex, race, and religious preference, unless they are shown to be bona fide occupational qualifications. And this is not likely. Discrimination on the basis of age is illegal under the federal Age Discrimination in Employment Act for individuals over age 40 and under 65. Age as an indicator of competence (for example, physical abilities) may be used for individuals not protected by the law. Some states, including New Jersey and Alaska, prohibit discrimination at any age.

Because competencies are not easily identified by objective measures, companies rely on education as an indicator. Education may be relevant, but only if it represents specific skills, knowledge, or abilities shown related to the outputs or behaviors on a job. It is a surrogate for the more subjective aspects of experience and actual skills, abilities, and knowledge.

Work analysis normally seeks to define competencies required by interpreting the required behaviors. For example, typing manuscripts may be interpreted as a competency showing "ability to type manuscripts." Of course, this general competency involves a number of subcomponents which may be further analyzed as considered necessary and appropriate in a given application.

Reward Structure

Job evaluation systems used in salary administration typically consider several factors included in the above categories, such as outputs, educational level, and company tenure. Among the additional factors often used, and therefore subjects for work analysis in support of salary administration, are reporting relationships, number of directly reporting subordinates, and assets or budget controlled. These are directly measurable or identifiable, although there is some question whether they are the most appropriate factors to be used in evaluating job worth. Also, some systems use subjective management estimates of the problem solving and difficulty involved in a position. While these factors are significant, they do involve subjectivity.

What to Analyze?

The aspects of work listed on the left side of Exhibit 7-3 are the least complex and the most objectively measured. They are therefore attractive for study, but provide an oversimplified and incomplete view of the work in a job. Some aspects, such as actual work behavior, are not accessible (although highly objective); others, such as age and service, are accessible but not necessarily relevant.

The aspects on the right side are the more complex and the most subjective, requiring considerable judgment in conducting work analysis. They are difficult to study, yet represent the full complexity and scope of the work on a job.

A logical strategy in work analysis is to begin at the left side and continually strive to retain the objectivity while moving into the more realistic and complete, but less easily defined aspects of the work. Thus activity analysis often begins with surveys of perceived (reported) activities and is then used as a basis for definition of desired (normative) and planned activities based on inputs from management and consideration of likely changes in the technology, the work systems, and the organization.

ALTERNATIVE WORK-ANALYSIS METHODS

To gather information about work requires a choice of methods. And the range of methods is limited: interviewing either the incumbents or the managers, sending out a questionnaire of some kind, or directly observing the work performed in some way. No one of these methods alone seems to be best in all situations, and each has its advantages and disadvantages (McCormick, 1976; Pierce and Dunham, 1976; Prien and Ronan, 1971; Wilson, 1974).

Experience in work analysis reflects six basic techniques that have been used in organizations. Several of the techniques involve a combination of data-gathering methods. Properly applied, each permits development of an in-depth understanding of the content and requirements of a position. The techniques are:

    1 Description—the use of interviews, group discussions or open-ended questionnaires to obtain information about work
    2 Observation or self-reporting—directly observing the work performed or obtaining a record from the incumbents through diaries or logs
    3 Functional analysis—examination of the work by a trained analyst using an established procedure such as functional job analysis (FJA)
    4 Published activity checklist—the use of published questionnaires such as the position analysis questionnaire (PAQ) or the management position description questionnaire (MPDQ) to be completed by the incumbents
    5 Tailored activity checklist—detailed questionnaires designed to fit the specific circumstances and types of work in a given organization (for example, Control Data Corporation, U.S. Air Force, Inter-American Development Bank)
    6 Comprehensive questionnaire—detailed questionnaire including both narrative questions and tailored activity checklists

Selecting a Work-Analysis Technique

Each work-analysis technique has particular advantages and disadvantages and is typically selected to fit the needs of a specific situation. In determining the appropriate method to use for work analysis, the following criteria are considered.

First, a method should generally be *empirical.* That is, it should obtain information about actual work activities on the job, so that the findings can be demonstrated to be "job-related." This is important for compliance with EEO guidelines and other government regulations governing employee selection, upgrading, compensation, terminations, etc. It is important to seek information directly from the source—and the best source is the person actually doing the work on a job. Additional inputs may be provided by managers, individuals in other positions, customers and other outsiders, and subordinates, but the incumbent remains the focus of empirical work analysis. Each source has the potential of providing realistic information about the work, based upon empirical data collection.

Also, the method should seek to define *actual behavior,* not what people think they are doing or should be doing. The aim is to describe actual, current behavior, in its full diversity. This means that the method should not direct or confine information gathering in a way that would restrict the surfacing of actual behavioral patterns and other tasks composing a job. It is important that work analysis concentrate on actual behavior—that is, what people really do—and not on job scope, duties, responsibilities, accountabilities, and other factors, although these factors may be pertinent aspects of a total position description used for salary administration and organization planning.

A work-analysis method should provide data in a form that is suited to *efficient analysis.* That is, the data should be obtained, summarized, and classified in such a way that they can be processed and classified for the intended purposes with ease. Thus the emphasis should be on codable, concise information rather than narrative, descriptive data. For this reason, questionnaire techniques are usually favored over interview and observation techniques. However, the latter techniques have the advantage of being more empirical and capturing kinds of behaviors that might not be covered by a questionnaire or other predetermined method. Useful work-analysis techniques also weight the activity components in terms of priority, time allocation, perceived importance, relationship to other functions, or other factors useful in the analysis and classification of the findings. It is important to be able to examine relationships among jobs and between jobs at different levels in an organizational system.

At the same time, work-analysis methods should be relatively *easy to administer,* with tools that are simple and understandable to the individuals using them. If at all possible, the techniques should be simple and pragmatic and should involve a minimum of paperwork. While more sophisticated, complex instruments and techniques may provide a greater detail and degree of accuracy of data, such esoteric qualities may scare the incumbents and reduce access to the information desired. As a rule, work analysis gathers far more data than are ever effectively used; therefore, concise, simple methods are generally preferred.

Work-analysis methods should allow easy *updating.* A single sample in a point of time may serve the needs of one application, but it is important to be able to refine and update the results of the study without having to do it all over again. Coded, quantitative data are more readily updated, particularly using questionnaire approaches, than are qualitative approaches based upon observation or open-ended questionnaires. Also, the method should provide for consistency (that is, reliability of responses) in the patterns of work between times of data collection.

Above all, techniques should be tailored to fit the particular organizational circumstances and the desired applications. As a result, there is often a trade-off of the above factors in favor of the specific needs of a specific application and in favor of an open and less formal structure for data collection. The focus, in a pragmatic sense, should be on the applications served, not on the methodology applied.

In summary, work analysis should capture realistically the actual behaviors displayed on a job in a way that is efficient, understandable, and practically relevant for the intended applications.

ALTERNATIVE TECHNIQUES COMPARED

The basic characteristics of each of the six types of work-analysis techniques are summarized in Exhibit 7-4.

Job Descriptions

The description method is the simplest technique and the one most commonly used today for developing position descriptions for salary administration. It is

Exhibit 7-4 Alternative Work-Analysis Techniques

	Descriptions 1	Observation or self-reporting 2	Functional analysis 3	Published activity checklists 4	Tailored activity checklists 5	Comprehensive questionnaire 6
Techniques/ developers	• Description questionnaires • Interviews • Group discussions • Delphi technique	• Observation • Incidents • Diary or log	• Functional job analysis • Other analyst studies of jobs	• PAQ • MPDQ • JDS	• Control data • Air Force • ASTD study	• A proposed method
Summary	Subjective statement of work activities and requirements based on available data and perceptions	Statement of work activities based on reported or observed sample of actual behavior	Characterization of activities and job requirements based on structured study by trained analyst	Weighted profile of work activities based on self-administered task checklist	Weighted profile of work activities and other work characteristics based on checklist/questionnaire tailored to needs	Comprehensive checklist/questionnaire provides data base for multiple purposes of work analysis
Realism	Allows greatest empiricism—all kinds of work aspects can surface—but subjectively	Potentially realistic and detailed but depends on depth and perception errors	Primarily designed for nonmanagerial jobs; follows constraining analysis procedure	Tends to capture only the broad dimensions of work	Probes in detail the various aspects of work in a specific situation	Can obtain and contrast multiple perceptions of the work
Applicability	Usually for a single purpose, but can be broad enough to apply to multiple needs	Usually conducted for only one purpose in a study's limited applicability	Limited to job classification for defining job requirements and performance standards	Usually job description/evaluation only; depends on design	Can be designed to serve more than one purpose	Designed to serve multiple purposes

Adaptability	Mostly narrative; difficult to analyze and update but highly adaptable	Usually entirely narrative data; highly adaptable to different situations; updating means starting over	Limited to those types of jobs covered by the methodology; not adaptable	Constrained by published instrument designing; poor adaptability; easily updated	Can be designed or adapted to fit any situation; easily updated or modified	Should be designed to fit all situations and anticipated needs; can be modified as needs change
Cost	Initial data collection and maintenance time-consuming	High cost for observation; low cost for self-reporting	High cost because of analyst involvement	Usually low; depends on costs of published materials	Initial costs high; low maintenance and updating costs	Highest initial costs; lowest maintenance costs

also often used in studies of job design and organization planning. A structured questionnaire may be used to collect information from job incumbents regarding the basic duties, activities, and responsibilities in a position. The results obtained may serve as a basis for conducting job-analysis interviews. Alternatively, interviews alone may provide the information needed to prepare job descriptions. The resulting data are used for evaluating job worth, for establishing performance standards or objectives, and for identifying relationships among the activities performed in different positions (McCormick, 1974).

An example of a work sheet used to obtain job information from exempt employees in an insurance company is shown in Exhibit 7-5. Other forms of questionnaires typically involve detailed listing of job responsibilities and activities performed. The work sheet or questionnaire is often used by managers

Exhibit 7-5   Job description work sheet.

JOB TITLE _____   YOUR NAME _____

DEPARTMENT _____   LOCATION _____

REPORTS TO (TITLE)_____   DATE _____

JOB ACTIVITIES

Outline below the primary parts of your job and indicate the relative proportion of time and importance applicable to each. Use a typical month as a 100% time-frame. Time and importance need not correspond.

	TIME %	ORDER OF IMPORTANCE
_____	_____	_____
_____	_____	_____
_____	_____	_____
_____	_____	_____
_____	_____	_____
_____	_____	_____
_____	_____	_____
_____	_____	_____

JOB QUALIFICATIONS REQUIRED

Outline below the skills, knowledge, abilities and experience necessary to perform your job effectively. Be as specific as possible and refer back to the activities outlined above.

_____

_____

_____

_____

_____

_____

COMPLEXITY AND DIFFICULTY

A. Give examples of type and extent of problems encountered in the position:

B. Give examples of requirements for judgment, analytical skills and creativity, which are needed to develop workable solutions.

C. What guidance is available in the form of established practices or supervision?

ACCOUNTABILITY

A. How do you affect net operating profits through the work you perform on your job? Explain.

B. What is your responsibility for custody or control of corporate assets or inventory items? Explain.

C. Do you supervise the work of others? Explain below or attach an organizational chart, if applicable.

JOB CHANGES

A. What changes have developed in the job during the last year?

B. What future changes do you anticipate during the year ahead?

as a basis for discussing and clarifying job requirements and performance expectations with employees (Dayal, 1969).

The success of the approach depends heavily on the quality of the responses—the ability of the incumbents to provide meaningful, specific, and accurate job information. Also pertinent are the interviewers' skills in obtaining and interpreting the information needed. Because the data are largely narrative, the description method is the least subject to analysis, updating, and control of all work-analysis techniques. However, it allows the greatest degrees of empiricism and flexibility as the questionnaires and interviews may cover a wide range of subjects and may be tailored to reflect job circumstances.

Job descriptions are more likely to be valid when the following guidelines are followed:

Focus on job content. Describe the way the job is actually performed as reported by the job incumbent.

Specify outputs of the job. Give quantitative indicators of results expected as a normal requirement (for example, sales, documents processed).

Avoid vague language. Use specific terms to describe activities, not fuzzy terms describing general duties (that is, avoid phrases like "handles," "managers," "responsible for").

Rate components of the jobs in order of importance and the time to be devoted to each. Avoid laundry lists of duties by using a weighting format such as that presented in Exhibit 7-4.

Use a separate description for each position. Combine jobs only when separate descriptions demonstrate that they are actually similar in content and requirements.

Narrative job description is the work-analysis technique most commonly applied for salaried positions. The technique, therefore, is important as a basis for developing useful job information in many companies and is the starting point for introducing more refined techniques.

Self-Reporting and Observation

A less widely used method is the collection of information through self-reporting by job incumbents or data collection by observers. Time logs or diaries may be used by incumbents to analyze where their time actually goes and what activities they actually perform each day. This of course requires a degree of discipline and commitment on the part of the individuals, but it has the potential of providing a highly empirical record of on-the-job behavior. The results are largely perceptual data, but they are usually quite detailed.

An analyst must go through the diaries and logs and tabulate the types of activities and the time devoted to each. In some instances, analysts identify the types of incidents or "behavioral anchors" which describe key job behaviors. These behaviors may then be converted to dimensions (with "desirable/ undesirable" behaviors portrayed). This technique has the apparent advantages of being empirical, having methodological structure, and yet remaining very much job-related (Kearney, 1976; Millard, Luthans, and Otteman, 1976).

As a substitute for self-reporting, observers may watch individuals work and record a brief description of the activities performed. The record may then be used in the same way as a diary. The pioneering studies of managerial work by Rosemary Stewart in England (1967, 1977) and by Henry Mintzberg (1973,

1975) used this technique. Their studies revealed the actual patterns of behavior, constraints, and choice of managers. Standardized job observations could be useful in job analysis within companies (Jenkins et al., 1975).

The method offers a maximum of realism, but it is potentially costly because the information collected needs to be reviewed and classified before it can be analyzed. Also, the intervention of an observer or the demands for maintaining a time log may be considered an imposition on an individual's time. The results are difficult to update and are not particularly applicable to some needs, such as salary administration, job requirements analysis, or employee selection. This method is most useful for analysis of job structure, organization structure, staffing requirements, and training needs. Because it is a flexible approach, it is easily tailored to fit the needs of different circumstances, but it is difficult to apply when a large number of different positions and individuals are involved.

Functional Analysis

A third method calls for the analysis of work activities by a trained analyst. The analyst may observe actual behavior or may interview the job incumbent using a standardized procedure to develop a comprehensive definition of the job and its requirements. A procedure for analyzing the functions of a job was developed in the 1930s by the Department of Labor. It was subsequently adapted by Sidney A. Fine as Functional Job Analysis (FJA) in 1948 (Fine, 1971, 1974). Developed as a task list to establish the government's *Dictionary of Occupational Titles* (DOT), the system has been expanded to cover a wide variety of types of work (see Korn, 1974). It classifies jobs into an established scheme, provides for establishment of career ladders, development of training curricula, vocational counseling using the DOT, and derivation of job requirements for employment placement.

Originally applied to the U.S. Air Force, it has since been applied to thousands of jobs across all industries. However, the method has only recently been applied to managerial, professional, and technical jobs and remains applicable largely to lower-level positions (Fine, Holt, and Hutchinson, 1975).

FJA relies upon an analyst's determination of an organization's goals and what needs to be done in the jobs under study to attain them. Each job is described in terms of three basic functions: data, people, and things. Each functional dimension is coded in terms of level of complexity and rated as to importance.

The methodology is easily updated and is widely applicable to given occupations. But it tends to be costly due to the role of the analyst and is not highly applicable to managerial and professional positions (Spirn and Solomon, 1976).

The United States Training and Employment Service uses an approach for obtaining and recording job analysis data that is an adaptation of the Fine FJA method (U.S. Department of Labor, 1972). It involves a systematic study of worker performance and worker trades covering:

Worker functions (in relation to data, things, and people)
Work fields (techniques and methods employed)
Machines, tools, equipment, and work aids
Materials, products, subject matter, or services
Worker traits

Jobs are characterized by information in the above categories. Again, this method is applied primarily to lower-level positions, not managerial or professional positions.

Published Questionnaires

Published questionnaires may be administered at relatively low cost and offer the potential of gathering a large amount of data from a large number of individuals in a relatively short period of time. Data are usually collected in a structured "task inventory"—a listing of the various activities believed to compose the job. The results are therefore amenable to ready analysis and classification.

Ernest McCormick and his associates at Purdue University developed one of the best-known published activity checklists (McCormick, 1974; McCormick and Jeanneret, 1969). The Position Analysis Questionnaire (PAQ) is a checklist of 194 job elements against which a job may be compared (applies/does not apply). A six-point rating scale may also be applied. The PAQ emphasizes human behaviors more than technical job tasks as is the case in FJA. The PAQ's six categories of tasks are:

Information input
Mental processes
Work output
Relationships with other workers
Job context and work satisfaction
Other job characteristics

The elements are rated by professional "raters" by importance to the job and based on extent, time, applicability, or special scales (a 0–5 scale is often used) and job attributes associated with individual job satisfaction. The jobs are then classified by thirty-two job dimensions with a behavioral emphasis. The PAQ methodology allows for comparision of jobs across all occupational groups including managerial, professional, and technical.

Studies based on the PAQ have been conducted over more than a decade, resulting in several versions of the questionnaire. Most of the studies have focused upon the identification of job attributes and associated individual satisfaction. The fundamental purpose of the published questionnaire is to characterize work activities in terms of common quantitative denominators that permit research for generalization and theory formulation in the psychology area.

The PAQ has been used by companies to contract different jobs by the thirty-two dimensions and as a tool for examining job content and structure in relation to worker motivation. But many companies find that the PAQ is not sufficiently specific to meet other needs such as job classification or job evaluation. It emphasizes low-level job characteristics. Also it is not easily tailored to fit unique circumstances or to capture information not built into the questionnaire design.

Building on the foundation provided by the PAQ, J. D. Hemphill designed a questionnaire for the analysis of mangerial-level jobs (1960). The 575-item questionnaire covers the physical and social demands of a manager's job, the subject matter of the work, the principal responsibilities involved, and the activities required. This 1959 study analyzed the responses of ninety-three managers to the questionnaire, called the Executive Position Description Questionnaire (EPDQ). A factor analysis provided ten dimensions for clustering activities:

Providing a staff service
Supervision of work
Business control
Technical concerns with products and markets
Human, community, and social affairs
Long-range planning
Exercise of broad power and authority
Business reputation
Personal demands
Preservation of assets

This early work by Hemphill set the stage for subsequent development of management-level position analysis questionnaires by companies, the U.S. Air Force, and other researchers. The MPDQ serves as a useful reference in constructing an inventory of managerial activities, but the factor structure itself varies with the nature of the work under study (see Mintzberg, 1973).

Other questionnaires have been developed and made available for use in describing and analyzing jobs. The Position Description Questionnaire (PDQ) is a simple, 191-item instrument developed primarily for job evaluation and identification of job families. The PDQ utilizes twenty-seven dimensions to describe a job. The Job Diagnostic Survey (JDS), developed by Hackman and Oldham at Yale University, measures several characteristics of jobs, employee reactions to jobs, and the need for growth felt by the employees (1974, 1975). The questionnaire is based on earlier work by Hackman and Lawler and by Turner and Lawrence in studying employee perceptions and feelings about their work (Hackman and Lawler, 1971; Turner and Lawrence, 1965). The JDS emphasizes the following variables:

I Job dimensions
  A Skill variety
  B Task identity

          C   Task significance
          D Autonomy
          E   Feedback from the job itself
          F   Feedback from agents
          G Dealing with others
   II   Experienced psychological states
          A   Future of the work
          B   Responsibility for the work
          C   Knowledge of results
  III Affective responses to the job
          A   General satisfaction
          B   Internal work motivation
          C   Specific satisfactions (pay, security, etc.)
  IV Industrial growth and satisfaction
   V   Motivating potential of the job

The JDS has been used primarily in job design/job enrichment studies (Dunkan, Aldas, and Brief, 1977; Hackman et al., 1975). A simpler instrument, the Job Characteristic Inventory (JCI), was developed by adapting the JDG. The final version uses only thirty items to describe employees' perceptions of their jobs (Sims, Szilagy; and Keller, 1976).

Tailored Questionnaires

One attraction of standard questionnaires is the ease of updating job information by use of the tools on a continuing basis. Another is the quantitative nature of the results. The advantages of a published questionnaire are extended in the use of a tailored activity checklist. Under this method an activity checklist questionnaire is constructed to fit the types of activities performed in an organization and to serve the specific applications desired.

    The U.S. Air Force Human Resources Research Laboratory, for example, has sponsored an active program of occupational research for more than a decade (Christal, 1974; Mayo et al., 1976; Morsh, 1967). The program has examined a wide range of occupational groups within the Air Force through use of tailored job inventories. With a large number of individuals involved, the collecting of work information was considered possible only through the use of quantifiable information. The task checklist developed for each occupational category provides data which are stored, manipulated, and recorded by computer. Further, the results of each study can be validated and checked for stability over time.

    A typical questionnaire has two sections. The first asks the worker about the job and personal experience, qualifications, attitudes, etc. The second section is a detailed list of all the activities that may be performed by workers in the occupational area or job type being surveyed. If the list is properly constructed, each individual should be able to define his or her job adequately in terms of a subset of the activities listed.

    The job incumbent is asked to estimate the significance of various tasks or activities listed on the inventory. The ratings may focus on the amount of time spent on each, the frequency with which each is performed, or the importance attributed to each. In some studies separate scales are used for each of these factors. Commonly, however, a combined rating is used to cover both time allocated and rated importance, as in this example:

0   Does not apply, is not a part of my job
1   A minor aspect of my work, occurs rarely and is unimportant
2   A small part of my work
3   A substantial part of my work (either frequent but not necessarily important or infrequent but highly important)
4   A major part of my work
5   A most significant part of my work (both highly frequent and important)

The distribution of ratings given the activity or task statements represents a relative weighting of the job content. Jobs may thus be described by a simple frequency listing of activities performed either for the total job or within activity categories (for example, technical specialist, leader, administrator, coordinator/ team member, external representative). The Air Force methodology provides a method of converting the ratings into time allocations by a sum-of-digits technique. If the total points assigned to activities on a scale (0 to 5) are 150, a rating of 5 would represent approximately 3.3 percent time allocation to that activity. A rating of 2 would represent a 1.3 percent time allocation. The resulting percentage time allocations may then be grouped by activity categories and ranked to provide a profile of the position.

The Air Force inventory data are processed through a Comprehensive Occupational Data Analysis Program (CODAP). The set of programs provides a variety of statistical analyses of the data as well as descriptions of positions and occupational groupings using the task inventory as a basic format. Similar computer programs have been developed by private organizations to meet their needs. Many time-sharing computer service firms also provide the tabulations and reports necessary for interpretation of such information.

Diverse organizations have developed tailored questionnaires to meet specific work-analysis needs. Control Data Corporation developed the Executive Position Description Questionnaire to check compensation levels and to identify management position requirements. The EPDQ was an attempt to replicate and build on Hemphill's pioneering work (Tornow and Pinto, 1976). A major New York commercial bank developed a series of questionnaires obtaining information on time allocations by activity area and product or service category of banking officers (Walker, 1977). The instruments involved the use of a time allocation matrix, with the respondent required to estimate the hours spent (per day, week, month, or year) in each cell. The estimates were then converted to percentages and totaled for activity areas (for example, business development, loan administration) and for product or service category (for example, business development, loan administration) and for product or service category (for example, commercial loans). The methodology was used as a planning tool and as a means of determining officer staffing requirements.

In a study sponsored by the American Society for Training and Development (ASTD) a questionnaire was developed to find out "what training and development professionals really do." The results provided a definition of basic professional roles and competencies, useful in planning professional development activities and developing self-assessment tools. The study methodology demonstrates how a tailored activity inventory/checklist can be used to analyze work and define job requirements (Pinto and Walker, 1978).

In each of these cases, the questionnaires were developed through review of pertinent organizational materials and interviews. This served to identify the types of activities that should be included. Each inventory was tailored and pretested so that it was specifically related to the jobs under study. Accordingly, the questionnaires are far more job-specific than such published questionnaires as the PAQ. The larger the variety of jobs and job levels covered by an instrument, the more general it must become, or the more lengthy (and unwieldy).

Tailored questionnaires serve multiple purposes, including job evaluation, training needs analysis, job classification, career path design, definition of selection requirements, and organization and job design. The scope of the questionnaire depends on the intended design and applications as well as the nature of the jobs studied. Naturally the experience of one organization may be used by another in developing questionnaires. As a rule, however, activity lists are not transferable and need to be verified through review of job descriptions, interviews, and pretesting.

Comprehensive Questionnaire Method

Imagine a single questionnaire that satisfies all desired applications of work-analysis information, allows easy updating and analysis with minimal time and cost, and covers a broad classification of salaried positions in an organization. A comprehensive questionnaire of this type has not been developed, but is conceivably a potent and cost-effective means of obtaining job information.

The instrument itself would include both activity checklists and narrative questions. Categories of items would include:

Factual job characteristics: number or size of projects, number of subordinates, reporting relationships, asset or budget responsibility, machines or tools used, etc.

Outputs: measures or indicators of the products or services resulting from the work

Activities: 200 or more tasks that may be performed, each with a time allocation and importance weighting scale

Attitudes: perceptions of the respondents to various characteristics of the work and the job design

Competencies: specialized skills and knowledge requirements not reflected in the activity statements

Essentially, it would be a combination of tailored questionnaires that might be needed for different purposes in an organization. Considerable resources and effort go into job evaluation and into the updating of job descriptions for that purpose as well as for identifying training needs, forecasting staffing requirements, and developing content-oriented selection and placement tools. And because these work analyses are fragmented, they are not always consistent or complete. It makes sense to develop and maintain a single base of information about the work in an organization, using a few well-designed tools on a continuing, long-term basis. Comprehensive questionnaires may be developed to cover all managerial positions in an organization (following the example set at Control Data Corporation), particular specializations (such as research, marketing, finance, or personnel), or specific classifications of jobs. Activity lists may be the primary part of the questionnaire that varies with the jobs covered.

In addition to the various uses of work information noted in this chapter, the comprehensive "work facts" methodology provides a way of comparing differing views of a job. The results may be tabulated and compared over time and among different position incumbents. A manager may complete the questionnaire to provide his view of subordinates' positions, and the resulting profile may be contrasted with that provided by the subordinates. The profiles offer a valuable tool for reconciling different views of job expectations and job requirements.

In summary, a comprehensive work-analysis questionnaire could be the flexible, easily updated, *dynamic* job description that companies have sought for decades. The technology for developing and applying such a questionnaire clearly exists, as indicated in this chapter. Whether the desire to have a single, consistent, current information base on jobs is strong enough to support development of the method depends on how strongly management cares about managing the work itself, and not just the people as employees.

Part Three

Performance Management

Chapter 8

Improving Organizational Performance

KEY POINTS

- A primary aim in human resource management is the improvement of productivity—the output created through the utilization of limited resources.
- Improvement of productivity of high-talent personnel requires subtle strategies which influence the essential functioning of the organization, and not merely individual performance.
- Control over the work context, the activities performed, and the objectives of performance influences the effort expended by employees. Motivation to work is also important, but is only indirectly controlled by management.
- Individual skills, abilities, and knowledge, controlled through selection practices and training and development, combine with expended effort in influencing the actual work performance.
- The reward systems, controlled by management, in tandem with work performance, influence the actual accomplishments and the tangible rewards given employees.
- The motivation to work is an aggregate of the satisfactions sensed by the employees with these variables. Efforts to improve motivation must therefore concentrate on the controllable management variables.

A fundamental management concern is the conversion of resources into useful products and services. The company survives by satisfying the needs of its customers, and thereby its stockholders, employees, and other "stakeholders." Human resource planning helps management identify opportunities to improve organizational performance and to develop strategies for achieving productivity gains.

The average factory worker in the United States today produces more than six times as much in an hour of work as did his or her grandparent at the turn of the century, and in most cases with far less physical effort. Improvements are due to new technologies and advances made possible by capital investments over the decades, to the ambition and rising levels of education and skill of the worker, and to steady improvements in management practices. People in an organization are not often extraordinary in their talents. The purpose of an organization, observed Peter Drucker, is to "enable common men to do uncommon things." It is a task of management to organize, motivate, equip, and direct rather ordinary people to perform at their highest possible levels.

The manner in which individual performance is managed is a key factor, but the wider context of *what* individuals are supposed to do is even more important. Management may influence the structure, systems, resources, and other organizational factors so as to expand or constrain the horizons of individual achievement. This implies a concern for *productivity:* achieving greater results with the same amount of human effort. The term "productivity" has various meanings, and some are explored in this chapter. The focus, however, is always upon the output gained through the management of resources: natural resources, capital (financial) resources, and human resources.

The focus of this book is, of course, on managerial, professional, and technical employees. And the greatest opportunities for increasing productivity today lie in the improved utilization of this talent. Capital, technology, and natural resources (particularly energy sources) have been increasingly used to reduce reliance on manual labor and to achieve productivity gains. Hence gains through industrialization and, more recently, automation, have been dramatic. While direct labor productivity has risen over the decades, the major expansion of jobs in our economy has been with the "knowledge workers," in indirect work: services, administration, research, engineering, marketing, etc. Our economy has successfully expanded to accommodate the swelling labor force in these areas, while manual labor employment, employment in certain crafts, and employment in agriculture have declined.

How do we improve the productivity of high-talent personnel? How do we define and measure productivity at these levels? Does individual job satisfaction contribute to improved organizational performance? Can improvements in the quality of work life benefit an organization as well as the employees? These questions are addressed in this chapter. The issue for management is not so much one of techniques for performance improvement, for many are available. It is, rather, a planning issue: What should be done and why?

A framework is proposed to guide management in the analysis of factors constraining improvement of organizational performance. Four principal controllable variables are relevant: the *objectives* perceived as important to individual employees and their managers, the *activities* that are actually performed on the job, the demonstrated *competencies* (skills, abilities, and knowledge) applied to the work by the individuals, and the *rewards* related to performance which act as incentives for improved future performance. The model proposed for understanding and improving productivity is a simple one, but of central importance to effective human resource planning.

PRODUCTIVITY

Chairman Richard C. Gerstenberg pledged General Motors to seek "creative and fresh approaches in our work practices and techniques to achieve a more effective interplay of human and capital resources." Productivity is a corporate concern and a basic objective of management improvement efforts. "We will do our utmost to provide the innovation, the technology, the tools, the facilities, and the leadership that are essential ingredients of productivity improvement" (Gerstenberg, 1972, p. 4).

Productivity is something of a vogue word in our society today. It is a concern because of inflation, the threat of economic downturns, the constant challenge of foreign competition (whose productivity gains seem to be superior), and a national desire to maintain a strong economy which provides full and satisfying employment. Productivity gains are widely seen as necessary if Americans are to sustain the high standards of living to which we have become accustomed, not to mention our prestige standing in the world economy.

But what are we doing about productivity? Gerstenberg observed:

> The President appointed a commission on productivity; Congress right now is conducting hearings on productivity. Economists measure productivity; they analyze it; they record it. Management traditionally urges more productivity; and labor leaders at times seem to resist it, even though they publicly advocate it. The effect of productivity on the daily lives of everyone is nothing less than enormous; yet few people appreciate it, or even understand it—and even fewer are trying to understand it (Gerstenberg, 1972, p. 4).

Productivity is a complex subject. Many varied perspectives are available as aids in understanding it. And while some perspectives may seem conflicting, the overall result is an appreciation of the factors that can be affected by management through improvement of organizational performance.

Defining Productivity

In essence, productivity is a measure of the efficiency of management: a ratio between what is put into anything (machines, money, raw material, human effort, etc.) and what is gotten out (refrigerators, education, health, automobiles, satisfaction). If the output has increased relative to the input, then we say that productivity has increased.

The economist likes to make comparisions of productivity among companies or industries. To do this, a common denominator (usually labor input) is necessary. Thus productivity is expressed as output per manhour. Outputs are frequently defined in terms of total sales value of goods or services, or in terms of value added (total sales value less the value of external purchases). The use of labor as a denominator, while convenient, is often misleading because it implies that utilization of labor, or individual performance, is a contributor to productivity improvement. In fact, technological improvements or capital investment may account for improvement while individual performance may have declined. The economist's view is more useful at the aggregate scale than within organizations; thus it is a measure of limited usefulness to managers, and particularly so for high-talent workers.

The accountant views productivity as a financial index, with particular attention to the dollar costs and the return on capital invested. It is true that the costs of productivity improvements may outweigh the value of the increased output. Also, at nonproduction levels, outputs are not often easily identified, as figures are influenced by many factors and many contributors. But financial measures are necessary to budgeting and control and to financial planning.

The engineer prefers to consider how resources are used, particularly physical resources such as equipment, space, materials, and energy. In seeking an optimal combination and utilization of resources, he gives little attention to the financial and broad economic figures. The engineer typically is not very interested in behavioral outcomes of work: job satisfaction, career development, etc.

However, the personnel manager typically concentrates on employee attitudes. He is concerned with such issues as turnover, absenteeism, adequacy of training, employee communications, and individual performance appraisal as indicators of productivity problems. The "quality of work life" may very well be considered an important organizational objective, and thus one of the outputs to be considered in studying productivity (Davies and French, 1975; Wooten and Tarter, 1976).

From the top-management perspective, productivity is a concern encompassing all of these aspects. The overall objective is to assure optimal earnings from the combined activities of the total business. The concern is overall organizational performance, including technological, structural, financial, and behavioral components (Burch, 1974; Kendrick and Creamer, 1975; McBeath, 1974).

Factors Affecting Productivity

Many factors contribute to productivity. As shown in Exhibit 8-1, various categories of factors may be important. Technical factors such as technology, raw materials, job layout, and methods may have a significant impact in some jobs. Robert Sutermeister, the creator of this model, argues that in some organizations, such as manufacturing plants, these factors may be the most important. The relative piece of the "pie" attributed to technical factors may be larger than all of the other organizational and behavioral factors combined (Sutermeister, 1976).

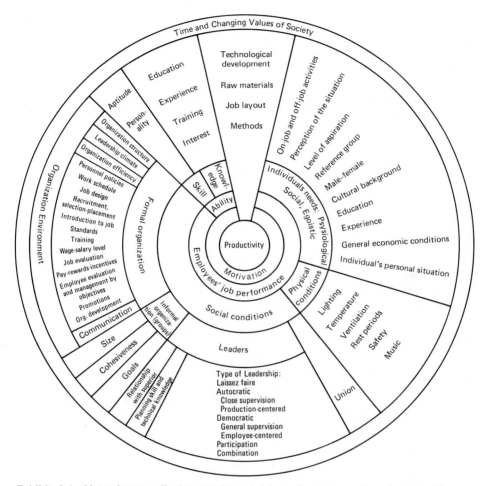

Exhibit 8-1 Major factors affecting employees' job performance and productivity. (*Source:* Reprinted by permission from Robert A. Sutermeister, *People and Productivity,* 3d ed., McGraw-Hill, New York, 1976.)

In other organizations, such as sales organizations or staff units, the technology may be less important than human factors. In a commercial bank, for example, the adoption of advanced computer systems and operating practices may be beneficial (indeed, competitively necessary), but the greatest opportunities for improved customer service, quality and quantity of work, and reduced costs lie in the ways personnel are organized and managed. The broadening of teller assignments, for example, to involve a variety of jobs allows improved utilization of personnel while also making the work more interesting and satisfying.

Technological breakthroughs can have widespread effects on technical processes, and therefore on productivity, in entire industries and types of work. The advent of the photocopier certainly revolutionized office work (if not productivity) in recent decades, while the minicomputer word-processing unit will have similar potential impact in the decade ahead.

But technological advances are uncommon, and cannot be relied upon as means of productivity improvement. Similarly, engineering applications have rather finely tuned production processes, product design, and materials usage. Accordingly, attention has turned in many organizations to behavioral factors for potential improvement in organizational performance. The variables are not as easily measured and influenced, but the potential gain is believed to be great.

Managerial Productivity

On managerial and professional jobs, structural and behavioral factors are clearly the focus of performance improvement. To a considerable degree, managers and professionals "make their own jobs," and hence the structure of the job and the goals and objectives to be achieved are not entirely controlled by management. Similarly, performance is not clearly defined or supervised, and hence motivation and direction of effort are targets for improved management.

For example, an American Management Association survey of 1,275 managers explored ways to improve managerial performance. The findings presented in Exhibit 8-2 indicate a concentration on improvements in the organization of work and the management of individual performance (Jacobs and Jillson, 1974). The remedies identified in group A, which had the highest response rates, require direct involvement of the individuals. The group B factors represent changes in working conditions for managers.

The respondents further indicated that productive managerial work is primarily dependent on the following factors: clear understanding of goals and objectives, participation by individuals and their supervisors in setting these goals and objectives, strong managerial working relationships, logical organization of the work (with proper assignment of responsibilities and delegation of authorities), and effective communications with others involved in achieving the goals and objectives (Jacobs and Jillson, 1974). Individual behavior is the key, therefore, to performance improvement at the managerial levels.

MOTIVATION OF INDIVIDUAL PERFORMANCE

In 1972, *Newsweek* published a brief article with the headline, "Too Many U.S. Workers No Longer Give a Damn." The article attributed America's faltering competitive stance in the world to worker malaise. "Whether they are overworked or underprivileged, pampered or oppressed, dehumanized by the demands of their jobs or just plain bored—whatever the reason—the evidence is strong that the traditional work ethic of the U.S. is showing signs of senility" (*Newsweek,* p. 65).

Such news has not been received with surprise among managers. So much has been said of the "restless generation" and the "new work ethic" that most managers readily acknowledge that attitudes toward work have changed, and

Exhibit 8-2   Respondents' Evaluation of Which Remedies Are Most Likely to Contribute to Improvement in Managerial Performance

	Remedy	All respondents (each respondent selected 3 remedies)	Presidents	Managers
Group A	More meaningful and challenging managerial work	45%	50%	41%
	More effective management control methods and techniques affecting budgets, scheduling, personnel relations, information flow, etc.	42	47	39
	Better management education programs to improve managerial competence	39	39	41
	"Financial incentives programs" for managers at all levels	37	35	38
	Greater dissemination down the line of information pertaining to executive-level decisions and the reasons for them	37	34	38
	Increased organizational decentralization wherever possible so as to delegate more responsibility and authority down the line	36	34	37
	Better managerial performance appraisal approaches	29	30	29
Group B	Higher standards in the hiring of managerial personnel	9	11	7
	Higher salaries for managers	8	6	9
	Better benefits	6	4	7
	Better managerial working conditions (environmental)	4	3	5
	Other suggestions	3	3	4
	Formal (and equitable) grievance procedures for management personnel	3	3	3
	"Contracting" of all management personnel to provide job security	2	1	2

Source: Reprinted with permission from Herman S. Jacobs and Katherine Jillson, *Executive Productivity* (An AMA Survey Report). Copyright 1974 by AMACOM, New York.

will likely continue to change. And attitudes toward work directly affect on-the-job performance, as well as personal career aspirations and development.

In the early 1970s, the "war babies" were just leaving school and entering the work force. America was still fighting in Vietnam, and a youthful counterculture was still in flower. It had become fashionable to challenge the traditional working patterns and work values. Many young workers sought to earn enough money to be able to "drop out" of the establishment career system, at least for a while. Alternative life-styles were valued more than upward career mobility (Sheppard and Herrick, 1972; Working Loose, 1971).

Over the years, effects of attitude changes have been felt as younger workers challenged established ways of managing. Absenteeism and turnover soared in many companies; dress codes and hairstyles changed; young women started to seek traditionally male job assignments.

In the 1960s, organization development programs sought to integrate the individual with the organization. In the 1970s the quality of work life commanded national attention, right along with attention to productivity. Company programs were widely adopted to enrich jobs, improve communications and teamwork, provide pay incentives, and upgrade managerial and employee interpersonal relations. Implicit all along has been the assumption that somehow employee satisfaction is an important factor in sustaining and improving performance.

Motivation, Satisfaction, and Performance

Does job satisfaction lead to improved performance? What motivates employees to work on a job? Are "turned-on" employees always good performers? These are basic questions regarding the meaning of motivation, satisfaction, performance, and the relationships among these factors.

From a commonsense viewpoint, job performance is obviously affected by job satisfaction. The impact may, however, be considered a constraint rather than a positive factor in that strong dissatisfaction with the work or working conditions may impede performance. Hence we often concentrate on *exceptions* to performance—performance problems or deficiencies—rather than positive effects of increased satisfaction on prospectively increased performance (Mager and Pipe, 1970; Rummler, 1972). On managerial, professional, and technical positions, signs of employee dissatisfaction are often more visible than performance problems—expressed in the form of turnover, absenteesim, and verbalized attitudes. We assume, also, that satisfaction is key to motivation to work. If motivated, most high-talent individuals have the capabilities necessary, so it is largely a matter of putting in the effort.

However, research studies over the years have shown little relationship between measures of job satisfaction and performance outputs. Highly satisfied workers may be poor performers; highly dissatisfied workers may be good performers. The relationships among these variables is compounded by a number of other variables.

Exhibit 8-3 identifies the primary determinants of individual performance, satisfaction, and motivation. The model is adapted from performance-motivation models developed by researchers (Cummings and Schwab, 1973; Nadler and Lawler, 1971, Reif, 1977; Steers and Porter, 1978; Vroom, 1964). The model is useful in thinking about the performance process and its relationship to job satisfaction and motivation.

Clearly certain variables are controllable by management, to a degree, which have a direct impact on performance. The work context (supervisory style, organization of the work, physical working conditions, commutation, hours of work, etc.), the tasks or activities to be performed (job content), and

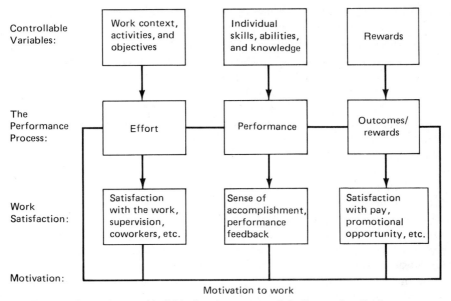

Exhibit 8-3 Determinants of individual performance, satisfaction, and motivation.

the job objectives (related to organizational objectives, presumably) all have a direct effect on the extent and nature of an individual's efforts devoted to a job. From effort itself employees may gain certain satisfactions—with the work, the supervision, coworker relationships, etc. To put it simply, there are folks who enjoy their work whether they accomplish anything or not.

Performance Determinants

Effort is a prerequisite for performance, which we may define as the accomplishment of certain defined tasks or objectives. But individual competence also comes into the picture. Hardworking individuals without the necessary skills, abilities, or knowledge are not likely to achieve much on their jobs. Performance is a function of both effort and abilities (and there may be some trade-offs, as for overachievers). Individuals may gain job satisfaction from a personal sense of accomplishment through work and also from feedback about their performance (Cummings and Schwab, 1973; Porter, Lawler, and Hackman, 1975).

Performance results in outcomes—productivity for the organization and personal rewards in the form of pay, benefits, job security, recognition from coworkers and superiors, and promotional opportunities. Employees often measure their job satisfaction largely in terms of these rewards, which are the most tangible ones received from the job.

Work satisfaction therefore has several distinct dimensions. Each, of course, is a matter of perceptions, as satisfaction depends on the needs of the individuals. Typically, research approaches to measuring job satisfaction are

based on surveying employee feelings or attitudes toward various job characteristics (Locke, 1976; Scanlan, 1976; Smith, Kendall, and Hulin, 1969). The
dimensions noted above are typically used in such studies. Locke has defined job
satisfaction as simply a pleasurable or positive emotional state resulting from the
appraisal of one's job or job experiences (Locke, 1976, p. 1300).

Work satisfaction results, according to Locke, from the perception that
one's job fulfills or allows the fulfillment of one's important job values. That is,
work is satisfying if it fits one's personal desires and needs (Locke, 1976, p.
1307).

Work satisfaction itself is a legitimate objective for an organization.
However, managers are interested in work satisfaction as a factor influencing
future performance. No direct causal relationship appears to exist, but extensive
research and theoretical work has concentrated on the performance-satisfaction
link (Greene, 1972; Scanlon, 1976; Schwab and Cummings, 1970). The link
which is necessary is "motivation." There are many definitions of motivation,
depending on the term's context of usage, but it seems most meaningful to view
motivation as a summary factor—"a label for the determinants of the choice to
initiate effort on a certain task, the choice to expend a certain amount of effort,
and the choice to persist in expending effort over a period of time" (Campbell
and Pritchard, 1976, p. 78). Hence the loop is closed. Motivation has to do with
a set of factor relationships that explain an individual's behavior, holding
constant the variables controlled or influenced by management and individual
skills, abilities, and knowledge (Campbell and Pritchard, 1976; Nadler and
Lawler, 1971; Vroom, 1964).

If performance is a function of effort and competence, it is important that
the individuals believe that they are able to perform at the desired level (Nadler
and Lawler, 1971). Effort depends on the expectancy that effort will result in
accomplishment of defined tasks, the expectancy that accomplishment will
obtain or avoid certain outcomes or rewards, and positive or negative feelings
about these outcomes or rewards. This "expectancy theory" of performance
motivation says that employees' perceptions and values are important determinants of the effort they will expend.

An alternative explanation of performance motivation holds that employees
need not perceive what is going on. Rather, effort is initiated by certain stimuli
in the work context (for example, supervisory practices) which are reinforced by
subsequent rewards for performance (for example, pay, recognition). Feelings
about the work, accomplishments, or rewards are irrelevant to the performance
process. Organizational behavior modification is founded on operant condition-
ing theory and has been widely applied (Luthans and Kreitner, 1976; Reif,
1977).

The relationships among performance, satisfaction, explicit rewards, and
effort are complex and have not been fully explored through research. Rewards
certainly cause individuals to extend effort on a job, but there are also other
factors. Perceptions of the job and the job context, personal competencies,
and satisfactions from various aspects of the performance process all influ-

ence the end results of performance. Managers may focus on any one or a combination of these variables, illustrated in Exhibit 8-4, in attempts to improve performance.

THE QUALITY OF WORKING LIFE

During the 1970s, much of the interest in work satisfaction and performance focused on the quality of working life. In his 1971 Labor Day address, President Nixon said, "In our quest for a better environment, we must always remember that the most important part of the quality of life is the quality of work, and the new need for job satisfaction is the key to the quality of work" (O'Toole, 1974, p. 712). This concern was heightened by changing attitudes toward work and a challenging of traditional work roles and career patterns, and by an influx of

Exhibit 8-4   A performance improvement framework.

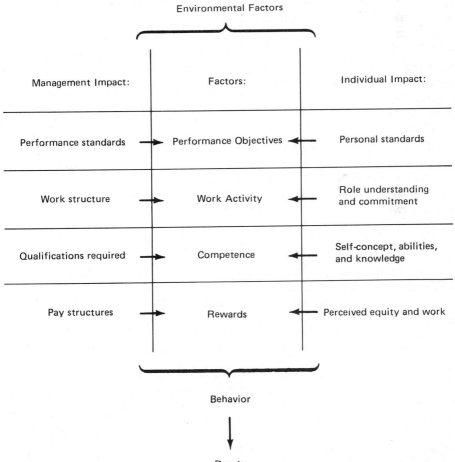

young people into the work force. Employers were also concerned about a potentially deteriorating work ethic among American workers and feelings that job dissatisfaction was high.

A special task force study was commissioned by the Department of Health, Education and Welfare to study work in America. The study report, published in 1973, provided a focus for consideration of ways to enhance the satisfaction-generating qualities of work and thereby contribute to an improved national well-being. James O'Toole, chairman of the task force, observed that "the issue of job satisfaction transcends the narrow methodological and ideological debate in which it is entrapped. As *Work in America* sought to document, efforts to improve the quality of working life can have positive effects not only on the nation's health but on such diverse issues as democratic participation, equality, family life, and economic productivity" (O'Toole, 1974, p. xiv).

Quality of Working Life Defined

Quality is a matter of perception, and widely differing viewpoints have been expressed about the important dimensions of working life. Some people are concerned with job content, others with working conditions and wages. Some feel that career mobility opportunities are important, especially opportunities to advance to higher-status occupations. Certainly, to many people, the quality of supervision (considerate and thoughtful) and peer relationships (working as members of a congenial group) are important factors. Each of these factors may be a determinant of job satisfaction or dissatisfaction (HEW Task Force, *Work in America,* 1973).

The quality of working life represents a consensus regarding the adequacy of such factors in an actual work situation. A more formal definition says that quality of work life is "the degree to which members of a work organization are able to satisfy important personal needs through their experiences in an organization" (Walton, 1974).

Ten major aspects of the concept are usually considered in efforts to improve quality of working life in organizations (Walton, 1974):

   1   Adequate and fair pay: fair and equitable pay relationships and equal pay for equal work performed
   2   Benefits programs: adequate and competitive retirement, health insurance, vacation, and other employee benefits
   3   A safe and healthy environment: clean and safe working conditions
   4   Job security: continuity of employment so that the employee is reasonably secure about the future
   5   Free collective bargaining: the right of all employees to organize in unions or other associations to represent themselves as a group or profession
   6   Growth and development: consideration of the employee as a growing, developing human asset of the organization
   7   Social integration: a working climate that fosters a feeling among employees of belonging and being needed in the organization
   8   Participation: employee involvement in the operations and decision making of the organization

9   Democracy at work: a recognition of employee rights and privileges compatible with their responsibilities to the organization

10   Total life space: a balance between working life and other parts of human life: leisure, education, and family life

Essentially, an emphasis on the quality of working life requires attention to individual employee needs and group needs as critical management values. These factors warrant attention on their own merits, as ends in themselves and as means to increased individual satisfaction. They are not primarily valued because of their potential contribution to organizational efficiency or productivity improvement, although these may be possible side benefits of QWL programs (Suttle, 1977).

Management Practices

Quality of work life projects are concerned with the structure and processes of the work itself and of the organizational context within which work occurs. The choice of factors to be acted upon depends on an assessment of employee attitudes and activities and upon the opportunities for improvement perceived by management. Projects are usually based on careful diagnosis of problems and opportunities and an evaluation of the organization's receptiveness to change.

Approaches vary and may involve management by objectives or similar participative goal-setting processes, job restructuring or enrichment projects, processes involving cost-saving sharing or productivity-sharing plans, and behavioral change or organizational development processes. The variety is nearly as great as the number of organizations reporting quality of working life improvement efforts.

Most projects have been experimental in nature and have been initiated by management as means for improving organizational effectiveness and productivity, rather than merely employee satisfaction at work. Cases involving long-term development and periodic evaluation of results are few, although this may be due in part to the relatively recent emergence of interest in QWL projects. Finally, most projects have concentrated on operating-level workers, particularly production workers and clerical personnel, rather than on managerial, professional, and technical workers. A major focus in the reported experiments is upon innovative organization, managerial relationships, and job structuring in production organizations (Davis and Cherns, 1975; Fairfield, 1974; E. M. Glaser, 1976; National Center for Productivity and Quality of Working Life, 1975). The best of the published descriptions of quality of work life improvement projects is the two-volume set of books edited by Davis and Cherns (1975). For explanation of the underlying concepts, the reader *Improving Life at Work* is recommended (Hackman and Suttle, 1977).

A PERFORMANCE IMPROVEMENT FRAMEWORK

We have identified in this chapter a number of variables which are believed to impact performance in organizations. We have indicated that management may act to increase productivity by introducing new technology, equipment, or improved operating practices. Management may also act to enhance employee satisfaction at work by modifying working conditions and job content. But such variables as employee motivation to work and overall organizational performance remain elusive.

A rather simple model may be helpful to managers in considering how to improve overall organizational performance and where to direct attention. The same model helps explain how employees view management actions and the factors determining organizational performance. This framework is presented in Exhibit 8-4. The model is useful as a diagnostic tool—to pinpoint the strengths and opportunities for improvement in managing performance.

Four principal factors are identified as determining employee behavior at work, and thus performance results. Performance objectives are critical, as they provide the direction for effort: What is to be accomplished and how will we know it is accomplished? The structure and content of work activities is the second key factor: job design, organization structure, and working relationships. Third, the skills, abilities, and knowledge—competencies—of the individuals are critical as a performance factor. And finally, rewards are necessary as incentives and recognition of performance. Any one of these factors may be a weak link, contributing to suboptimal organizational performance. And there is a common tendency of managers to zero in on one or two of the factors, such as performance objectives, as the central focus of performance improvement efforts while neglecting other factors. Or attention may be given to job design and organization without adequate consideration of the objectives to be achieved or the need for competent people to do the work. A balanced consideration of the four factors is necessary to achieve optimum organizational performance.

Who Controls the Factors?

Certainly management has an important influence on performance through control over these factors. As noted in Exhibit 8-4, these factors are the controllable variables in the individual performance, satisfaction, and motivation processes. Management defines the acceptable standards of performance or objectives to be achieved. Management controls the structure of the jobs and the organization. Management selects and promotes individuals for job assignments based on individual qualifications. Management controls the policies and systems governing wages and salaries, the principal rewards for performance.

At the same time, however, it is realistic to observe that the individual employees have a significant impact on these factors, as well. The performance standards an employee adopts may differ considerably from those intended by management. They may, in fact, be higher where professionals or managers are dedicated to their work. Mutual agreement on performance objectives or standards is necessary for effective organizational, as opposed to individual, performance. The goal-setting and review process is discussed in the next section of this chapter.

Work activities, too, are influenced by the individuals as well as by management. Particularly on professional and managerial jobs, employees "make their own jobs." That is, they spend time on those activities and perform their work in ways they feel is appropriate. The individuals have considerable autonomy and flexibility in shaping their day-to-day work and what they do may not square with management's impressions of what they should be doing (see Chapter 7). Employees perform those activities which they understand to be important to their organizational and professional roles and to which they are personally committed. In this regard, it is useful to consider the applicability of job design and job "enrichment" techniques to the management of work activities. This topic is also addressed in this chapter.

Competencies may seem objective enough, as management weighs individual work experience, past performance, education, and other indicators of ability to perform. Yet education and experience are not always indicative of future performance, especially where the work is not the same. Further, individuals can overachieve or become lax (or technically obsolete) in their jobs. A person's self-image and feelings of capabilities are extremely important in determining overall ability to perform. Competence is not a general matter, as the EEOC has pointed out in its uniform selection guidelines, but rather a matter of specific ability to perform specific job-related tasks. Competence has objective qualities, but its subjective aspects are also important, as will be discussed in Part Four of this book.

Finally, the pay structures that management believes to be motivational and equitable may not be seen that way at all by the affected employees. Management may have little idea of employees' perceptions of the value of the rewards provided for work and their equity in relation to the pay of others. These problems are addressed in Chapter 10.

Can Optimal Performance Be Achieved?

Because of the necessary cooperation and mutuality of both objectives and processes between individuals and their managers, it is possible that optimal performance simply cannot be achieved. Business enterprises are human organizations, and suffer the foibles of any association. Each individual "member" comes with a different set of needs, expectations, and behavioral patterns. The likelihood of everyone working together smoothly for the common good is low.

For this reason, some observers have suggested that the concepts are idealistic, and will never fully work out in practice. Certain realities of organizational life suggest that efforts to improve organizational performance may have limited impact. Nord and Durand (1978) suggest that such efforts are based on five assumptions, widely accepted but probably fallacious. These are as follows:

1 There is a great deal of compatibility between the goals of individuals and the goals of the organization. And personal development and job satisfaction are goals compatible with organizational goals.

2 It is possible to have high levels of interpersonal trust and openness. This is important to the well-being of the individuals and the organization.

3 Managers will involve employees in the decisions of the business because they see it as in their best interest. They will be willing to share power and give recognition to the wants and interests of subordinates.

4 Authoritarian and bureaucratic management structures are no longer viable because of rapidly changing demands on management.

5 Employees want to get involved in more interesting, enriching, ego-involving work on their jobs.

Perhaps these are pitfalls to implementation of performance improvement practices. Alternatively, they are explicit challenges management must face (see also Kotter, 1977).

PERFORMANCE GOAL SETTING

In *The Practice of Management,* published in 1954, Peter Drucker observed that "What the business enterprise needs is a principle of management that will give full scope to individual strength and responsibility and at the same time give common direction of vision and effort, establish teamwork and harmonize the goals of the individual with the commonweal. The only principle that can do this is Management by Objectives and self control" (Drucker, 1954).

The process of "management by objectives" is a formal management process through which individuals and their managers jointly define common goals, define major areas of responsibility in terms of the results expected, and use these measures as guides for future performance and subsequent review of performance (Odiorne, 1965). Common elements in the process are:

1 Formulation of clear, concise statements of objectives
2 Development of action plans for their attainment
3 Systematic monitoring and measuring of attainment
4 Corrective actions necessary to achieve the planned results

MBO is concerned with *what* is to be accomplished as a starting point in planning *how* it will be accomplished. It is a results-oriented way of managing which links individual performance goals with the long-range and strategic goals and plans of the enterprise (Raia, 1974).

Types of Objectives or Goals

Performance goals or objectives are the essence of the process. Goals are usually set by identifying areas of individual responsibility considered important to the organization and then defining key results for each. Specific performance measures are identified for each goal—for example, quantity or quality of production output; cost performance, as measured by direct and indirect expenses; and resource utilization, as measured by return on investment, turnover of inventories, and equipment utilization. The third step is to set specific objectives to serve as standards against which performance is measured (Reif and Bassford, 1973).

A firm may identify key results areas as market position or market share. Another may concentrate on generation of short-term profits. Individual objectives should relate to the organizational objectives and overall strategic plans. Yet some organizations do not have clearly defined corporate objectives and strategies, and this makes an integrated management-by-objectives process difficult. Nevertheless, as Drucker has pointed out, the process may result in the clear realization that the organization has no objectives and what passes for objectives are merely good intentions (Drucker, 1976).

Objectives, most authors contend, should be clear, concise, realistic, measurable (and quantifiable where possible), ambitious enough to be challenging, but achievable. They should be guides to action, stating what to achieve, not how to achieve it; they should take into consideration constraints not within the influence of the individual (such as budget constraints or adverse market conditions). Of course, they should be mutually agreed upon by the individuals and their managers (Odiorne, 1965, 1974; Raia, 1974; Reif and Bassford, 1973).

Objectives may be regular or routine, representing achievement of ongoing job responsibilities. They may call for innovative or creative achievements, such as development of new products, systems, or programs. They may focus on problems such as reduction of energy usage, reversing a decline in share of market, or reduction of excessive employee turnover. Finally, they may be concerned with personal development—acquiring additional knowledge, skills, and experience that will enable improved future performance (Raia, 1974).

When such objectives are established through individual and managerial discussions, however, there may be disagreement about which objectives are important. MBO advocates assume that the organization's objectives are truly those of the individual and that, by setting personal objectives within those of the organization, a formal commitment is made and the individual will strive to attain those objectives. While this assumption may be valid, it is important for managers to recognize that personal objectives may conflict, or at least compete, with valued organizational objectives. Considerable tact and skill are required to discuss objectives openly and candidly and to achieve agreement on specific objectives that are important to both the individual and the organization (H. Levinson, 1970, 1972). Sometimes the resulting objectives are set too low. If managers establish high performance expectations in setting goals with individuals, employees will usually rise to the challenge and achieve better performance results (Schaffer, 1974).

Individual Performance Planning

Goal setting is the crux of individual planning. But for goals or objectives to be useful as guides to performance, they must be used as a basis for periodic progress review and final review or appraisal of performance. Performance appraisal itself does not directly help improve performance. Rather, it is the periodic evaluation of *past* performance results which is used to determine compensation, advancement, and other personnel actions, as well as to provide a basis for future goal setting. The process must be a complete, closed loop.

A detailed outline of the steps involved in the process of managing and appraising by objectives is illustrated in Exhibit 8-5. This view indicates clearly the importance of joint participation by the managers and individuals in planning and monitoring of performance (Koontz, 1971). Making an objectives-based performance process work effectively requires attention to all the steps, with emphasis on setting high-quality, achievable, well-defined objectives (Koontz, 1977). Company studies have found that attention to personal development goals is important to the success of the process, because these goals are usually very important to the individual employees. To ignore them is to overemphasize the organization's interests and objectives. Also, studies have stressed the importance of training, both for the managers and for the employees, in the skills of goal setting, coaching, counseling, and performance evaluation (Carroll and Tosi, 1973; Ivancevich et al., 1978).

Because the performance planning process focuses on the individual, it is often useful to view the tasks from the individual perspective. Exhibit 8-6 illustrates the logical process that individuals follow in planning for performance improvement. The employee has the option of being passive in the goal-setting process and of ignoring the efforts, however well-meaning, of managers to set challenging performance goals. Further, performance planning in many companies is driven by a formal, annual performance appraisal, rather than by an integrated goal-setting process. In such instances, goals for performance improvement may be better set by starting with the performance appraisal data, viewing past performance rather than future goals (Schlesinger, 1976).

MBO, as a pure system, has not been uniformly successful in its implementation, often because of the difficulty of changing established management practices (Koontz, 1977; Odiornie, 1977; Stein, 1975). Working from an established appraisal system may be an effective strategy for gradual implementation of the goal-setting concept. Chapter 9 examines the performance appraisal process and requisites for its effective application.

WORK ACTIVITIES

The objectives or goals of work are important, but the actual tasks undertaken by individuals are also important to effective performance. In considering the ends-means debate, it is not enough to set targets for desired results and assume that these justify the means. The means, or activities, and the "how" of a job are equally important. The activities performed by individuals are identifiable, tangible, and controllable. Objectives and results are often elusive.

Accordingly, a model for guiding management of performance needs to consider the structure and content of the work activities performed by employees. How employees spend their time, what tasks they consider important enough to receive priority attention, which activities are considered

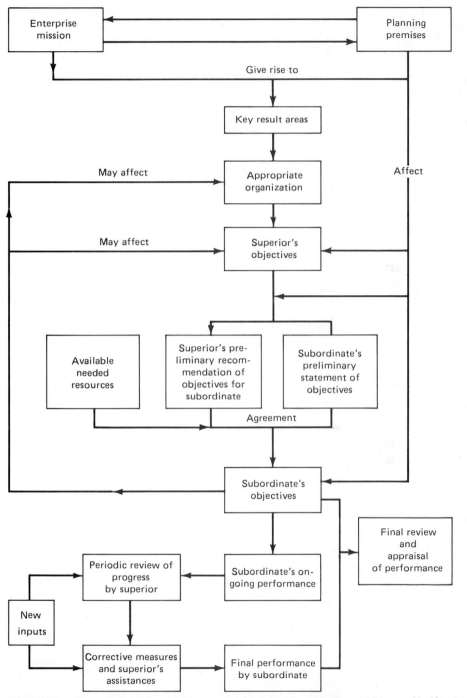

Exhibit 8-5 The system of managing and appraising by objectives. (*Source:* H. Koontz, *Appraising Managers as Managers,* McGraw-Hill, New York, 1971.)

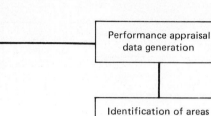

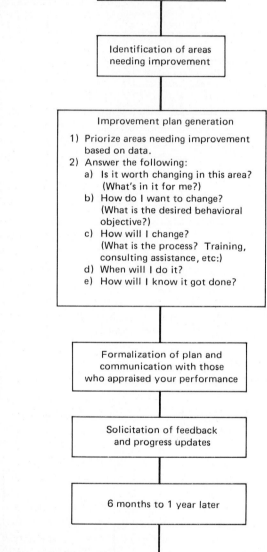

Performance appraisal
data generation

Identification of areas
needing improvement

Improvement plan generation

1) Priorize areas needing improvement
based on data.
2) Answer the following:
a) Is it worth changing in this area?
(What's in it for me?)
b) How do I want to change?
(What is the desired behavioral
objective?)
c) How will I change?
(What is the process? Training,
consulting assistance, etc:)
d) When will I do it?
e) How will I know it got done?

Formalization of plan and
communication with those
who appraised your performance

Solicitation of feedback
and progress updates

6 months to 1 year later

Exhibit 8-6 Performance improvement plans. (*Source:* Len Schlesinger, "Performance Improvement: The Missing Component of Appraisal Systems," *Personnel Journal,* June 1976, p. 274.)

primary sources of job satisfaction, and which activities help prepare individuals for future tasks and job assignments are all pertinent issues.

During the past decade there has been considerable research and experimentation with regard to job design, and particularly job "enrichment," and to innovative organization structures which have the potential of enhancing employee motivation and performance. The primary techniques involve restructuring jobs and organizational relationships, but improvements in performance have been achieved in some instances by merely changing employees' perceptions of the work and thus their attitudes toward work and work relationships.

Job Design

Jobs are defined by job descriptions. But job descriptions do not necessarily tell what a person *actually does* on a job. Managers think they know what their subordinates do, but when confronted with data are often surprised to find their assumptions do not fit with reality. Managerial, professional, and technical employees have considerable influence over the actual activities they perform on their jobs, as long as the goals or objectives (or standards of performance) are satisfied. Thus there is no established, single definition of the jobs, no agreement between the individuals and their managers about what the job involves.

A large commercial bank, for example, conducted a study of the activities of its lending officers. Assigned to branch offices around the world, these individuals performed their jobs as they felt appropriate to achieve their targeted results. Through an analysis of the ways they reported they spent their time on their jobs, however, efforts were redirected toward those activities that made the greatest contribution to branch objectives (for example, obtaining new deposits or short-term corporate lending). It was necessary to rely on information provided by the officers themselves, through interviews and a data-collection questionnaire. The application of the findings required reassignment of certain tasks, adjustments in staffing at both officer and support staff levels, and setting of new performance objectives geared to the actual activities to be performed on the jobs (Walker, 1977).

In other cases, organizations have reorganized work being performed, resulting in modifications in jobs and reorientation of employees to these changes. Reorganizations happen all the time, and individual jobs are restructured to meet changing needs of organizations. Given that jobs are often haphazardly conceived and defined in the first place, particularly professional and managerial positions, it makes sense to accept changes over time as the organizations change. One observer described "organizing," a basic managerial process, as "the process of grouping activities and responsibilities, and establishing relationships that will enable people to work together most effectively in determining and accomplishing the objectives of an enterprise" (Sherman, 1967, p. 53). Changing job design and organization structure is normal, not exceptional, in a healthy, adaptive organization.

At the heart of such change is the design of jobs. Job design involves "specification of the contents, methods, and relationships of jobs in order to satisfy technological and organizational requirements as well as the social and personal requirements of the jobholder" (Woodman and Sherwood, 1977, p. 402). Thus organizational change and job design are closely aligned as management tools. And the motivational impact of job design is a central concern, often as great as the technological or productive impact of job design. An aim of job design is "to build increased challenge and autonomy into the work for the people who perform it. By creating job conditions that motivate employees *internally,* gains might be realized both in the productive effectiveness of the organization and in the personal satisfaction and well-being of the workforce" (Hackman, 1978, p. 15).

Job Enrichment

Job design can stretch individual performance. Jobs can help individuals stretch and grow as human beings and increase their sense of competence and worth. This means that jobs can, and perhaps should, be designed in ways that will provide the greatest motivational impact.

Research studies have indicated that five characteristics of jobs are worthy of attention:

1 Skill variety
2 Task identity
3 Task significance
4 Autonomy
5 Feedback

A tool developed based on these studies, called the Job Diagnostic Survey, is used to measure these job characteristics and provides a "motivating potential score" for a job (Hackman, 1977). Other tools have been developed and applied, but all focus upon the meaningfulness, challenge, development potential, and feedback characteristics of jobs (Aldag and Brief, 1979; Woodman and Sherwood, 1977). Job enrichment requires giving individuals greater planning and control responsibilities over their work, as opposed to greater simplification and specialization in work.

The concept of job enrichment, developed and applied primarily to clerical and production jobs, was widely acclaimed as an important technique for improving the quality of working life and, indirectly, individual performance and organizational productivity. Reports of experiments and ongoing company applications indicated that the concept offered considerable promise, where the circumstances were right and the techniques effectively applied (Davis and Taylor, 1972; Hackman, 1975; Hamner, 1977; Rush, 1971). Some studies have focused on ways to diagnose whether jobs are amenable to "enrichment" and the most appropriate job-design changes to introduce (Reif and Monczka, 1974; Walters, 1977).

Job enrichment typically entails building greater individual planning, decision making, and control into jobs. Job enlargement, a related technique, merely involves expanding the scope of a job, adding more activities to it. Job design may entail work simplification, where some activities are felt to be repetitive, dull, or routine, thereby minimizing relatively unsatisfying work.

Changes in the job context can also improve job design. For example, job rotation can give work more variety without changing the particular jobs themselves. Flexible working schedules and an abbreviated work week may also improve work motivation and job satisfaction, while balancing somewhat job commutation patterns. Managerial and professional employees have often enjoyed a degree of autonomy and flexibility regarding working schedules, particularly the choice of tasks to be performed. But the four-day work week, for example, is clearly an innovative departure from common practice. In some jobs, job sharing has also been introduced, allowing multiple part-time jobs to satisfy full-time job requirements (Elbing, 1974; Nollen and Martin, 1978).

Organization Design

Activities performed in an organization also are affected by the structure of the organization—organizational design. Traditional concepts of organization call for unity of command ("one boss for each employee"), assignment of a function to only one unit, authority to act commensurate with the responsibility assigned, limited span of management (number of positions supervised by a manager), and other rather fixed organizational patterns. Such "rules of thumb" serve to help managers maintain a relatively simple, formal organization (Dale, 1952; Scott, 1969).

Over the years, however, managers have acknowledged that the formal organization structure tells only part of the story. The *real* organization is as the employees perceive it to be, regardless of how the lines are formally drawn. Also, research has confirmed that organizational forms are best when they are adapted to fit the peculiar qualities of the members, the clients served, the technologies applied, management strategies, and other forces influencing behavior. An early study by Alfred Chandler pointed out the variations in structures among organizations, depending in large part on their strategies (Chandler, 1962). Today, emphasis in organization design is upon finding the organizational characteristics that appear to make a difference in performance. On what factors does organizational performance depend? How important is coordination across the organization for completion of the tasks? How important is the division of work into relatively autonomous units that can respond freely to market, technological, and other forces for change? Organization design is viewed as a continuing process of balancing demands for individual and work group performance, enabling performers to work together as effectively as possible in the achievement of overall objectives (Galbraith, 1977; Mintzberg, 1979; Taylor, 1975).

There is no optimal way to organize work. In fact, any organizational structure, however perfect at one time, becomes inappropriate as conditions and needs change. Organizational design must therefore be concerned with flexibility, with adaptivity to pressures requiring changes in structures and practices. Organizational design has to consider many variables, including the obvious structure of jobs, job relationships, and reporting relationships. Integrating roles of managers, lateral relationships and information flows, team relationships and interteam linkages are also important. The focus could be on structure; it could be on information flow and communications; it could be on controls and planning; or it could be on management and supervisory patterns.

Organization design efforts have even focused on influence and power as key variables, subsuming all other considerations under this underlying theme which integrates and differentiates organizational performance. Drucker once observed that corporations have a common habit of rigidifying an organization structure and then overhauling it when it becomes intolerable, with the consequent effect of an earthquake. It is generally preferable to gradually adapt organizational patterns to changes, so that upheavals are minimized.

One organizational pattern, in particular, allows a great deal of flexibility. Matrix organization recognizes the need that often prevails for individuals to interact with two managers, rather than one. Developed in aerospace companies, matrix management is now applied in many industries where dual responsibilities are necessary (for example, production and product, engineering and production, product and market). Matrix relationships may have long been practiced, but within a formal, traditional chain of command organization structure. The matrix design legitimizes behavior that is necessary for effective organizational performance, but which contradicts traditional organizational "rules of thumb" (Galbraith, 1976; Lawrence, Kolodny, and Davis, 1977; Sayle, 1976).

Organization Development

Activities performed in an organization are also influenced by the manner in which managers effect change. Leadership, communications, and day-to-day interpersonal relationships are potent variables affecting organizational performance. What people perceive as expected or desired behavior will serve as guides to their behavior, regardless of defined job or organizational designs.

During the 1960s, a body of techniques was developed and applied in a wide variety of organizations to bring about improved performance and working relationships through behavioral intervention. Even without changing organization structures or job activities, changes could be effected in the way individuals *perceive* their roles and relationships and their expected behaviors. Organization development, in its pure form, is concerned primarily with the process of organizational change, and not so much with the content factors such as the activities or tasks, technology, or the formal structures of the organization.

Techniques applied include team building, survey feedback, various group training techniques (for example, laboratory training), diagnostic interviewing aimed at problem solving, task forces, and management training. Varied techniques are used.

The management techniques unique to organization development include employee attitude surveys and feedback, diagnostic interviewing and other forms of study of organizational conditions and opportunities for improvement (including "action research"), various forms of team building and group training aimed at changing attitudes and increasing group relations (and perhaps also conflict resolution and intergroup relations), and management training (aimed at improving management styles). Organization development assumes that change agents (third-party facilitators or consultants) can help an organization better understand its behaviors and adopt new individual, group, and total organizational qualities. Change in all parts of the *culture* of the organization is a major goal in the change process. A cardinal value of the process is *shared or distributed influence,* fostered by open and candid relationships. The focus is change in *behavior,* supported by related changes in systems and structures (Margulies and Raia, 1972; Margulies and Wallace, 1973; Rush, 1973; Short, 1973; Selfridge and Sokolik, 1975; Strauss, 1976).

Organizational performance is influenced by many variables, most within the influence or control of management. Productivity, the quality of working life, and individual satisfaction at work depend on the effectiveness of management's efforts in managing performance. This chapter has examined the central issues in this important area of human resource planning and has reviewed the principal techniques available to management for managing performance improvement.

In 1909 Central Leather Company was the seventh largest in the nation in assets. At the same time, a small company called Ford Motor was about to introduce its Model T. Organizational performance clearly has many dimensions, and the capacity to adapt and change is crucial. An organization must have the ability to scrutinize its strengths, its limitations, and its prospective weaknesses in the face of changing demands. Further, management must be able to identify and influence those variables that have the greatest effect on future performance, including most particularly the objectives, activities, competencies, and rewards influencing individual performance.

Chapter 9

Appraising Individual Performance

KEY POINTS

- Objective appraisal of individual performance is a necessary basis for planning performance improvement and justifying personnel actions such as promotions, transfers, terminations, and salary changes.
- Most companies experience difficulty in implementing objective appraisals. Too often appraisals are subjective and involve paperwork rather than candid evaluation and helpful feedback.
- Appraisals serve two purposes: evaluation of past performance and planning for future performance improvement and personal career development. These dual purposes make effective appraisals difficult for managers because they create rather conflicting roles.
- Each of the various appraisal techniques available has certain advantages and disadvantages: narrative appraisals, goal setting and review, rating scales, checklists, critical incidents, and ranking.
- Effective performance appraisal programs must designed and administered so as to be reasonable in the view of their users and critics, relevant to actual job behaviors required, and reliable in application over time.
- The courts have taken increased interest in appraisal programs as a possible source of discrimination and therefore are subjecting them to scrutiny by these criteria.

Probably the oldest technique used by management to improve individual performance is the appraisal. Employee motivation to perform, to develop personal capabilities, and to improve future performance is influenced by feedback regarding past performance and development.

Of course the oldest form of appraisal feedback is direct perception of results achieved. Workers building the pyramids, fighting in armies, tilling soil, and performing other work eons ago were able to see what was achieved through their contributions. Negative feedback, severe in some instances (for example, death), was also given by supervisors to particular workers deserving singular considerations for performance judged inadequate.

In modern organizations, appraisals provide an important mechanism for management to use in clarifying performance goals and standards and for motivating future individual performance. It is a key component in the personnel administration process of most companies and provides a basis for decisions affecting pay, promotions, terminations, training, transfers, and other employment conditions.

Companies have practiced performance appraisals for decades, and have adopted various techniques in the process. Yet even today most companies are not fully satisfied with the effectiveness of their appraisal processes and are alert to opportunities for improvement. Additionally, court interpretation of equal employment opportunity and age discrimination laws has focused attention on the legal aspect of appraisals—their objectivity, reliability, and fairness.

As a result, the old subject of performance appraisals is one of contemporary concern. This chapter examines the purposes served by appraisal processes, the techniques being used, and the experience gained through appraisal practices. Specific company practices and pertinent research studies are discussed as a basis for guidelines in the design and implementation of effective appraisal programs.

The trend in performance appraisal practice appears to be toward emphasis on the basics—the rudimentary purposes and techniques of appraising performance and planning for future performance and development. Hopes for development of sophisticated new appraisal techniques have largely been dashed by the experience of companies that have found them unwieldy, misunderstood, time-consuming, and costly to implement. For most companies, more effective appraisals means better use of basic tools and techniques, not more complex, advanced tools and techniques.

APPRAISAL OBSTACLES

There are no particular problems inherent in performance appraisal techniques. Most any technique can be made to work effectively by conscientious managers. But that is like saying that automobiles are not inherently dangerous, only the drivers are.

In a recent survey by the Conference Board, three out of four companies reported having appraisal systems covering at least some of their managers

(Lazer and Wikstrom, 1977). In other surveys, appraisal systems have also been found to be in widespread use (Bureau of National Affairs, 1974, 1975). In these surveys, however, the companies having systems reported experiencing various difficulties. It appears that performance appraisals are not given the full, conscientious attention by managers that the designers of the systems assumed would be given. Often, appraisals are viewed by managers as necessary exercises to be tolerated—as paperwork requirements imposed on managers to justify salary changes and other differential treatment of employees.

Further, it is recognized in these studies that appraisals are usually highly subjective, even though formal systems may be used. This means that error in judgment and personal bias are potential problems. Managers may try to be objective in appraising individual performance and capabilities, but they may simply not have all the pertinent facts regarding job requirements, actual qualities of individual behavior, and relative standards among appraisers.

Design and Implementation Problems

The problems with management performance appraisal systems identified by twenty-five personnel executives in the Conference Board survey reflect limitations in both the design and the implementation of appraisal systems (Lazer and Wikstrom, 1977, p. 17). Among the problems identified in that survey were the following:

> Conflicting multiple uses
> Unclear goals of the system
> Ratings biased by pay considerations
> Lack of clear performance criteria (standards)
> Reliance on ratings of personality rather than performance
> Rater biases such as halo persistence in ratings
> No validation of performance appraisal system
> No conceptual justification of the system
> Managers not trained to administer appraisals
> Managerial dislike for giving feedback
> One-way communication between superior and subordinate
> Rater biases
> No developmental or performance follow-up
> Susceptibility to manipulation by managers
> No built-in reinforcement for doing the appraisal
> Conflicting coach and evaluator roles
> No use of appraisal systems for top management
> No credibility of appraisal systems in the organization
> No impact of appraisal on performance
> Regarding appraisal as an administrative chore not related to business goals.

Nevertheless, about two out of three of the appraisal systems described in the survey were thought by the employers to be effective. That is, the programs were considered to be accomplishing the purposes for which they were designed. Managers often concede there is "no such thing as an infallible appraisal system" and therefore accept their system as probably as good as any other.

New personnel managers often zero in on appraisal programs as a great opportunity to make a change in systems that will be both widely visible in the organization and generally welcomed as a potential improvement. Revamping appraisal forms and procedures and providing new guidelines and supporting training are surefire ways to get attention, and usually have some degree of positive impact on an organization. Merely changing the appraisal program is often a stimulus for improved appraisal practices. If nothing else, it keeps appraisers off guard and they have to stop and think about what they are expected to do.

Can We Abolish the Performance Appraisal?

A few years ago, an article raised this possibility (Schrader, 1969). Appraisals, the author observed, are often valued more for form than for substance. An appraisal is something that must be done merely so the company can say it has been done. And the results of this "tortured and damaging ritual" are not particularly beneficial to the company.

What is performance appraisal like in practice? Too often, the scenario is as follows:

> My boss asks me to sit down in his office and says he wants to talk with me. He begins with some idle chitchat and questions about "How's my family?" and "How's the job going?" I guess he's putting me at ease, or more likely to put himself at ease for something awkward he wants to talk about.
>
> Then he tells me he just wanted me to know what a fine job I've been doing and that we don't take time to talk about our progress often enough. And he points out, with some embarrassment, several of my "strong points" which have been obvious to me. Now I'm wondering what the negatives are going to be. Something bad is going to be coming up.
>
> I can't do anything about some of the points because they reflect our different personalities, but others are ones I'm willing to work on. He urges me to try harder and apologizes for having to bring up the negatives. I thank him for being frank with me and promise to do an even better job in the year ahead.

The routine is difficult for managers because they are uncomfortable in the role of appraiser. Further, they are acting not only as appraisers or judges, but also as coaches and counselors. They normally dislike criticizing a subordinate (and having to justify criticisms) and then trying to turn the discussion around to a positive note. They usually lack the skills necessary to handle the interviews effectively, as these skills are quite different from other day-to-day contacts with the employees. Also, they are not always sure of the judgments they are making about the individual's performance and personal qualities; it is hard to take back opinions you later reverse as invalid.

These difficulties have been acknowledged for decades (McGregor, 1957).

And yet companies continue to require appraisals, and struggle to overcome (or minimize) the problems noted. Appraisals, for all their potential faults, are vital for the management of performance and improvement of productivity in an organization, as discussed in the previous chapters.

Formal appraisals could be abolished as systems and procedures, but the guts of appraisals—the clarification of job expectations, the reviewing of accomplishments, and the planning of future performance and development efforts—are central to effective management. And as will be discussed later in this chapter, objective performance evaluations are necessary as a legal defense to charges of discrimination on the basis of age, sex, and race.

PURPOSES OF APPRAISAL

One of the basic problems encountered by employers in appraising employee performance is the dual purpose of appraisals. On one hand, employers need objective evaluations of past individual performance for use in making personnel decisions. On the other hand, employers need tools to enable managers to help individuals improve performance, plan future work, develop skills and abilities for career growth, and strengthen the quality of their relationship as manager and employee.

Managers find it difficult to serve both as judge and counselor simultaneously—the dual roles required by these dual goals (Meyer, Kay, and French, 1965; Sloan and Johnson, 1968). Where both purposes are served by one appraisal program, the results are often driven by salary administration needs. Justifying a given salary adjustment often overrides all other purposes of appraisals. Thus performance appraisal programs tend to be used for one or the other of these purposes.

As a result, many companies have separate appraisal programs for performance *evaluation* and performance *planning and review*. The former involves the manager's judgment of past performance for administrative decisions. The latter involves goal setting and review for employee development.

At Corning Glass Works, for example, the appraisal programs are structured as follows:

> Evaluation interviews of a subordinate's performance, potential, promotability, and salary increase are distinct from MBO and appraisal sessions. It is best to make these evaluations when the subordinate is due for a salary increase. The manager rates each subordinate's overall performance and potential. The ratings which are shared with subordinates and endorsed by the supervisor at the next level, reflect both the whats and hows of performance (Beer and Ruh, 1976, p. 64).

A single appraisal program is rarely devised that can serve these multiple purposes. Some companies have concentrated on the goal-setting (MBO) process and tried to stop *evaluating* performance, but came back to doing both as separate programs (Patz, 1975).

The dual appraisal aspects, *evaluation* and *development,* clearly require different characteristics to be effective. Exhibit 9-1 highlights the key differences in emphasis regarding purpose, focus, method, responsibility, subject matter, and applications. Because of the difficulty of objective evaluation and the more obvious payoff of developmental performance planning and review, attention in the past decade has focused on the developmental aspects (Kellogg, 1975; Thompson and Dalton, 1970). But now, with concern about possible discrimination in appraisals, employers are giving the evaluation aspect of performance appraisal careful attention once again.

A Coordinated Process

Performance appraisal cannot be a stand-alone process. To be effective, it must interface with the other human resource management activities which rely on appraisals. Exhibit 9-2 indicates these interfaces and the emphasis of each (development or evaluation). This exhibit illustrates the relative importance of appraisals as a human resource management tool. If used, appraisals are a vital tool in many applications. If not used, and merely filed away as a personnel paperwork requirement, they are irrelevant and unworthy of time or attention. Therefore, coordinating the use of appraisals with use of other management tools is important in establishing a reliable, objective process.

One way to help managers visualize the important points of coordination between management processes is a flowchart or model of the appraisal process vis-à-vis other processes. One simple example from a management consulting

Exhibit 9-1   Dual Approaches to Performance Appraisal

	Evaluation approach	Development approach
Purpose	To assess past performance as a basis for personnel administration decisions	To motivate and direct individual performance and career development efforts
Focus	Review of past	Planning for future
Method	Judging	Counseling/discussing
	Ratings/descriptions	Goal-setting and review
Responsibility	Manager as appraiser	Manager and employee share joint responsibility
Subject matter	Past accomplishments	Future goals and plans
Applications	Work planning	Salary administration
	Improving performance	Transfers, promotions
	Developing capabilities	Layoffs, terminations
	Planning of	Other personnel
	training activities	actions

Exhibit 9-2   Dual Approaches to Performance Appraisal

Human resource management activity	Interface	Emphasis
Internal placement	Identifying readiness	Development
Promotion	Identifying outstanding performer	Evaluation
Termination	Identifying inadequate performer	Evaluation
Career planning	Discussion, career guidance	Development
Training	Identifying training needs	Development
Salary administration	Merit judgment	Evaluation
Policies	Discussion clarification	Development
Communications	Two-way discussion	Development
EEO/AA	Formal	Both development and evaluation
Management change	Identifying needs for management changes (style, systems, structure, etc.); motivational and goal-directed activity	Development

Source: Adapted from E. Allen Slusher, "A Systems Look at Performance Appraisal," *Personnel Journal,* February 1975, p. 114.

firm's appraisal guidebook is presented in Exhibit 9-3. A more elaborate example is given from McCormick & Company, Inc., in the Conference Board report (Lazer and Wikstrom, 1977, pp. 73–82).

APPRAISAL TECHNIQUES

Companies use many different forms of performance appraisals, according to their needs and management preferences. Even in a single company, multiple techniques may be used, to fit the needs of different employee groups and the preferences of different organization unit managers. The fact that techniques are so varied represents the lack of agreement on the "best way" to appraise employee peformance.

Any formal appraisal process is believed superior to informal appraisal with no established form or procedure. The various techniques that have been developed represent attempts to provide informal appraisals. How much better they actually are depends on their job-relatedness, reliability, adaptability, objectivity, and (last but not least) the cost of introduction.

Exhibit 9-4 summarizes the merits and limitations of the principal techniques for performance appraisal. As a summary, the assessments are necessari-

Exhibit 9-3   Coordination of Appraisal with Management Processes

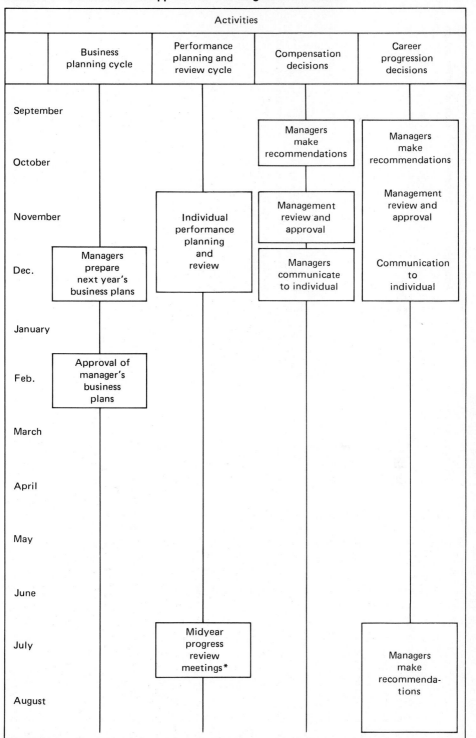

*Additional conferences scheduled throughout the year, as appropriate.

Exhibit 9-4 Principal Techniques for Performance Appraisal

Technique	Description	Job relatedness	Reliability	Adaptability	Objectivity	Cost of introduction
Narrative appraisals • Using job descriptions • Role analysis • Question/answer	Open-end essays on individual performance	Depends upon use of job requirements	Difficult to assess, often not reliable	High	Low (highly subjective)	Low cost, easily introduced
Goal setting and review • Management by objectives (MBO) • Budgets • Direct measures of outputs or results	Establishment of goals at beginning of period and then comparison of performance against these goals	Highly relevant, but may focus on only part of a job	Higher for specific, direct output measures	High	Can be high or low; depends on appraisers	Requires extensive training and several years time to fully implement
Rating scales • Single word or phrase anchored • Paragraph anchored • Behaviorally anchored	Performance evaluated against predetermined factors, on three, four, five, or more relative levels	Highly relevant if scales designed properly	Easily monitored, results compared	Relatively inflexible, scales must be revised	Can be high if reasons for ratings documented	High cost to develop anchored scales
Checklists • Task checklist • List of qualities • Weighted • Forced choice	Performance rated against list of normative factors	Depends on relevance of checklist, functions to tasks, not personality traits	Easily monitored; simplistic	Low, applicable to jobs with specific tasks	Depends on how used; "simple" may mean "superficial"	Moderate cost
Critical incidents	Examples of good and bad performance written down by appraiser as they occur and retained for periodic review	Reflects only a few observed aspects of performance	Difficult to assess or compare evaluations	High	Low	Low cost, but time-consuming for appraisers
Ranking • Alternation • Paired comparisons • Multi-rater • Forced	Appraisers' comparisons of relative performance, either individually or by group consensus	Only indirectly related to job content/standards	Easily monitored	High	Tends to be subjective; depends on vigor of process	Low cost, time-consuming for multirater rankings

ly general. Any of the techniques may be strengthened in practice by diligent design and implementation efforts.

The principal techniques are grouped as follows:

Narrative appraisals: Descriptions of the strengths and weaknesses of the employee's performance or behavior. Good job descriptions or analyses of desired roles and behaviors are valuable to appraisers in making judgments under this approach (Hopkins, 1975). Without useful criteria for evaluating performance, narrative appraisals tend to be highly subjective and to focus on qualities of the person appraised rather than on actual performance. Also, narrative appraisals are the most time-consuming to prepare and the most difficult to analyze and interpret. Nevertheless, they are commonly used as a technique and allow the appraiser the maximum of flexibility in considering the overall performance of an individual.

Goal setting and review: Not to be confused with the overall process of managing by objectives discussed in Chapter 8, this appraisal technique is a specific technique of appraising individual performance in relation to goal-based criteria. When practiced as part of a broader management-by-objectives process, the criteria (goals and measures) flow from larger work group and organizational goals. But a larger process is not essential for appraisal by results of achievement of preestablished goals.

The technique merely requires agreement between the manager and individual on the specific goals to be achieved and subsequent comparison of actual achievements by these standards. Often, achievements are directly measurable (sales, outputs, wastage, etc.), or are easily identified by comparison with standards (for example, budget compliance). This popular appraisal technique has the advantages of flexibility and high relevance to specific job demands. It suffers risks of deteriorating into subjective appraisal and of focusing on only the most obvious (and easily measured) aspects of job performance.

Rating scales: Evaluation of performance against established factors on a multipoint dimension. One of the oldest formal appraisal techniques used, the rating scale has gained considerable favor because it is quantitative and reliable, and can be designed to represent empirically identified performance factors. In the past, scales typically represented personality traits (for example, integrity, dependability, sociability) which were not necessarily job-related. Today's scales, anchored with brief descriptions of desired and undesired behaviors, provide a tailored, objective basis for appraisal (Campbell et al., 1973; Prien, Jones, and Miller, 1977; Schwab, Heneman, and DeCotiis, 1975). The chief drawback is the cost of developing the scales based on empirical analysis of jobs.

Checklist: Listing of job factors against which individual performance may be evaluated. Checklists are commonly used for routine jobs with well-defined tasks, such as clerical jobs, keypunch operators, technician jobs, or saleswork. They provide a useful standardized appraisal tool that is easy to complete for large numbers of employees. The chief drawback is the risk of a halo bias—of rating an individual on an overall basis, and not appraising objectively all aspects of performance.

Critical incidents: Records of specific examples of good and bad performance, maintained by an appraiser during the year. The idea is to develop a continuing record of specific incidents of on-the-job performance rather than to appraise total performance periodically (Scott, 1973). The incidents are clearly job-related and provide a basis for employee development counseling. The problems typically experienced are a tendency to gather only negative incidents and to consider only a portion of the job performance (only what is visible to the appraiser and often only what is seen toward the end of the year). Incidents tend to be more useful for performance improvement purposes than for documenting evaluations of performance.

Ranking: Comparison of employees by relative performance levels. This technique is a natural way for managers to appraise their employees. A straight ranking involves ordering employees from best to worst, either based on overall performance or on a number of factors. Alternation (or alternative) ranking involves identifying the very best performer, then the poorest, then the next best, then next poorest, and so on. Paired comparisons require comparisions between randomly assigned pairs of employees, resulting (when consolidated as a list) in overall ranking. A forced distribution involves assigning employees to classes based on performance levels (as students in school grading). Each ranking technique is attractive because of its simplicity, but is limited by the risk of subjective judgment. Multirater ranking techniques (wherein a group of appraisers together rank a group of individuals) strengthen the reliability of appraisals, but job relatedness remains an indirect consideration.

Further discussion of performance appraisal techniques is provided in the published literature (Cummings and Schwab, 1973; Lazer and Wikstrom, 1977; Whisler and Harper, 1965).

THE APPRAISAL PROCESS

As discussed above, a major purpose of performance appraisal is to motivate and guide the individual employee toward improved future performance and purposeful personal development of skills and capabilities. To some managers, this is the sole purpose of appraisal and an important tool for managing.

The objectives of performance review in a large insurance company are as follows:

To define the responsibilities and appropriate activities for each individual

To clarify the performance expectations (levels or standards of performance) through discussion between the manager and the individual

To provide an input to various personnel decisions (salary changes, promotion, transfer, etc.)

To provide for self-analysis to initiate the process of self-development planning under the guidance of the managers.

The company's process serves both development and evaluation purposes, but the primary emphasis is on individual development and performance improvement. "The Company faces challenges of improving profitability, strengthening its competitive position, and improving its varied services to customers. Management firmly believes that effective management of our business requires effective management of the performance and development of our employees."

Any of the appraisal techniques described above may be used as a basis for such a program. However, those techniques that have high job relatedness provide a more realistic basis for planning of future peformance and development activities. Goal setting is the most commonly used technique, followed by narrative appraisals (which in turn are supplemented by job descriptions and other job requirements and performance criteria) (Lazer and Wikstrom, 1977).

Keys for Appraisal

The keys to effective planning and review for individual performance and development seem to be the following:

1 Clearly stated job requirements or performance criteria
2 Employee self-review of performance, interests, goals, and plans
3 Independent judgment by the manager as appraiser, using available indicators and measures of actual performance
4 Discussion between the manager and the employee, comparing the results of their independent reviews and developing together a mutually agreeable review of past accomplishments and a plan for future activities and targeted accomplishments

Without any one of these four key components, the process of mutually discussing and planning performance progress breaks down. The effective developmental appraisal is a job-oriented, mutually shared, discussion-based planning activity. Whereas in performance *evaluation* the responsibility rests primarily with the appraising manager, the responsibility in the development process rests on both the employee and the manager. This shift in roles, of course, is often difficult for both employees and managers to adjust to and represents a major obstacle to effective performance and development planning.

The process adopted by the insurance company mentioned above illustrates the application of these important points. Identifying information has been removed at the request of the company. Similar processes have been developed and applied in many other companies.

Specific job requirements are clarified through the use of a job description work sheet, as illustrated in Exhibit 7-5 in Chapter 7. The work sheet allows employees to update their job descriptions, which do not always reflect the current job demands. The work sheet serves as a starting point in self-appraisal by the employee and for appraisal by the manager.

Performance Planning

After completing or reviewing the work sheet, the employee is equipped to complete a performance planning work sheet (Exhibit 9-5). This narrative questionnaire guides the employee through a structured analysis of activities

NAME _____   POSITION TITLE _____

LOCATION _____   DATE _____

PERFORMANCE REVIEW

A. DESCRIBE ACTIVITIES
   The important activities I perform on my job are:

_____

_____

_____

_____

_____

_____

B. MAJOR ACCOMPLISHMENTS
Since my last performance review, I have achieved the following specific accomplishments on my present job:

_____

_____

_____

_____

_____

_____

_____

_____

C. MAJOR STRENGTHS

My most significant areas of strength on my present job are: (Be specific and explain)

_____

_____

_____

_____

_____

_____

Exhibit 9-5   Performance planning work sheet.

D. MAJOR AREAS FOR IMPROVEMENT

Areas for improvement on my present job are: (Be specific and explain)

_____

_____

_____

_____

_____

_____

_____

E. IMPROVEMENTS IN MY JOB

Following are some things that would make my job more effective and more satisfying:

_____

_____

_____

_____

_____

PERFORMANCE PLANS

A. PERFORMANCE GOALS

The following are my goals for performing my job during the year ahead:

_____

_____

_____

_____

_____

_____

B. PERFORMANCE MEASURES

For each of these goals, here's how my performance should be measured:

_____

_____

_____

_____

_____

Exhibit 9-5 Performance planning work sheet (*continued*).

C. ACTION PLANS

I will take the following steps to achieve these goals (plan specific actions needed and the timing of each—e.g., learn a new skill needed on the job, target dates for reviewing progress):

_____

_____

_____

_____

_____

CAREER DEVELOPMENT PLANS

A. CAREER OBJECTIVES

The following are my career objectives: (indicate types of work, life style or personal accomplishments)

Short range: (one to three years) _____

_____

_____

Long range: (three years or more) _____

_____

_____

B. JOB TARGETS: Specific positions I would be interested in and feel I could handle are:

_____

_____

C. DEVELOPMENT NEEDS: I need to develop the following skills and knowledge either to improve performance in my present job or to prepare for my future career:

_____

_____

_____

_____

_____

D. PROPOSED DEVELOPMENT ACTIVITY: I propose to do the following to meet my development needs over the next 2-3 years:

_____

_____

_____

_____

_____

Exhibit 9-5 Performance planning work sheet (*continued*).

performed, past accomplishments, strengths and areas for improvement, suggested improvements in the job itself, proposed performance goals and performance measures for the year ahead, and specific actions plans both for performance and for personal career development. Although the work sheet is open-ended, experience indicates that salaried employees generally have sufficient information on their future goals and activities.

The work sheet is primarily a self-analysis tool which the appraiser may give an employee in advance of a review discussion. It also serves as a useful starting point in conducting the performance review discussion. The work sheet is a planning tool, and includes a heavy dose of goal setting as an inherent technique. It can be as quantitative as the job and relevant performance measures allow; it may be tailored to fit the circumstances of particular types of jobs or employee skills. It is not used as a formal appraisal document, but it can help to improve the appraisals and encourage employee involvement in the appraisal process.

Experience indicates that the self-review is a useful element of performance appraisal and that employees often tend to be more critical of their own performance than managers are. It also communicates to employees a company commitment to disclosure about performance appraisal information, while not necessarily limiting the objectivity of formal performance *evaluations* submitted by managers (Bassett and Meyer, 1968).

Appraisal Discussion

The appraisal discussion itself is the crux of the process. Here the manager and the employee compare their work sheet notations and discuss points of agreement and disagreement. The purpose of the discussion is not to make an evaluation of individual performance or to communicate such a unilateral judgment. Rather, the intent is constructive—to clarify, motivate, and direct. If the discussion has been candid and thorough, there remains little need for any unilateral communication of appraisal results, or any direct discussion of pay actions as they relate to appraisals. The mutual discussion should eliminate the potential of surprises later in the year when compensation changes are communicated or other personnel actions are taken which relate to performance (terminations, transfers, training, etc.).

Many articles and books have been written providing guidance to managers in the skills of conducting performance review discussions (Burke, 1970; Kellogg, 1976; Meyer, 1977). Exhibit 9-6 presents one company's guidelines. In general, the suggestions include:

Review what has been achieved since the last review and examine reasons for successes and failures.

Stimulate and discuss ideas about what can be done to improve results achieved.

Help the individual analyze personal performance and underlying factors affecting performance such as skills and knowledge, job structure, standards, resources available, etc.

Exhibit 9-6 Summary Guidelines for Performance Planning and Review Conference

---

Purpose

- To clarify expectations through job analysis (compare job analysis record)
- To review individual's effectiveness in specified performance categories (compare performance category checklist)
- To compare actual performance with performance goals (compare previous performance planning and review record)

- To agree on necessary development activites and, when appropriate, to discuss career goals (compare performance category checklist and previous performance planning record)
- To mutually agree on performance goals, criteria for measurement, and progress review date (compare performance planning and review record)

Recommended frequency

One performance planning session and one progress review meeting each year, or more frequently if appropriate

Recommended timing

Performance planning and review: November–December
Progress review: July–August

Preparation

Supervisor and individual separately:
- Review records of previous planning and review discussions
- Compare actual performance against goals
- Consider career status, development plans, and performance goals, as appropriate

Individual alone:
- Prepares job analysis
- Completes performance category checklist
- Identifies proposed performance and development objectives for coming period
- Develops goal accomplishment plan

Agenda

Supervisor and individual together:
- Review records of last performance planning and review discussion
- Agree on actual levels of achievement against goals
- Agree on performance and development, goals basis of measurement, and dates of progress review as appropriate
- Consider career status and development plans, as appropriate

Follow-up

Individual completes performance planning and review record as documentation of performance and development goals and gives copy to supervisor.

Strengthen the individual's commitment to the job.

Learn about the individual's interests, goals, and long-range career plans, and help the individual relate these to the current job.

Strengthen the understanding between manager and individual, and foster an open line of communication.

Discuss and resolve specific anxieties, uncertainties, or misapprehensions affecting job performance plans and directions for future career development; plan specific activities in support of these plans and directions.

Get feedback from the individual on how well you have managed.

In the developmental approach to performance appraisal, the discussion between the manager and the employee is critically important. It requires a great deal of work on the part of both the manager and the employee to be effective, but it can provide both with a sense of accomplishment, a sense of future direction and priorities, and a commitment to specific developmental activities that strengthens both their relationship and the overall organization.

PERFORMANCE EVALUATION

Of the two aspects of performance appraisal, performance evaluation serves as the basis of management actions such as salary administration decisions, terminations, layoffs, promotions, and participation in training. Evaluations must therefore provide an accurate definition of individual performance relative to actual job requirements and performance standards.

In practice, this means that employers aim to design evaluation tools that are compatible with the tools being used for development-oriented appraisal and planning and that are defensible as reasonable, relevant, and reliable indicators of employee merit.

In the insurance company, for example, the manager is required to complete a performance review form following the review discussion. This form (Exhibit 9-7) serves as the formal performance evaluation for administrative purposes. It also provides an assessment of the individual's readiness for alternate assignments and of specific development needs. The review is signed by the manager (but not the employee) and is reviewed by at least one other reviewing manager, usually the next-level manager.

This review procedure is fairly typical of the way performance evaluations are obtained in large companies. In this case the job description work sheets and the performance planning work sheets provide the relevant information on the important elements of the jobs performed. In others, the appraisal criteria are provided in scales or checklists built into the appraisals. In fact, a special version of the appraisal is used in this case for clerical positions, and other forms are being designed for underwriters, adjusting, and other groups of positions.

Effective Performance Evaluations

Performance evaluation techniques have come under fire from the courts, from employees, and from skeptical managers in instances where appraisals have a high risk of being subjective. To be effective, the appraisals must be carefully prepared. Three basic characteristics are important.

An appraisal needs to be *reasonable* in the view of its users and its critics. This means the program must be generally understood and accepted as reasonably useful, fair, necessary, and objective. The purpose or purposes of the

Exhibit 9-7 Performance review.

NAME	(Last)	(First)	(Initial)	DATE
JOB TITLE		DEPARTMENT	LOCATION	

PERFORMANCE *Indicate below the key performance areas for which the employee is responsible and indicate the level of accomplishment in each.*

Performance Areas:	Accomplishments/Comments	Distinguished	Exceeds Expectations	Full	Marginal
1.					
2.					
3.					
4.					
5.					
6.					

Overall Performance Appraisal _____
Opportunities for Improvement/Future Objectives.

_____

_____

_____

_____

_____

_____

_____

_____

DEVELOPMENT

Has this individual, in your estimate, the ability to go beyond present responsibilities? Please estimate, to the best of your ability, the individual's development potential.

_____

If this individual does not hold a management assignment, where would you direct his/her development, the alternatives being specialist or management?

_____

_____

Is the individual a possible candidate for another position as a planned next assignment? When would the person be available and fully qualified?

Position: _____

Timing: Immediate _____ Within 2 years _____ Within 5 years _____

Alternate Next Position: _____

Timing: Immediate _____Within 2 years _____ Within 5 years _____

If no information is given, explain (e.g., near retirement, new on position, career position, not promotable).

_____

_____

What are the individual's development needs, for improved performance on the present position? For future career progress?

_____

_____

_____

What training and development experiences are planned to help the individual? Please indicate specific actions (special assignments, training programs, etc.):

_____

_____

_____

Has this review been discussed with the employee?   Yes ____   No ____

REVIEWER'S SIGNATURE: _____   DATE _____

EVALUATOR'S SIGNATURE AND COMMENTS: _____   DATE _____

_____

Exhibit 9-7   Performance review (*continued*).

process are clearly stated and procedures for the implementation have a minimum vagueness. Employee participation in the design of the process and subsequent communications are also important.

A second important factor is relevance. A program is *relevant* if it covers those aspects of work that are important and only those aspects. Relevance is assured by clear statements of job requirements and the kinds of on-the-job activities of behaviors that are necessary for successful performance. Personality traits, race, sex, and age are usually not job-related. The focus should be on how employees go about their work and the nature of the outputs or results created.

Third, appraisals need to be *reliable*. This means they should be free of significant defects. Evaluations of performance for the same individual at the same time should be consistent among different raters. They should contain a minimum of subjectivity that leads to distortion. Direct measures of output (units produced or sold, for example) are highly reliable, but such measures are not always available or applicable. And so rating or narrative assays are used as indirect measures and are highly dependent on the quality of information available about performance, on the ability of appraisers to make reliable judgments, and on the use of consistent standards (criteria) against which ratings are made.

The Legal Context of Appraisals

These characteristics are important considerations in any appraisal program, if it is to satisfy management's needs for performance evaluation information in making personnel decisions. In recent years, however, the pressure for effective appraisals has increased due to new legal requirements.

Under the Equal Protection Clause of the Fourteenth Amendment, the Civil Rights Act, and the Age Discrimination in Employment Act, courts have ruled that appraisal systems must be justified where they have an adverse impact on protected employees. Where terms or conditions of employment are affected by an appraisal system, the system is, in effect, an employment test. And tests must be validated to demonstrate that they are significantly correlated with important elements of work behavior relevant to the jobs for which the affected individuals are being evaluated.

Under the Uniform Guidelines on Employee Selection Principles validity studies of selection procedures are not required where no adverse impact results. Where there is no injury, there is no cause for action. If the personnel actions based on appraisals (compensation, promotions, etc.) fall evenly without regard to age, sex, or race, a company need not fear legal scrutiny.

Even if there is an adverse impact, appraisal could be justified as a "business necessity"—a procedure "essential for the safe and efficient conduct of the business." But the courts construe this justification narrowly and would require the company to substitute some other system for achieving the same necessary business purpose with less discriminatory effects.

In a number of cases, courts have ruled that performance evaluation systems having an adverse impact must be reasonable, reliable, and relevant. The defendant companies have been required to demonstrate that their appraisal systems met these criteria in order to be accepted as a basis for layoffs and other adverse effects on protected employees (Basnight and Wolkinson, 1977; Holley and Feild, 1975; Lazer and Wikstrom, 1977).

Until recently most of the court rulings dealt with racial discrimination. For example, an appraisal system was subject to scrutiny in *Wade v. Mississippi Cooperative Extension Service* (1974). The court held that the employer had the burden of showing that the appraisal process was job-related and served legitimate needs—and that the inference of discrimination had to be removed by clear and convincing evidence. In the ruling, the court found that:

> . . . Objective appraisal of job performance . . . is based upon scores received by subordinates rated by supervisors on an evaluation instrument according to a

number of factors. For example, a substantial portion of the evaluation rating relates to such general characteristics as leadership, public acceptance, attitude toward people, appearance and grooming, personal conduct, outlook on life, ethical habits, resourcefulness, capacity for growth, mental alertness, and loyalty to organization. . . . These are traits which are susceptible to partiality and to the personal taste, whim, or fancy of the evaluator . . . and obviously susceptible to completely subjective treatment.

In *Brito v. Zia Company* (1973), the courts pointed out the need for "identifiable criteria based on quality or quantity of work or specific performance that were supported by some kind of record." Also, the need for standardized and controlled administration and scoring of evaluations was noted.

Age Discrimination Cases

The actual number of cases involving performance appraisals under issues of race and sex discrimination are relatively few. But the courts appear to be much more alert and active in rulings concerning age discrimination. For one thing, employers have often tended to dilute performance evaluations as employees grow older, as an act of kindness and respect for long service. When layoffs and forced retirements have been necessary, older workers have frequently been affected in greater proportions. As a result, courts observe a clear pattern of age discrimination.

In the case of *Mistretta v. Sandia Corporation* (1977), the theme of Sandia's defense was that performance appraisals were the main ingredient in layoff decisions which adversely affected a number of older employees in 1973. In the court's decision, District Court Judge Mechem concluded:

> The system is extremely subjective and has never been validated. Supervisors were not told to consider specific criteria in their ratings . . . the evaluations were based on best judgement and opinion of the evaluators, but were not based on any definite identifiable criteria based on quality or quantity of work or specific performances that were supported by some kind of record. Courts have condemned subjective standards as fostering discrimination.

Other age discrimination decisions which have pointed to the need for valid performance appraisals include *Brito v. Zia Co.* (1973), *Muller v. U.S. Steel* (1975), *Rich v. Martin-Marietta* (1975), and *Sarcini v. Missouri Pacific Railway Co.* (1977).

Judge Mechem noted several problems with the system used by Sandia, which was derived from Bell System policy (Sandia is a subsidiary of Western Electric Company, Inc.). He observed:

> . . . Subjective systems are often corrupted by personal bias. . . . When a decision involves an individual in the protected age group, the decision must be based on abilities rather than age. Management's concern about the increasing age of its staff,

reduced hiring, new technical developments, emphasis on recruiting and advancing young Ph.D.s might not violate ADEA in themselves, but these policies and attitudes could easily be reflected in subjective performance ratings.

In ruling against Sandia, he concluded:

> The evidence presented [by Sandia] is not sufficient to prove or disprove the contention that at Sandia performance declines with age, but there is sufficient circumstantial evidence to indicate that age bias and age based policies appear throughout the performance rating process to the detriment of the protected age group.

In addition to court cases, it is noteworthy that the proposed extension of mandatory retirement to age 70 (and to eliminate the upper age limit for most federal employees) would bring a large number of additional individuals under the protection of the law. And the proposed elimination of the (4f(2)) exclusion for employees covered by bona fide seniority systems or employee benefit plans will protect many additional employees against involuntary retirement. The proposed ban on mandatory retirement for these groups will bring increased pressure on personnel decisions and the performance appraisal systems supporting them.

State laws are also an important consideration. California enacted a statute that bans mandatory retirement at any age. Similar laws are being considered in New York, New Jersey, Massachusetts, Pennsylvania, and other states. These laws go beyond federal legislation by expanding the protected group. There is activity in some states to drop the protected age threshold from age 40 to age 18. The need for objective performance appraisals may be greater, therefore, in states with liberal statutes.

GUIDELINES FOR PERFORMANCE APPRAISAL

Although the obstacles may sometimes seem considerable to employers, performance appraisal systems may be designed and implemented in a manner that satisfies the above requirements. In large measure, it is, in fact, the *manner* of design and implementation that determines effectiveness (and legal justification) of an appraisal program more than it is the particular set of techniques adopted. Accordingly, the guidelines below focus upon the *manner* of designing and implementing performance appraisal programs.

1   *Apply specific performance standards.*
To be job-related and free of age bias, performance evaluations need to be based on specific, empirically derived job requirements. In many companies job descriptions prepared for salary administration purposes serve as a starting point for performance evaluations. Too often they are the ending point as well, and the appraisers are left to conceive applicable performance standards in the course of evaluating individual performance.

The Conference Board survey mentioned earlier found that only half of the companies studied had analyzed the requirements of the positions covered by the appraisal systems. Companies are not accustomed to devoting time and resources to job analysis for purposes other than salary and wage administration. Some argue that goal-setting techniques reduce the need for defined job standards, but appear to have little defense against charges of subjectivity and bias in appraisals.

Job requirements should cover both the *what* and the *how* of job performance (Levinson, 1976; Oberg, 1972). They should therefore include:

Basic activities (or roles) required on the position and other similar positions

Special activities required unique to a given location, project, technical requirement, etc.

Identifiable or measurable outputs or products resulting from performance

Skills, abilities, and knowledge necessary for successful performance

The courts appear to favor job performance standards that are based on some form of empirical analysis—examination of the actual job requirements. Interviews, questionnaires, observation, or any other work-analysis technique may be used to provide empirical evidence of job-related performance standards (Walker, 1977). The results need not be lengthy, detailed job descriptions, but the relevant aspects of job performance need to be accurately defined.

2 *Assure that the program is rationally designed.*

The courts favor the view that a performance appraisal program should be rational. That is, the judge must feel that the system is designed for specific purposes which are reasonable and clearly identified and that the techniques adopted have the capacity to achieve these objectives.

The courts have not dictated what type of program or what techniques are most acceptable. They have not dictated parameters for the design of appraisal programs. It is incumbent on employers, then, to reconsider the multiple purposes being served by appraisals, and to define carefully a philosophy and program (or programs) that effectively serve the objectives they have in mind.

Many large companies, for example, periodically review all appraisal programs being used and audit the results being obtained from them. Programs found deficient are overhauled; others are updated and reinforced for increased effectiveness. Different programs, involving various techniques, are commonly used in companies to meet diverse needs and circumstances.

3 *Document performance evaluations.*

Performance appraisals are often viewed as burdensome paperwork imposed by the personnel staff primarily for salary administration purposes. While effective appraisals of performance need not involve any paperwork, the courts appear to feel that documentation is important. And written evaluations provide a company with a record of judgments underlying personnel actions.

An employer should obtain a written performance evaluation for each employee at least once each year. These evaluations should be retained for at least three years, even though the information may not be used in personnel decisions. The evaluations should reflect consideration of the performance standards and be consistent with the rationale of the appraisal program. They need not be lengthy (one handwritten page may suffice) as long as they are thoughtful and complete.

Summary ratings retained on computer files are not sufficient because they lack the detailed information revealing the judgments relating to job requirements. Summary ratings are useful for monitoring appraisal applications and rater consistency, however, and for examining patterns in employee performance by units or job categories.

It should be noted that employees may have access to their evaluations; California, Alaska, Maine, and other states have disclosure statutes.

4 *Administer the program systematically.*

It is important to maintain a regular schedule for evaluations and to obtain complete participation by all appraisers. In many organizations, evaluations are reviewed by managers one or more levels above the appraiser to assure proper administration of the program and to strengthen the objectivity of appraisals. If some employees are given an opportunity to discuss their evaluations, it should become policy for all.

In short, the courts appear to favor appraisal programs that are systematically administered. This reflects concern for equitable treatment of all groups of employees and a concern for regular, recurring appraisals as a matter of routine management practice. Ad hoc, haphazard appraisal programs do not carry much weight with the judges.

5 *Train the appraisers.*

Appraisal programs are often faulted because of inadequate appraiser abilities. In many organizations, managers have never been given training on how to conduct performance appraisals. Where they have, the training typically involved only a brief orientation on the administrative procedures required by a new program, followed by periodic procedural memoranda.

Certainly training should cover the administrative aspect of a program—the forms, rating scales, the use of job standards, the linkages with salary administration, timing, etc. However, it should also help appraisers understand the objectives, problems, and behavioral aspects of performance evaluation. Appraisers control the quality of appraisals, and thus need to be guided and motivated to give the program the necessary attention (Prather, 1970).

Monitoring of appraisals by personnel staff can be useful in maintaining high-quality appraisals, if the results of monitoring are fed back to the appraisers. Conversely, appraisers can make valuable suggestions for the improvement of the program itself.

Above all, it is important that management support for appraisals be evident. In many companies, the appraisal program begins with top management and cascades through the organization. The most powerful force in performance evaluation is the example of the appraiser's own manager as appraiser. Hence the best form of training is the proper use of the appraisal program, beginning with top managers appraising their subordinates.

Chapter 10

Compensation Planning

KEY POINTS

- Planning for compensation programs should be integrated with human resource planning because of the interrelationships of compensation practices with other management practices.
- The process of defining job worth has long been accepted as having some degree of subjectivity. Now, however, EEOC requirements are likely to demand increased objectivity based on job analysis and a refinement of the evaluation process.
- Merit compensation gives employees incentive to achieve goals the organization considers important. However, managers find it difficult to recognize and reward the outstanding performers and to penalize the poorer performers. Here, too, equal employment opportunity requirements demand a justification for pay differences. Hence merit compensation is a great concept, but it does not always work out as well in practice. It needs to.
- Bonus plans are a form of short-term management incentive arrangement which require substantial effort by management if they are to have the desired motivational effects. Long-term incentive arrangements help bring about longer-term corporate growth and success, but tax regulations are a primary design parameter in these programs.
- Flexible benefits programs are the most noteworthy innovation in the

management of "fringe" benefits (pension, insurance, vacations, etc.). Allowing employees greater participation in the allocation of their benefits is believed to increase the motivational value of the benefits.

Compensation planning is important as part of human resource planning because the demands upon management practices in this area are changing rapidly. Marshall McLuhan said, "Our Age of Anxiety is, in great part, the result of trying to do today's job with yesterday's tools—with yesterday's concepts." This aptly characterizes the challenge of managing employee compensation and benefit programs.

Companies have developed elaborate compensation systems and procedures over the years with the aim of attracting, retaining, and motivating people necessary to help achieve organizational goals. Rewards are considered necessary as incentives to employees, in exchange for the services provided. And systematic programs for administering rewards have been considered necessary to ensure a sense of equity within the organization, external competitiveness, and efficient use of the company's resources.

Compensation is a generic term, including various sorts of rewards given employees. The most obvious component is pay, which may be wages or salaries. Benefits, which used to be called supplemental but now are hardly that, include insurance, pensions, medical benefits, time off for vacations, and other indirect rewards which still bear direct costs to the employers. Finally, "total compensation" is usually viewed as including nonmonetary rewards such as recognition, working conditions, titles, and praise (Belcher, 1974; Mahoney, 1979; Patten, 1977).

Pay itself is of central importance to life in our society. It is the means of acquiring the necessities as well as luxuries that constitute life-styles. But it is inherently a yardstick used to judge individual worth and importance. From a company viewpoint, pay and other compensation elements constitute an important source of costs. In some labor-intensive service companies, payroll and benefit costs exceed 70 percent of total operating costs. Even in manufacturing and other capital-intensive companies, the percentage may exceed 40 percent.

Concern over the effectiveness of compensation programs surrounds the benefits gained from each dollar spent (or invested). "The most important aspect of compensation is behavioral and motivational," observes a compensation director of a large bank. "This is the tough part and the aspect that is ignored. In salary administration, action is totally rearguard and we end up using money with minimal effect" (Bull, 1973, p. 23).

Fundamental questions are being raised in compensation planning regarding the assumptions, strategies, and approaches being applied in the various aspects of compensation management. The basic question of "What is a job worth?" has been raised again and defies a ready answer, because of new equal-pay-for-equal-work considerations stressed by federal equal employment legislation. Merit pay is followed in concept in many companies, but with heightened interest in productivity, the results of merit programs are being weighed and often found wanting. Similarly, incentive compensation, now a common component of compensation for executives, continues to tend toward being "additional compensation" with little direct incentive impact on performance. And with soaring costs of providing medical, retirement, and other benefits, companies are rethinking their philosophies about indirect compensation.

These questions are exacerbated by environmental circumstances impacting costs and employee perceptions of compensation. Greatest among these is inflation, which has all but consumed pay adjustments for salaried employees in recent years. Pressures for cost control and productivity improvement are being widely experienced in different industries. Recent federal legislation and court decisions have given new significance to several areas of compensation practice, such as job evaluation and salary comparisons, employee benefit plans, and executive incentive plans. Further, varying economic, legal, and cultural conditions affect compensation practices of companies operating internationally. Finally, from employees themselves are coming pressures for greater disclosure of pay practices and even participation in the planning and administration of compensation programs.

This chapter reviews these issues affecting human resource planning and points to their possible solutions. Compensation issues need to be linked with other human resource planning concerns, including performance appraisal, job analysis and career path design, and career management. Compensation planning is vital for the development of the more complex, job-related, cost-control-oriented, and motivational compensation practices.

ISSUES IN COMPENSATION PLANNING

The issues that influence compensation programs change over time. In the mid-1970s wage and price controls, recession, inflation, and job mobility were characteristic influences on policies and practices. In the 1980s, inflation will quite likely continue to be an important factor, unfortunately accompanied by economic recession or at least economic pressures on businesses. Depending on economic conditions and employee attitudes, mobility may be tempered by a desire among employees for security in employment.

During the decade ahead we are likely to see a continuation of the trend of proliferating legislation. The regular flow of federal legislation seems never-ending. Following ERISA (Employee Retirement Income Security Act of 1974), ADEA (Age Discrimination in Employment Act of 1967) Amendments (1973), and several tax reform acts, we may look forward to prospective legislation on health insurance, ERISA improvements, and equal pay. Court decisions and EEOC and other agency guidelines and rulings may supplement the work of Congress in adding demands upon compensation practices (Ellig, 1977).

Attitudes of employees will also shape future compensation policies and practices. Early signs of pressures for disclosure of compensation information, for a voice in the setting of salary levels and the allocation of pay adjustments, and for a general improvement in egalitarianism of compensation practices (except by the high-paid performers) appear likely to develop into major forces. Concerns about salary compression, cost of living differentials and adjustments, and pay practices for international assignments will also require attention, if not easy solutions.

Economic Conditions

Inflation does not help companies provide financial incentives to employees. The merit pay system, which has been used for decades within United States industry, is in trouble. Pounded by double-digit inflation and forced into higher income tax brackets, the salaries of many employees have hardly held their own, let alone increased with merit increases. For many employees, the net real income has declined over the years of high inflation.

Add to this the effects of spiraling starting salaries. Companies find it difficult to raise the salaries of experienced workers by greater proportional amounts than initial hiring rates. In some companies engineers with five years experience and training find their pay levels only slightly ahead of those of inexperienced engineers fresh from the campus.

Companies are restrained from raising salaries by cost economics, but also by government controls, which seem to have the habit of coming and going with regularity (and may one day simply come and stay). While companies with collectively bargained hourly rate plans seek to make similar adjustments to salaries as those negotiated with the unions, many companies allow a compression to develop between these broad groups as well (*Business Week,* 1977; Ellig, 1977).

As individuals we are accustomed to following the CPI (Consumer Price Index). This barometer of nationwide inflation now dictates adjustments to many negotiated pay levels, to social security and food stamps recipients, and to others with cost-of-living adjustment provisions (COLAs) affecting their pay. Compensation planners must also take account of CPI changes, and plan for substantial adjustment to salaries if pay is to be kept whole.

Company problems under inflation are particularly acute as they concern white-collar professionals. Dozens of new pay arrangements, including incentives, benefits, and direct pay approaches are conceived and adopted each year with the hope of resolving the problem by dealing with the quality of the technique instead of the amount of money.

It is clear, though, that employees are less likely to accept nonfinancial rewards as substantial when their consumer buying power is declining. And when recession exists as well, job security comes to the fore, complicating management efforts to reward the high performers and discourage the poorer performers.

Relocation of employees, particularly professionals and managers, is also compounded by economic conditions. Substantial differences in cost of living, including tax and commutation costs, may be taken into account in adjusting individual salaries. But the added complexity of salary administration, the difficulty of trying to "take away" such adjustments later when an employee relocates, the nonperformance differentials that are added to the system, and the sheer costs involved all make employers reluctant to make such adjustments. As a result, adjustments are often made *unofficially* as exceptions, adding a different sort of compensation management problem (*Business Week, 1977;* Runzheimer, 1977).

New Legal Requirements

The advent of HMOs (health maintenance organizations), SPDs (summary plan descriptions required under ERISA), and maternity leaves paid as disabilities are among the innovations brought to us largely through federal legislation. Responding to the expressed concerns of voters who feel that employer arrangements should be changed, Congress enacts legislation that must be implemented by the employers. ERISA, for example, was passed at least partially because of popularized fears of failed pension plans under conditions of corporate bankruptcy or inadequate funding by companies. Whether or not justified by the facts or risk, the law establishes minimum standards for pension plans and sets guidelines for their design and administration.

Similarly, court decisions have influenced compensation practices. Under the Age Discrimination act, for example, a court awarded double damages to former employees of a company found to have been subjected to age bias in pay raise practices. The employer had a practice of slowing the time between minimum salary increases as employees aged, a practice viewed as a "willful violation" of the ADEA by the courts (*Mistretta v. Sandia Corporation, 1977*).

Administrative guidelines for equal pay and equal employment opportunity also influence compensation policies and approaches. Consideration of new guidelines governing job analysis and job evaluation grew out of public perceptions that traditional practices were inherently biased. Similarly, consideration of merit pay programs as a form of "test" covered by the federal employee selection guidelines would create significant new demands for validation of pay-adjustment practices, especially as they are related to performance appraisal systems.

Taxation regulations, seemingly constantly under revision, control the financial impact, and therefore the desirability, of various compensation arrangements. Most notably affected is executive compensation, where the relatively more attractive pay arrangements continually shift as tax provisions change. Innovations are called for to take advantage of the most favorable prevailing situations.

International Practices

International compensation practices also vary frequently, with differences among countries widening as currencies gyrate. The weakness of the United States dollar has caused United States executive talent to become relatively inexpensive on the world market, as illustrated in Exhibit 10.1. Each salary

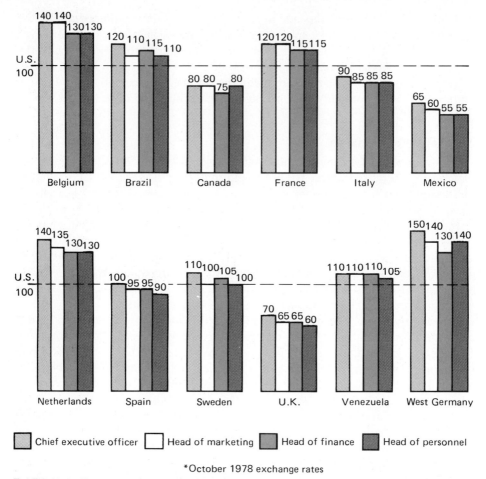

*October 1978 exchange rates

Exhibit 10-1   Base salary indices for selected countries.* (*Source:* Reprinted with permission from Towers, Perrin, Forster & Crosby, *Worldwide Total Remuneration,* New York, 1979.)

index in the table relates pay in a given country, expressed in United States dollars, to the "going rate" in the United States for the same job in typical medium-sized companies. The graph shows salaries among four managerial positions in thirteen countries. In seven of these nations, at least two of the four jobs command higher pay than in the United States; in six, all four surpass 100 percent.

The salary differences pose a problem for multinational companies. An executive in, say, West Germany, may well earn substantially more (in United States dollars) than his counterpart at headquarters back home. Pay differences may be complicated further by variations in employee benefit entitlements in different nations, including differences in perquisites provided (for example, paid car, special allowances).

Such problems are even more complicated for those truly international employees known as TCNs (third-country nationals). A TCN is a non–United States citizen transferred across national frontiers by a United States–based employer (or a similar pattern from another national viewpoint). For these employees, even accruing a pension can be a complex matter, because of different pension provisions and statutory employee benefits (Social Security) provided. Multinational corporations typically maintain a multiplicity of benefit programs tailored to the requirements and conditions of the various countries in which it does business.

At the same time there are pressures to consolidate the various compensation arrangements provided worldwide into a single, common, uniform system. Just as variations may be made for cost of living in different cities within one country, so could adjustments be made elsewhere as necessary. The desire to control costs associated with staffing, particularly expatriate and TCN staffing under varied economic conditions around the world, has impelled centralization of human resource policy formulation and compensation administration in some companies.

Employee Attitudes

Compensation practices are often more attuned to administrative needs than to desires or motivational needs of employees. Most organizations seem hesitant to abandon or change traditional approaches to wage and salary administration, or to disrupt established employee benefit programs. Consequently the results gained from the money spent fall short of the motivational potential of compensation (Bull, 1973; Lawler, 1976; Weeks, 1976).

Attention during the 1960s and 1970s to job enrichment, organization development, team building, and nonfinancial aspects of *motivation and reward systems* seemed to imply that pay was less important. But pay is important, and the total compensation program of a company has a potent influence on employee decisions to join, stay, and perform in a company. Pay seems to have a strong impact on employee satisfaction and consequently on absenteeism and turnover. Further, when pay is linked with performance, evidence suggests it also contributes to motivation to perform and grow (Dyer, Schwab, and Fossum, 1978; Lawler, 1976, 1977). Lyman Porter observed, "In the future, organizations can assume a much more vigorous and imaginative role than they have in the past in motivating employees. Organizations can provide work incentives that will make the work situation more rewarding and more satisfying for the individuals as well as helpful to organizational goal attainment. They can motivate employees by actively structuring rewarding environments" (Porter, 1973, p. 113).

Employees are pressing for more innovative compensation systems and policies. There is clear evidence that employees consider the magnitude of pay when joining an organization, the relative equity of compensation across jobs in a company, and differential rewards actually paid that are linked to performance. There is evidence that they know full well what the cost-of-living factor is and the extent to which their pay adjustments exceed this factor. And they question the need for management secrecy in compensation matters: Does management have something to hide? (Dyer, Schwab, and Fossum, 1978; Lawler, 1977b).

Innovations in compensation practices are responsive to changing employee desires. The all-salaried work force is one example. Increased disclosure of pay practices, and in some instances actual salary data, is another. New incentive and merit arrangements such as lump-sum payments are restoring incentive linkages to pay. Flexible benefits give employees a voice in the combination of insurance, vacation, savings, cash, or other benefit forms within defined cost parameters. In some instances, employees are asked to participate even in the design and administration of pay practices (Lawler, 1977a).

Greater flexibility in compensation plans also allows greater responsiveness to employee needs. Giving managers greater authority and latitude over compensation decisions affecting subordinates does much to increase the motivational impact of the plans without necessarily increasing their cost or sophistication. Getting managers to differentiate among better and poorer performers, for example, requires not only an adaptable system for merit pay, but a sense of responsibility and willingness to make merit judgments among the managers (Mruk and Giblin, 1977; Weeks, 1976).

There seems to be a relentless drive toward egalitarianism among many employee groups. Equity in compensation practices seems to be an important objective; merit pay practices that differentiate among employees are frowned upon. Special privileges (including perquisites) for executives are increasingly criticized by some factions. Even our federal income tax practices, once intended solely as a means for raising public funds, are now perceived by many as a means of leveling incomes as a social goal. Clearly, changing attitudes must be considered in compensation planning.

DETERMINING JOB WORTH

The traditional job evaluation program, used in 75 percent of all large companies, entails analysis of jobs, writing of job descriptions, evaluation of job information against a job evaluation plan of some sort, grouping and grading of these jobs into pay levels, development of a structure, and then pricing of this overall structure and the jobs slotted in it against comparable data from other companies.

In practice, job evaluation has served its purposes well. It is a formal process which provides a rational, justifiable explanation for the pay levels assigned each position in the company. At the same time, it has run into a number of difficulties along the way. It is a costly and time-consuming process. It arrays jobs within a structure based on subjectively defined management values of what the jobs are worth (not always wholly separate from the subjective evaluations of the job incumbents). And the use of job comparisions in the marketplace assumes that jobs are fairly evaluated elsewhere. Jobs may therefore be paid more or less than their "real worth" because of bias or error inherent in the process.

The sophistication and complexity of job evaluation have increased over the years, but the fundamental issue remains unresolved: How can we fairly and objectively determine the worth of a job?

Job Evaluation Techniques

Every self-respecting salary administration system has always involved the writing of job descriptions. They are the bedrock, the basis for subsequent building of the salary structure and for pricing of positions relative to one another and the market. The basic duties or activities, responsibilities (including assets and subordinates), and accountabilities (including measures or indicators of results by which successful performance is noted) are defined.

But the time and labor required to write and update job descriptions has widely been judged onerous for the sole purpose of salary administration. As a result, job descriptions have tended to be more structured (using questionnaires or checklists) and simpler. Rarely are job descriptions maintained for multiple purposes of human resource management, as discussed in Chapter 7.

Approaches for evaluating jobs have therefore also varied over the years. Ranking systems and classifications systems (such as used by the federal government) tend to be global and subjective, but provide a basis for perceptions of a structured approach that has objectives of fairness and equity. Point-factor and factor-comparison methods assign points to various perceived characteristic aspects of jobs and benefit from a degree of quantification. But they are frequently no less subjective in the manner of applied judgment (Husband, 1976; Patten, 1977).

Newer techniques have been proposed, and applied experimentally. These include Jaques' "time-span of discretion" approach which uses as a single evaluation factor the amount of time that an individual works on his or her own without supervision (Jaques, 1961). Alternate methods have focused on decision making (the Patterson technique), or problem solving (Charles, 1969), or other facets of jobs (as in Guttman scaling) (Belcher, 1974; Elizur, 1978; Patten, 1977).

All approaches require learning a system and then applying "good managerial judgment" in making it work. All require periodic updating and revision, usually including the job description itself; and this implies that job evaluations are inherently always out of date to some degree. There is often little concern for external labor market patterns in considering such jobs, along with a tendency to perpetuate past judgments of job worth. Evaluations always weigh the job, not the incumbent, and thus either ignore the influence of the incumbent on the job or inherently violate the rule by considering the person as well.

Participative job evaluation has been proposed as a way to obtain a consensus of employees regarding the relative importance of a number of jobs in an organization. Rankings by individual employees are combined into a composite rating. The value is thus that perceived by the members. The approach takes the mystique out of job evaluation but lacks any analytic basis (Carey, 1977; Younger, 1978).

Finally, computerized job evaluation has been attempted by several companies, including Control Data Corporation (Gomez-Mejia, Page, and Tornow, 1979; Pinto and Tornow, 1976). Here incumbents rate a job using a position description questionnaire comprising 300 items (for example, decision making, supervision). A committee identifies the key factors and their weights, benchmark jobs, and norms. Multiple regression analysis is used to aid these judgments and can be used to verify the subsequent results.

A similar multiple regression approach has been developed by TPF&C which bypasses the tedious steps of writing job descriptions. Instead, only a few variables are used to identify job worth, relative to market data available in a multiple company data bank (Risher, 1978). The variables were identified through research utilizing multiple regression analysis. Simply, the following factors were observed to be the primary ones accounting for job values:

Average number of employees the managers supervised
Average reporting level (number of levels from the CEO)
Company's annual return on equity, after-tax profits, and sales volume
Average job-family composition, that is, the average number of managers in the job functions reported

In a study of management compensation in twenty-two companies, a multiple correlation coefficient of .95 was found between average total compensation paid and the values estimated by the model (Foster and Kanin-Lovers, 1977). The multiple regression model provides a way to determine the worth of jobs, relative to prevailing market value, without having to go through detailed job analysis.

EEO Implications

Each of these job evaluation approaches is systematic and objective. The approach provides a logical, rational basis for deciding what jobs are worth to a company. Experience indicates, also, that managers in different companies, using a similar system, will assign quite similar scores to the same jobs.

But job evaluation also has a high degree of subjectivity: in the writing of job descriptions, in the slotting of jobs in grades, in the choice of factors to be used, in the choice of benchmark jobs to be compared externally, and in the very fact of basing job worth on prevailing pay rates. Such sources of subjectivity are seen as potential sources of discriminatory practices. The median pay of full-time women workers in the United States was $8,227 a year, only 60 percent of the $13,693 median pay of men (A. B. Smith, 1978). The disparity may be due to traditions and prejudices that have channeled women into lower-paying, lower-value occupations such as clerical and secretarial work, but it may also be partially due to bias.

The Civil Rights Act of 1964 prohibits "discrimination against any individual with respect to his compensation . . . because of such individual's sex." Also, the Equal Pay Act of 1963 requires that men and women performing equal work must receive equal pay. Specifically, the Act prohibits discrimination between employees on the basis of sex by paying less "for equal work on jobs the performance of which requires equal skill, effort, and responsibility, and which are performed under similar working conditions, except where such payment is made pursuant to (i) a seniority system; (ii) a merit system; (iii) a system which measures earnings by quantity, quality, or production; or (iv) a differential based on any other factor other than sex. . . ."

The job evaluation system and the manner in which it is applied may have the effect of causing or perpetuating employment discrimination. A bias-free system would focus solely on skill, responsibility, and effort, as demonstrated to be required by the actual duties of the job. Do existing job evaluation systems fall short of this standard? The Equal Employment Opportunity Commission seeks to attack systems now in use, charging they are inherently prejudiced against jobs traditionally held by women. Additionally, the commission seeks to stretch the equal-pay-for-equal-work concept to read "equal pay for work of equal value," which has the effect of broadening the scope of discrimination inquiries (Bates and Vail, 1978; Lee Smith, 1978; Thomsen, 1978).

In 1978 the EEOC commissioned the National Academy of Sciences to study whether it would be feasible and desirable to develop job evaluation methods that are "fair, objective, comprehensive, and bias-free." A preliminary report issued early in 1979 raised a number of issues. Regarding factors and factor weights, the report observed that while there is no systematic evidence that the way of measuring these factors is sex-biased, "sufficient grounds exist for suspecting a relationship to preclude uncritical acceptance of the appropriateness of the indicators . . . in currently used job evaluation plans. There are drawbacks to accepting existing wage rates as the criterion of worth and to find the factors (and weights) that best predict this existing wage hierarchy. The fact that job evaluation rests on subjective judgments and factor ratings on vague features of jobs (such as responsibility and experience) is the basic problem. Bias can enter the process at two points: in the preparation of descriptions and in the evaluations based on these descriptions" (Wendt, 1976, p. 447).

In the future it may very well be that increased disclosure of job evaluation practices to employees and greater participation by employees in the process itself will minimize risks of bias. Too often job evaluation decisions are made by committees of white male managers, implicitly indicating the potential for bias. Shedding more light on job evaluation practices may be the single most important step toward allaying fears of discrimination and building more objective, bias-free approaches (Carey, 1977; Lawler, 1977a; Patten, 1978).

Salary Compression

With inflation, starting rates for employees tend to rise. This is necessary in order to attract qualified candidates. And with recurring wage control guidelines imposed by the federal government, many employees are induced to change jobs in order to attain substantial salary increases.

So, with a lid on available increases for existing employees, but pressure for higher starting salaries dictated by the marketplace, the company finds itself subject to salary compression. First, companies push salaries up at the supervisory levels to assure adequate differentials over the wages of subordinates (who also earn overtime pay). And if they push the adjustments up the hierarchy, the whole structure is adjusted. The automobile companies have made cost-of-living adjustments to salaried positions following union-negotiated settlements on pay increases, but these companies also strive to emphasize merit pay as the primary way of correcting compression (Miller, 1978a).

If inflation is only partially taken into account by adjusting pay rates, the question arises, "Are we distorting our pay structure?" Where young engineers command initial salaries of $20,000 or more per year, what becomes of the relative worth of ten or twenty years of experience and supervisory responsibilities of project managers who earn $25,000 but started at salaries of $8,000 as young engineers fresh from college? To maintain a structure with fully adjusted differentials is costly and may end up overpaying some positions relative to individual expectations. To allow partial adjustments is cost-effective but results in distortions.

Geographic differences in pay rates, influenced by differences in costs of living, also have an effect on the salary structure of a company. There are wide differences in taxation, housing costs, commutation costs, and other personal costs which add pressures to salary levels. The need for adjustments in major cities with high costs of living (New York, Boston, San Francisco, etc.) is a problem in compensation planning. And the problem is of even greater significance internationally, where taxation, living standards, and economic conditions vary even more widely (Runzheimer, 1977). The Consumer Price Index jumped 38 percent in Brazil in 1978; 20 percent in Spain, 7.4 percent in the United States and the United Kingdom, 3.5 percent in Japan, and 2.5 percent in West Germany. The value of the United States dollar in these countries has also fluctuated greatly. Such factors cannot be ignored in determining rates of pay; the resulting pay levels for individual executives assigned overseas are rarely accepted as wholly equitable, even though the costs to the company are high.

Finally, compression problems will be aggravated by the fact there there is such a flood of talented young executives (or would-be executives) moving through organizations. The highly educated group of 30-to 40-year-old employees will compete aggressively for relatively few managerial and high-professional positions. As a result, pay rates may be eased: companies will have a pick among such individuals for sought-after positions of responsibility and status. That situation, if it materializes, will create compression in relation to a shortage of younger workers available to take the less desirable technical, trade, and semiskilled jobs. Prices will be bid up at these lower, but critical levels. Should a young millwright be paid as much as or more than an MBA office manager with five years of experience? Job worth reflects both the supply and demand situation and the inherent value placed on the work performed.

MERIT PAY

The principal means of adjusting salaries in American industry is the merit pay process. Once known and expected as an annual "service increase," the adjustment to individual salaries is now aimed at motivating and rewarding individual performance. Salary adjustments, whether merit-based or not, become a permanent part of an individual's salary. They are not withheld in the future as are incentive payments. Hence the manner of awarding salary increases is an important planning issue: How can a merit pay concept really work?

Obstacles to Pay for Performance

The merit pay concept requires making distinctions among those who perform and then making pay adjustments to recognize these distinctions. But adjustments must be within the limits of "ranges," which in turn reflect job worth and external labor market rates. Compression must also be taken into consideration. Hence the freedom of managers to reward performance is constrained by the other compensation variables considered important.

Employees are generally more concerned with perceived equity of pay as compared to others within the organization than they are with external comparability of pay or even the recognition of outstanding performance. There is therefore a tendency toward the norm, or a leveling of salaries toward the average. Managers are reluctant to give extraordinary increases to outstanding performers because of the lack of precision of performance evaluations and because increases become permanent, creating potential future equity problems.

Additionally, merit pay funds are narrowing as increased living costs are perceived as the dominant reason for the bulk of salary increases. Where merit pay funds represent 6 or 8 percent of payroll, it is difficult to persuade any employee that an increase is for outstanding performance. With inflation in double digits, any increase barely keeps the employee's compensation whole, let alone recognizing performance. And to give an outstanding increase to an outstanding performer (for example, 20 percent), the manager is forced to give other employees less, which is really an insult in the face of inflation.

Nevertheless, some companies are making big distinctions in the raises they give. Digital Equipment Corporation gives increases ranging from nothing to 30 percent. Westinghouse pays up to 19 percent and Xerox pays up to 13 percent. Timing is also a factor that can be varied. Some firms have moved to giving increases at intervals ranging from six to eighteen months, depending on performance.

The system used at Atlantic Richfield illustrates the dilemma. The range of raises possible is from 4 to 15 percent with an average increase of 10 percent (1977–1978). But managers are reluctant to give one employee substantially more than another. They are equally reluctant, however, to merely give across-the-board increases. Thus recognition of merit is infrequent, but meaningful. At Security Pacific National Bank, outstanding performers are given somewhat (but not greatly) larger increases, and more frequently. Additionally, Security believes that open communications about salaries and salary practices aids the motivational impact of merit raises.

Some companies, including Citicorp, have admitted that they merely try to keep average performers whole in the face of inflation. The focus of attention is on the "winners," who can receive up to four merit increases during a single year. "We believe in smaller, more frequent increases rather than large rewards with a long time in between," indicated a Citicorp executive (*Business Week,* 1977).

One technique used for years was the forced distribution of increases. Managers were required in some companies to give increases like grades, on a normal "bell" curve. Only 10 percent of the employees could receive a substantial raise, and an equal proportion would receive a small raise or none. Forcing raises into such categories had the effect of guaranteeing dissatisfaction, both among the employees who question the merit basis of awards and among the managers forced to make the distinctions within such rigid parameters.

Linking Raises with Performance

Organizations must have a defensible performance appraisal system or they will have problems with merit pay practices. In fact, under equal employment opportunity guidelines, pay practices are subject to validation where they have an adverse impact on women or minorities. Defending a performance appraisal process as objective and bias-free is difficult enough, as discussed in Chapter 9. Demonstrating a clear linkage of pay raises with performance, in the context of a complex salary administration system, is another challenge (Lawler, 1977b).

For decades, companies have attempted using various appraisal techniques as a basis for rewarding performance: trait or global ratings, critical incidents, rankings, management by objectives, and forced distribution arrangements. The central requirement of defining the standards or expectations of performance as criteria for subsequent evaluation has remained elusive in practice. Attempts to structure job-related criteria as behavioral scales were hailed as a potent tool for guiding objective managerial judgment, but the costs of developing and maintaining such job-specific instruments make it questionable as the solution to the broad problem. A question of cost-effectiveness is raised when given the knowledge that $40,000 must be spent to develop a way to allocate merit increases to 400 employees in a job category (Hamner, 1976; Meyer, 1975; Patten, 1977b).

Appraisal techniques become institutionalized quickly, and consequently are ineffective. They may be effective at spotting the few outstanding performers and the clearly marginal or inadequate performers, but they do not help managers differentiate the performance of the majority of employees in the middle.

Management by objectives and other goal-setting approaches have proved useful. But they tend to work best where performance is geared to specific, measurable, or identifiable results that can be targeted, such as projects completed, sales, or output. Goal setting is ineffective when goals are set too "easy," when goals do not compose the total job, when goal attainment is difficult to prove or measure, and when performance is the result of team efforts. A bank lending officer, for example, can set a number of meaningful goals (for example, new accounts, loans made), but other banking officers and staff have a hand in achieving these results. Everyone likes to take credit for a team result (Mobley, 1974; Weeks, 1976).

Alternative Merit Approaches

Clearly, the merit pay concept has value. The principal criticisms have to do with its implementation. Thus if adequate merit funds are made available, managers are trained to make fair appraisals and reward performance fairly, the merit portion of increases is identified for employees, and employees are open and trusting as participants in the whole performance-based process, merit compensation can work. It is likely that companies will continue to work toward this ideal, revising the tools and policies being used in the hope of developing an effective process.

Other alternatives, or variations, have been proposed. One is the lump-sum bonus. One difficulty of granting pay raises, however substantial, is that they are spread out over a whole year as increments in base pay. After deductions there is not a sizable amount seen by the employee; after several months, the new base is assumed normal. The incentive value of a raise would be greater if a portion of the increase were given all at once. One company, for example, gives the first six months' increase in cash in advance. Pitney Bowes gives a wholly cash payment of up to 15 percent which must be earned all over the next year.

Another alternative is to rely on performance contracts. A normal but substantial increase would be given to all employees to achieve the specific results and perform as promised during the year. Those who did not perform would receive less increase, if any. The argument is that the employees are paid to do a job and that superior performance is neither sought nor encouraged. Full performance is easier to judge and should be rewarded (Meyer, 1975).

Given inflation, less than full increases constitute a pay decrease. Any employees who are given smaller rates of increases, or increases "stretched out" over time, may feel they are being discriminated against if the specific performance problems are not openly discussed. Many declining performers or those on a plateau are over age 40, and are thus protected by the Age Discrimination in Employment Act. Where performance shortcomings are not clearly communicated, affected individuals may cry age discrimination and be upheld in courts. Age may not be a factor in the terms or conditions of employment, says the act, which protects employees through age 69. Thus giving increases to the younger employees "with potential" is not permitted; allowing older employees to 'ride out" their careers without rigorous performance or merit pay consideration is no longer an acceptable practice (See Chapter 9).

Performance contracts may be one way to minimize the risk of litigation, if not fully comply with the spirit of the Age Discrimination law. This calls for candid discussion with employees regarding their own goals, performance standards, and pay expectations.

The merit pay concept is viable. Even the federal government has adopted a program and a reorganization of the civil service system to encourage differentiation among performers. In an era of limited resources, it becomes quite important to have the best-quality people performing at their best and to control overall payroll costs at the same time. Merit pay is a necessity for achievement of this goal. The only real alternative is strengthened job analysis and performance evaluation; this requires management commitment and hard work. It also will require a willingness to give the outstanding increases called for by outstanding performance, and to give them in substantial sums as long as inflation continues to consume increases in salaries.

INCENTIVES

One of the simplest and best compensation systems is that used in the sports and entertainment worlds. Pay is directly and immediately linked to the performance of the individual. It is not likely that industry would or even could emphasize such direct rewards, because employees need a degree of income stability and because performance is not usually so easily identifiable. But the concept of an incentive payment directly tied to behavior has appeal.

The purpose of company incentive pay plans is to encourage employees to perform or produce at extraordinary levels. In most cases, incentives are supplements to base pay based on performance and are not permanent additions to compensation. They are contingent on current performance, whether individual or organizational.

Types of Incentives

We are all aware of piecework programs, whereby employees earn all or a portion of their pay based on measured output (sales, production, volume, etc.). Sales commissions are a form of incentive compensation, and usually a highly effective one because of the direct link to individual performance.

We are also aware of group incentive arrangements such as the Scanlon Plan, in which the financial gains resulting from employee suggestions and productivity are partially shared with the employees as a group. Profit-sharing plans are supposed to have a similar effect, but often lack the immediacy to yield an incentive impact on performance. They are therefore usually categorized as an employee benefit rather than as an incentive tool, which they were originally conceived to be in many situations.

The primary application of incentives of concern in compensation planning is at the management level. These are the most complex and controversial, due to taxation implications, the difficulty of measuring management performance, and the sheer size of awards. Also, the variety of management incentives is great, representing a continuing flow of innovations for compensating key managers in companies.

There are short-term incentives (usually cash payments), perquisites, and long-term incentives (for example, stock options, deferred cash awards, stock awards, performance shares). While a more attractive reward than cash has never been conceived, noncash elements of executive pay have grown in popularity. The combination of incentives best suited for a company depends on the preferences of the managers affected, and hence there is always a high degree of discretion applied in designing and modifying executive compensation programs (Crystal, 1978; Lewellen and Lanser, 1973).

Short-Term Incentives

Of the nation's top 100 companies, 96 use short-term awards. Most are paid on a current basis (not deferred payment); virtually all involve cash awards, although many involve a combination of cash and stock. Only one company pays short-term awards in stock only (Eastman Kodak gives stock on a deferred basis).

Cash awards are paid either immediately following the close of the year on which the award is based or in installments beginning in that year and continuing for a number of years thereafter. Deferred cash awards are not paid until termination or retirement. Similarly, stock awards may be paid immediately or deferred (TPF&C, 1979).

Such awards are designed to stimulate attainment of annual goals and objectives in a company. Normally, only those managers who are in positions to have a significant impact on annual results are allowed to participate, although there is a tendency for participation in such plans to expand somewhat over time. Sometimes companies have special one-shot "spot" bonus arrangements to reward outstanding performance of other managers not included in the formal bonus plan (Crystal, 1978).

The bonus fund is determined by a formula which is normally tied directly to the annual profitability of the business or return on investment. The allocation of individual awards is usually determined through measured achievement of specified goals or budgets. Naturally, quantitative, financially indexed formulas are more easily administered because there is less subjectivity (except as implied by accounting practices).

Performance-based bonus plans have been widely implemented and are believed to be effective. Careful planning helps assure that the program is perceived as equitable to the participants, cost-effective to the shareholders, and incentive for the results desired. Often such plans are overhauled periodically to correct problems that have emerged: eligibility is reviewed, evaluation and allocation procedures are changed, and the potential size of awards is realigned (Hrabak, 1978; McConkey, 1974; E. W. Miller, 1977).

Among the problems that arise in bonus programs, the most difficult relate to organization. Centralized bonus awards promote corporate synergy but reward the poorer-performing managers at the expense of the better performers; decentralized awards are difficult to administer evenhandedly. Where acquisitions are involved, it is difficult to compensate old and new employees on the same par because standards may differ. Where venture managers are included, high reward must accompany high risk, but it often does not do this in a large organization. There is also the problem of managers making their results look good one year at the expense of future years (for example, by cutting back on maintenance) or not having full control over the results they are judged by (this is the situation for regional insurance managers who do not have responsibility for claims). Such organizational issues are key to short-term incentives and are clearly human resource planning problems, as well (Crystal and Walker, 1973).

Long-Term Incentives

One aim of long-term incentive programs is to help balance the attention given short-term results, rewarded by short-term bonus programs. Another aim is to provide the executives with tax-favorable compensation arrangements usually involving capital appreciation paralleling company growth and success.

Stock options are the most common vehicle for long-term incentives. Qualified stock options, which allowed long-term capital gain treatment on stock appreciation, were once widely popular but were doomed by the 1976 Tax Reform Act. Nonqualified stock options remain popular and are widely supplemented with stock appreciation rights. Such rights allow the executive to receive a payment equal to the amount by which the fair market value of the stock, on the date the stock option otherwise would have been exercised, exceeds the option price.

Also common are cash or stock awards geared to indicators of company performance. Performance share awards are earned by meeting preestablished performance goals over a period of three to six years. The shares are converted to common stock or may be paid in cash equivalent. Goals are usually stated in earnings per share. There are other variations on the performance unit award concept.

The variety of exotic compensation arrangements will likely continue to grow as executives and compensation specialists seek ways to give incentives to long-term company performance through its key managers, consistent with an ever-changing legal and tax environment. Of the top 100 companies, 93 provided long-term incentive awards in 1978. In fact, 89 provided both short- and long-term incentive awards.

Perquisites

Personal benefits are frequently provided to executives as part of the total compensation package. These are deductible to the corporation but are taxable to the individual. The most frequently reported perquisites are:

Financial counseling and estate planning
Income tax preparation

Payment of private club fees and dues
Personal use of company cars
Personal use of empty seats on company aircraft
Annual medical examinations
Supplemental medical and life insurance coverage
Personal use of company property (for example, a New York apartment)

Perquisites are a human resource planning concern because they represent important status or recognition symbols. Determination of who receives which perquisites defines to a considerable extent the perceived management hierarchy, just as does participation in bonus and long-term incentive plans. They are also important because in the international environment, perquisites are even more popular, including augmented pensions, elegant offices, entertainment allowances, extra vacation, and housing assistance.

Perquisites are under scrutiny in the United States and elsewhere. In the United States, perquisites must be reported in corporate proxy statements, and it may well develop that these benefits will be subject to regulation. There is little, if any, tax advantage to the executive.

EMPLOYEE BENEFITS

Just as executives desire perquisites, all employees like to have supplemental forms of compensation. Retirement benefits, life and medical insurance, profit sharing, and other benefits have grown in popularity over the years and are now commonplace. The expenditures by employers for employee benefits have steadily expanded and now exceed 30 percent of payroll.

Benefits Provided

Exhibit 10-2 presents the component employee benefits provided by 748 companies surveyed by the Chamber of Commerce of the United States. The particular benefits provided and the costs paid by employers vary somewhat by industry. However, the trend in employee benefits is toward higher costs, and this does not even require significant liberalization of benefit programs. Inflation alone accounts for much of the rising dollar costs of benefits.

Inflation has a strong impact on the value of benefits to employees. Where there are fixed ceilings on benefits (for example, hospitalization, retirement income), the value of the benefits may diminish. For retirees covered by private pension plans, inflation is a severe problem, and companies must strive to upgrade the benefits with cost-of-living adjustments. There is the question whether companies should spend large amounts of funds for individuals who are no longer contributing to the organization's success. Benefits are widely seen as a social responsibility of an employer, and less as an investment ultimately yielding some performance incentive or payback.

With the growth of private pensions and related benefit programs, the government has expanded its role. Social Security is now a substantial form of

Exhibit 10-2   Employee Benefits, by Type of Payment, 1977

Type of benefit	Total, all companies
Total employee benefits as percentage of payroll	36.7%
1. Legally required payments (employer's share only)	8.5
a. Old-age, survivors, disability, and health insurance	5.4
b. Unemployment compensation	1.5
c. Workmen's compensation (including estimated cost of self-insured)	1.5
d. Railroad retirement tax, railroad unemployment and cash sickness insurance state sickness benefits insurance, etc.	0.1
2. Pension, insurance, and other agreed-upon payments (employer's share only)	12.7
a. Pension plan premiums and pension payments not covered by insurance-type plan (net)	5.9
b. Life insurance premiums, death benefits, hospital, surgical, medical, and major medical insurance premiums, etc. (net)	5.9
c. Salary continuation or long-term disability	0.2
d. Dental insurance premiums	0.2
e. Discounts on goods and services purchased from company by employees	0.1
f. Employee meals furnished by company	0.2
g. Miscellaneous payments (compensation payments in excess of legal requirements, separation or termination pay allowances, moving expenses, etc.)	0.2
3. Paid rest periods, lunch periods, wash-up time, travel time, clothes-change time, get-ready time, etc.	3.5
4. Payments for time not worked	9.8
a. Paid vacations and payments in lieu of vacation	5.0
b. Payments for holidays not worked	3.2
c. Paid sick leave	1.2
d. Payments for State or National Guard duty, jury, witness and voting pay allowances, payments for time lost due to death in family or other personal reasons, etc.	0.4
5. Other items	2.2
a. Profit-sharing payments	1.1
b. Contributions to employee thrift plans	0.4
c. Christmas or other special bonuses, service awards, suggestion awards, etc.	0.4
d. Employee education expenditures (tuition refunds, etc.)	0.1
e. Special wage payments ordered by courts, payments to union stewards, etc.	0.2
Total employee benefits as cents per payroll hour	226.4¢
Total employee benefits as dollars per year per employee	$4,692

Source: Chamber of Commerce of the United States of America, 1977.

employee benefit (paid for by both employees and employers). And now Social Security benefits have a cost-of-living adjustment factor built in, so that the costs of this public benefit are guaranteed to rise. The problem of inflation is well known to the government, and it may be that benefits will be provided to meet the problem. Advocates of expanded Social Security benefits, national health insurance, and other social programs believe that the government is in the best position to provide such protection. Others feel the government should regulate private benefit programs. Tax legislation and such acts as ERISA have this effect, and are responsive to public calls for governmental regulations.

Projections suggest that in the future employee benefits will become blended together so that employees will not see where one ends and another begins. Employees are concerned with security, and will be increasingly so as economic conditions constrain employment opportunities and dampen purchasing capabilities of incomes. Employees will thus demand more benefits, regardless of costs and regardless of their incentive effects for the employer (Gordon and LeBleu, 1970; Meyer and Fox, 1974).

Public awareness and litigation have forced employers to disregard pregnancy, childbirth, or related medical conditions in employment practices. Here is an example where the law did not require employers to consider pregnancy as a disability under employee benefit plans. Yet Congress responded to public interest by enacting a law requiring employers to provide the same medical benefits and disability leave as would otherwise be provided under their plans.

Employee benefits, once viewed by employers as a gratuity to employees, are now viewed by employees as an earned component of total compensation. As a result, it is difficult for employers to modify benefits or to control the costs. Integration of benefits and refinement of program provisions help control the costs and enhance the benefits provided, but the planning questions deal largely with the technical design and administration of programs (Allen, 1977).

Flexible Benefits

The most valuable strategy open to management is increased communication with employees regarding benefits and increased employee participation in the allocation of benefit expenditures. Too often employees are unaware of exactly what benefits they are being given, nor do they care—until they need to use them. Surveys of employee preferences for particular combinations of benefits are helpful in planning benefit programs. Direct communications to employees regarding their benefits is also high priority today.

However, the greatest potential involvement by employees may come from an innovative approach to benefits administration: flexible or cafeteria benefits. Long considered impractical under taxation regulations and administrative complexities, this approach is now being shown to be feasible. A new federal tax law (1978) paved the way for expansion of such plans, which allow employees to choose from an assortment of different fringe benefits.

Under such a program, a company provides minimum core requirements in such areas as health, life insurance, vacation, and retirement. Then it allocates a fixed amount of money, often expressed in terms of credits, to employees so they may opt for additional benefits suited to their needs. Some employees may wish expanded medical and dental coverage; others may prefer increased vacation time. A person near retirement may wish to enrich the pension coverage.

American Can Company adopted the program for all of its 9,000 salaried employees in the United States. TRW and other companies have applied the concept, and the outlook is that flexibility may be the most noteworthy change in the way benefit plans are handled (*Business Week,* 1978; Perham, 1978; Werther, 1976).

GUIDELINES FOR COMPENSATION

In conclusion, the planning of compensation programs is necessary because of changes occurring in the business environment. Inflation, changing employee attitudes, international complexities, and legal requirements all directly affect the needs for compensation arrangements and the way they are designed and administered.

It is important to be attuned to the taxation effects on pay arrangements. It is not only in the company's own interest, but also in the individual employee's interest. Particularly in the area of incentive arrangements, the tax implications are changing rapidly and are highly complex.

It is important to tailor compensation programs to company philosophies and objectives. The expenditures should be investments, to the extent possible, in future employee performance. Bonus plans and long-term incentive plans should give incentives to what the company wants to give incentives to. Sometimes such plans actually work against the company's goals. Programs should also be cost-effective. Fifty percent bonuses are no more effective than 5 percent bonuses if they are not geared to the desired motivational factors. Participation in programs and the administration of programs should be geared to the organization's management style and organization.

At the same time, it is important to tailor programs to the interests and needs of the employees themselves. As individual expectations change, so should the compensation programs of a company. Competitive practices such as cost-of-living adjustments, dental benefits, or early retirement provisions need to be weighed but not automatically adopted. Benefit surveys among employees and flexible benefit programs are ways of finding out what employees feel they want and need (Applebaum and Millard, 1976; Salter, 1973).

Finally, the nonfinancial aspects of compensation should be considered as part of the total program. Perquisites for executives, training opportunities, job design, status symbols such as titles and offices, and other factors can be controlled to enhance employee loyalty and motivation. As the standard of living of employees rises, these other factors become increasingly important.

The planning for the compensation programs and policies of a company should be conducted as part of overall human resource planning within the context of strategic planning. Compensation has a major impact on the management of the company, plus it usually constitutes a major area of expense. The effectiveness of compensation programs, further, is dependent not only on its own program design, but also upon the interfacing systems and programs: performance appraisal, job analysis, career management, management succession, and organization. It is not, as some assume, a highly specialized area of management. It does involve considerable technical complexity, but it is very much a part of the management process.

Part Four

Career Management

Chapter 11

Managing Careers: Policies and Systems

KEY POINTS

- Managing careers, as opposed to merely staffing jobs, is increasingly a necessity in organizations. Changing employee attitudes, tight labor markets, and increased pressures to control employee retention and productivity have stretched out the time frame for considering actions affecting employee careers.
- While there has developed a considerable body of theory and technique regarding recruitment, placement, selection, training, and other career management practices, significant human resource planning issues remain largely unresolved.
- In recruitment and selection, major concerns are determination of work-related criteria and application of valid prediction/decision processes. Equal employment opportunity guidelines impose broad demands on management for such objectivity.
- In internal placement (including transfer, promotion, and demotion practices), objectivity is also sought. But there the concern is about the degree of employee involvement in decisions, the degree of openness of the career systems.
- Career development activities, including training and development programs, should be planned in accordance with needs identified through human resource planning, or specific diagnostic studies. Individual career planning

plays a potentially central role in guiding company training and development activities.

• Privacy is also an increasingly important consideration in career management. The ethical aspects of management actions influencing individual careers, including the privacy of employee career-related information, are not well defined and need to be weighed by management in human resource planning.

The concept of the career is relatively new to management. Historically, individuals were employed to perform specific tasks and any adjustment of duties was determined on an ad hoc basis. At best, as illustrated in Whyte's *The Organization Man,* employees aspired to longevity of employment (achieved through conformity and loyalty of service) and advancement through the corporate hierarchy by achievement on each job assignment.

With increased employee mobility, particularly among managerial, professional, and technical talent, company needs have changed. It has become increasingly difficult to attract, retain, and develop the high-talent personnel needed to staff growing, dynamic organizations. Development of managers, particularly, requires substantial investment by a company in training and diverse job experiences. Such investment calls for a long-term *career* payout.

From the employee viewpoint as well, careers are more important than jobs. Preference is given the employers that hold out attractive *long-term* opportunities for advancement and growth; turnover is less in organizations that track and nurture career development of employees. Greater objectivity in management actions affecting careers is also sought, with associated calls for explanation by management of its career actions and policies. Objectivity and disclosure are impelled, too, by increasingly demanding equal employment opportunity and affirmative action program requirements, as well as other federal and state regulations governing employment, terminations, etc.

And the appropriate strategy for management is not clear-cut. For example, in attempting to develop managers in a company, management may move some individuals along rapidly for developmental purposes. Managers who have been around a while feel they are bypassed, while younger employees also are dissatisfied. "If the institution with which they're affiliated is active in moving employees around to broaden experience, they may claim their privacy is invaded, their right to manage their own lives is threatened, or they are victims of a manipulative system. If, on the other hand, companies follow a cream-will-rise-to-the-top policy, they say industry is uncaring and abandons its human responsibilities" (Kellogg, 1972).

Techniques for recruitment, selection, placement, training, and development, and terminations are abundant. Research and advanced practices in these areas have yielded increasingly sophisticated tools that may be used by management. However, what is of concern is a resolution of the human resource planning issues relating to the choice of such techniques. It seems sometimes that no matter how a problem is approached, there are negative consequences as well as benefits. How can a company satisfy needs for long-term, strategic planning for its human resources and an open and participative career systems approach for its professional employees, and at the same time satisfy its short-term staffing requirements?

This chapter examines the human resource planning issues relating to career management policies and practices. At the same time, a broad review is provided of the state of the art regarding the techniques used in managing careers.

CAREER MANAGEMENT: CONCEPT AND PROCESS

The management of careers is a process that involves managers, human resource staff, external parties, and the individuals themselves. It is a broadly inclusive process without a specific designation of sole responsibility. Further, it is a process that includes many activities, varying in intensity by organization and the needs of particular employee groups.

The obvious question arises, then, "What is career management and whose responsibility is it?" While there can be no clear-cut answer, the question may be addressed by considering the principal issues concerning career management being addressed in human resource planning. As the process which guides management of human resources, the planning process serves to integrate the various functions contributing to the management of careers and provides a useful focus on the alignment of implementation responsibility.

Career Management Issues

Every employee is influenced by management actions at each step of his or her career: The choice of an organization is influenced by recruiting programs; the choice of job assignment is influenced by internal placement and selection practices; the peformance on the job and opportunities for personal development are influenced by the design of the job and the performance standards or objectives established; retirement or termination is influenced by the benefits and other inducements provided. Accordingly, the company's efforts parallel individual career decision making (Walker, 1973).

At the same time, however, such career management practices in most companies are not closely integrated as a unified system. Nor are the policies and practices applied always carefully thought through as to their potential impact. Further, career management practices are subject to the same dynamic forces as other management functions, and thus must be responsive to changing legal, social, and economic conditions.

As shown in Exhibit 11-1, each of the aspects of career management discussed briefly in this chapter entails certain issues of human resource planning importance. To the extent that these issues may be addressed, company practices will be strengthened and the benefits to both the organization and the individuals will be increased. This exhibit serves as a summary of the principal points raised in the sections that follow.

Exhibit 11-1   Career Management Issues

Career management aspects	Human resource planning issues
Recruitment • Attracting a flow of applicants • Defining hiring requirements • Selection • Induction and orientation	Knowing/influencing the supply of talent available Use of agencies or search firms Defining staffing needs Defining bona fide job requirements Providing realistic information to recruits Validation of selection process Shortening of the learning curve Minimization of early turnover
Placement • Defining job requirements and career paths • Inventories and placement systems • Job posting and bidding • Selection procedures • Fast track programs • Management succession programs • Relocations	How to define professional and managerial job requirements and job families/career paths What to put into an inventory and how to put it to use How much employee involvement is desired/appropriate Validation of internal selection procedures and practices Managing accelerated career progress for high-potential employees Minimizing disruptive effects of relocations, controlling relocations
Training and development • Individual career planning • Training needs analysis • Program design and development • Research and evaluation	Equipping employees with tools to do their own effective career planning Managing raised expectations Defining training and development needs objectively Weighing alternative approaches for meeting these needs Evaluating the costs, benefits, and quality of programs
Decruitment and alternatives • Terminations • Retirements • Demotions and transfers	Policies and philosophy regarding reverse or lateral career steps Policies governing terminations and ensuring legal compliance Effecting flexible retirement policies and practices

Responsibility

Clearly, the responsibility for career planning rests with the employee. The employee has, in fact, the ultimate control over the critical variables: whether to join and stay in the organization, whether to seek or accept specific job assignments, and whether to strive for high performance and personal growth on the job. All management can do is try to provide systems and information that can influence these personal career decisions.

In a more structured view, the responsibility is shared. As shown in Exhibit 11-2, individual needs flow from broad personal objectives and career/life plans, and are translated into company-relevant career development plans. Company needs flow from broad business objectives and plans, as represented in human resource plans. The systems, often devised primarily to satisfy the company's management needs, also serve the individual's needs. The responsibilities for administration and maintenance of the systems and the effective use of these systems to serve management and individual needs are therefore mutually shared (Alfred, 1967).

This is a conceptual perspective, of course, and in many organizations there is little significant linkage with the individual side of the equation. In other instances, the absence of human resource plans and of particular human resource systems has fostered the emergence of strong informal systems. For example, identification of job opportunities within a "closed organization" is sometimes effected through very powerful informal communication lines based on personal contacts and gossip chains. "Who knows who" can work as a powerful force in internal search and placement. In the absence of formal, objective criteria for employee selection, informal criteria will be applied, representing personal perspectives of the important variables (which may sometimes include school ties, age, ethnicity, and other non-job-related factors).

Privacy as an Issue

By saying that the responsibility is shared, the issue arises whether the individuals risk the company meddling in strictly personal affairs, and, vice

Exhibit 11-2 Career management: a dual linkage.

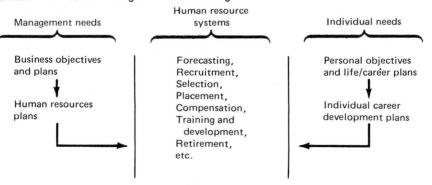

versa, the company risks individuals gaining too much involvement in strictly management matters.

As in the case of secrecy in compensation matters, the fundamental questions are "Who needs to know?" and "Who benefits from more open disclosure?" Many managers feel that career management systems are intended to serve management needs primarily, and therefore employee needs for information and involvement are minimal and largely unjustified (Tronsen, 1976).

Yet legislative action in some states, initiated by California action, has forced open company personnel files for disclosure of all information maintained which has had an effect or potential effect on employment conditions—and that includes every career management action. The legislation reflects employee attitudes that they have a stake in the company's systems and that loyalty, service, and performance have a quid pro quo: candid and objective management behavior (Linowes, 1978; Murg and Maledon, 1977).

On the flip side of the issue is the preservation of individual confidentiality: the right to privacy. Should career-related data be made available widely in an organization? Should questionable selection techniques such as the polygraph (lie detector) or psychological tests be permitted to invade private aspects of lives? Should information on performance or even reason for termination be shared with outsiders, as in employment reference checks? The trend is firmly toward the answer "no." Increased state and federal legislation is likely, in response to widespread concerns about the invasion of personal privacy. Companies have limited need for personal information, as evidenced in the pruning of employment application blanks. Access to personal information will be more strictly controlled in the future (Rahiya, 1979; Schein, 1976).

The effects on companies are compounded by public concern about data banks established by credit firms, the Social Security Administration, the Internal Revenue Service, and other agencies and organizations. The fears of lost privacy carry over to the employment context. Management must be prepared to allay such concerns and maintain a balanced posture regarding the need for data and the use of data in both the giving and the taking sides of the process (Ewing, 1978; Westin and Baker, 1973).

RECRUITMENT

The first logical element of career management is the recruitment of people who can be expected to fill an organization's staffing needs. Of course, it is one thing merely to satisfy quantitative requirements; it is another to recruit the desired talent for qualitative requirements of the organization. Also, recruitment is complicated by management's desire to recruit employees in such a manner that the new employees will have realistic expectation regarding their jobs and their career opportunities, so that turnover will be minimized.

The primary issues in the recruitment process of concern in human resource planning are the strategies for attracting sufficient flows of desirable applicants, defining and applying relevant recruitment requirements and job qualifications, applying valid selection methods, and smoothing the "joining up" process of new hires.

Attracting Qualified Applicants

Any human resource management textbook details the usual sources for recruitment, including schools and institutes, college and universities, the government and military, and the experienced labor market. The methods of identifying prospects are also described: advertising, referrals, employment agencies and search consultants, etc. (Glueck, 1974; Wernimont, 1974). The process appears rather direct and obvious.

Complications arise in recruitment, particularly for professional and technical talent, when these sources fail to yield an adequate flow of candidates considered to be qualified. Shortcomings are not necessarily due to the sources, or to the methods used for tapping them, but rather to changing labor market availability circumstances. There is sometimes a tendency to "kill the messenger who brings bad news" and hence question the utility of particular sources that seem to have dried up.

The recurring shortage of engineering candidates, for example, is no fault of the recruitment process, but is due, rather, to fluctuations in the supply of engineering graduates and experienced engineers (in turn related to demographics and past educational patterns) and to fluctuations in the overall demand for engineers. In the 1973–1975 period, aerospace and other employers cut back engineering employment markedly. Boeing alone reduced its employment from 100,000 to 30,000. This spurred many talented engineers to leave their profession and discouraged young people from specializing in engineering. Yet the pattern became a principal factor in the problem of recruiting engineers a few years later (1977–1980) when aerospace was a booming industry again.

Related to the problem of availability is the matter of retention. Churning of recruits increases recruiting demands and also impairs a company's recruiting effectiveness. Hence an important consideration in planning a company's recruitment process is the development of sources which demonstrate good retention after employment (low turnover) and avoidance of sources which demonstrate higher turnover. Too often companies get into a routine of recruitment (for example, at colleges and universities or through search firms) which sustains a recruitment problem.

The use of search firms or employment agencies is a concern also because of the expenses involved. While these external agencies provide a valuable service in identifying and screening prospective candidates, the costs are high. And the criteria used by the firms may not be wholly consistent with the employer's, if for no other reason than that the agencies' primary criterion of success is *placement,* not subsequent performance or retention. As a result, some corporations have placed stringent controls over the use of agencies as a recruitment source, including centralized direction over all managerial-level searches. Some large companies may be using several different agencies for different executive positions; efficiencies may be gained by coordinating these sourcing activities (Meyer, 1978).

In summary, the problems experienced in attracting the desired numbers and types of applicants require consideration of wider issues than merely the recruitment techniques applied. Knowledge of the labor market conditions, competitor requirements, and excessive recruitment demands imposed by poor retention of hires are essential factors that should be incorporated in human resource planning as a context for recruitment.

Defining Requirements

While job specifications have been the subject of much attention at blue-collar, clerical, and some technical levels, they have not been well defined at the managerial and professional levels (Schneider, 1976; Wernimont, 1974). On these higher-level, "fuzzy" positions which require more conceptual, analytic and managerial competencies than specific technical or physical competencies, specifications are more difficult to draw up.

As a result, typical specifications call for certain educational backgrounds ("college degree required, M.B.A preferred"), specified work experience ("three to five years in sales management"), and parameters governing maturity or youthfulness ("minimum ten years experience, management potential sought"). Related statements of responsibilities and duties do not provide a useful definition of the skills, abilities, and knowledge actually required for effective performance of the positions. In fact, recruitment of candidates at managerial and professional levels tends to be based on general parameters rather than on specific job-related criteria.

Recruitment would be strengthened by the use of specifications that are more precisely defined, based on analysis of the work actually expected to be performed on the positions. These would provide a more specific set of criteria for searching out prospective applicants and also for initial screening. Communication of such criteria to prospects aids self-screening, and for those who become viable candidates, they serve as a basis for more realistic expectations which, in turn, will help minimize subsequent turnover.

Selection

The recruitment process is a part of the selection process. The manner in which prospects are identified, solicited, and drawn into the employment process is clearly a procedure which influences the characteristics of resulting recruits. In turn, the procedure is also subject to employment discrimination. Specification of opportunities to prospects has the potential effect of encouraging or discouraging some applicants or prospects.

One way to minimize the risk of inadvertent exclusionary screening in the initial recruitment process is to sweep widely. Broad advertising and broad penetration of candidate sources may help ensure that all prospects are aware of the opportunities. A series of self-screening steps may then be applied, using realistic information about the nature and conditions of the work as a basis (Murray, 1979; Wanous, 1975, 1979).

At the same time, communications may be tailored to enhance the subsequent selection of individuals who are likely to be good performers or likely to stay on the job (retention). Items may be built into the recruitment information which stress the expectations in these regards, using specific characterizations of the demands of the job (Freund and Somers, 1979). As long as such factors are demonstrated to be job-related and not to have a disparate impact on protected classes, they may be useful in self-selection.

Federal EEO requirements and affirmative action plans usually call for detailed information on the flow of applicants and the disposition of their applications. Such requirements can be a burden to employers that are not equipped with adequate records systems and analytic procedures. Yet applicant flow information can be valuable for research aimed at improving the recruitment and selection process, as it includes the full net of initial prospects. Too often selection research has only the data on successful hires available. The requirements also provide impetus to the development of full-scale human resource information systems vital for human resource planning.

Orientation and Job Entry

A topic of some interest in recent years has been the possibility of aiding professional and managerial employees in the "joining-up process." If new employees can be aided in the process of learning "the ropes" of an organization, the learning curve is improved and productivity ultimately improved for an organization. Various suggestions have been made for the improvement of this initial period of learning and adjustment. Few companies, however, have devoted resources or attention to the issue (Frohman and Kotter, 1975; Kotter, 1972; E. H. Schein, 1968; Van Maanen, 1978; Wanous, 1979).

Wanous has identified four stages in the socialization process, as it is called by academicians. First, employees confront and accept the organizational realities (confirming or adjusting expectations). Achieving role clarity follows, with an induction into the tasks to be performed. Individuals then must learn how to behave, to present themselves, and to resolve interpersonal conflicts as they arise. Finally, signposts of progress are needed, including those of achievements, acceptance, satisfaction, feelings of influence, job involvement, and sustained work motivation (Wanous, 1979).

SELECTION AND ASSESSMENT

In the mid-1960s, a major oil company arrayed the criteria used by regional sales managers in the selection of sales representatives. Among the criteria were the following:

College graduate (four-year) required, with high grades preferred
Previous business experience preferred
Married preferred, ideally with children (but not if wife an only child)
References of previous employers checked thoroughly and found clear
Athlete preferred

Tall man preferred

Ex-clergy, schoolteacher, government employee, or union employee considered unsuitable

Such are the criteria used for generations in judging the abilities and potential of professional employment candidates. Not always stated explicitly, judgments have been largely subjective.

During the past two decades, selection and assessment practices have become more systematic and more objective. This is due in part to management's desire to validate the selection procedures so as to upgrade the overall quality of talent selected and promoted. But it is also due to the pressures induced by affirmative action plans and federal equal employment opportunity regulations.

Selection and Assessment Techniques

For more than half a century, industrial and organizational psychologists have been devising, studying, and applying techniques for employee selection. "The traditional role of the industrial-organizational psychologist is to provide information to be considered in making that decision. To this end he develops and tests hypotheses about applicant characteristics that can be used to predict employee performance and shows how to assess them. Presumably, where valid tests are available, the employment decision is itself made more valid—a presumption rarely checked since the decision process itself is rarely studied" (Guion, 1976, p. 177).

The selection process applied by managers is judgmental. But judgment may be enhanced by the use of selection tests. "Tests," in professional and legal usage, refers to all steps in the selection process: recruitment of prospective applicants, application forms, interviews, paper-and-pencil tests, work-sample tests, physical examinations, etc. Typically, the selection process represents a series of such tests, acting as successive hurdles. The systematic use of various types of tests, shown to be related to performance, is believed to be a valuable supplement to managerial judgment (Dunnette, 1966; Guion, 1976; Miner and Miner, 1978; Stone and Ruch, 1974).

The nature of the desired performance that selection procedures are used to predict may be defined by particular management objectives: quantity and quality of output, appraised performance, tenure, attendance, effectiveness in customer relations, etc. These performance factors serve as the criteria for the construction of the various selection tools (or tests) and are also used as the basis for evaluating the effectiveness of the selection procedures.

The employment interview is the most difficult "test" in the selection process to specify. Its measures are drawn from judgments and perceptions of interviewers. Nevertheless, interviews are probably the selection method most widely relied upon in the employment of managerial, professional, and technical employees. For interviews to be more job-related and defended as such, the judgments inherent in the interviewing procedure must be anchored to criteria determined to be important in the jobs themselves. Structured interviews are one way to establish a framework for decision making and to provide a basis for validation studies (Byham, 1978; Dipboye, 1976; Gatewood and Ledvinka, 1976; Jablin, 1975).

Other selection tools more readily yield measures that can be used as predictive data for validation studies. The popularity of psychological tests over the years has rested in large part with the suitability of resulting selection data for predictive validation studies. One noteworthy exception is the application of clinical psychological judgments, derived primarily through interviewing (but supplemented with testing and biographical data) in selection decisions. These judgments are accepted largely on faith by executives, and are used primarily at managerial-level selection decisions (Koten, 1978).

Another noteworthy selection tool, increasingly used but rarely justified as a valid selection technique, is the polygraph. Although not used widely at managerial and professional levels, the polygraph (lie detector) is used as a "test" influencing the selection decision. Reportedly, one-fifth of the nation's largest companies use the technique. A number of states have laws curtailing use of the polygraph; nineteen others have laws requiring licensing. Sixteen states prohibit the use for preemployment purposes. Without evidence of its reliability, Congress is likely to enact legislation restricting business use of such machines. The Privacy Act of 1974 recommended a prohibition and the EEOC has studied the machines, but no such legislation has yet been passed (Business Week, 1978; Quindlen, 1977).

Validity

The various selection tools are considered useful only if the results of their application are related to the desired performance criteria, preferably criteria shown to be required on specific jobs or types of jobs. Such selection procedures are considered job-related, or in the psychologist's term, *valid*.

Attention has largely focused on the validity of the more obvious selection tools, such as paper-and-pencil tests. These have included psychological tests (interests, aptitudes, intelligence, etc.) as well as tests that measure skills, abilities, and knowledge. Determining whether such tests are valid requires specification of the criteria considered important (and job-related) and relating the test results (predictors) statistically to these (Dunnette, 1966; Guion, 1976).

The need for convincing proof of the validity of selection procedures has been generated by laws and regulations, principally those governing equal employment opportunity. Generally, if an employer can demonstrate that the selection process is job-related and is necessary to the needs and objectives of the business, the legal requirements will be met. Of course, the demands for such evidence are greater where such selection processes have a disparate impact on protected employee classes. Valid selection procedures, then, are necessary for legal reasons, but also as management tools for selecting talent capable of satisfying the organization's bona fide needs.

There are various validation procedures that may be used. Two involve empirical validation: *predictive* and *concurrent*. Predictive validation studies involve comparison of selection data with subsequent measures of performance to determine whether the "high scorers" were also substantially higher achievers. Concurrent validation compares test scores of present employees, segmented in groups of high and low performers. Empirical validation is highly regarded (for example, in the courts), but it is slow, costly, and methodologically difficult.

Two other validation methods are also recognized, and are currently in vogue because they meet the tests of job relatedness without the empirical analysis problems. *Content* and *construct* validation both require careful observation and analysis of job requirements and activities. Content validation involves comparison of the content of the tests with the observed content of the actual jobs being staffed. Tests of knowledge in aerodynamics would be valid if the subject jobs in fact demanded the specific knowledge covered. Construct validation involves showing that tests measure "theoretical constructs" or qualities shown important in the jobs (through job analysis). For example, conceptual skills, sales management attributes, or planning might be applicable constructs (Gatewood and Schoenfeldt, 1977; Guion, 1978; Otteman and Chapman, 1977).

In reality, there seems to be a fourth type of validity which determines the legal acceptability of selection processes: *judicial* validity. Court rulings have been so varied, at times seemingly contradictory (even the various federal agencies concerned with establishing uniform selection guidelines have been in conflict), that selection procedures may be considered valid *when judges say so*.

The common requirement of all forms of validation, however, is that "there should be a review of job information to determine measures of work behaviors or performance that are relevant to the job in question. These measures or criteria are relevant to the extent that they represent critical or important job duties, work behaviors, or work outcomes . . ." (Uniform Guidelines on Employee Selection Principles, 1978).

Equal Employment Opportunity and Selection

Since the passage of the Civil Rights Act of 1964, United States employers have made a lot of progress toward eliminating discrimination in employment. But this effort has had the side effect of making the process of hiring, advancing, and terminating employees more complex, time-consuming, and frustrating.

The 1978 Uniform Guidelines on Employee Selection Procedures is a 14,000-word catalog of the do's and don'ts for hiring and promotion. The guidelines give employers the benefit of a single set of rules to follow (they were negotiated among the EEOC, the Civil Service Commission, the Labor Department, and the Justice Department), but they are not necessarily clear. Also, they are just that—guidelines. Court decisions on specific suits may negate particular aspects of the guidelines; the guidelines are merely administrative interpretations of the law (Miner and Miner, 1978; Schlei and Grossman, 1976; A. B. Smith, 1978).

The primary focus of governmental attention to employee selection is upon the "bottom line"—the final tally of a company's hiring of minorities and women. The bottom line is considered "good" if a company hires minorities at least at 80 percent of the rate at which it hires from the demographic group (usually white males) that provides most of its employees. If a company hires 20 percent of all white males that apply for a particular job category, for example, it must hire at least 16 percent of all blacks and 16 percent of all females that apply (H. J. Anderson, 1978). If a company has an affirmative action plan and meets this hiring test for all job categories, the federal government is likely to leave it alone.

However, if the minority hiring rates are below 80 percent or if there is other cause for scrutiny (for example, complaints or suits), the federal agencies may ask for proof that the selection procedures used are genuinely related to the jobs being staffed. Here the challenge of demonstrating validity of selection tests becomes a preoccupation and may well become a "cosmic search"—a never-ending quest for tests that do not discriminate but that screen in the candidates who are able to perform the jobs (A. B. Smith, 1978). The guidelines place this responsibility squarely on the shoulders of the employer.

Finally, the guidelines encourage the use of "alternative procedures" of selection when the objective is to increase the rate of selection of minorities up to the 80 percent level. Selection procedures may be modified in order to select candidates "from a pool of disadvantaged persons who have demonstrated their general competency." The pitfall is that once this is done, the employers may be subject to reverse discrimination charges. Whether this aspect of affirmative action hiring as permitted by the guidelines is *constitutional* is as yet unresolved (Loomis, 1979).

INTERNAL PLACEMENT

While much attention has been devoted to recruitment and selection, less attention has been given the ways employees are promoted or transferred among jobs in a company. Equal employment opportunity demands have focused on external hiring, but are shifting toward the internal career progression process. The advancement of protected employees into management positions is a particular concern of the federal agencies and of company affirmative action programs.

At the same time, companies are seeking more efficient, rational processes for matching individuals with the kinds of work they are best suited to perform. The aim of optimally utilizing the skills available among managerial and professional employees remains elusive, as there is considerable subjectivity in the definition of job requirements as well as individual capabilities and potential.

Inventories for Job Matching

Systems for inventorying talent and identifying job candidates are needed for several reasons, among them:

To provide targets for individuals in their personal development

To assure management of an adequate, prepared supply of talent to meet projected needs

To assure objectivity and fairness in considering alternative individuals as candidates for a vacancy or anticipated vacancy

To expand the career progression possibilities for individuals by providing a formal, organizationwide inventory

Increasingly, emphasis is being given the planned *career progression* of individuals from one job to another, based on career plans, career paths and job requirements, and individual appraisals.

Informal candidate search, backup identification by each manager, and sourcing by personnel staff are the most common approaches for internal placement. Informal search is the most subjective and limited in scope. Backup planning by each manager usually formalizes the traditional informal consideration of talent to fill vacancies from within the organizational unit. Identification of prospective candidates by personnel staff may turn up a wider range of persons, but remains subjective and informal.

The preferred approach for planning developmental moves from one job assignment to another (whether promotional or lateral) is data-based inventories and management succession planning incorporating targeted individual development plans. Employee request systems or job posting/bidding systems may be used as supplemental systems, but fall short of meeting the whole requirement because they involve virtually no advance planning or preparation of individuals for targeted positions (except to the extent individuals themselves initiate this through personal career planning).

With computer-based personnel information systems, companies are now able to record, store, and retrieve data on individual qualifications and target positions. A candidate inventory can be maintained manually if there are fewer than about 1,000 employees included; this is usually the case for the salaried exempt group of employees, which may constitute a separately defined labor pool in a company (Anthony, 1977; Ferguson, 1966; Thomsen, 1976).

An inventory should include basic work experience, education, pertinent skills data, and target positions. Target positions are those positions (or families of similar positions) agreed upon by the individual and his manager as logical and possible next job assignments. Timing of the target positions may be grouped into immediate (0 to 2 years) and long-range (assumes some further experience or training) categories. The inventory can then provide names of employees identified as possible candidates for designated positions or job families and individual biographical summaries.

In the 1960s a number of companies established inventories for job matching which were based largely on detailed tables of skills and experiences. The data were reported by the employees and usually included an estimated skill level, the number of years "used," and the years elapsed since the last use. They were most useful in the aerospace companies, which conceived the technique to

match definable, specific technical and engineering skills with technical requirements of short-term projects requiring staffing (R. A. Martin, 1967; Murphy,
1972).

Collection and maintenance of extensive skills data for such systems is
costly. To make the system cost-effective, the skills contained in the system
should be limited to those called for on the various jobs in the organization; job
requirements should be defined so that the inventory may be used to identify
qualified candidates. The skills inventory is of limited use in targeting individuals
for possible future jobs or in guiding individuals toward alternative career
opportunities. It tends to look backward toward an existing base of capability
rather than ahead toward career development (Seamans, 1978; Shelbar, 1979).

In a 1975 survey of 850 companies, only 8 percent reported having
automated skills inventories. However, of 99 companies with more than 10,000
employees, 28 had manual systems, 37 had some kind of automated system, and
22 were in the process of developing an automated system (Hay Associates,
1975). IBM was one of the first companies to create an automated skills
inventory. Their vast system was started in 1963 and finally abandoned in 1971,
to be replaced with a less ambitious, more development-oriented system
(Foltman, 1973).

Job Posting and Bidding

Job posting is a system which allows employees to apply for other positions in a
company. It calls for employees to respond to announcements (posting) of
positions and then be considered, just as if they were external job applicants.
Individual qualifications are considered, and the hiring manager goes through an
interviewing process, usually following an initial screening by the personnel staff
operating the posting procedure.

Bank of America, for example, publishes a Job Opportunities Bulletin each
week, resembling a help-wanted section of a newspaper. The bulletins list
various job openings and also publish brief descriptions of the work involved and
the qualifications required. Additionally, they give salaries, grades, and the
departments, subsidiaries, or branches offering the jobs. Copies are placed in
staff lounges, hallways, and other points frequented by employees. On the back
of the bulletin is an application form. Employees who are interested fill out
forms, mail them in to a coordinator, and are then considered.

Such systems have been adopted widely, primarily for nonmanagerial
salaried positions. The preponderance of usage is for office and clerical,
administrative, and technical positions. Job posting is pervasive in life insurance,
banking, and many governmental organizations. One reason for the popularity
is the implicit openness of the system, enabling all employees, including
protected employees, to nominate themselves for positions for which they
consider themselves qualified. Posting is a valuable tool incorporated in many
affirmative action programs (Connelly, 1975; Hughes, 1974; Miner and Miner,
1978).

A variation on the posting approach is the employee request system. In this system, each employee indicates the position or positions he or she is interested in and feels qualified for. Positions may be selected whether vacancies exist or not. A personnel staff member reviews the individual's record of training and experience and determines whether the individual is qualified for the position requested. If the answer is affirmative, the request goes into an inventory as a target position, and the individual is automatically considered as a candidate when a vacancy occurs. If the answer is negative, the individual is targeted for specific training or other experience to provide the needed skills and knowledge.

Such a system is operating in the Bell System of AT&T. The Upgrade and Transfer (U&T) System is widely regarded as a significant step beyond job posting because it involves a shared responsibility and commitment to future actions. Appraisal of qualifications leads to positive developmental actions and thereby enhances the availability of candidates in the future, as needs arise. It is a planning-oriented approach. Nearly 150 staff personnel are required to maintain the system in AT&T, responding to employee requests and tapping the system for candidates to fill positions (Shaeffer, 1972).

Relocations

Another aspect of the career management problem that is of concern is the increasing difficulty of moving employees from place to place. Promotions and transfers usually involve relocation, and with this comes disruption of personal lives and considerable company expense.

The corporate custom of shifting managers from one location to another to meet prevailing staffing needs or to provide developmental experience creates a lot of stress. Nearly one in five families moves each year, and many of these moves are induced by employers. In one major company it was noted that the middle management group had an average rate of relocation of once every four years. The rate was more frequent among the younger, "high-potential" individuals. With each move, spouses and children suffer uprooting and are forced to adapt to changes, making new friends and adjusting to often radically different life-styles and attitudes. The employee has responsibility for the move and for family adaptation as well as adaptation to a new working situation (Tiger, 1974).

There is little question but that achievement-oriented employees accept relocations as necessary (as reflected in the joke that IBM stands for "I've Been Moved"). But the personal toll can be great. As a result, there has been some questioning by individuals about the need to relocate and some resistance to company-requested transfers among individuals who feel that other values should be weighed. Changing attitudes toward work careers, and private life-styles have tempered employee readiness to relocate.

One factor is certainly the costs incurred in moves. Companies have been compelled to aid employees and their families substantially to minimize the adverse financial effects of relocations. In fact, many companies are outright generous in relocation benefits, as a way to make relocations attractive. In addition to the usual moving costs, some companies are providing interest-free loans to help buy homes, allowances to cover differences in old and new mortgage rates, money to cover unusual moving expenses (boats, piano tuning), home purchasing services (to remove the burden of selling a home), and sums designed to offset the increased income tax liability resulting from these assistance payments. With inflation and tight housing and mortgage circumstances, such liberal benefits are becoming common among large corporations (Robins, 1979).

The problems of relocation are compounded in international assignments. Cultural differences, economic differentials, and sheer distance from familiar settings make moves among countries particularly straining on families and costly to employers. As a rule of thumb, a domestic base salary is multiplied by 2.5 or 3 for overseas costs. But added problems of language, adaptation, loss of time, and family strains add to company costs. And the difficulties do not end when an assignment is completed; for then occurs the difficulty of reentry, particularly after a period of years when "home isn't the same anymore." For these reasons, companies are relying more on local staffing of international assignments and minimizing the use of expatriates for managerial assignments. Complex arrangements are made for those executives assigned overseas (Lanier, 1979).

TRAINING AND DEVELOPMENT

Training and development is a human resource planning concern for several reasons:

It is a central element of human resource management and the principal vehicle for developing skills and abilities of employees other than through job assignments.

It is a major area of expenditure, both in out-of-pocket costs and in the time devoted by staff and participants.

It is an important means of influencing management values, attitudes, and practices in human resource management; it is a communications medium controlled by the company.

It is becoming a subject of concern with regard to legal responsibility.

Underlying these concerns is the nagging question whether training and development efforts are effective and whether, through improved planning, they might be better directed to the needs of the organization and the employees.

Needs Analysis and Diagnosis

The principal problem in training and development is knowing what training and development is needed. Too often programs are planned as "programs" and announced to recruit participants. Human resource planning calls for the tailoring of programs to fit needs, not the marketing of programs within a company. Yet many training and development professionals seem concerned with refining programs and then "selling" them to prospective clients within the company.

Normally as part of the appraisal process, each employee establishes some specific needs for training or development. These designated needs relate to:

Specific needs for improving performance on the current job
Needs for preparing the individual for the next (target) job
Needs for allowing the individual to consider alternate career choices (for example, an individual who wishes to move into data processing)

These needs result, ideally, from discussions between the individuals and their managers. One technique calls for the individual to identify his or her own needs, followed by a formal appraisal process. A final appraisal document presents an agreed-upon development action plan (Mager, 1970).

An alternate approach is to conduct needs analysis surveys. Whether by interviews with managers or by use of a survey questionnaire, a needs analysis study can identify the perceived topics requiring attention in an organization. Such surveys may be open-ended, soliciting viewpoints and suggestions regarding training and development, or they may be structured, asking for ranking of topics as to relative needs. Surveys may address both general needs (for example, planning, control, writing ability, oral communications, decision making) or specific functional, product, or job-related needs (Berger, 1976; Rimler and DeGenaro, 1978).

A pitfall in surveying needs, however, is ending up polling *interest* in various topics, not bona fide needs. A survey may simply end up being an endorsement of various programs already offered, thus failing to yield definition of changing needs. To minimize the risk, the requirements of the jobs should be used as basic criteria for identifying skill and knowledge gaps (opportunities for improvement), hence training and development needs.

Program Planning and Development

Often, programs are readily identified to satisfy an organization's needs. That is, the solutions are found all too quickly, often without adequate consideration of the appropriate training approach, the content and structure, and whether the resources should be developed internally or purchased externally.

The full-blown training and development process includes specific steps devoted to these issues. A study conducted by the American Society for Training and Development identified fourteen roles of training and development practitioners, based on responses from 2,790 members. Of the roles, shown in Exhibit 11-3, the first seven deal with needs analysis (a and g) and program planning and development (b, c, d, e, f). These planning roles are extremely important in providing direction to the overall process and for ensuring that specific programs are attuned to real organizational needs (Pinto and Walker, 1978; White, 1979).

In 1978, American Telephone and Telegraph Company alone spent $700

Exhibit 11-3   Training and Development Practitioner Roles Identified through Factor Analysis

a   Needs analysis and diagnosis
  - Construct questionnaires and conduct interviews for needs analysis, evaluate feedback, etc.

b   Determination of appropriate training approach
  - Evaluate the alternatives of "ready-made" courses or materials, use of programmed instruction, videotape, computer-managed and other structured techniques versus a more process-oriented organization development/team-building approach.

c   Program design and development
  - Design program content and structure; apply learning theory; establish objectives; evaluate and select instructional methods.

d   Development of material resources (make)
  - Prepare scripts, slides, manuals, artwork, copy, programmed learning, and other instructional materials.

e   Management of internal resources (borrow)
  - Obtain and evaluate internal instructors/program resource persons, train others how to train, supervise their work.

f   Management of external resources (buy)
  - Hire, supervise, and evaluate external instructors/program resource persons; obtain and evaluate outside consultants and vendors.

g   Individual development planning and counseling
  - Counsel with individuals regarding career development needs and plans; arrange for and maintain records of participation in programs, administer tuition reimbursement, maintain training resource library, keep abreast of EEO.

h   Job/performance-related training
  - Assist managers and others in on-the-job training and development; analyze job skill and knowledge requirements, determine performance problems.

i   Classroom training
  - Conduct programs, operate audiovisual equipment, lecture, lead discussions, revise materials based on feedback, arrange program logistics.

j   Group and organization development
  - Apply techniques such as team building, intergroup meetings, behavior modeling, role playing, simulation, laboratory education, discussions, cases, issues.

k   Training research
  - Present and interpret statistics and data relating to training; communicate through reports, proposals, speeches and articles; design data collection.

l   Management of working relationships with managers and clients
  - Establish and maintain good relations with managers as clients; counsel with them; and explain recommendations for training and development.

Exhibit 11-3   Training and Development Practitioner Roles Identified through Factor Analysis *(continued)*

---

m   Management of the training and development function
   • Prepare budgets, organize staff, make formal presentations of plans, maintain information on costs, supervise the work of others, project future needs, etc.

n   Professional self-development
   • Attend seminars/conferences, and keep abreast of training and development concepts, theories, and techniques; keep abreast of activities in other organizations.

Source: Reprinted with permission from P. R. Pinto and J. W. Walker, "What Do Training and Development Professionals Really Do?" *Training and Development Journal,* vol. 32, no. 7, July 1978, p. 61.

million on educational programs for its employees, or more than three times the budget of the Massachusetts Institute of Technology. McGraw-Hill runs sixteen courses for its employees which are approved for college credit by the New York State Department of Education. Honeywell enrolled 3,500 of its employees in 183 courses ranging from solar heating and cooling to women in business.

Such companies spend considerable sums of time and money in training and development programs; they design courses, develop new educational techniques, and carefully monitor the results. The bulk of the programs are carefully designed to help employees contribute to desired business results.

It is important, first of all, to determine the training approach that is suited to the objectives (or needs) being served. Self-study or use of university courses may be the preferred approach over development of an internal program. Some topics require a high degree of structure; others call for more flexible, open discussion approaches.

It is important also to make a significant investment in the design and development of the program. Often neglected, this aspect of the process can make or break a program. Programs can be easily put together and run, but they may not adequately meet the needs they are to satisfy. At the same time, there is a risk of overdoing the program design, pouring time and money into refining programs when the marginal benefits are slim (for example, supervisory training, other standard programs).

Finally, it is important to weigh objectively the relative merits of making, borrowing, or buying the necessary program materials. In-house education offers the greatest potential control, some companies believe, but may not be the most economical in the long run, nor the most creative. External packages offer advantages, but sometimes fail to fit company needs precisely. Similarly, external seminars and courses may be less expensive, but only if they are of adequate quality and coverage to meet the needs. There is no pat solution to the problem of program planning and development, and it warrants specific attention as part of human resource planning (R. L. Craig, 1976; Goldstein, 1974; McGehee, 1977; Odiorne, 1970).

Legal Aspects of Training

Just as legal compliance is an important planning issue concerning employee selection and placement, it is also an issue concerning training and development. However, companies are less likely to take notice of these implications because they receive less publicity and are less often the subject of litigation. The requirements stem from Title VII of the Civil Rights Act and from affirmative action program guidelines.

The first aspect is access to training. If there is little dissemination of information about company training programs among women and minorities or if the decision to participate is based on subjective, nonreviewable factors (attitudes, interest, rated promotability, etc.), a legal complaint may be filed. Any parameters used to decide about participation are also subject to review (for example, job categories, levels, age or service levels, course prerequisites). Even on-the-job development activities may be subject to review when there are EEO charges (Pinto, 1978; Gordon, 1978).

A second concern is the use of training programs either as assessment tools or as a basis for preparing individuals for promotion or new job assignments. Under these circumstances, training and development programs are considered "tests," as previously discussed, and are subject to validation requirements. Even the designation of "management trainee" may be challenged as discriminatory if there is no bona fide training and development program that would warrant the distinction, any pay differences, or any advantage gained for career advancement.

Another issue is copyright. As heavy users of materials produced by others, trainers should be aware of the legal impact of copyright protection. The new copyright law protects even unpublished materials. The planning concern must be whether copyright holders' rights are being violated by the development of materials which draw heavily from protected works. It may be impractical to purchase or obtain permissions for everything used or adapted for use. But trainers are clearly vulnerable to legal charges, or at least ethical charges on this matter.

Other issues include the respect for confidentiality and privacy of participants, for ensuring the informed consent of participants in programs (even implied consent may be challenged if participants feel adversely affected or coerced, as in a team building program), and liability (for example, a divorce resulting from an in-depth career development seminar). These issues are of emerging significance and are not easily resolved. They should be taken into consideration in the planning and design of programs.

DECRUITMENT AND ALTERNATIVES

Every career must end sometime, and everyone must leave employment in an organization sometime. Death or disability take some, with little notice or choice. Other employees voluntarily retire, whether at the normal date or earlier; some are forced to retire at a mandatory age. Some resign to pursue other interests or continue careers elsewhere. Still others are terminated by the company, either on an individual case-by-case basis or as part of company programs to reduce staffing or to reorganize.

A certain amount of turnover is desirable throughout an organization, to ensure a flow of new talent and to open vacancies for internal career progression. However, the turnover is usually greater among the new employees and far lower among the longer-service employees. It is higher in many companies among the more talented employees and lower among those employees whose performance has declined, who have few external career options, and who see their careers as having reached a plateau.

It becomes a necessary human resource planning concern, then, to induce turnover, to remove blockages in career paths in an organization, and to foster career development and optimal performance.

Retirements

Retirement has traditionally been considered a reward for long and faithful service to a company. Normally at age 65, an employee steps out of his or her job and assumes a life of leisure. Or so goes the stereotype. In fact, retirement now has various meanings to employees, including the traditional view for some. Early retirement may very well mean a shift to a second career, or merely a reduced level of activity in one's career (as in a part-time post-retirement job). To some, it represents a forced termination—an unwanted separation from one's lifework—and is highly resented.

Although the perceptions of retirement have changed and varied, this way of leaving an organization remains a positive and financially supported one. Under most company benefit plans, a substantial retirement income benefit is accrued (given certain service requirements) by age 60, and certain life insurance and medical insurance benefits are continued into retirement. Employees may retire voluntarily prior to the age considered "normal" in the benefit plans (usually age 65), in some instances as early as age 50 (although with some reduction in benefits). Salaried employees typically retire from major companies at age 62 or earlier. The average age of employees retiring from Pacific Telephone Company, as one example, is actually 58 (due in part to generous benefits).

Few employees stay on in their work beyond age 65. Many retire because of failing health or chronic conditions impairing abilities (such as hearing, eyesight, or arthritis). Some who stay physically strong and in good health and continue to be capable performers. Others probably should retire but want to "hang on" to their work and have difficulty accepting the idea of retirement.

Under the Age Discrimination in Employment Act of 1967, as amended in 1978, these older employees are protected from forced retirement. Company-initiated retirement prior to age 70 is tantamount to termination, and must be justified on the basis of documented inadequate performance. It is necessary, then, to induce employees to retire early, but without inducing the capable, desired, high-level performers to leave as well. This highlights a dilemma for human resource planning and retirement policy (Rhine, 1978; Walker and Lazer, 1978).

From a management point of view, the different quality of performance must be reckoned with. As shown in Exhibit 11-4, superior performers should be induced to stay on and perform. Poorer performers should be induced to retire early. If they are not inclined to retire early, the company has the option of terminating them (for cause) or tolerating their presence indefinitely.

Inducing retirements involves providing retirement preparation assistance, whether formal programs or individual counseling. It involves ensuring that retirement benefits are adequate and attractive, and that the policies of the company make it "okay" to retire early, as a legitimate and socially respectable action. Retirement should be a positive career decision, made by individuals in the context of broader life and career planning. It is that context that may need to be built for employees who have not thought about their careers, let alone the retirement decision.

Terminations and Outplacement

The Age Discrimination in Employment Act protects employees between the ages of 40 and 70 from adverse actions where age is a factor. In some states (for example, California and Connecticut), there is no upper age limit at all. Hence management has a responsibility to determine the basis for terminations and to defend (or justify) such actions with proper documentation.

Inadequate performance is just about the only defensible basis for termination. A reduction in force for economic reasons is not justified when those adversely affected are primarily in the protected age group. Severance for cause requires evaluation of individual performance against established performance standards or objectives. And such evaluation must be over a period of time, to avoid the impression that the case was "trumped up." Further, evidence should be maintained of efforts to otherwise reassign the individual to a job better suited, or to develop the individual's capacities to satisfy the job demands. Affirmative action is not called for, but termination actions where age is a factor indicates intentional discrimination based on age.

Guidelines for handling terminations should be complete and clearly

Exhibit 11-4   A Mixed Bag of Performers

	Inclined to retire early or at normal age	Inclined to stay on working
Superior performers	Motivate them to stay and work through attractive career opportunities and superior compensation.	Utilize their talents well and keep them motivated and up to date in needed skills and knowledge.
Poorer performers	Induce them to retire through early retirement provisions.	Terminate or tolerate.

communicated to managers involved in such actions. Each individual case should be reviewed to ensure that the action is necessary and that all alternative courses have been exhausted. In the future, terminations of poor performers will likely affect younger employees, as companies face up to individual problem situations earlier in careers. This is particularly likely as organizations move to trim staffing levels and operate with fewer people for higher overall productivity.

To ease terminations of managers, some companies use the services of *outplacement*. Outplacement is the use by the company of a specialized, professional consulting firm that assists terminated employees in their search for new employment. Acknowledged users include Lever Brothers, Union Carbide, Singer, Citibank, Bankers Trust, and many other large corporations. At the company's expense, individuals terminated by a company are provided with counseling and day-to-day assistance in adjusting to the termination and obtaining a new position elsewhere (Gooding, 1979; Kase, 1976; Scherba, 1978).

Alternatives

What alternatives are there to retirement or termination? Companies have long suffered the delusion that every employee must steadily and surely rise through the organization. The up-or-out attitude is entrenched in our society's attitudes toward careers.

The reason Professor Lawrence Peter wrote about "the Peter Principle" was to point out the ludicrousness of such an attitude. We are not supposed to be merely amused by the poignancy of his humorous treatise. Rather, we are called upon to allow individuals to reach plateaus in jobs where they can perform ably *without* having to be promoted one further level, where they cannot perform ably. If advanced too far, they should be allowed to move back or laterally to other positions which are better suited to their abilities.

Downward career mobility is a realistic option. Plant managers may be delighted to become crew leaders in another plant. An engineering manager who is a good engineer but a poor manager may welcome a move back to "the bench" for the balance of his or her career. An assertive and bright person who was promoted too rapidly into management may welcome a less demanding job which offers career stability. But company policies and social attitudes militate against demotions.

Similarly, lateral moves (across locations, functions, or organizational lines, without pay increases) are rare in companies and scorned by employees. "They simply don't get anywhere." Nevertheless, they may help management balance out staffing, facilitate career mobility for others, and reduce the need for forced terminations.

Finally, career renewal is a realistic alternative. Being a poor performer or an older employee does not preclude the potential for learning. Given basic mental capacities, many "problem" employees can be stimulated to develop new skills, acquire new knowledge, and learn to perform new tasks. Many people are far more adaptable, even in old age, than given credit for. They respond to socially defined expectations: "I'm too old to learn a new job." Yet colleges and universities are being sustained by women and older persons returning to earn degrees that may make career renewal possible. Second and third careers are commonplace, involving dramatic shifts in occupational emphasis and shifts in life-styles. Given the chance, some employees will seize the opportunities to start anew.

A major factor to be dealt with is motivation. Perceptions of individuals, managers, and peers are difficult to change. An important human resource planning concern, then, is the changing of organizational cultures to permit more rigorous performance appraisals, terminations when justified, and compassionate counseling to guide capable individuals toward more fruitful career paths.

Chapter 12

Management Succession and Development Planning

KEY POINTS

• Management development is increasingly important, yet also increasingly difficult because of rapidly changing demands on managers in a growing, adapting organization.

• "Grooming your replacement" simply is no longer adequate as an organization's succession policy. It is good to check on the availability of backups periodically, but this process does not assure the availability of future management talent needed.

• Corporate policies and leadership are needed in large, diversified, and decentralized organizations to overcome potential obstacles to the development of managers: tendencies toward fragmentation, informality, subjectivity, short-term perspective, and manipulation.

• Criteria for assessing managerial candidates and for guiding succession and development planning should be based on an analysis of the requirements expected on specific management positions, given the organization's strategic plans.

• Assessment of managerial potential and ability remains a line management responsibility. Research-based techniques may be helpful, but the important guideline is to evaluate demonstrated performance (against the criteria), and not personality traits or other subjective factors.

• Developmental programs should be tailored to the needs identified, first at the organizational level, and then for the specific individuals covered. Too often programs have been developed and conducted without adequate needs analysis.

The need for management development is widely acknowledged. As companies grow and mature, the pressures for high-quality management talent are frequently found to be critical. Emphasis on decentralization, aggressive marketing and product innovation, technological advances, complex governmental relations, and increasing customer demands all are cited as factors impelling attention to the development of managerial talent. The more rapid rate of change experienced in many organizations today, compared with a generation ago, also creates strains on managerial abilities and adaptivity.

To meet this need, most companies have provided management education programs to its senior managers and high-potential management candidates. Participation in programs, whether external or company-sponsored, is supplemented by on-the-job appraisal and coaching, developmental job assignments and rotational programs, and special assessment or tracking processes. Such practices are not particularly new or innovative, and have been available for decades.

What is relatively new, and the critical aspect of concern in human resource planning, is a more systematic process of defining future management requirements, identifying candidates, and matching this demand and supply as a basis for planning developmental actions. The process of management succession and development *planning* is an important element in strategic business planning. Organization planning, as well, is inevitably intertwined with judgments about the availability and capability of available managerial talent.

It used to be considered that management succession planning was important because of a shortage of managerial talent. But in the decade of the 1980s, there will likely be a surplus of well-educated, ambitious young men and women competing for relatively few managerial positions. The task of selecting prospective managers and of arranging desired developmental job assignments will become more difficult as a result. The challenge will not be merely "replacing" managers, but developing the best possible managers to meet changing requirements imposed by organizational strategies (Murray, 1977; Neilson, 1978).

Yet the basic tasks of management development remain largely the same. "Developing managerial competence occurs on the job," reported a 1964 Conference Board study report. "Recognizing this, many firms mold the work experiences of their managers by paying attention to sound organization planning, coaching by superiors, and the use of special assignments as a means for getting tasks done. Performance appraisal is used to stimulate and encourage managers to develop further. Off-the-job methods are used to supplement the growth that occurs at work" (Wikstrom, 1964, p. 8). Planning and tracking individual progression through relevant developmental experiences remains the key to building management capabilities.

The development of managers is more complex today; it requires a greater degree of specific definition of needs (development for what?) and longer-range planning of assignments and organizational changes. Also, development plans are much more situational than in the past. It is difficult to develop managers "as general managers" within the constraints of a dynamic, performance-oriented organization. Hence the need for systematic succession and development planning.

This chapter reviews the basic techniques used by companies in meeting their needs in this area. Traditional replacement planning techniques are the starting point, followed by a discussion of succession planning, which is aimed at broadening the capabilities of managers and increasing organizational succession flexibility. The chapter also examines the state of the art and practice in the areas of defining managerial position requirements (development criteria), identifying and assessing management candidates, and planning management development programs.

THE SUCCESSION PLANNING PROCESS

What activities and systems should compose management succession planning depends on the type and size of an organization, the organizational climate and management style, and the nature of changing demands for managerial talent. However, there is wide agreement that the process of developing managers is a line management responsibility, a long-range process, and dependent on the initiative and effort of the individuals. Clearly, the bottom line results desired from the process are the anticipation of future managerial staffing requirements and the development of high-talent employees as managers to satisfy these needs (Desatnick, 1970; English and Marchione, 1977; Kellogg, 1977; Mahler, 1973; Ostrowski, 1968).

Elements

The following activities are considered necessary for the effective development of managerial talent in a large organization:

1 Consideration of the biographical data on prospective managerial candidates, including career progress, experience, relevant education, and self-reported interests and preferences regarding future career steps. Individual attitudes regarding relocation, dual-career situations, and specific career interests and aspirations are often highly relevant in realistic management succession planning.

2 Evaluation of individual performance against established goals or standards. Performance on challenging positions is regarded an important indicator of future performance and, broadly, development potential as managers. Feedback of appraisal results to individuals and constructive dialogue for future performance (and development) planning is also an important ingredient.

3 Determination of future management staffing requirements through forecasting, business planning, and organization planning. At senior management levels, this is often a highly subjective and sensitive activity, but nevertheless an important one in defining the "demand" for managerial talent.

4 Definition of qualitative requirements of future managerial positions. A "position profile" may define the activities to be performed on a management position as it is expected to change in the future and thereby provide criteria for assessment and development of prospective successors.

5 Review and discussion of these data by the responsible managers, whether at a local unit level, divisional or group level, or corporate management level. Discussion is vital to allow sifting, challenging, and interpreting of the data on needs and available talent.

6 Specification of actions for training or development of each succession candidate. Such actions may include a targeted job assignment, a temporary developmental assignment or project, a formal training program, or external activity.

7 Plans for progressively broader job experiences and evaluation of high-talent candidates under different supervising managers. "Fast-track" candidates are moved along these developmental paths at an accelerated pace.

8 Summaries of the availability of candidates and their readiness to step into the various management assignments considered in the succession planning. This typically involves the use of summary listings, tables (by position and by individual), or "snapshot" organization charts indicating successors identified.

9 Tentative plans for meeting any identified shortages or surpluses for managerial staffing (for example, through recruitment, special assignments to meet gaps, terminations).

The relationships among these activities composing the succession planning process are represented in Exhibit 12-1. The first four activities represent inputs to succession planning. The managerial review and discussion activity represent the heart of the process; staff may help provide the inputs, but the operating managers are in the best position to develop plans affecting future succession. The plans developed may be implemented by these managers, through staff action, or, as appropriate, by the individuals themselves. The process is an integrated set of activities, and therefore, the outputs of one cycle contribute to inputs for the next. Ideally, the process feeds upon itself, resulting in more and more comprehensive and objective plans and more fully developed individual candidates each year.

Implicit is a commitment to an investment in the development of employees as managers and the intentional movement of individuals among job assignments for developmental purposes, even where short-term business necessity may dictate that an individual should stay put to maintain critical performance. In turn, a high degree of support from senior management and involvement in important succession decisions are also assumed to be important requisites of succession planning.

INPUTS: Supply and demand information   OUTPUTS: Plans to meet requirements

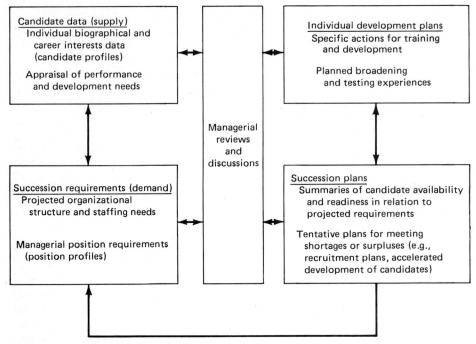

Exhibit 12-1   The management succession planning process.

Obstacles to Management Development

In many organizations, the development of employees as managers does not entirely fit this model. Customs and practices that have grown up over a period of years may impede systematic management succession planning. Resistance to changes in management practices tends to block efforts to move employees around and give them the broadening experiences needed.

One obstacle is *fragmentation*. Departments or divisions operate as largely autonomous business units, looking after their own talent supply and requirements. Career progress is typically vertical and locally arranged. Search for candidates typically begins at "home" and may end there with minimal external search. Decentralized organizations experience particular difficulty with fragmentation because it is considered legitimate under this management structure.

Informality is also a common obstacle. Managers often rely on their personal knowledge of candidates and act as sponsors or mentors for those considered to be promising. Formal systems for search, evaluation, or career development planning may be neglected as peripheral. The extent of counseling, developmental (challenging) job assignments, and other training and development depends considerably on the styles of the particular managers in charge and the pressures of day-to-day work loads.

Individual development potential and needs are often judged *subjectively* by criteria important to the managers, and not by criteria defined by objective job requirements. Criteria sometimes reflect the qualities and career experience of the managers themselves, or qualities the managers would like to see in their successors (Livingston, 1969). The value of an M.B.A. degree or particular experience may be weighed inordinately; sex, race, religion, political affiliation, age, or community activities may bias judgments about individuals and thus influence career plans. There are also subjective viewpoints that "managers really make their own jobs" and that "managers should be selected to complement others on the team." Subjectivity is a basic ingredient in managerial judgment, but it remains a potential obstacle to managerial development.

Many managers have a *short-term* planning perspective. First things come first. Profits and current operations may limit the time and resources managers devote to longer-range developmental activities. Where operations are lean and margins are thin, there may be little slack for developmental activities. Particularly, the best performers who are succession candidates may be the ones least easily spared, even for short courses, let alone long developmental reassignments. Also, with the crunch of business demands, there never seems to be enough time to implement the various individual development plans that were conscientiously formulated.

Sometimes, too, careers are *manipulated* for the convenience of the business, at some expense of individual development or utilization long-term. Individuals may be reassigned, relocated, or locked into an assignment, as if they were pieces in a chess game. Individual aspirations, goals, and preferences may not be considered fully; turnover of high-fliers may be rationalized by management. Aggressive individuals are sometimes quelled and rewards go to those who do an "adequate" job but who are not a "threat" to the system. "Most corporate practices," wrote Theodore Alfred in a *Harvard Business Review* article on this problem, "make it possible for managers to hoard good people to the detriment of the total organization. Most corporate practices make it possible for a manager to promote from within his own department or from among his own acquaintances without considering others in the organization. An individual's opportunity to be considered for other jobs in the organization depends far too much on his present supervisor's opinions and knowledge" (Alfred, 1967, p. 157).

Employees also may raise obstacles to effective succession planning and development. An increasing prevalence of dual careers, reluctance to relocate, and concern for "quality of work life" add to the factors constraining developmental activities. Many talented management candidates simply do not wish to pursue management careers if the price is severe dislocation of their personal lives.

Implementing Succession Planning

It is possible, indeed vital, to surmount these obstacles. The keys to implementation are twofold: introduction of policies and systems that will make succession planning part of the ongoing management process and introduction of attitude shifts in support of developmental objectives. Tools need to be practical and results-oriented, tailored to fit the style of management and characteristics of the organization. Usually organizations start with a rudimentary replacement planning or charting procedure and evolve toward a more comprehensive succession and development planning process. With this evolution, companies mold managerial attitudes to give recognition and support to management development and succession planning as an important responsibility. It is noteworthy that the companies often cited as doing a good job in this area (for example, GE, GM, IBM, ITT, and Exxon) are large corporations that have been working at it for a good many years (*Business Week,* 1975).

The following sections describe the techniques involved in replacement planning and in the broader approach to succession planning.

REPLACEMENT PLANNING

"A manager's first responsibility," some executives have held, "is to identify and prepare his replacement." This traditionalist viewpoint acknowledged the need to assure continuity in management and the primary placement of responsibility for managerial development on each key manager. Development, by this viewpoint, occurs primarily on the job and is planned and monitored by the immediate manager. If each manager has a qualified backup, the organization will not be caught with a short management team. Further, a manager who has a qualified replacement may be considered better suited for promotion because his or her former role will be ably filled.

Replacement planning has been formalized in many organizations by the use of charting techniques. Organizational charts provide a quick picture of the key management positions, their relationships, and the availability of replacement candidates. Smaller companies usually do not need formal procedures for keeping track of candidates and following their progress. Managers know each other's strengths and weaknesses, and senior managers are able to use this knowledge in deciding who is to be transferred, promoted, or given new responsibilities. Replacement charts allow these judgments about performance and capability to be documented, an aid in larger organizations when informal knowledge becomes less complete and less reliable or objective (Wikstrom, 1961).

The Replacement Planning Process

Replacement planning is typically implemented by requiring the division managers in an organization to prepare detailed organizational reviews. Human resource staff and other operating staff supply data concerning changing staffing requirements as well as incumbent managers and prospective candidates. The process is a systematic evaluation of the management organization and description of plans for the development of needed managers.

The process applied in a large industrial products company is illustrative. The process "looks at managers and helps identify the top 10 to 20 per cent who are above standard and who can be promoted at a faster-than-average rate; the middle 60 to 80 per cent who should be developed through normal position growth; and the bottom 10 to 20 per cent who are not qualified for present jobs and should be moved" (Tullis, 1969). At the heart of the program are annual review meetings for each division. Here division managers appear before top corporate management and review their organization and management development plans in relation to current annual operating plans. The plans described cover a minimum of the top three levels of the divisional organizations. The corporate group acts as a review and advisory committee.

In the meetings, the divisional reports begin with a review of the organization structure and pertinent progress toward established goals and objectives. Organizational changes, new or changed positions, and deleted positions are reviewed. Then appraisals of key managers are discussed on a position-by-position basis. Personal histories and appraisal forms on all the individuals are on hand and are referred to during the course of the presentation. Development plans for managers are described using the organization chart. In this particular company, a large fabric-covered board is used, with plaques for the positions at the top three levels of organization and for outstanding candidates below. The division manager can thus move the plaques around to show anticipated or optional moves being considered.

Each such plaque has the name, photograph, age, service record, and performance appraisal rating of the incumbent and the names of likely replacements. Appraisal ratings are color-coded to highlight strengths and weaknesses (that is, blue represents above standard, green is standard, yellow is questionable, and red is critically below standard).

Replacement planning has been applied in this general manner in dozens, if not hundreds, of corporations, many for several decades. The formats and procedures have evolved, benefiting from refinements developed through usage. Elaborate wall charts are not always used; in fact, simpler paper copies of replacement charts are widely preferred. Exhibit 12-2 presents an example of a forecast review chart used for many years in a major oil company.

Information systems technology has also been brought to bear on replacement planning in some companies. In one company, for example, a fully automated time-sharing system maintains a complete management inventory. Replacement charts are generated as required and are kept up to date by automatically adjusting for promotions, transfers, and terminations. Management inventory data are displayed on computer-generated organization charts. Additionally, anticipated staffing changes may be considered by printing out projected future organization charts.

Guidelines for Replacement Planning

Most systems call for the incumbent or higher-level managers to select the potential replacements. There is logic to having incumbent managers make the choices since they know the candidates and the job requirements best.

The candidate best suited for advancement on short notice is not necessarily

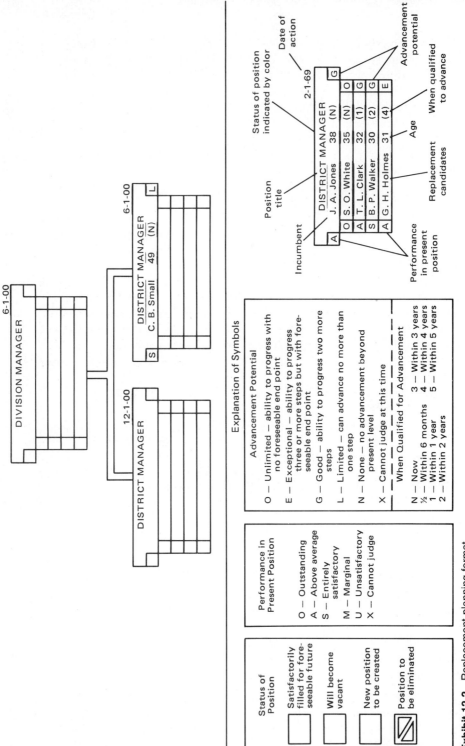

Exhibit 12-2 Replacement planning format.

the one you would want for the job, given additional time for development. Replacement planning focuses on the short-term "backup" availability, however, while providing for identification of additional potential succession candidates.

Some individuals may be considered qualified replacements for several managers, giving a false sense of depth in the organization. It is a good idea to limit the number of times the same individuals are named in replacement plans.

One way to minimize both the multiple counting of capable replacement candidates and the risk of focusing unduly on the short-term planning for replacements is to use a work-sheet format rather than the organization chart format. Exhibit 12-3 presents such a work sheet that calls for long-range replacements (one to five years) as well as immediate replacements. In the example (an actual company form), birth date is used to *estimate* retirement timing and thus anticipate vacancies and the availability of replacements.

Replacement processes often focus on the "high-potential" candidates in an organization. "Crown prince" and "super star" are terms that imply efforts are being directed exclusively toward an elite group of employees believed to have exceptional potential for management advancement. The idea is to concentrate attention on those few individuals who "have what it takes to move ahead rapidly." Such a selective approach is simpler, requires less attention and investment on the whole, and helps expose candidates to senior management. However, the approach assumes that individuals displaying strengths early in their careers will remain strong. Conversely, many capable managers may be overlooked through such a selective approach.

Of course, the benefits from replacement planning lie in the resulting developmental actions. The idea is to prepare individuals as candidates for key management positions by job experience, off-the-job training, and personal coaching. It may be that none of the replacement candidates identified is well suited to the job and thus external recruitment is called for. Replacement planning provides a picture of the strengths and weaknesses of an organization's management staffing. Only when the picture is used as a management action plan is the process worthwhile.

Limitations

In the absence of an alternative formalized program, replacement planning is a valuable tool for management development. However, it suffers from several inherent shortcomings:

- There is little consideration of the actual requirements of the positions, or of the prospective changes that will occur in the jobs when the incumbents are succeeded.
- Identification of backups or replacement candidates is largely subjective, based on personal knowledge of the nominating managers. There are rarely objective indicators of performance, individual capabilities, or past achievements. Even basic biographical data are often not considered.

Div., Subsidiary, or Corp. Ser. _____ Dept. _____ Plant _____

POSITION TITLE	INCUMBENT		POSITION CHANGES CONTEMPLATED		IMMEDIATE REPLACEMENTS FOR INCUMBENTS		LONG RANGE REPLACEMENTS (1–5 Years)	
	Name	Birth Date	Immed.	L.R.	Name	Birth Date	Name	Birth Date

IMPORTANT
This is to be used as a confidential personal work sheet only. Complete in longhand with no copies.
DO NOT TYPE.

Exhibit 12-3 Management manpower planning work sheet.

- A high-potential candidate may be qualified for more than one management position, but may be "boxed in" by the vertical, line-oriented replacement planning or, alternatively, may be named as a backup for several positions, giving a false impression of management depth.
- The planning is fragmented and vertically oriented; rarely is there provision for lateral or diagonal moves across organizational units.
- There is rarely any input from the individuals themselves regarding their own self-assessments and career interests.
- Most significantly, the charts rarely result in the moves planned or in other developmental activities; the process is often a static, annual paperwork exercise.

To achieve management development, the supportive planning process needs to be broader, longer-range, and more development-focused.

To overcome the shortcomings, companies have succeeded simple *replacement* charting with more intensive *succession* planning—with more intensive management review of job requirements and the dynamics of changing organizational needs, candidate information, appraisal information, and specific assignments and developmental decisions for the candidates.

Exhibit 12-4 represents the primary contrasts between replacement planning and succession planning. The former tends to concentrate on immediate

Exhibit 12-4   Contrasts between Replacement and Succession Planning

Variable	Replacement planning	Succession planning
Time frame	0–12 months	12–36 months
Readiness	Best candidate available	Candidate with best development potential
Commitment level	Designated preferred replacement candidate	Merely possibilities until vacancies occur
Focus of planning	Vertical lines of succession within units or functions	Development of a pool of talent; candidates with capability to take any of several assignments
Developmental action planning	Usually informal; merely a status report	Usually extensive; specific plans and goals set for each person
Flexibility	Limited by the structure of the plans, but in practice, decisions reflect a great deal of flexibility	Plans are conceived as flexible; intended to promote development and thinking about alternatives
Experience base applied	Each manager's best judgment based on personal observation and experience	Plans are the result of inputs and discussion from multiple managers
How candidates are evaluated	Observation of performance on the job over time; demonstrated competence; progress through the function	Multiple evaluations by different managers of the candidates on varied job assignments; testing and broadening early in careers

needs and a "snapshot" assessment of the availability of qualified backups for key management positions. Succession planning, by contrast, is more concerned with longer-range needs and the cultivation of a supply of qualified talent to satisfy these needs. The two are not in opposition; succession planning is a logical and natural evolution beyond the rather simplistic charting of *static* requirements and supply.

SUCCESSION PLANNING AS A BROADER PROCESS

Replacement planning is a useful process for gaining management attention to management staffing needs and to the prime candidates for management positions. Its limitations are overcome by the broadening of the process to consider longer-range management succession rather than immediate backup availability. The major payoff of succession planning—advance activities in developing or recruiting needed management talent—is thereby enhanced.

Succession planning involves a more flexible, longer-range, developmental view of future management staffing. It calls for more systematic planning for the broadening of individuals involving assignments under different managers in different functions or units. It confronts directly the major obstacles to succession planning noted earlier in this chapter. And because of its qualities, it is more difficult to implement. It is far easier for most managers to deal with a crisis, a problem that demands immediate, urgent resolution, rather than to anticipate possible future problems and to plan ahead to avoid them. It is also far easier to be a mentor and sponsor for your own selected successors than to work with other managers in a systematic process of evaluation, rotation, and career guidance for a pool of management candidates.

A Case Illustration

As identified earlier, the principal components of a succession planning process are individual data, data on requirements, management review and discussion of these data, and resulting development plans and summary succession plans. The following brief case, actually a composite of facts from several corporations, illustrates how the process can be applied.

AMERICO is a diversified manufacturer of industrial equipment with sales of $575 million. The Power Systems Division, the major operating unit, represents the original company, American Machinery Company, which dates to 1881. The company had pioneered in production of steam power units for agricultural and stationary industrial applications. In this century the company grew through acquisitions and through introduction of new products, now composing its Industrial Equipment Division. A major growth step occurred in 1956 when the company acquired a food-processing equipment company (the Beane Machine Corporation), which now represents AMERICO's third arm. Expansion has been dramatic during the past two decades as the company has applied its engineering capabilities to energy recovery systems, pollution control equipment, and commercial and industrial water conditioning systems, each now a part of the business.

Today, the company operates fifty-two manufacturing facilities, controlled through the six product-oriented divisions. The company's growth and diversity necessitated a divisional structure with a small centralized management group. Since 1976, when George Sherman became president, however, some stronger corporate direction and controls have developed. A budgeting and planning system was installed in 1977, and new corporate staff functions for marketing, international, and operations effectiveness have been established, following product lines. The diversity of products, the large number of locations, and the sheer size and rapid growth of the company necessitated a divisional structure with a centralized corporate management group. A comprehensive planning and budgeting system was installed; staff functions for marketing, international, and operations effectiveness have been established.

Management Development Characteristics/Needs

The character of management development in AMERICO stems from the traditions of American Machinery. The company has always rewarded loyalty and good service of its employees. Terminations were rare, and there was little pressure to move people around for the sake of moving them around. Executives and middle-level managers tended to be older and highly experienced individuals who had worked their way up the ladder of jobs in the company over twenty or thirty years. Candidates for management vacancies were identified largely by personal knowledge, as the stronger performers were well known to the senior executives.

With the strains of growth and acquisitions, this approach seemed to be breaking down. "People used to know everyone but we don't anymore." Further, the supply of capable managers to fill new positions and assume greater responsibilities was felt by top management to be very thin. As a rule, the company had promoted from within, but in the past few years, Sherman had felt the need to bring in new executives from other companies, notably the vice presidents for international and for marketing. "We need to keep abreast of the latest techniques available if we are to take full advantage of our opportunities for growth," he said.

A major obstacle to a corporatewide management development effort was the diversity of management styles in the company. The old Power Systems Division had not changed appreciably over the years, and continued to emphasize technical competencies and on-the-job performance as the keys to development. The Food Equipment Division had a somewhat different style, reflecting the strong marketing orientation of its general manager who had joined the company prior to the merger. This division has applied a management-by-objectives philosophy in all aspects of its activities, reflecting the division's underlying concern for aggressive marketing of its products. The other four divisions, formed as ventures or acquired as small companies, lack any formal management development systems. The general managers feel they do not have the time or resources to give this function attention, even though they agree it is highly desirable over the long term.

In a planning meeting involving all the general managers, Sherman expressed concern that the company needs to identify and develop its high-potential employees. "Somebody really has to take responsibility to know these people, follow them, make judgments on them, and promote them." During the next five-year period, he observed, the corporation would need 275 managers for new positions and as replacements for those retiring. "We talk a good game in management development," he said, "but we frankly lack the follow-through."

Actions Taken

Sherman appointed a management development committee, comprised of ten managers and chaired by the labor relations vice president. Over a period of six months the committee reviewed the company's practices, policies, and needs, with the assistance of external consultants.

Upon recommendation to top management, the following actions were taken:

Adoption of a corporate philosophy of management development, stressing the need to provide developmental assignments and defining the responsibilities of managers and staff.

Establishment of specific objectives and accountabilities for management development as part of the one- to three-year business planning and budgeting process.

Establishment of an annual management succession planning and review process ("management depth reviews") whereby each division presents an analysis of its management talent supply and planned development activities. Reviews examine both short-term replacement availability for key positions and longer-range development plans for succession candidates.

Development of guidelines for a uniform approach to performance appraisal and assessment of development needs for application by all divisions. Minimum standards were established by which divisions could tailor their own programs.

A search and placement procedure was adopted whereby candidates from other divisions would be considered along with local candidates for management vacancies; a corporatewide search would precede external hiring. A centralized inventory system used by Power Systems was expanded to serve all divisions.

A series of specialized management education programs was developed and conducted to meet specific needs identified by the committee. Also, a central file of information on specific external programs was established as a service to the divisions in selecting programs.

The corporate employee development staff was expanded to provide direction and support in the implementation of these activities. Positioned as an internal "consulting" unit, the professionals have responsibility for coordination and monitoring of the overall management development process.

None of the actions taken is particularly profound or unusual. But together they provide the foundation necessary for the divisions to build the structures of management development consistent with a "large company" viewpoint. Previously the division managers had neither the incentive nor the direction for such change. Above all, the actions created an awareness of the priority of management development among the many management responsibilities and placed it squarely in view of top management.

The strategy introduced new policies and ways of thinking without undermining the strong decentralization characterizing the company's management. Roles of corporate staff were retained as consultative, rather than as operational, for management development. Through the committee approach, the changes were accomplished by persuasion, and not by dictates from top management or imposition of corporate staff systems and procedures. The process resulted in greater acceptance of managerial mobility and other aspects of management development as an integral aspect of managing the business. The obstacles remain, but the succession planning process provides a mechanism for continually knocking them down to allow headway in developing managers with multiproduct experience.

GUIDELINES FOR SUCCESSION PLANNING

Such applications are not uncommon among large companies, and numerous articles have been written describing the lessons learned (W. E. Bright, 1976; Digman, 1978; Levinson, 1974; Pitts, 1977). The details of the procedures applied may vary among organizations, but the basic elements are constant.

Of these elements, adequate data on individual candidates and adequate definition of management requirements are certainly prerequisites to planning. These elements are discussed below. The determination of developmental actions for individuals is also key, and is discussed below. But the crucial element is the sensitive review and discussion element—the role of management, usually acting as panels or committees, in making and applying the rules of the "game."

Assigning Responsibilities for Succession Planning

As in replacement planning, each organizational division has the responsibility for its own employees (particularly in a decentralized management organization). But at some level, to be determined by management, there needs to be coordination among managers for management development activities. Too, personnel or human resource staff professionals may get into the act by facilitating assignments and the succession planning process.

Responsibilities of divisional management include the use of procedures for recruitment, selection, placement, appraisal, and development of their employees either as prescribed by the company or as are deemed appropriate to the business. Divisions are expected to analyze their own human resource needs, constraints, and opportunities as part of their business planning activity and to identify development actions planned for key individuals as part of these plans.

Succession planning is, therefore, a process that may be applied at any hierarchical unit level of an organization. Plants or office units within a division may conduct replacement planning, but the division (or other integrative organizational level) may act to pull these plans together and broaden them as succession plans. Reassignments of high-talent individuals may cut across unit lines, contradicting the more restrictive replacement plans formed (whether formally or informally) by particular unit managers.

A similar integration occurs at the corporate level of an organization; at least this is the way the process is believed to work best. Senior corporate management believes that there are needs of a corporate nature, warranting involvement of senior executives and senior divisional executives in the succession planning for "corporate positions." Typically, the chief executive officer and the president assume responsibility for management succession and development for division manager positions, positions reporting directly to division managers (at least in larger divisions), and other positions selected for organizational or business reasons.

Similarly, there is a pool of talent identified as "corporate property"; that is, individuals whose careers should be managed to serve the total corporation's needs, not merely those of a particular business unit. These individuals (often numbering 1 percent or more of salaried employees) are to be reviewed and discussed by a corporate-level, interdivisional committee. Their job assignments are to be planned at this level, and not by immediate unit management alone.

This notion of "corporate talent" and "corporate positions" is a troublesome one for companies that merely plan for replacements. Yet it is a crucial response to the obstacles blocking the development of broadly experienced managerial talent. Exhibit 12-5 illustrates the way these levels of responsibility overlap and shows the focus of responsibilities at each level.

Incidentally, it should be noted that the human resource staff role in the process is to serve as a resource to the divisions and to corporate management to

Exhibit 12-5   Responsibilities for management succession.

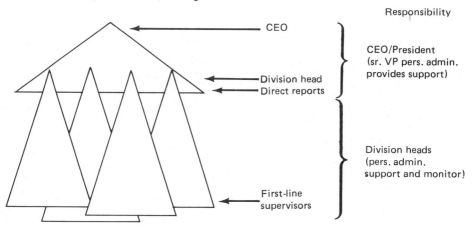

assist in their succession planning and in the implementation of developmental actions planned. The staff may develop, implement, and monitor the processes necessary for succession planning and may also be responsible for arranging interdivisional transfers in accordance with succession plans and corporate policies.

The Functions of the Review Committee

The management development or succession committee at the corporate level serves several functions:

1   To ensure that the divisions do their own succession planning adequately to meet business needs and priorities; to evaluate the results of these programs against corporate standards.

2   To establish and maintain a succession planning process for identifying, evaluating, and developing high-potential talent as a corporatewide management talent pool.

3   To directly track the development progress of selected individuals considered to be successors for key corporate positions. Such positions would require senior management approval for appointment.

At the corporate level, the focus of discussion is upon corporate needs and upon long-range strategies regarding organization and management succession. The focus in divisions is more operational, and is confined to the talent requirements within each. The committee develops policy guidelines for management development and standards for evaluating candidates. Requirements for developing candidates for key corporate positions would be clarified as a basis for facilitating developmental assignments across divisional and functional lines.

A major function of the committee, then, is to formulate corporate policies regarding management succession and developmental actions. How will the organization go about overcoming the obstacles? The following are issues that may be considered, subjected to research, and ultimately interpreted as guidelines or policies.

1   *Forecasting:* What are our likely management staffing needs?

What organizational changes do we anticipate?

Which management positions should be directly considered by the committee as "key corporate positions"?

To what extent should each organization attempt to define position requirements and qualifications sought in advance of vacancies?

What will be required of a successful manager in the future, given our current strategies?

2   *Inventory and appraisal:* Whom do we have as possible management candidates and how good are they?

Do we have adequate biographical and performance appraisal data on our managers and candidates?

How will we identify corporate management potential in a candidate? What do we mean by "high potential"?

Should candidates be appraised against specific position requirements or more general management criteria?

Should candidate wants and self-assessments be solicited and considered? Should individuals be told they are candidates?

3 *Development and training:* What can we do to enhance the capabilities of our candidates and better meet our changing needs?

What do we consider to be a good *developmental* assignment?

Should we have (or create) positions for developmental purposes?

Under what conditions should interdivisional assignments be made to help develop candidates? What incentives can be offered divisions giving up candidates?

Should we pay for potential as well as performance?

How shall we handle "peaked" managers who are adequate performers but who are blocking paths and expected to become less adequate performers in the future as company needs change?

Should we restrict participation by management candidates in external university and other long-term development programs?

Should we have guidelines regarding frequency of reassignments and relocations for management candidates (to avoid too rapid movement and disruptions)?

4 *Recruitment:* How will we find the talent we need and do not have?

What is our policy regarding external search versus promotion from within? When will we take a chance on a known internal candidate who is not fully qualified, over an external recruit (80 percent)?

Should we aggressively hire "young high potentials" on an explicit basis as promotable management candidates?

Should we pay higher initial salaries to attract desired talent even though we are contributing to internal salary compression?

The succession planning reviews conducted at the divisional and corporate levels remind managers to look at managerial development as a business need. A steel company noted that as a result, "Key openings should not be filled until consideration is given to all qualified people in the corporation, thus increasing the lateral movement of personnel and widening their experience. In the long run, this will provide more people in management who are capable of taking the broad view. To the individual the approach provides challenging opportunity; to top management, it insures an increasing number of personnel alternatives—the key to change and progress."

There is an added benefit of the committee approach: It is a developmental experience for those participating. One company president noted, "As we look ahead, I expect the work of the committee to stimulate and encourage even more thought and effort at all levels, not merely to develop managers but to build a management that is resourceful and adaptable to change." If changing management development practices is so tough, maybe that is a good place to try remolding management attitudes toward change, to help managers accept new ways of managing and to work as part of a larger corporate management team.

The focus of the committee reviews and discussions is upon change. What organizational changes, new management positions, or changes in management positions are planned? The scope of the process typically covers no more than 30 to 50 key executive positions and 100 to 150 candidates, although this may vary with the size of the organization. Are there any losses of key people (retirements, terminations) that have succession planning implications? What developmental assignments (transfers or promotions), including moves across lines, are proposed? Such changes may surface through review of divisional succession plans as well as through direct consideration of the corporate management structure. Succession planning is not a conceptual or academic exercise; it is an action-oriented management tool.

Also in the discussions, the committee may consider broad human resource needs indicated in the plans. Supply-demand imbalances, apparent common training needs, significant needs for external recruitment, patterns in performance appraisal results, affirmative action plan shortfalls, and other common patterns may indicate need for corporate actions or policies. The committee, then, may help be a sensor and guide for corporatewide human resource policies and practices. Management succession is a logical focus, but the broader process is relevant.

In performing its functions, the committee needs to consider (1) the changing managerial requirements, particularly qualitative requirements of management positions, (2) the capabilities and development needs of individual candidates, and (3) development activities that may be adopted for these individuals. Tools and guidelines in these three areas are discussed below.

DEFINING MANAGERIAL REQUIREMENTS

The first concern in management succession planning must be defining exactly what the organization is looking for—what it expects of its future managers. To be able to assess the development potential and needs of individuals as management candidates and to plan for developmental activities, a definition of requirements is needed. "Development for what?" is the first important question. The advantage of broader succession planning over simple replacement planning is its flexibility in allowing a changing definition of the criteria for considering candidates: The requirements of the position may change, and thus the obvious immediate candidate may not be best suited as a longer-term successor, or may not be properly prepared for the changing requirements.

Historically, companies have sought to promote those individuals who displayed certain qualities thought to be predictive of strong managerial capability. Often these qualities represented personality traits beyond the reach of development programs ("Either you have it or you don't"). Education, job experience, specialization, and other factors such as height and age played roles as factors considered indicative of managerial competence.

Increasingly, however, the criteria used to judge managerial potential and individual development needs are *behavioral* requirements, based on analysis of actual activities performed on the positions. The qualitative requirements of managerial positions stem from the actual demands of the position and not from subjective criteria that relate more to the people judging and being judged than to the work being performed.

Attribute-Based Requirements

A study conducted by Syntex Corporation aimed at identifying criteria for assessing and developing managerial candidates through its corporate "career development center." The study resulted in agreement among managers on a series of traits seen as important for effective management. Seven of these were seen as highly critical:

Accepts full responsibility for the performance of the work unit.
Works toward building teamwork among subordinates.
Establishes high standards of performance for the work unit.
Sees that the work unit achieves established goals, evaluates subordinates' performance against the goals, and provides frequent feedback.
Possesses good technical skills specific to his or her functional area.
Inspires subordinates to establish a success pattern for the work unit, which provides a sense of pride and achievement among them.
Is honest with subordinates and superiors and communicates things as they really are.

These traits were believed applicable in selecting middle managers, regardless of functional specialization.

Similar studies have provided the basis for assessing candidates in other corporate management development and assessment programs. Various criteria and related characteristics have been used to assess prospective managers (Norton, Gustafson, and Foster, 1977). Such factors as self-confidence, creativity, energy, risk taking, drive, intellectual ability, and persuasiveness are often cited as criteria used in judging management potential (Finkle, 1976).

One author has argued that "a strong constitution and a juggler's finesse are assets in what may well be the major challenge of a rising manager's career" (Uyterhoeven, 1972). Such criteria are derived from the perceptions of the appraisers—managers in charge. From their perspectives and experience, the need for strong personal attributes is the basis for replacement or succession planning judgments. Indeed, there has long been the view that certain traits or personality attributes do exist which differentiate managerial talent from nonmanagerial talent. The only difficulty perceived is isolating the critical factors to be used as reliable criteria.

Requirements for advancement among management positions also sometimes reflect general views of logical career progression. An individual may be expected to move first from making an individual contribution (as a technical performer) to managing functional work or project work. Then the progression moves to managing a business or profit center to managing several businesses and ultimately to leading an institution (Mahler, 1973). It is easier to move an individual geographically, across product or even functional specializations, than it is to progress among these managerial stages.

However, considering personal attributes and generalized perceptions of managerial demands is not adequate as a basis for succession planning. As discussed in Chapter 7, job requirements need to be based on *actual activities performed,* not on subjective managerial perceptions of requirements. Chapter 13 explains how job requirements may be empirically defined and jobs classified for career planning and succession planning purposes.

Management Activities and Roles

Most large organizations have managerial position descriptions. These descriptions cover the basic function of the position (purpose, mission, objective), duties and responsibilities, accountabilities, reporting relationships, and limits of authority. As discussed in Chapter 10, these are written for organizational purposes and as a basis for determining job worth for compensation purposes (Wortman, 1975).

But such descriptions are rarely helpful in defining what the positions actually call for in managerial behavior. Managerial activities are not easily pinned down and specified, as they are subject to changing business demands and to the abilities and interests of the incumbents. Position descriptions tend to look at jobs as static and finite when, in practice, they are dynamic.

What is needed is direct observation of the positions, so as to obtain a more complete perspective of the activities performed. Job descriptions may be supplemented with a description of managerial activities performed, or entirely separate "profiles" of positions may describe activities and the implied requirements for succession and development (Campbell et al., 1970; Mintzberg, 1973; Stewart, 1967).

There have been numerous research studies examining managerial behaviors with the aim of defining generic roles and requirements of managers. Leonard Sayles (1964) found three major activities composing the managerial function: leadership, monitoring, and interacting with other managers. Hemphill (1959, 1960) identified ten clusters of activities by using a 575-item activity checklist questionnaire. Mintzberg (1973) also identified ten clusters of activities, or "roles," but through direct observation of five chief executive officers of middle- to large-sized organizations. Mintzberg's work, incidentally, is probably the most complete in terms of thoughtfully considering the process and problems of studying managerial work.

Many of these studies summarize the activities performed by managers as a set of roles. A role is simply an organized set of behaviors belonging to a position (Mintzberg, 1973)—a grouping of activities performed as part of a job. Personal attributes may influence *how* a role is performed, but not *that* it is performed. Hence requirements for managerial positions must start with the work to be

Exhibit 12-6   Position profile.

```
POSITION PROFILE


POSITION TITLE: _____


INCUMBENT NAME: _____


UNIT: _____  LOCATION: _____


REVIEWED_____  DATE: _____


REPORTS TO (POSITION TITLE): _____
```

Please read instructions.

```
POSITION SUMMARY: Summarize the overall function and purpose of this position.
```

performed first, and then consider attributes as they influence performance on the job (Hodgson, Levinson, and Zaleznik, 1965; H. Levinson, 1968).

It is important to examine the specific activities performed on each managerial position, and not to generalize about roles or activities. The reason so many different role models of management behavior have been developed is that each study examined different managerial positions. There are commonalities, to be sure, but for succession planning, a job-specific description is essential. Position descriptions may be quite adequate, if they are sufficiently detailed and realistic. A position profile may be used to summarize the pertinent information for succession planning purposes, with the information

Exhibit 12-6 Position profile (*continued*)

II. POSITION ELEMENTS

Describe briefly below the principal work activities (duties and responsibilities) of the position. Indicate where applicable the titles of positions with which contact is required.	Time %	Order of Importance
1. TASK SPECIALIST:	_____	_____
2. TEAM MEMBER:	_____	_____
3. LEADER:	_____	_____
4. COMPANY REPRESENTATIVE:	_____	_____
5. ADMINISTRATOR:	_____	_____
6. CHANGEMAKER (ENTREPRENEUR):	_____	_____

Exhibit 12-6 Position profile (*continued*)

III. QUALIFICATIONS

Indicate the skills, knowledge that you believe necessary for performance of the position activities:

a. Specialized or technical knowledge or skills required?

b. Education or experience normally required?

c. Oral or written communication skills?

d. Skills of persuasion (e.g., negotiating contracts, selling, purchasing)?

e. Coordination and team skills?

f. Ability to direct the work of others without direct authority?

g. Direct supervisory and management skills?

h. Knowledge of company policies, procedures, organization, and people?

i Knowledge of industry practices?

j. Basic administrative skills?

k. Creative abilities or ability to introduce change?

gathered through interviews, questionnaires, or observation. Exhibit 12-6 presents a basic format used in a number of companies for this purpose. (The roles indicated are offered as broad headings to aid in the classification of activities and are often adapted to fit the situation). Alternatively, some organizations use activity checklist questionnaires to help define managerial positions, although rarely for management succession planning purposes alone (see Chapter 7).

IV. JOB DIFFICULTY

---

a. Give examples of the type and extent of problem solving required in carrying out the position responsibilities.

b. Describe decisions and recommendations required to be made and indicate the degree to which others share this responsibility.

V. ACCOUNTABILITY

---

a. Indicate the extent to which this position influences the production of net operating profits or company growth through the development, sale, manufacture, or distribution of a product or the conversion of sales to gross profits and net profits to usable funds.

b. Describe the responsibility of the position for the custody or control of corporate assets and inventory items.

c. List the number and type of personnel for whom you are responsible.

	Number	Type of Personnel
1. Employees reporting directly to you		
2. Employees reporting to your direct subordinates		
3. Employees for whom you have functional responsibility		
4. Total		

VI. ORGANIZATION CHART

Attach organization chart.

Exhibit 12-6 Position profile (*continued*)

Position requirements serve as the criteria for judging individual candidate qualifications and identifying gaps that may be bridged through individual development actions. Accordingly, the requirements must reflect reality, both in terms of the activities performed on specific positions and in terms of the changes anticipated in the work relating to business plans and future organizational changes. Position requirements are typically defined to reflect current requirements as an initial step, and then modified in successive cycles of succession planning to take into account the changes anticipated. As discussed in Chapter 4, succession planning needs to be attuned to the broad changes taking place in an organization, reflecting business strategies (Neilsen, 1978).

ASSESSING MANAGERIAL TALENT

A Columbia University conference in 1955, attended by senior executives of a number of large corporations, suggested the following policies for executive development: (1) Graduation from college is a first criterion for selection of a potential executive. (2) Participation in formal programs designed to train future executives is imperative. (3) General training at various levels and phases of management is questionable, and special training for specific assignments is all that is necessary. (4) On-the-job training from the immediate superior is desirable, particularly if the superior is considered a "good boss." (5) Evaluative feedback with the trainee is desirable to further development, but without letting the individual know he or she is identified. (6) The key to training and development is to be found in work assignments. "The key to an effective career development program . . . is to place promising young men in a sequence of jobs, each one of which adds concretely to their knowledge and experience" (Columbia University, 1955).

Such a view of management succession has the effect of precluding many individuals from being considered as possible management candidates or from obtaining the experience necessary to become qualified candidates. Excluded would be non–college graduates, individuals who were not selected for formal training early in their careers, individuals without "good bosses," individuals who did not receive performance appraisals, and any who were not on jobs that allowed them to develop and display their abilities. The ideal candidates "fit the pattern."

In twenty-five years, we have added pressures for objective decision making in assessing individuals as managerial candidates. Minorities and women challenge the objectivity of managerial judgements, believing that the criteria informally applied may have discriminatory effects. Further, many companies are increasingly concerned that high-talent employees be identified early and accurately, so that training and development efforts may be wisely invested.

A multitude of research studies has attempted to apply prediction techniques to identify those individuals who ultimately become effective managers. Such techniques as assessment centers have been developed and widely used for this purpose, and other innovative assessment techniques have been used. But the results have not been encouraging: Correlations between assessment measures and managerial effectiveness have rarely exceeded .40 (Campbell et al., 1970). The assessment of managerial talent is a complex process involving both personal attributes and the variables of differing management situations and requirements.

Accordingly, the assessment task continues to require improvement of managerial judgment, subjective though it may be. But judgments regarding the abilities, performance, and development needs of subordinates need not be prejudiced. It can be made highly objective by defining the pertinent individual qualifications that should be considered in relation to the activity-based requirements of specific positions.

Assessment Techniques

The most commonly applied techniques in assessing the development needs and potential of management candidates involve consideration of individual qualities and circumstances. A specific position is considered as a prospective assignment for an individual; the readiness of the individual for this assignment is considered; the net gap is defined. If the gap is not too great, developmental actions may be taken to better qualify the candidate (Campbell et al., 1970).

Individualized assessment strategies are typically flexibly applied, and differ from candidate to candidate. Standardized biographical data sheets, performance appraisal inputs, and summary evaluation forms may be used, but the judgments take into account individual candidate variations and position requirements. The assessors are typically immediate superiors, although assessments may also be made by higher-level managers, personnel staff specialists, or external assessors such as managerial psychologists. Documentation may be gathered and maintained in support of an assessment of potential and development needs, but the judgments are inherently *clinical*.

How is objectivity encouraged in such assessment techniques? Some companies obtain assessments of individuals from more than one appraiser (for example, functional managers, clients, peers, subordinates). Training and the monitoring of assessment practices and results are, of course, basic ways of strengthening the assessment processes. Validity studies, however, are rare because such clinical assessments involve a multiplicity of assessment variables and the criteria used are not always spelled out—and if they are, they are likely tailored to specific position requirements and organizational circumstances.

Such an assessment procedure is troublesome to those who prefer a more controlled, systematic, or even *mechanical* approach. Some assessment specialists, particularly measurement psychologists, seek predictive tests and interviewing formats that may sort high-talent managerial candidates from those less likely to succeed (Ghiselli, 1971; Guion, 1965). Mechanical approaches require the application of rules or statistical equations developed by prior research, and these rules may be applied to the information collected by anyone (with training). This type of procedure minimizes the need for managerial judgment. Unfortunately for advocates of such systems, the assessment task has been complicated in most instances by so much variation in the facts to be considered that judgment (clinical judgment) seems to be inevitably required.

A promising assessment approach which combines both mechanical and clinical aspects is the *assessment center*. Each participant in an assessment center is observed and evaluated by a team of managers (or other assessors). Candidates go through a series of exercises and in-depth interviews, as well as team projects, as a basis for demonstrating their managerial ability and potential. The team's evaluations result in a written assessment report on each candidate, including numerical ratings on a series of behavioral dimensions. The report is then used as an input to succession planning and management development decisions (Bray, 1976; Finkle, 1976; Finkle and Jones, 1970; Moses and Byham, 1977; Rics, 1978). Assessment centers are used in nearly 2,000 companies, including IBM, General Electric, J. C. Penney, Sears, General Motors, and Standard Oil of Ohio. Perhaps the most noteworthy application has been at American Telephone and Telegraph, where a program has been underway since 1957. This "management progress study" has tracked the career progress of 274 employees who went through an assessment center program (Bray, Campbell, and Grant, 1974; Campbell, 1970). An aim of this program and some others is to determine predictive patterns that may suggest a valid mechanical process for assessing managerial potential. Bray has called the assessment center "the most elaborate, most expensive assessment method known to man" (Bray, 1976, p.6). At the same time, assessment centers remain highly clinical and subjective, merely pooling the judgments of a team of observers (Bucalo, 1974; Howard, 1974).

The benefits of a team approach are gained by the involvement of a management succession committee in the process of reviewing the performance, career progress, and capabilities of identified high-talent employees. At the unit or corporate level, a committee of managers provides a valuable forum for discussion of specific individual qualities and developmental needs. At a minimum, it provides a useful cross-check with the immediate managers' assessments. In some instances, the committee may act much like an assessment center and get deeply involved in judging the capabilities and development needs of individual succession candidates.

Above all, assessments are most useful when applied to the planning of individual development activities, as well as the broader decision making regarding long-term succession prospects. They are most valuable, then, when they are keyed to specific managerial position requirements, rather than broad managerial qualities. While progress is being made in developing valid, systematic assessment approaches, the heart of the matter today rests on managerial judgment. The responsibility remains inescapable.

MANAGEMENT DEVELOPMENT ACTIVITIES

Succession planning helps companies ensure that the best available managers are considered to fill key managerial positions. But more than that, it directs training and development activities toward the pressing needs of high-talent managers. No longer need executive development programs be created and individuals "sent." Rather, training and development activities may be specifically tailored to individual needs, based on assessments and succession plans.

Management development occurs on the job, of course, but also in programs off the job, both in-company and externally. Challenging job responsibilities—combined with coaching and performance appraisal and feedback—is a potent development tool and the focus of basic management development. Rotational assignments, special assignments, task force assignments, and transfers across functional or unit lines all pose additional developmental experiences. Off-the-job training and development resources include courses, seminars, conferences, professional meetings and conferences, interaction with consultants and other external representatives, management meetings, and committee assignments, as well as career planning and "assessment center" programs.

Many books have been written espousing management development activities, and this chapter need not recount the options or their merits (R. L. Craig, 1976; House, 1967; Mahler and Wrightnour, 1973; Wikstrom, 1964). What the books do not always point out is the approach for defining individual development needs and matching alternative programs or resources to these needs.

Individual Development Planning

It is vital that each individual management candidate have a personal development plan tailored to his or her target job's requirements. The development plan should represent the program for bridging the gaps in individual capabilities relative to targeted position requirements. Such a development plan may be highly informal and may represent merely a small section in the performance appraisal form (see Chapter 9). In other instances it may be more formal and detailed (Luthans, 1978; Rodgers, 1971).

Prudential Insurance Company has used a more detailed "Prudential development grid" for some of its high-talent employees. This grid calls for identification of development needs in five areas: administrative skills, communications, situational skills (for example, managing time, problem solving), technical job knowledge, and experience. For each need identified, developmental activities are outlined as ways to gain new skills, knowledge, or experience. These activities are then listed down the left side of a grid; timing for completion is indicated for each by months which are listed on the horizontal side of the grid. The activities are thus scheduled for completion during the year ahead.

To guide the selection of suitable programs, many companies provide descriptions of available programs. Exhibit 12-7 presents a description of a university executive development program, highlighting the subject areas covered by the program. Such descriptions are prepared by the training and

MANAGEMENT DEVELOPMENT
MASSACHUSETTS INSTITUTE
OF TECHNOLOGY

PROGRAM FOR SENIOR EXECUTIVES
Cambridge, Massachusetts

PROGRAM ADMISSIONS/REQUIREMENTS

Level: Vice President — Senior Vice President
Age: 40 — 50
Education: College degree preferred but not required

OVERVIEW

This program, geared to senior officers on a corporate policy-making level, focuses on improving
the function of managerial problem solving and decision making. Through the use of qualitative
and quantitative tools, participants analyze planning, control, information systems, and financial
accounting as they relate to management decisions. Studies of external environmental factors and
human resources development are also significant components of the program.

SCHEDULE/DURATION/FEE

8 weeks   2/11–4/13/79 $9,625
              9/17–11/16/78   9/16–11/16/79

PROGRAM PROFILE BY SUBJECT AREA

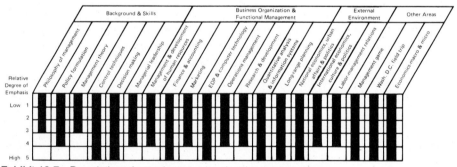

Exhibit 12-7   Description of sample executive development program.

development staff, although some published descriptions are available. Also,
some companies provide guidelines for the types of courses or programs that
are suited to different stages of managerial careers. Exhibit 12-8 presents an example of such a "curriculum matrix" developed in a large paper
company.

American corporations now spend an estimated $1 billion or more each
year sending hundreds of thousands of managers to developmental programs.

The benefits in increased skills and knowledge are great, but there are questions whether the expenditures are entirely worthwhile, whether programs are adequate to meet the needs, and even whether more money ought to be spent, but in different ways. Management education is a growing business, and it is easy for growing companies to get caught up in the excitement of "growing" managers. In fact, few companies have any clear idea how much money is actually dedicated to management development activities, let alone how much time is spent by managers in these activities (*Business Week,* 1977; T. Murray, 1979).

Guidelines for individual participation in programs usually call for a review of the particular programs in terms of their content, the level and representative mix of participation, and the reputation of the sponsoring organization. Checking word-of-mouth opinions of particular programs is helpful, as is a debriefing of executives after they have attended them. It is impractical to attempt to measure a participant's learning, but directed questioning may be able to sense more than merely attitudes. Participation in developmental programs is costly and should be viewed as an investment, with the same dollars-and-cents evaluation as every other corporate expenditure.

A study of development program participation by managers in a large, diversified corporation found that a relatively small percentage of the managers attended a relatively small variety of programs. Some managers found it desirable and quite permissible to attend four, five, or more seminars and other programs during a year. Other managers attended none. On the average, each attended a program less than three days per year. The variety of programs was considerable, but participation concentrated in programs dealing with leadership, problem solving, teamwork, and other behavior-related subjects. Upon examination of overall corporate needs, it was concluded that more emphasis should be given to basic functional skills needed in management and to programs focusing attention on economic, technological, and social changes affecting the business. It was also felt that the target (or guideline) participation rate should be five days per year. In this company, it was felt that too many of the programs were conducted in-house, for company employees only, at the expense of managerial interaction with people from other companies. For certain program needs, therefore, participants would be directed outside. A cost analysis indicated that while certain economies were gained by designing and conducting certain programs internally, costs were more easily measured and controlled when contracted externally.

The use of formal training and development programs for managers should be planned on the basis of organizational patterns and needs, focusing ultimately on each individual management candidate's strengths and development needs. Succession planning provides the specific, evaluation-based process for determining these needs and plans, linked with realistic expectations of future organizational changes and managerial staffing requirements.

CURRICULUM MATRIX

Exempt Level	Functional, Disciplinary				
Entry and Early Career	Finance	Marketing	Manuf./Engin.	Forest Econ.	Infor. Systems
	Cost accounting Auditing Consolidations and advanced accounting International finance Reporting techniques Accounting computeriza-tion model	Basic sales and territory management Sales forecasting and profit planning Paper industry overview	Industrial security and safety Industrial rela-tions at IPCO Foreman-supervisor program Paper industry overview	Woodlands management Timbering dif-ferences by region Harvesting economics Reforestation practices Woodlands products technology Computer usage in econometrics and planning	Systems design Management science techniques Management science appli-cations at IPCO Data base theory Information retrieval
	All Introduction to International Paper Company philosophy Effective communications workshop Professional employees seminar (technicals only)				
Middle	All Review Courses Functional Conferences International Business Seminars Fundamentals of Finance for Nonfinancial Executives				
Senior					

Exhibit 12-8 Curriculum matrix.

Planning	Special Skills	Middle	Advanced
Statistical techniques Strategic and tactical planning Acquisition strategy Risk analysis, concepts and applications Management science techniques	Speed reading Languages Negotiation seminar COBOL	New Manager Program Organization of the corporation Responsibilities of a manager Motivation and leadership styles Decision making Business management Management skills Introduction to Middle Management Corporate business objectives Managing corporate assets Management issues Workshop I (High Potentials) Advanced sales technology Management skills Management workshop Introduction to corporate management	
		IPCO finance Management skills Strategic planning Management practices Management by exception Middle Management School Management issues Personnel policies and practices Performance evaluation and coaching Organization realities Managing company assets	Workshop II (High Potentials) Introduction to advanced management business concepts IPCO legal environment Corporate domestic and international strategies Economics Industrial relations Interrelationship of government and business Decision making Effective managerial leadership
		All Review courses Functional conferences	Management Conferences Management Methods Workshop Awareness Program Urban management Impact of domestic trends on international scene U.S. foreign policy Commercial and industry relations Racial America Personnel plans and programs Current corporate litigation Executive college programs

Chapter 13

Defining Career Opportunities

KEY POINTS

- Information about career paths, expected vacancies, and position requirements is essential for realistic career development planning.
- Career paths are objective descriptions of sequential work experiences, usually different job assignments. Paths may be described as experienced historically in an organization, as determined by management to meet prevailing needs, or as shown to be logically possible based on an analysis of behavioral job requirements.
- Most organizations use career paths in planning the development and promotion of employees. However, the paths may very well be historical or managerial rather than behavioral.
- The structure of career paths, represented in a comprehensive grid of jobs by units and levels, provides a useful framework for forecasting of needs and vacancies.
- Job requirements are best stated in terms of skills, abilities, and knowledge required to perform designated activities in a job. Experience and training may thereby be provided to help individuals qualify for consideration. Age, years of service, educational levels and degrees, and other credentials are unlikely to be useful as job-related development and career management criteria.

Many employees want to know more about the career opportunities available in an organization to help them set realistic career objectives and plan practical steps for their personal career development. Recent proliferation of career-planning materials, workshops, and company-sponsored counseling programs indicates a growing employee awareness and activism regarding careers. However, the information available to employees regarding career paths is usually quite limited, and does not tell "the whole story" about job progression possibilities and associated qualifications requirements.

Many managers also want career paths to be defined, so that an adequate number of individuals may be identified and prepared to fill future vacancies. Once career progression patterns are identified, more systematic forecasting of staffing requirements is possible. For the development of senior management talent, career paths are needed as guidelines for career development assignments across functional and organizational lines. Increasingly, senior executives are the product of varied job experiences, and not necessarily the product of lifelong careers within a single function or unit.

In addition to employee and managerial interest in career paths, the federal government is requiring action in this area. To assure equal employment opportunity and affirmative action program compliance, companies are advised to describe jobs in terms of actual requirements: work content and related qualifications. Employee selection and upgrading decisions are to be based on job-related factors, which nets out to mean a definition of possible career paths.

In summary, career path information is important for employee career development and human resource planning, but it needs to be realistic. And this means career paths need to have a realistic basis and realistic applications. This chapter briefly discusses approaches to satisfying those needs.

CAREER PATHS DEFINED

Career paths are not a new phenomenon invented by human resource planning professionals. In many companies quite a bit of work has been devoted to the formal defining of career paths, but that does not mean that the career paths were created in the process. Career paths do not need to be described in writing in order to exist. Rather, employees move through a patterned sequence of positions or roles, usually related to work content during their working lives. This is the crux of the notion of a career path.

For purposes of career management and other aspects of human resource planning, however, career paths are useful only when they are formally defined and documented. Career paths are more appropriately defined, then, as objective descriptions of sequential work experiences, as opposed to subjective individual feelings about career progress, personal development, status, or satisfaction. For example, an individual may view increasing responsibilities or changing work assignments within a single job as a career, but this subjective view of a career does not constitute a career path, as defined above.

Career Paths in Practice

An organization needs to move individuals along career paths, to develop the diversity of capabilities necessary to staff various levels and types of jobs. At the same time, not all individuals need follow career paths. There is a need for "career professionals" in many specialist positions. An oil company study a few years ago, for example, found that stability, not mobility, was preferred for staffing of sales representative positions. Neither do individuals need to follow upward career paths. Lateral paths provide exposure to multiple functions and activities and thus develop broader capabilities among individuals. Many individuals find lateral careers highly satisfying.

Career paths have emphasized upward mobility within a single occupation or functional area of work. In many companies career paths have meant step-by-step progression tied to years of service. If an individual deviated from the prescribed lockstep pattern and timing, he or she faltered. Such career paths were developed in the following manner:

1   Examination of the paths followed in the past to the top "rungs of the ladders"
2   Identification of entry and exit points into the career path, usually at the bottom only
3   Definition of requirements for the entry positions, normally in terms of educational level and specialization, experience, and years of service
4   Identification of the important job experiences leading to the top "rung," and benchmark timing for reaching each "rung"

This process described a generalized or idealized route for advancement within the unit or function. It made career paths explicit, and no longer just subjective.

Various organizations have developed career paths. Notable are the efforts of the U.S. Navy, the U.S. Air Force, and several major industrial and banking corporations (R. J. Greene, 1975; Idema, 1978; Pearson, 1966; Saxon, 1973). Many of these applications may be characterized as "traditional approaches." They have described paths largely followed by employees in the past, are based on subjective managerial views of the work involved, and are usually restricted to a single function or organizational unit (for example, sales, accounting, engineering). The practical utility of such paths, therefore, depends on the realism and scope of these key factors.

A typical career path within the sales function, for example, might include five steps, shown in Exhibit 13-1. Each step in the progression is largely paced by years of service (Pearson, 1966). Such a restrictive path might be improved by recognizing a flexibility regarding the years of service; otherwise the progression is a simple age-and-service lockstep which would prevent young salespeople from progressing even if they were quite capable. Further, the path could acknowledge other options which might provide valuable experience in developing district and regional managers. Assignments in finance or marketing

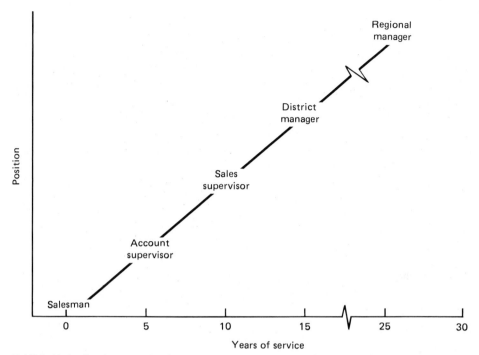

Exhibit 13-1   A sales career path.

research, for example, or in production might be valuable in sales management. The path implies that this is the only way to move ahead in the organization.

Another problem with career paths is that they imply the necessity of moving ahead—of climbing career ladders and the corporate hierarchy. Lateral moves, downward moves, or staying at a given level on a career basis are not indicated as attractive options. The bias toward promotions as the only meaningful career direction is clearly built into this traditional perspective of a career path.

An Alternative Approach

Rather than defining paths as linear, narrow progression lines, it is possible to pinpoint each position in an organization within a grid framework. In this way various career movement options are displayed as paths. Traditional vertical paths within functions or units are represented in each column, but the juxtaposition of other vertical paths provides a way of identifying a multitude of lateral, diagonal, and even downward career progression alternatives. The possibilities are limited only by the vacancies that actually occur and by the individual's qualifications relative to the position requirements.

Exhibit 13-2 presents such a grid, adapted and excerpted from a career planning grid actually used in a commercial bank. The numbers indicate the

Exhibit 13-2 Career Planning Grid for Major Divisions of a Bank

Level	Retail banking (title/no. of positions)	Corporate banking (title/no. of positions)	International (title/no. of positions)	Operations (title/no. of positions)
D	District manager 12 Branch manager A 6 District lending manager 4	Department manager 8 Senior account manager 9	Regional manager 4	
C	Branch manager B 38 Lending manager A 4 Branch operations manager A 5 Branch manager C 66	Institution manager 6 Senior account manager 21		Section manager 6
B	Commission lending manager 11 Branch operations manager 12 Branch manager D 40 Branch operations manager B 19 District trainer 11	Account manager 12 Associate institutional manager 5 Associate account manager 4	Area manager 12 Liaison representative 5 Area specialist 4	Senior programmer 5 Service representative 4 Analytical programmer 25 Operations supervisor 9
A	Branch operations manager B 11 Commission lending officer 27 Operations specialist 12 Retail lending officer 69 Operations supervisor 9	Account administrator 11	Account representative 16	Industrial engineer 5 Operations analyst 12 Associate programmer 19 Technical writer 4 Buyer 3 Procedures analyst 2

Source: Adapted and excerpted from an actual grid of all multiple incumbent positions in a commercial bank.

number of positions existing for each title. Related manpower forecasts show the number of vacancies anticipated for each title based on turnover, mobility, and projected growth in the bank. The levels indicated are broad organizational levels and are not directly linked to salary levels. The intent is to avoid confounding the career planning activity with compensation administration factors.

Using the grid, employees and managers may consider the various alternatives to the usual "up-the-ladder" career progression. A commercial lending officer in the retail banking division, for example, could most easily move to any of the other titles in level A within that division. The second most likely progression would be to level B positions within that division. Other alternatives might be positions in level A or level B in the other divisions.

For each position title a brief profile of the position activities and qualifications required is provided. Thus the employee or manager has available a sort of catalog of job options to consider in career planning and in considering career development activities. Qualifications are stated in terms of skills, abilities, and knowledge required, interpreted from the statements of activities performed (for example, "ability to . . ."). Appropriate kinds of job experience, educational specialization, and other indicators of these capabilities may be indicated, but educational degrees, years of service, age, personality characteristics, and other such factors not clearly job-related are not included.

ANALYZING CAREER PATHS

An organization that has no career information at all would benefit from even traditional descriptions of career paths. It is instructive to managers to consider past career progression patterns and their own subjective views of possible alternative career paths for employees to follow. In view of today's demands on career management, however, more realistic career information is needed. Career paths need to be specific, not general. They need to be practical, not idealized. They need to be anchored to reality—actual work activities and skill and knowledge requirements.

Career paths should:

Represent real progression possibilities, whether lateral or upward, without implied "normal" rates of progress or forced technical specialization

Be tentative and responsive to changes in job content, work priorities, organization patterns, and management needs

Be flexible, to take into consideration the compensating qualities of a particular individual, managers, subordinates, or others influencing the way work is performed

Specify acquirable skills, knowledge, and other specific attributes required to perform the work on each position along the paths, and not merely educational credentials, age, or work experience which may preclude some capable performers from career opportunities

The Analysis Process

To define career paths in this manner, empirical data are needed. Positions are analyzed and grouped on the basis of their actual work content. This does not mean that job descriptions necessarily have to be rewritten, or that the organization structure has to be changed. Job titles do not even have to be changed. The following steps are required:

1   Gather data on actual work activities, their relative importance, and the relative time allocation to each.

2   Determine, through analysis of these activities, the skill, knowledge, and other qualifications required to perform these activities effectively.

3   Identify patterns of similarity among positions, based on their content and skill-knowledge requirements, and grouping of similar positions as job families.

4   Identify logically possible progression lines among these job families, representing career paths.

5   Integrate the overall network of these paths as a single, career system depicting progression possibilities.

This process is illustrated in Exhibit 13-3.

Analysis of positions may be an extensive, ongoing process in large organizations. Where advanced approaches are used, professionals may be engaged full time in this process of "occupational analysis and classification." For most organizations, however, the challenge is to move simply from a "traditional" approach toward "defined" career paths. This means accomplishment of the above steps as efficiently as possible to yield useful career information.

To provide a "realistic basis" for career paths, an organization need not conduct an extensive, expensive study. A basic approach includes a review of

Exhibit 13-3   How to develop realistic career paths.

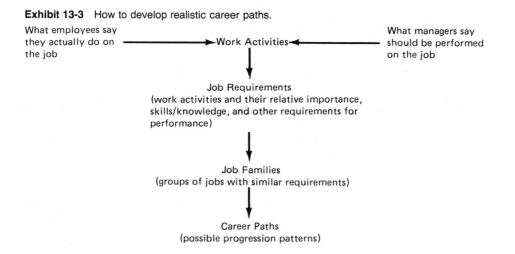

What employees say they actually do on the job → Work Activities ← What managers say should be performed on the job

Job Requirements
(work activities and their relative importance, skills/knowledge, and other requirements for performance)

Job Families
(groups of jobs with similar requirements)

Career Paths
(possible progression patterns)

job titles by the personnel staff, grouping the positions on the basis of the staff's knowledge of the nature of the work involved. The common characteristics of jobs in each family are identified, and specific activities and qualifications differentiating positions within each family are noted in a summary chart. This information is reviewed by selected managers. Position data are refined and positions are reclassified accordingly. Simply providing a fresh, objective consideration of realistic career possibilities in an organization improves the career development process.

The basis for career paths is further strengthened, of course, by additional substantive data on actual work activities on the various types of positions covered. Data may be gathered through selected interviews with incumbents, the use of widely distributed questionnaires or time logs, direct observation of work activities, or use of task checklists. These are all methods of activity analysis applicable to salaried positions. (See Chapter 7.)

A Behavioral Approach

Job descriptions rarely represent actual on-the-job behaviors. They tend to emphasize duties and accountabilities and are, at any rate, written for purposes other than considering career development requirements. Job descriptions, organizational manuals, operating procedures, training manuals, and other existing data may be useful inputs to the process. In most instances, however, some form of data gathering directly from employees is necessary to provide a sufficient basis for analysis of job similarities and differences.

In a sense, positions have always been grouped on the basis of similarity. Geographic location, organizational unit lines, technical specialization, and business function or product are typical bases for grouping jobs and thus prescribing career movement possibilities. Often when career paths are first described they are restricted by one of these particular dimensions. This may make sense, if the employer feels it is impractical to relocate employees across great geographic distances, or if the organization is composed of autonomous operating units. For managerial, professional, and technical talent, however, most organizations are discounting the significance of these barriers to career development.

The dimension that is being used today to "open up" career paths and give them greater realism is the behavioral aspect. By examining actual work activities—behaviors—it is possible to identify striking similarities in job content, even where the functions or technical specializations are different. A common example is the sales representative for a particular product line. It has been demonstrated in many situations that persons with the necessary skills can represent varied types of products, regardless of technical, product or industry knowledge, or territorial differences.

Another common example is the traditional career specialization of engineers. Exhibit 13-4 shows the traditional career progression patterns within a group of engineering positions in a major oil company. In this example, mechanical engineers normally progress through path A, chemical engineers

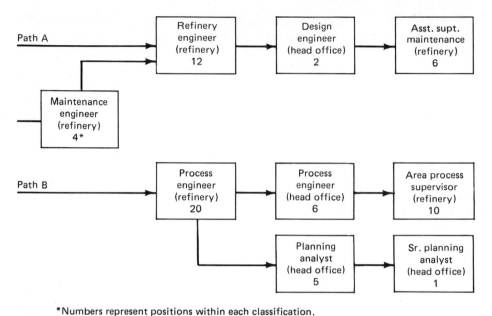

*Numbers represent positions within each classification.

Exhibit 13-4   Engineering position analysis: traditional career paths among positions.

through path B. This created an impression among engineers in the refineries that career opportunities were quite restricted. There has been resulting turnover and expressed dissatisfaction among the younger engineers. When the positions are grouped according to behavioral activities, however, the career paths offer a wider range of job progression possibilities and greater flexibility of assignment by management. These revised career paths are shown in Exhibit 13-5. From the data gathered, it was concluded that engineering specializations, per se, should not be barriers to career movement among these engineering positions.

This process assumes that individuals can acquire necessary technical skills or specialized knowledge that may be needed on a position. The progression from one behavioral role pattern to another is viewed as the critical dimension in career paths—from task specialist to manager. Experience suggests that employers tend to underestimate an individual's adaptability to different types of specific tasks, and to overestimate an individual's ability to change roles and become a supervisor, coordinator, administrator, or manager. Changing role behavior patterns is the most difficult aspect of management development, starting with the instance of promoting the "best worker" to a foreman role. This view does not demean the importance of maintaining or developing adequate technical competence on a position. In developing career paths, both dimensions need to be examined.

The behavioral approach provides greater flexibility in career planning, offering individuals a wider range of career options and management a larger pool of job candidates. Realistic moves along lateral career paths and moves

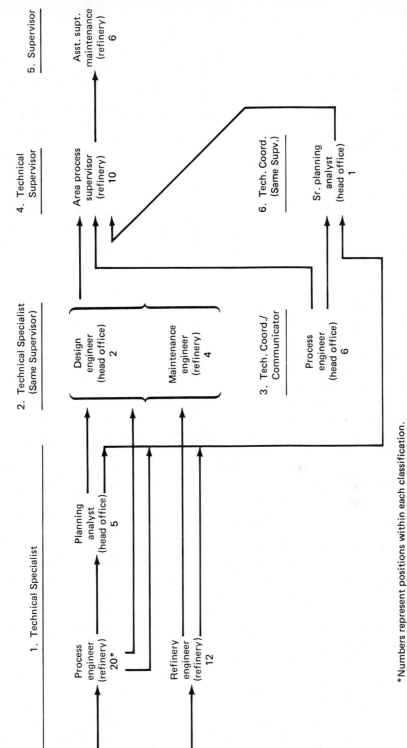

Exhibit 13-5 Engineering position analysis: career paths suggested by behaviors.

*Numbers represent positions within each classification.

317

among positions within the same job family are also explicit options as part of the overall career system. Further, positions may be reclassified in groups and paths as their work content changes, in response to individual differences, managerial styles, organizational, or other forces. The career system, then, serves as a realistic framework for keeping track of jobs and the planned movement of individuals.

TOWARD BEHAVIORAL PATHS

As shown in Exhibit 13-6, it is possible to summarize the characteristics of three kinds of career paths: historical, organizational, and behavioral. This chapter argues the merits of behavioral career paths while recognizing that historical and organizational paths exist as a matter of fact and necessity.

Historical paths are the informal paths that have always existed in the past and are represented by the past patterns of career movement among the incumbents of senior positions. These paths have guided promotions and transfers over the years as managers have promoted subordinates through their own footsteps. These paths are easily analyzed by examining biographical histories, although exceptions to the rules are often found (Glaser, 1968; H. White, 1970a).

These paths represent the social influence in an organization over the years, and to define paths of this type or in this way has the effect of perpetuating past practices. In a sense, these paths are the actual paths in an organization, worn well over time (often becoming ruts), and are the most factual. Few managers, however, would openly admit that these are the types of paths that are desired in the future, for needs are viewed as changing and "career paths must be modified to take into account the changing characteristics and needs of our employees and our company's circumstances."

Organizational paths are those defined by management, often through negotiation among the managers concerned. They are the paths considered pragmatic by management and are reflected, therefore, in the business plans, needs, and organizational structures. These paths clearly reflect the prevailing values of management in an organization. Such paths are represented in the relationships noted in job descriptions prepared for salary administration purposes; vertical paths are likely to be consistent with the salary progression patterns followed in practice. Career paths and job evaluation practices both are influenced by the same expedience-oriented management judgment. Organizational paths are often retained as confidential information by management (Glaser, 1968; Jennings, 1971).

Behavioral Paths

Behavioral paths, in contrast, represent the logical and possible sequences of positions that could be held, based on an analysis of what people actually do in an organization. The paths are, therefore, rational definitions of what is possible

Exhibit 13-6   Three Kinds of Career Paths in Contrast

Historical	Organizational	Behavioral
Past patterns of career progression; how the incumbents got where they are	Paths defined or dictated by management to meet operating needs; progression patterns that fit prevailing organizational needs	Paths that are logically possible based on analysis of what activities are actually performed on the jobs
Actual paths created by the past movement of employees among jobs	Paths determined by prevailing needs for staffing the organization	Rational paths that could be followed, management willing
Perpetuates the way careers have always been	Reflects prevailing management values and attitudes regarding careers	Calls for change; new career options
Used as basis for promotions and transfers	Usually consistent with job evaluation and pay practices	Used as basis for career planning
Basis is informal, traditional	Basis is organizational need, management style, expediency	Basis is formal analysis and definition of options

(neither what has been in the past nor what is desired by management). And the emphasis in defining behavioral paths is upon change: Such paths inherently challenge historical patterns and prevailing management assumptions (and career restrictions). Mobility across functions, geographic lines, and organizational lines may be expanded by applying behavioral paths.

Career paths based on empirical analysis of actual job requirements represent the "state of the art" in this area of human resource planning. Federal EEOC guidelines regarding employee selection practices call for job-related criteria for promotion, transfer, and other personnel actions. Behavioral paths, based on job analysis, provide a documented, objective, and defensible basis for career management. They provide, too, a strong reference point for individual career planning and development activities. The approach is certainly more difficult, and imposes greater challenges to management, but it is the potentially more comprehensive and formally defined.

Job Families

One feature of the behavioral approach to analyzing and defining career paths is that it examines jobs in terms of similarity of content. Accordingly, all jobs in an organization might be classified according to the similarity of activities performed using some form of taxonomy.

One such behavioral framework for classifying positions into job families is presented in Exhibit 13-7. Step 1 in this classification scheme sorts positions into

Exhibit 13-7   Classification of Positions into Families

Step 1	Step 2

A Task/technical specialists
• Analyst and evaluator role
• Predominantly task specialists
• Implementation through others
	1 Task specialists—minimal supervisory activity:
	  a Limited contact with others; tending to operate independently
	  b Significant contact/interaction—primarily internal with limited number of people
	  c Significant contact/interaction—primarily internal with many people
	  d Significant external contact
	2 Predominantly task specialist—some supervisory activity:
	  a Jobs having a significant innovative contribution
	  b Awareness of interpersonal relationships required
	  c Significant degree of supervisory skills required
	3 Predominantly supervisory and managerial within task specialist activity.

B First-line supervisors • Supervision of hourly/nonexempt people • Assignment of work to others • Day-to-day planning and scheduling • Basic paperwork • Meeting production schedules • Labor grievance/union activities	**1** Technical experience essential. **2** Experience of a less technical nature. (Experience may be needed more to gain credibility than to do the job.)
C Schedulers/coordinators • Interface among many groups • Primarily an intermediary resource • Working through others	**1** Specific task work with some coordination activity. **2** True coordination—scheduling/interacting with many people; not concentrating in task specialty necessarily; general staff assistance, organizer, administrator. **3** Coordinator with direct activity as well.
D Assistant superintendents; general line supervisors • Supervision of shift supervisors • Intermediary to second-line supervisors • Planning organizing, scheduling, coordinating, training	**1** Detailed/comprehensive knowledge of machines/processes essential. **2** Concentration on scheduling and planning; can rely on first-line supervisor for detailed task specialist knowledge.
E Second-line supervisors; superintendents; report to managers • Planning and controlling supervision through others • Interaction with corporate staff or regional management	**1** Supervision and control based on technical knowledge; task specialist predominant. **2** Balance of task specialist work and planning and controlling activities. **3** Primarily an administrator; can rely on support staff for technical expertise.

five categories representing the proportion of technical work or expertise required versus managerial and supervisory work or ability required. The distinctions are made through analysis of the roles comprising each position (see the position profile method described in Chapter 12). Step 2 represents a further subclassification within each major grouping.

In the case where this exhibit was developed, approximately 350 managerial and professional positions were classified using this framework. Once classified, the positions could be readily identified as "more similar" to some positions than to others by virtue of the job family concept. Positions with similar work content (activities) but concerned with different products, functions, or placed in different organizational units or locations are identified now as related. Seemingly strange bedfellows emerged through the analysis, but were acknowledged as realistic family members when reviewed by management.

As a result of job analysis, new career options are opened that might otherwise have been ignored. In some instances, as in the engineering career path analysis, the task of redefining paths is relatively simple and direct, although profoundly difficult to implement in change-resistant organizations. In others, a more comprehensive, complex process of analysis, job classification, and career path description is necessary. The career planning grid, illustrated in Exhibit 13-8, is a tool that serves all levels of scope and complexity. It provides a format for displaying all options in a single format (although the grid may extend several pages). In a highly complex organization the grid may be coded and maintained on a computer information system, where it can provide the structure for computer modeling of projected personnel flows as well as highlight options for individuals in specific positions (Air Force, 1975; Elster, 1973).

The combination of the job family analysis and the grid presentation of job relationships allows the definition of specific career paths in a straightforward

Exhibit 13-8 Career Planning Grid

Functional path (plant engineering)	Other engineering functional opportunities	Other related technical opportunities
Plant engineer (large plant)	Corporate engineering	Technical director Production superintendent Corporate staff positions
Senior project engineer	Engineering superintendent Senior project chemical engineer Maintenance superintendent District engineer	Technical supervisor Quality control supervisor Process control supervisor
Project engineer	Construction engineer Safety engineer Project chemical engineer	Production foreman Senior operations analyst
Junior engineer	Industrial engineer	Field technician Operations analyst

manner. Exhibit 13-8 is a final summary of an engineering career path and various alternative options at each career step. Again, this is an example adapted from an actual case, and is for illustrative purposes only. If such presentations of career paths could be prepared for the principal functional areas of an organization, career planning would have a highly realistic and flexible foundation. The paths would reflect historical and organizational practices, particularly in the vertical path, but also acknowledge the possible behavior-based career path alternatives along the way.

Some human resource planners become concerned with the precision and validity of particular classifications of positions. They presume that there is some objective or "right" answer when attempting to classify positions and define job families and career paths. Such concern is not warranted, as the purpose is to provide a logical, realistic framework for management and personal action. Even in biology the elaborate taxonomic schemes developed during the past century are not rigid nor wholly objective. Even Darwin, in *The Origin of Species,* argued that classification systems are intended to be pragmatic: "I look at the term species as one arbitrarily given for the sake of convenience to a set of individuals closely resembling one another."

REALISTIC APPLICATIONS

Career paths are worth developing only if they are used in career planning and development. Individuals should consider career information in conjunction with their own self-analysis of career interests, abilities, and aspirations. The result is application of the career paths in the development of more realistic individual career objectives and plans. Similarly, through planning, appraisal, and counseling activities, managers may help individuals translate these personal career plans into career development actions. It is important that development activities—whether training, job assignments, or shifts in job activities—be realistically attuned to the organization's needs.

Career paths provide a vital link between the individual's own career aims and the organizations's actual talent requirements. The net result can only be positive: improved utilization of talent and less ambiguity in employee views of the employment relationship. Some managers have argued that communication of career paths, and particularly specific information, often frustrates employees by encouraging false hopes and expectations about career opportunities. This may be valid where such information is not realistic. But more employee turnover, underutilization, and frustrated career development have assuredly resulted from too little realistic information, not too much of it.

Input to Career Planning

Career paths, however realistic, are beneficial only if translated into individual career action plans. As shown in Exhibit 13-9, this process involves the application of career information by employees in career analysis/planning and by managers in appraisal and counseling.

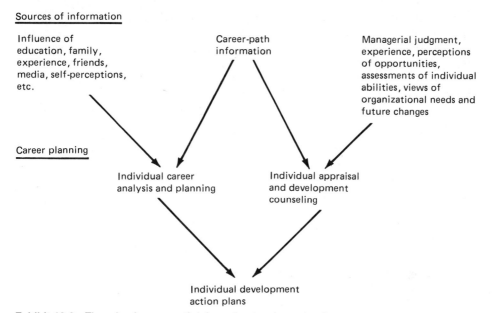

Exhibit 13-9   The role of career path information in career planning.

All too often, career planning is practiced as an isolated employee activity without either realistic career path information or relevant appraisal and counseling inputs. Techniques such as career-planning or life-planning workshops, structured individual planning exercises, and self-improvement materials are widely popular today. These provide a useful way for individuals to clarify personal interests, abilities, and aspirations, with consideration to such influences as their educational experiences, work experiences, family background and expectations, career plans and progress of friends, role examples suggested by television and other media, and personal feelings of competence and self-worth. However, individual career analysis and planning without career path information and other managerial inputs is like sailing without having a chart or knowing the seas. It is fun for a while, but becomes frustrating for individuals who wish to get somewhere.

Career path information may be communicated to individuals in several ways, including:

Publication, in digestible pieces, in employee magazines and newsletters
Inclusion in employee manuals
Publication as a special career guide or as part of career-planning workbooks
Presentation in cassettes, on videotapes, or live

At a minimum, a reference book should be provided to each manager, presenting the basic job families, career progression possibilities, and related requirements.

Through appraisals and counseling, managers (and professional staff) may communicate such information and, once they have the abilities and inclination, may actually help individuals evaluate their career development options. Responsibility for career development may rest with the individual, but the manager can have a significant influence on individual motivation, decisions, and actions.

Other Applications

Career information may be applied by managers in several ways, including:

Describing career opportunities to new recruits or internal job candidates
Identifying "target positions" for which individuals are ready now or are becoming developed in appraisals of so-called "promotability and potential"
Identifying specific training needs of individuals
Discussing with the individual realistic career alternatives: future jobs, long-term opportunities, or staying on the current position as a career professional

Managers also bring to employees additional information useful in career planning: experience, knowledge of changing organizational needs and business plans, and an independent (if not wholly "objective") assessment of individual abilities and potential. When managers fail to participate in the career development process, these benefits are lost, and plans are accordingly less realistic for the desired results.

In summary, employees should receive career path information directly and through their managers. In this context, specific plans may be made for realistic development actions.

Other applications of career path information are also possible, particularly substantive information on work activities and job requirements. These include:

Planning changes in job design or organization structure.
Considering applicable areas of performance evaluations and associated performance objectives or standards.
Double-checking salary levels, to assure that jobs are evaluated fairly. The job family approach may even be used as the core of the overall salary administration system, avoiding the need for point-factor type evaluations of job worth or separate job descriptions.
Forecasting the availability of qualified job candidates, either by examining past flows of personnel through the system or by analyzing appraisal data (in terms of targeted positions).

For years, personnel people have advocated the development of a single definition of work for all personnel applications. Now that there is an emerging demand for more information on career paths and job requirements, it is possible to apply this concept. Using career information for multiple purposes improves the cost/benefits relationship. It also tends to increase the reliability and consistency of management practices. There have been many instances in companies where a supposed transfer and promotion involved a move to a lower authorized salary level, and exceptions were made to make the move attractive.

If management is to be rational and fair in human resource management, there needs to be rational, consistent definition of what jobs involve and require. Career paths need to be defined, based on actual work activities and requirements, so that employees and managers will have a realistic basis for career development planning.

Chapter 14

Individual Career Planning

KEY POINTS

• Career planning is a personal process of planning one's future work. It involves decisions regarding broad life plans (including the choice of occupation), development plans (job assignments, specializations), and performance plans (on the current job).

• Career planning issues vary as persons mature, with different concerns occurring at each stage of adult life: establishing identity, getting established, maintenance and adjustment, and decline.

• Human resource planning activities parallel individual career planning activities; companies may provide assistance and resources to individual employees in their personal career planning.

• The most prevalent company career planning practices are basic communication of information useful in career planning (for example, training programs, educational assistance, job requirements, salary administration) and informal counseling by personnel staff and by supervisors.

• Newer and less prevalent company practices include provision of self-analysis workbooks, conducting group workshops, and provision of specialized counseling and assessment programs.

• To be effective, career planning should be implemented as a comprehensive process, designed through a process of needs analysis, development of resources, and pilot introduction before full implementation.

- There are some risks in career planning, principally due to a raising of employee expectations and anxieties about career opportunities. These may be minimized by making career planning as realistic as possible. Also, the risks may be exaggerated; in fact, there are far more potential benefits than risks.

Career planning is the process of setting individual career objectives and devising developmental activities that will achieve them. It is a private, personal activity guided primarily by personal knowledge and impelled by personal initiative. In the broadest sense, it is the personal process of planning one's future work. In the process individuals analyze their interests, values, goals, and capabilities; consider the available opportunities; make decisions that may affect activities relating to the current job; and establish personal development plans that are likely to bring desired results (Dyer, 1976; Walker, 1977b).

The process results in decisions to enter a certain occupation, join a particular company, accept or decline job opportunities (including relocations, promotions or transfers), and ultimately leave a company for another job or for retirement. In a very practical sense, the individuals select their occupations, the organizations they will serve, the jobs they will hold, and the actual work they will perform. For example, we see employees frequently turning down career opportunities offered by management because of personal plans, life-styles, dual careers, or other factors.

Historically, personal knowledge and initiative have impelled career planning, while education and work experience, personal contacts, and generally "being at the right place at the right time" have been keys to career progress. Increasingly, however, companies are providing resources to help employees consider their career plans. Programs typically include career counseling by personnel staff or by supervisors; group workshops to help employees evaluate their skills, abilities, and interests and to form development plans; self-directed workbooks aimed at guiding career planning and analysis by the individuals; and communication of job opportunities and other information useful in career development.

To date, most career planning programs have been experimental and of limited scope. Many employers have been reluctant to intervene in matters such as personal assessments, life planning, and career goal setting. Accordingly, many programs have been limited to work-related matters, focusing on current job performance. In some companies, programs have been designed for nonexempt employees, in others, for managerial and professional employees. Sometimes career planning help is targeted to minority and female employees covered by affirmative action programs.

Career planning is the individual employee's counterpart to the company's overall human resource planning process. And the two processes need to be closely coordinated if the needs of both the individuals and the organization are to be satisfied (Schein, 1978). Increasingly, career planning is an important aspect of a company's overall human resource planning activity.

This chapter examines the way individuals go about personal career planning and the issues involved in the process. Company practices are reviewed and implementation strategies discussed. Specific tools and techniques available for management and individual use are reviewed. Finally, the risks and benefits of providing career-planning assistance to employees are considered.

THE PROCESS OF CAREER PLANNING

Comedian Steve Martin sums up his attitude toward careers and career planning rather succinctly in a song he sings to the accompaniment of a single, discordant banjo chord:

> We're havin' some fun.
> We've got music and laughter and wonderful times.
> And you know, I see people goin' to college for 14 years,
> Studying to be doctors and lawyers.
> And I see people gettin' up at 7:30 each morning
> To go to the drugstore to sell Flair pens.
> But the most amazin' thing to me is
> I get paid for doin' this.

Everyone has a career, but not everyone plans a career. A career is a commonsense concept that is widely accepted, but few people really have logically analyzed their careers or charted future career plans (Hall 1976; Van Maanen and Schein, 1975).

Since the days of the aspiring young Horatio Alger, the popular model of career success has been characterized by individual responsibility for personal development and career advancement. Hence individuals are encouraged to define personal objectives and pursue their achievement. They are encouraged to "succeed" in organizations by displaying their talents effectively, by obtaining the support of a sponsor or mentor, by changing jobs (or employers) whenever opportunities appear blocked, and by generally being savvy regarding organizational opportunities, constraints, and management practices.

In recent years, careers have also been the subject of extensive academic research (Hall, Hall, and Hinton, 1978; Jeliuek, 1979). The findings, while far from definitive, point to a number of qualities of careers that shed light on how careers are planned. There are different levels of career planning, representing different time frames of analysis. There are also different career stages, normally reached at relatively predictable points in life. These influence career-planning needs and practices. Finally, career-planning behavior is influenced by managerial human resource planning practices. Hence this linkage needs to be considered. This section cannot cover the full depth and range of career topics, but highlights the issues critical to human resource planning practices.

Levels of Career Planning

There are essentially three outcomes from individual career planning: (1) broad conclusions about one's own capabilities, interests, aspirations and objectives—

life planning; (2) targets for future job assignments, developmental activities to make that progress happen, and plans for other future career decisions—*development planning*; and (3) specific goals and plans, work priorities, and reward expectations on the current job assignment—*performance planning*. Individuals should consider these levels of career decisions so that day-to-day activities fit in with an overall career plan which, in turn, is consistent with personal feelings and expectations about life. A person needs to tie together short-range, middle-range, and long-range thinking about careers if personal development is to be effective.

As shown in Exhibit 14-1, the three levels of career planning integrate the various forces influencing career choices, the diverse bits and pieces of information available to a person, and the person's own attitudes. In developing life plans (or "themes") the individual draws primarily from introspection. In developing development plans and job-specific performance plans, the individual relies more heavily on managerial inputs.

As shown in the exhibit, individuals must largely be self-reliant in life planning, must expect a cooperative relationship with management in development planning, and must rely primarily on management in performance

Exhibit 14-1 Levels of career planning.

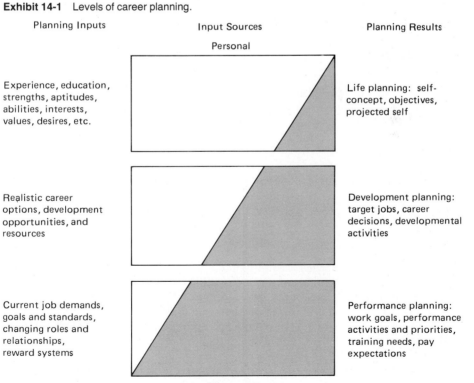

| Planning Inputs | Input Sources | Planning Results |

Personal

Experience, education, strengths, aptitudes, abilities, interests, values, desires, etc.

Life planning: self-concept, objectives, projected self

Realistic career options, development opportunities, and resources

Development planning: target jobs, career decisions, developmental activities

Current job demands, goals and standards, changing roles and relationships, reward systems

Performance planning: work goals, performance activities and priorities, training needs, pay expectations

Managerial

planning. While this may be a broad generalization, it serves to highlight the dilemma of many individuals: a lack of skills to do effective life planning, at the one extreme, and a lack of adequate inputs from management to do effective development or performance planning. When management fails to fulfill its role, individuals move in to fill the gap, making their own assumptions about opportunities as a basis for decisions. Attention also tends to shift toward voids at the more immediate levels. Hence if management plays its proper role, individuals are able to reach conclusions about performance and development more readily and can then concentrate on long-range life planning.

Few individuals do life planning except in times of personal crisis. When a person loses a job, becomes ill, is divorced or loses a loved one, or retires, life-planning issues become crucial. Individuals are thrust into basic self-review, and few have a firm enough foundation of self-understanding to withstand the storms.

At the same time, most of the popular publications readily available to individuals deal with life-planning issues, or at least a consideration of life and career issues in the context of the search for employment or advancement. Such books include: *What Color Is Your Parachute?* (Bolles, 1972), *Executive Career Strategy* (Schoonmaker, 1971), *Getting Yours* (Pogrebin, 1975), *Career Strategies: Planning for Personal Growth* (Souerwine, 1978), and *Where Do I Go from Here with My Life?* (Crystal and Bolles, 1974).

Influential Factors in Life Planning

An individual draws from many sources in developing a self-concept and life plan. Influences of childhood, family experiences, friendships, education, and successive work experiences are all noteworthy. Personality factors have a major impact on one's outlook, but these are heavily influenced by social interaction and acculturation. How much risk a person will take, the choice of life-styles, the level of achievement motivation, and energy are among the fundamental factors influencing a person's long-range career direction and development (Crites, 1969; Hall, 1976; Schein, 1978; Super, 1957).

In a 1974 study of management school graduates, Schein observed five dominant motives of what people wanted from their careers (Schein, 1975, 1977). These basic motives, which Schein calls "career anchors," help account for the different ways that individuals select occupations and long-range career goals. They are as follows:

1 *Managerial competence:* A person seeks and values opportunities to manage. This reflects further values for interpersonal competence, analytical competence, and emotional maturity.

2 *Technical/functional competence:* A person seeks and values opportunities to exercise various technical talents and areas of competence. Such a person resists being promoted out of a technically satisfying role into one that is primarily managerial.

3 *Security:* A person is motivated primarily by the need to stabilize his or her career situation, even if that means subordinating some personal work needs or desires to those of the employing organization or the profession.

4 *Creativity:* This anchor is difficult to articulate, but relates to entrepreneurial values. A person is driven by a need to build or create something that is entirely his or her own product.

5 *Autonomy and independence:* A person seeks work situations where he or she will be largely free of organizational constraints to pursue professional or technical/functional competence. These persons value autonomy more than the exercise of technical talents per se.

The most valuable assistance to individuals in considering life planning is a structured process for considering factors such as these, for obtaining feedback from others as a way of testing career alternatives, and for analyzing the often complex patterns of choices being faced. *The Three Boxes of Life* by Richard Bolles (author of *What Color Is Your Parachute?*—the most popular career-planning publication) zeroes in on the long-range issue of balancing lifelong learning, lifelong working, and lifelong leisure or playing. More fundamental ideas, but with less helpful structure, are found in *On Becoming a Person* by Carl Rogers (1961) and in various texts on theories of career development (Kroll, 1970; Osipow, 1973; Pietrofesa and Splete, 1975).

Life Stages

Individual thinking about careers is influenced by aging. In the process of maturing, a person normally progresses through a series of stages. These stages in life stem from basic biological facts of aging (as represented in physical and mental abilities, health, appearance, etc.), compounded by psychological feelings about recognition, status or status loss, opportunities for growth, and other needs satisfaction.

A good deal of research and writing has been done on life stages, and several different theories have been put forth regarding stages in adult life, the aspects relevant to career planning. The work of Erik H. Erikson, Donald Super, and Daniel Levinson are the most comprehensive (Erikson, 1961; D. J. Levinson, 1978; Super, 1957). The basic stages are summarized below.

1 *Establishing identity:* A period of exploration of alternative careers and of "getting into the adult world" (D. J. Levinson, 1978). This period of exploration typically ranges from age 10 to age 20 or older. It is largely concerned with life-planning issues: determination of self-concept and key objectives. It is a period of leaving childhood and adolescence and pulling up roots by leaving the family.

2 *Growing and getting established:* A period of testing different types of work, making a commitment to an occupation, selecting and adjusting to career paths in a working life (as opposed to the more transient life of a student), and generally becoming settled and self-confident in one's work. For some people, however, establishment comes early, with very minimal, if any, trial (Super, 1957). Becoming established is referred to by Levinson as "becoming one's own man" (Levinson's research included only men). During this stage, from age 20 to 40 or so, the person generally also establishes a home and rears children.

   3   *Maintenance and adjustment to self:* A period of acceptance of one's life, or serious questioning and renewed life planning. This stage, generally from age 35 to 45 or 50 (or even later), leads either to major changes in life plans (occupational change, divorce, etc.) or to acceptance of the career as a plateau. This implies a reassessment of life objectives, self-concept, and projected aspirations—the guts of life planning. The midlife transition thus becomes a potential crisis to some. (Heller, 1974; Persig, 1974; Sheehy, 1976 and in professional literature Blau, 1978; Golembiewski, 1978; Kets de Vries, 1978; Orth, 1974).

   4   *Decline:* A period of diminishing physical and mental capacities, and loss of aspiration and career motivation. Often this stage is socially induced, through forced retirement or other ways older workers are treated. As life expectancy and health at ages 55, 60, and older improve, more and more people are able to resist decline in their careers.

   Career development programs tend to focus attention on the needs of individuals who are getting established: the up-and-coming, young, "high-potential" employees. While this attention is worthwhile, particularly to attract the best available recruits and to help get them started on their careers, additional programs are needed to attend to the needs of employees who have moved on to stages 3 and 4.

   If middle-aged employees are not given help in coping with their career-planning needs, many good performers may be lost. Some may leave to join other organizations or occupations; others may simply "retire" on the job as a result of career frustrations in this stage of life.

   If companies are sometimes callous to the career-planning needs of middle-aged employees, they are more often neglectful of the needs of older employees. Technically, the Age Discrimination in Employment Act (ADEA) protects "older workers" (ages 40 to 70) from wrongful treatment in the terms and conditions of employment. However, stereotypes and prejudices regarding the capabilities of older people persist in our youth-oriented society. As a result, a new perspective of career development is needed to help employees in their fifties and sixties conduct positive, constructive career planning that will delay the onset of decline in life (Kimmel, 1974; Sheppard, 1971; Walker and Lazer, 1979).

   At each career stage the question arises whether the stress of pursuing a successful career is really "worth the price." Such books as *Type A Behavior and Your Heart* (Friedman and Rosenman, 1974), and *Confessions of a Workaholic* (Oates, 1972), and articles such as "What Price Success?" (J. Steiner, 1972) and "Business Careers as a Treadmill to Oblivion: The Allure of Cardiovascular Death" (Ogilvie and Porter, 1974) suggest the nature of the questioning that occurs. In some instances it results in a cutting loose from society-guided career paths (American Friends Service Committee, 1971; Kalins, 1973), but in most cases the adjustment is successfully accomplished by working within the conventional career options available.

Career Planning and Human Resource Planning

"The challenge of career development lies in equipping the employee with the necessary knowledge about himself and reality" (Salvagno, 1969). This simple statement says quite a bit about the linkage between individual career planning and organizational planning for human resources.

From the management viewpoint, career planning and development should remain an individual responsibility. However, many individuals lack the information, the skills, the insights, or sometimes the initiative to determine their own career plans effectively. While the "cream may rise to the top" in an organization, many employees with considerable talent may be overlooked or left behind.

As discussed in Chapter 11, management provides certain systems and activities aimed at building and maintaining a competent work force to meet the company's needs. As shown in Exhibit 14-2, however, aspects of this process directly relate to the key career decisions made by individual employees. The decisions, occupational and organizational choices, job choice (assignment), performance, and retirement, are iterative: Individuals may make these decisions several times in their careers (Walker, 1973).

COMPANY PRACTICES IN CAREER PLANNING

Many companies are establishing programs and systems to assist their employees in career planning. Systematic self-analysis and career development are viewed as beneficial to both the individuals and the company. Career planning practices are not aimed at planning people's careers for them, but rather at:

Helping employees conduct their own career planning by raising questions that need to be answered and providing information on available opportunities and resources

Exhibit 14-2 The career planning process and management. (*Source:* James W. Walker, "Individual Career Planning: Managerial Help for Subordinates," *Business Horizons*, vol. 16, no. 1, February 1973, pp. 65–72.)

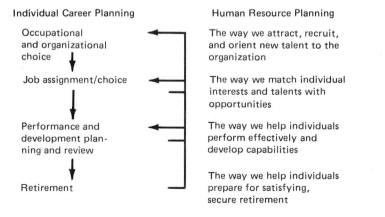

Individual Career Planning

Occupational and organizational choice

Job assignment/choice

Performance and development planning and review

Retirement

Human Resource Planning

The way we attract, recruit, and orient new talent to the organization

The way we match individual interests and talents with opportunities

The way we help individuals perform effectively and develop capabilities

The way we help individuals prepare for satisfying, secure retirement

Guiding employees in taking advantage of systems available for career development, such as job posting, performance reviews, training, and educational assistance programs

Increasing employee confidence in the company's career management and demonstrating to outside parties that the company is concerned with career development, particularly for minorities and females

Actual practices in career planning differ from company to company, and little hard information on company experience with formal career-planning programs is available. In fact, there is little agreement even on what career planning means. To some it is a wholly new management function; to others it is merely a new label for employee counseling and other employee development activities that have been around for a long time (Burack, 1977; Gould, 1978; Leach, 1977; D. Miller, 1978).

Why Get Involved?

Pressures for company-sponsored career-planning programs have emerged from several sources:

High-talent candidates (particularly minorities and females) often give preference to employers who demonstrate that career advancement opportunities exist.

Women, employees in midcareer, and college recruits are asking for career-planning assistance. Popular publications have raised their awareness of the need for career planning.

Affirmative action programs and court-approved settlements of discrimination suits frequently require companies to set up career development programs for protected classes.

Company growth and changing staffing requirements necessitate individual career development to help assure that needed talent will be available.

Some companies have adopted career-planning programs to reduce turnover, improve the "quality of working life," help minimize the chances of white-collar unionization, and improve on-the-job performance.

Others have initiated career-planning programs specifically to help those employees whose career expectations are *too low*. These companies have found that it is in their best interest as well as the employees' interests to stimulate career aspirations toward more ambitious career goals—to actually *raise* employee expectations. Several companies have focused on "career awareness" or "achievement motivation training" as a central component of career-planning workshops.

When asked to identify the reasons for offering career-planning programs in a recent survey, most respondents indicated that basic desires to aid employee development were the primary motives (Walker and Gutteridge, 1979). The most influential factors identified in this survey of 225 companies are as follows:

1 Desire to develop and promote employees from within
2 Shortage of promotable talent
3 Desire to aid career planning
4 Strong expression of employee interest
5 Desire to improve productivity
6 Affirmative action program commitments
7 Concern about turnover
8 Personal interest of unit managers
9 Desire for positive recruiting image

Few companies indicate that career-planning programs were developed as a result of attitude survey findings or research by personnel staff. The desire to avoid unionization was also reported a minor and infrequent factor.

It is to be expected that the prevalence of career-planning programs in companies depends in part on industry practices. As such programs become common, they are widely adopted as basic elements of human resource management systems.

Techniques in Career Planning

The basic techniques used to aid individual career planning include counseling, workshops, self-development materials, and assessment programs. Counseling may be provided by personnel staff (sometimes specialized staff counselors such as psychologists or trained guidance counselors), by supervisors, or by external counselors or related services (career centers, universities, etc.). Workshops encourage individuals to assess their interests, abilities, and circumstances; increase career awareness; and set personal development goals and plans. The group setting fosters interaction and mutual help among employees. Self-development materials include workbooks and reading materials, whether developed specifically by the company or published for general public use. They have the appeal of requiring self-initiative and investment of personal time and effort by employees. Assessment programs include tests on vocational interests, aptitudes, personality, abilities, and other attributes that have long been used by managers in making employee selection, promotion, transfer, and development decisions. They are used in career planning primarily to aid employee insight and self-assessment of qualities with respect to the requirements of alternative career paths.

Even more fundamental to career planning are communications regarding career opportunities and developmental resources available to interested employees. Communications provide the foundation upon which these other career-planning practices are built.

A 1979 survey of 225 companies by the American Management Association found that communications relating to career planning are more common than the other types of career planning aids (Walker and Gutteridge, 1979). Respondents were asked to indicate for each type of practice whether they were currently applying it, were planning to do so within one year, once applied it but have since discontinued it, or have never applied the practice. Exhibit 14-3

Exhibit 14-3 Career Planning Practices

Practice	Doing		Planning		Discontinued		Never done	
	Number	Percent	Number	Percent	Number	Percent	Number	Percent
Communication on educational assistance (n=223)	207	92.8	9	4.0	0		7	3.1
Informal counseling by personnel staff (n=222)	197	88.7	11	5.0	1	0.5	13	5.9
Communication of EEO and affirmative action programs and policies (n=220)	191	86.8	18	8.2	0		11	5.0
Communication on company's condition and economics (n=216)	183	84.7	13	6.0	0		20	9.3
Communication on salary administration (n=220)	168	76.4	24	10.9	1	0.5	27	12.3
Communication on job requirements (n=217)	153	70.5	41	18.9	1	0.5	22	10.1
Communication on training and development options (n=214)	137	64.0	40	18.7	1	0.5	36	16.8
Career counseling by supervisors (n=217)	121	55.8	38	17.5	0		58	26.7
Job posting and communication of job vacancy information (n=218)	118	54.1	33	15.1	4	1.8	63	28.9
Workshops on interpersonal relationships (n=213)	104	48.8	26	12.2	5	2.3	78	36.6
Job performance and development planning workshops (n=210)	89	42.4	46	21.9	0		75	35.7
Communication on career paths or ladders (n=212)	82	38.7	65	30.7	2	0.9	63	29.7
Outplacement counseling/related services (n=212)	79	37.3	4	1.9	4	1.9	125	59.0
Psychological testing and assessment (n=211)	74	35.1	17	8.0	40	19.0	80	37.9

Workshops and communications on retirement preparation (n=212)	71	33.5	51	24.1	0		90	42.5
Testing and feedback regarding aptitudes, interests, etc. (n=208)	68	32.7	20	9.6	28	13.5	92	44.2
Referrals to external counselors and resources (n=209)	61	29.2	8	3.8	8	3.8	132	63.2
Training of supervisors in career counseling (n=212)	53	25.0	67	31.6	2	0.9	90	42.5
Career counseling by specialized staff counselors (n=210)	43	20.5	16	7.6	2	1.0	149	71.0
Individual self-analysis and planning (n=211)	33	15.6	39	18.5	2	0.9	137	64.9
Assessment centers for career development purposes (n=213)	31	14.6	37	17.4	8	3.8	137	64.3
Life and career planning workshops (n=210)	24	11.4	36	17.1	2	1.0	148	70.5

*Bases of percentages vary with responses. Nonresponses are excluded from percentage calculations.

Source: James W. Walker and Thomas G. Gutteridge, *Career Planning Practices* (New York: AMACOM, 1979), pp. 11, 15. Reprinted with permission of the publisher. © 1979 by AMACOM, a division of American Management Associations. All rights reserved.

presents the ranking of practices reportedly applied with the percentage responses indicated for each practice.

As shown in the data, virtually all the companies provide certain basic career-planning aids to employees or intend to do so shortly. Informal counseling by supervisors or personnel staff is the most common form of help to employees. Communications on various career-related topics are the other most common practices.

There are several types of workshops, with interpersonal skills workshops and job performance and development planning workshops the more prevalent types. Life- and career-planning workshops were reportedly offered by only a few of the companies.

Practices in communicating job opportunities include job posting and communication of information on career paths or ladders. While each is reported by less than 40 percent of companies, both are also targeted for substantial attention in the future. This suggests that companies are recognizing the basic role played by job opportunities information in the career planning process.

Various types of testing and assessment are reportedly low in use and in many companies some of these practices have been discontinued. A number of companies reported concerns about the EEO impact of testing and assessment programs that are not validated. Others pointed to the high costs of assessment centers and some other programs as factors impeding or discouraging their use.

According to this survey, the primary activities being emphasized as newer practices include training of supervisors in career planning, career counseling by specialized staff counselors, workshops of all types, communications on career paths and outplacement counseling, and related services. Also, they report assessment centers are being used more for developmental purposes (Walker and Gutteridge, 1979).

While many of the companies studied report having several of the practices in use, but not all of them, some companies reported having broad-based, comprehensive career-planning programs. These companies provide an example to be followed in career-planning practices.

At Cleveland Trust, for example, a broad-based career assessment program provides a wide range of resources to employees. First, the individual works with a counselor to explore the concerns and goals. This is followed by a career assessment workshop, which involves the use of a workbook designed to aid self-analysis. In addition, the bank provides a career opportunities booklet which lists opportunities available at Cleveland Trust and provides background information on the various areas. If an employee feels that there are no attractive opportunities in the bank, an outplacement service is available to help him or her find another job elsewhere. This overall program is believed to foster retention, career development, and motivation of employees (Hastings, 1978).

Relative Merits of Career-Planning Activities

Just because companies provide certain activities does not necessarily mean that these are the most effective or beneficial. To the contrary, what a company may consider suitable may not be the most suitable for individual employee needs. Further, virtually every possible technique has both positive features and disadvantages.

Exhibit 14-4 presents a subjective assessment of the various techniques that might be used in aiding career planning. The exhibit is reprinted from an article by Donald Bowen and Douglas Hall and is not related to the previously presented survey results. The information, nevertheless, is useful in weighing the relative merits of alternative career planning practices (Bowen and Hall, 1977).

An Implementation Strategy

Implementing career-planning practices is a simple matter—if the practices are isolated communications, workshops, or other programs and if the scope of application is limited to small, defined groups of employees. In many companies, career planning is introduced as an experimental process, restricted in participation, scope, and resources. The survey results surely include many such levels of career-planning practices.

However, such a modest implementation strategy does not ensure an adequate depth or range of assistance to employees for career planning. Realistic career planning should be comprehensive, in-depth, guided by adequate information, and linked with pertinent management systems. Accordingly, a more comprehensive implementation strategy may be called for. Exhibit 14-5 illustrates the steps necessary.

First, an organization should conduct an audit to identify the needs it wants to satisfy and to develop a strategy for implementing the program. A large consumer products company, for example, conducted a series of interviews with employee relations staff members to find out whether employees wanted a career-planning program and what techniques they thought would be most applicable. The company obtained factual inputs from twenty individuals, including top corporate personnel executives, employee relations managers in the operating divisions, all members of the training and development staff, and representatives from compensation, data systems, manpower planning, and other employee relations functions. The result was a plan of action that became part of the following year's budgeted activity.

In other companies, inputs have been obtained from other staff and operating managers. This helps establish a supportive climate for introducing the program once it is developed. Participation by managers in the early development of a career-planning program helps allay concerns that it will burden them or otherwise "rock the boat" and also builds commitment to the program.

The second step is to develop the tools necessary to implement the program. Personnel systems supporting career development should be checked and any shortcomings corrected. For example, an insurance company had several performance appraisal systems in use, but felt that greater consistency was needed. A new appraisal process was developed that served both performance and development aspects, and this process was introduced through management workshops. In other companies, needs have been identified in

Exhibit 14-4   Characteristics of Various Career Planning Activities and Probable Contribution to Career Success

Activity	Potential advantages	Potential shortcomings	Probable impact on psychological success and identity integration
	Individual activities		
1 Personal planning with possible aid of self-help materials.	**a** For persons with strong motivation and adequate sources of information, may be adequate for goal setting. **b** Cost is minimal.	**a** Most people need interpersonal feedback to develop a complete and accurate self-evaluation. **b** No built-in mechanism for checking completeness of information on occupational opportunities or for correcting distorted views of self. **c** No opportunity to explore new occupational possibilities.	Considerable potential contribution because individual sets own goals. Actual contribution likely to be minimized, however, because the activity lacks mechanisms for exploration of new potentials, interpersonal feedback, and social support to maintain motivation.
	Counselor-client activities		
2 Testing approach: Guidance counselor administers vocational interest and aptitude tests and feeds data back to client; may also provide information on occupations, job market, and job-hunting techniques.	Test results and information supplied may be of considerable value for client.	**a** Usually expensive. **b** Client has no way of testing validity of counselor's views or test results. **c** Interpersonal feedback likely to be minimal.	Since people do not readily accept disconfirming data in situations where there is no opportunity to validate the information, contribution may be relatively limited.
3 Counselor approach: Emphasis on interpersonal exploration of client's needs with counselor.	Skillful counselor may provide valuable input for self-assessment.	**a** No mechanism for checking validity of counselor's perceptions. **b** Most helpful in exploring personal needs; minimal stress on occupational information. **c** Usually expensive.	Potentially helpful, subject to the limitations that client must experience insights produced as valid and must check validity with other persons outside the counseling situation.
4 Combination testing and clinical approach.	**a** Combines benefits of both testing and counseling approaches. **b** Checking test results	**a** Potentially very expensive. **b** Most counselors are not	Essentially the same as for number 3.

340

5 Superior regularly or periodically assesses subordinate's performance and provides feedback and suggestions for improving performance and/or career opportunities.

6 Assessment center: usually conducted by or sponsored by employer. Employee is tested by a number of pencil-and-paper tests and is presented with situational tests and interviews where performance is observed and evaluated. Evaluators are often other managers trained in the technique. Psychologists design center and interpret test results.

against perceptions of counselor provides some mechanism for "validating" information

Boss as counselor or coach

a Superior may have an excellent opportunity to observe subordinate's behavior in a number of work activities.

b Superior knows career opportunities within the organization.

c Superior can provide assignments to expand subordinate's capabilities.

Group activities

a Substantial amounts of data can be developed quickly.
b Multiple judges on panel and results of several tests provide variety of perspectives for candidate.
c Moderate cost—usually borne by employer.
d Some evidence for more valid predictions than available through counselor-client approaches.

equally proficient in both approaches.

c Counselor may experience a need to see client in a manner consistent with test results.

a The superior's power can be highly threatening, causing subordinate to be defensive, cautious, and closed to feedback.

b Superior's first loyalty is likely to be seen as to the interests of the organization, not the subordinate.

c Not likely to integrate nonwork aspects of subordinate's life with career issues.

a High-threat situation:
1 Employee likely to feel "on the spot" and anxious about results—not an optimal situation for feedback.
2 Center serves interests of employer first, which may be incompatible with interests of employee.

b Primary emphasis is not on setting of personal goals.

a If done as a part of performance appraisal, depends on format. Traditional performance appraisal unlikely to be productive. MBO with substantial self-evaluation by subordinate may be helpful, since subordinate sets own goals, etc., and takes lead in assessment.

b If done as informal coaching, can be very effective to the extent that superior provides relatively nondirective assistance which maximizes subordinate's freedom to choose.

a Likely to be minimized to the extent that employee:
• Cannot really choose not to attend.
• Is not involved in design of activities.
• Is threatened by long-term career implications of evaluation.
• Receives minimal or threatening feedback.
b No explicit provision for goal setting.

Exhibit 14-4 Characteristics of Various Career Planning Activities and Probable Contribution to Career Success: *(continued)*

Activity	Potential advantages	Potential shortcomings	Probable impact on psychological success and identity integration
		c Data generated primarily applicable to career with employing organization only.	**c** No support group for planning or dealing with career crises.
		d Interpersonal feedback frequently not a prime or major objective.	
		e Does not provide information on other job possibilities, especially outside employing organization.	
7 Life planning workshop: conducted within organization. A set of semistructural experiences are presented which encourage participants to assess their values, situation, etc.; to set goals; and to develop greater self-awareness through interpersonal interaction with other participants.	**a** No cost to participant. **b** Encourages personal goal setting. **c** Wide exploration of self and needs encouraged. Copious interpersonal feedback generated. **d** Supportive environment. **e** Development of "supportive groups" and opportunities to assess and develop job-relevant skills possible.	**a** Normally do not provide occupational information, especially for careers outside the organization. **b** Employers leery of processes which may encourage employees to leave organization. **c** Provision for periodic follow-up probably necessary to maximize value to most participants.	**a** Specifically designed to provide identity integration and psychological success through personal goal setting and enhanced self-awareness. **b** If conducted within organization, benefits may be somewhat limited by need for program to serve employer's needs and by reluctance of employees to open up in groups of colleagues.

f Other participants are frequently valuable sources of information on career alternatives.

g Goals developed and development needs can be integrated into parallel organizational programs.

h Can be a part of an organization development effort.

d Participants may not be encouraged to explore changing jobs or careers.

c This is the only design which explicitly requires small groups in order to maximize feedback and opportunity to validate data.

8 Life planning workshop: conducted outside organization.

a Same as 7b through 7g.

b Low threat situation.

c Potential for developing job-hunting skills possible.

a Moderate cost to participants unless underwritten by employer.

b Normally do not provide occupational information on job markets, nature of jobs, etc.

c See 7b and 7c.

See 7a and 7c.

343

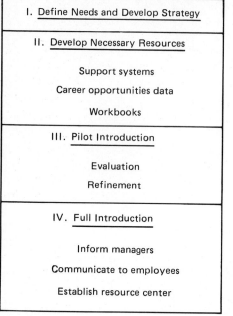

I. Define Needs and Develop Strategy

II. Develop Necessary Resources

Support systems

Career opportunities data

Workbooks

III. Pilot Introduction

Evaluation

Refinement

IV. Full Introduction

Inform managers

Communicate to employees

Establish resource center

Exhibit 14-5 Implementing a career planning program.

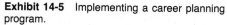

other areas: counseling staff, training and development programs, personnel data systems or inventories, job posting, job description, salary administration, manpower planning (staffing requirements), recruitment and selection, personnel policies, etc.

In another company, a sophisticated personnel data system was in place, but was not widely understood or used for purposes of identifying candidates for job vacancies. The company developed a "career profile" printout for each employee and strengthened the procedures for making use of the data base.

Perhaps the most common void in the resources needed to support career planning is realistic information on career opportunities. The best strategy is to build career information gradually, starting with simple charts that show job titles in each unit or function by organizational level. Salary level or grade need not be used, because the purpose is to identify only the possible job opportunities. To back up such a chart, a food products company published brief descriptions of the content and qualifications of each job. In another case, a bank published a manual containing all these basic facts, sorted by department.

With the basic data in place, refinements may be made. For example, job titles can be grouped into "families" of similar jobs, and possible job progression lines (career paths) among jobs and job families can be drawn. A computer company provides detailed information on levels and job vacancies. And an oil company has published career paths within its financial and engineering functions.

Career-planning workbooks are useful as basic, self-directed tools. Although many varieties of published workbooks are available, experience suggests that the tailored approach provides the realistic, in-depth information and exercises needed. IBM, Xerox, General Motors, and other companies have developed their own workbooks, tailored to their particular needs. These workbooks generally provide exercises on self-analysis, career planning, and career goal setting.

Information may also be included on the company's personnel systems, EEO and AA policies and practices, career opportunities, salary administration, and other policies. Articles may be included to stimulate and guide individual thinking; illustrations help maintain interest. A major oil company developed a series of five workbooks that included these features. Employees receive each in sequence over a period of weeks: "Know Yourself," "Know Your Interests," "Know Your Opportunities," "Know Your Job," "Develop Your Plan." A food products company developed a similar series of three workbooks: "Know Yourself," "Know Your Opportunities," "Know Your Plan."

It is also advisable to pretest workbook materials. In this way management can assess the effectiveness of the tools in achieving their intended purposes and make whatever modifications are necessary. Such a study may be limited to one location or may represent a cross section of all employees. In one company, employees from all divisions were included; in another, the pilot group was composed of the financial staff.

A career resource center may be established (usually as part of the employee development function) to conduct the program and handle referrals from supervisors. The center may provide:

Counseling on career matters and referral to other counselors for additional kinds of information

Group workshops

Additional reading materials and courses

Additional information on career paths and job requirements

Tests to identify skills, abilities, and aptitudes

Company and external training and development programs such as seminars and courses

Finally, all supervisors and managers should be informed about the program before it is initiated so that they can answer employee questions. The program should subsequently be communicated widely, so that all interested employees know that it is available, what is involved, and how to sign up. Under affirmative action requirements, communication is often a significant task. One company was required to inform certain employees in writing about the program. In addition, it had to receive a signed statement from each individual affirming that she or he had the opportunity to participate in the program.

The Information Systems Group of Xerox Corporation established such a career information center to provide resources to any employee on request. Included in the materials available are handbooks outlining career paths, workbooks for self-analysis, and videotapes on careers. Playback facilities are at every location, used for skills training programs. Such videotapes include interviews with key executives, panel discussions with groups of employees representing different kinds of jobs or interests (for example, female managers), and instructional tapes on how to do career planning. Xerox also uses an open job-posting system, counselors in headquarters locations, and a computer-based management replacement inventory with search capability.

Case Example: Mobil

An individualized career planning and development process has been applied at Mobil Oil Corporation. The process involves a number of interrelated procedures which assure uniformity throughout the company in career-planning practices. Additionally, the process is closely linked with management practices in other aspects of human resource planning. Exhibit 14-6 illustrates Mobil's framework for the career planning process.

The following are the principal components of the process:

Human resource objectives: This document continues to be a five-year

Exhibit 14-6 How career planning fits in at Mobil.

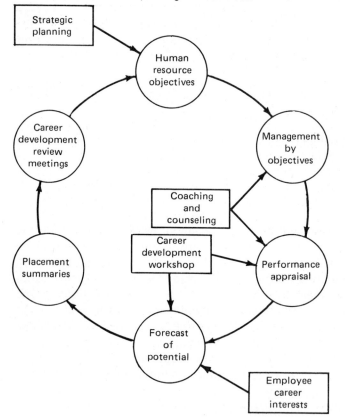

manpower forecast of both human resource needs and their costs. It starts from the smallest organizational unit and iteratively works its way upward.

Management by objectives: Individualized employee performance objectives, standards, and action plans are developed within the framework of a results-oriented MBO system. Long-range organizational objectives cascade downward to ultimately become individual job goals.

Coaching and counseling: The process of setting objectives within the MBO system, the monitoring of performance with respect to objectives, and the feedback of results all revolve around the supervisor's coaching and counseling abilities.

Performance appraisal: The performance appraisal process is an annual, multipurpose procedure that focuses on evaluation of results in terms of the objectives and standards developed through the MBO system. It is also used to establish a basis for individual salary administration.

Forecast of potential: This evaluation also occurs annually. Assessments are made about the employees' strengths and weaknesses as well as their likely effectiveness in higher-level positions or with increased responsibilities. Individualized developmental action plans are then developed.

Career development workshops: Two- and three-day workshops are conducted which focus on "how to" develop your own career within the system. They cover personal needs, career interests and goals, and the development of specific career plans.

Personnel development coordinators: In all cases the burden of career development is placed on the individual, and all supervisors are evaluated on their development of subordinates. In addition, coordinators work to facilitate the growth and movement of employees at lower organizational levels.

Placement summaries: These documents describe current and future staffing needs in terms of incumbents, ready replacements and forward replacements.

Career development review meetings: These meetings provide a form for organizational evaluation, and for review of an organization's requirements during the coming year and its ability to meet them. The review cycle begins with the smaller organizational units, which supply the next higher level of management with information necessary for human resource planning, and so on. The placement summaries act as the basic input document. The purpose of these reviews is to assure that adequate backup personnel exist for all key positions, both in numbers and in quality, and that appropriate plans for meeting individual development and organizational needs are formulated and pursued.

Mobil employees are expected to assume primary responsibility for their continuing growth and adjustment to organizational changes and opportunities. Developmental plans should be formulated by employees and their supervisors during objective-setting discussions, and performance and career development discussions. The company can and must encourage and assist these efforts through a variety of career development methods which include:

1 ON THE JOB
   Experience
   Position redesign

           Job change
           Special assignments
  2 **INTERNAL TRAINING**
           Management education
           Professional/technical
           Skill development
           Special programs
  3 **SELF-STUDY**
           200-plus courses
  4 **OUTSIDE TRAINING**
           University programs
           Conferences
           Workshops
  5 **EDUCATIONAL ASSISTANCE**

EFFECTIVENESS OF CAREER PLANNING

It is difficult to assess the benefits obtained through career planning or to judge the quality of the career-planning practices of companies. Results are largely a matter of attitudes of the participating employees. The quality of the programs themselves is relative both to management's standards and to prevailing industry practices which, as we have seen, are just taking shape and thus are an unsure basis for evaluative comparison.

Some managers have expressed fears that career planning "rocks the boat." They see the negative effects of raising expectations and stirring personal anxieties as far outweighing any substantial benefits that might accrue to the company. Yet such fears are not rationally based; facts are not considered in fearing raised turnover, burdened supervisors, and unrealistic employee expectations and job demands.

What Are the Risks?

Career planning has both positive and negative effects, as outlined in Exhibit 14-7. However, the problem is that some managers only see the risks in career planning and none of the potential rewards.

In some companies, supervisors are concerned that career planning will increase their work loads by requiring them to provide counseling and increased on-the-job development. Many already feel burdened by other personnel programs (appraisals, employee interviewing and selection procedures, job descriptions, etc.) and other administrative demands (budgeting, salary administration, etc.).

Career planning may also lead to increased strains on personnel systems such as training, educational assistance, internal placement, and job posting. Use of counselors may increase, and employees may request more information on job vacancies, pay practices, and career opportunities.

It is also feared that raised expectations may increase employee anxiety. Fundamental questions regarding personal strengths, weaknesses, and goals are

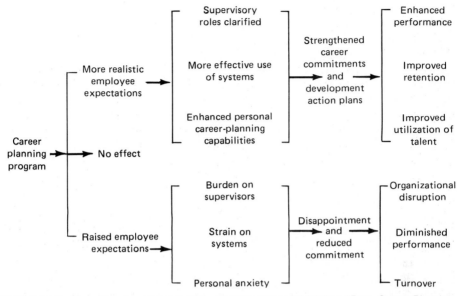

Exhibit 14-7 The effects of career planning. (*Source:* James W. Walker, "Does Career Planning Rock the Boat?" *Human Resource Management,* Spring 1978, p. 3.)

sometimes surfaced for the first time. Workshops, workbooks, and counseling rarely equip individuals to deal adequately with these issues. Accompanying the expectation that life somehow will be different is general anxiety about the *uncertainty* of career decisions and future events.

Anxiety caused by raised expectations can be beneficial if it leads to increased employee motivation. But unfulfilled expectations can lead to disappointment and reduced organizational commitment. As a result, some employees may become demotivated, performance may falter, and some may seek work elsewhere.

More Realistic Expectations

The key to effective career planning is in developing more *realistic*—not *raised*—expectations. Companies that have been successful in their career-planning efforts have guided employees toward opportunities and resources that are actually available and reasonable.

They have tried to dispel the "up or out" view of a career and instead promote other options such as lateral careers and careers within specialized job areas or locations. An employee need not feel it necessary to be promoted to "get ahead." And employees need not change jobs to have career progress. Promotional opportunities are, by definition, limited in a hierarchical organization. If career planning focuses on personal development in the current job rather than on promotability, potential, and career mobility, it can help create more realistic career expectations and help minimize potential dissatisfaction.

As shown in Exhibit 14-7, realistic expectations lead to a clarification of supervisory roles and responsibilities, more effective employee use of a company's career resources, and stronger individual abilities to carry out career planning in a practical, meaningful way.

Rather than burdening supervisors unduly, career planning can clarify and support supervisory responsibilities. The supervisor's primary role should be to discuss openly with each employee current job goals, requirements, and performance results. It is unlikely that all supervisors can or even should try to become career counselors in a broader sense. Nevertheless, many companies have been training supervisors to counsel employees on career matters as well as performance planning and appraisal. And the view is that the performance appraisal process is an important entree to career discussions.

Several large corporations require managers to meet with employees at least annually, more often if the employees desire, to review career progress and career plans. As difficult as the task may seem, the companies have found that managers do, in fact, have the abilities and that such reviews are not unduly burdensome. Supervisory training is essential, they report, along with adequate third-party staff support.

Career planning can also help equip employees to make *better* use of career development resources and systems. Many companies candidly report on expected vacancies and describe what the systems can and cannot do. Importantly, career planning gives management an opportunity to communicate how performance appraisal, training and development, performance incentives, compensation, and other systems relate to personal needs and plans. Employees are often unaware of many programs and do not realize how extensive the company's help really is.

Effective career planning does require information about job requirements and career paths, compensation opportunities, and available development resources. It is also important that employees learn about the company's business—what it is doing and why, its plans and objectives, and future career opportunities. The straight story helps avoid rocking the boat.

End Results

Experience suggests that the key to a successful process is *depth* of information, of employee thinking and analysis, and of management attention to career management needs. Employees need to develop their *personal skills in career planning,* not merely seek help and direction. It should not be a superficial exercise, nor merely another development program. To be effective, career planning needs to be an intensive, voluntary, recurring, and self-directed process of self-examination and planning. It must lead to development of realistic personal goals and action plans.

The primary aim of career planning is not to help employees lay out a career plan, per se, but to equip employees to help themselves. For example, when Gulf Oil Corporation designed a pilot study to evaluate its new career-planning program, involving self-study workbooks, a detailed questionnaire was used to measure changes in participant career attitudes, information adequacy, and specific career planning skills. The intent of the program, stated Gulf, was to equip employees with the skills needed to develop and achieve their own career plans.

At best, corporate career planning presents the company's needs and resources in an open, candid, and helpful way. Rather than disrupting an organization, it strengthens the commitment among employees who represent the core of its talent. Of course, the risks are greater for a stable or contracting organization than for an expanding one, because opportunities are limited. But even in these cases, career planning can help stimulate and guide employees toward the personal development and alternative work opportunities that are *available* and are best suited to them.

Part Five

Conclusion

Chapter 15

The Impact of Human Resource Planning

KEY POINTS

- Measurements are sought which will assess the worth of human resource activities, but they are elusive.
- Traditional measurements are readily available, but should be carefully applied to avoid misinterpretation.
- Human resource accounting represents an alternative, sophisticated way to track the impact of human resource activities on business results.
- Ultimately, however, measures of the impact of human resource planning are subjective judgments that can be made only by managers, with supplemental information provided by measurement efforts.
- One technique which provides both a benchmark and a forward perspective for human resource planning is an audit, which may be conducted within an organization or by external consultants.
- The essential impact of human resource planning is the extent to which it helps management maintain an effective and successful organization.
- Given the potential difficulties to be experienced in the 1980s, human resource planning will be come increasingly important as a management tool.

Human resource planning is itself a process of anticipating needs for change in an organization and of monitoring responses to these needs. Yet an organization also needs a way to assure that human resource planning is having its desired impact. This chapter briefly reviews the methods that may be used to measure the results of human resource planning and to evaluate the overall human resource planning process.

Human resource planning links a company's business planning and broad company objectives with the specific programs and activities that make up human resource management. As such, the principal measure of effectiveness must be the strength and adequacy of these linkages: Has the company adequately prepared for changing human resource requirements? Has the company been able to utilize its human resources effectively in conformity with corporate plans and with affirmative action plans?

Sometimes specific indicators of results are sought in evaluating human resource management efforts: vacancies filled, turnover rates, costs per hire, etc. The attitude sometimes exists, "If you can't measure it, it doesn't exist." But the results of human resource planning must also be viewed as complex and broad. The task is to evaluate the impact of a total system, not merely measure the costs or benefits attained from particular actions or system components.

Accordingly, efforts to measure results in the human resource area have become more sophisticated, and the state of the art calls for an integrated view of expenditures as costs and capital investments, and of the benefits attained as both measurable and subjectively identifiable. There is, in sum, no simple indicator of the impact of human resource planning.

Studies aimed at assessing the overall effectiveness of human resource efforts (and human resource planning systems) follow the pattern of an audit, comprising interviews, observations, and review of available information. Such comprehensive evaluation studies are valuable to companies in taking a periodic look at policies and practices, directions and emphases, and pressing needs for change. Just as audits of accounting practices, budgeting processes, or inventory systems provide an objective perspective of how well these processes are functioning, so an audit can guide a company's human resource planning efforts.

Of course, evaluating the past impact of human resource practices is only half the task. Assessment of human resource planning must also look ahead to impending changes affecting the management of the enterprise. The conditions expected in the 1980s are far different from those experienced at any time since World War II. Whether human resource planning will help management bridge the "awkward eighties" is a fundamental issue to be considered.

MEASURING RESULTS

Certainly companies look for practical benefits to flow from human resource management activities. It is one thing to say that "people are our most important asset." It is another to identify the return on this asset and, thereby, the cost-effectiveness of human resource management expenditures.

Results are of various types and some are more easily measured than others. Quantitative indicators are available for recruitment success, turnover, control of pay adjustments, participation in training programs, relocations, and other discrete activity patterns. Personnel costs may be tallied and tracked from period to period, highlighting achievement of desired cost-control targets. But other results are difficult to pin down, including improvement in the quality of management, the caliber of new recruits, the effectiveness of training, or the adequacy of career development activities. These require subjective judgments.

The contrasting views of human resource expenditures as expense versus investment provide a basis for considering the lasting value of expenditures. If training is an investment, what is the measurable return? And how do we define the bounds of the investment: Do we include opportunity costs? Even defining the cost of developing training programs requires judgments of time and resources devoted and then some way to allocate or amortize these costs over the program's useful life. It may be far easier to consider many expenditures as current operating expenses and simply question whether they were worthwhile and appropriate.

Traditional Measures

An effort to measure the results of human resource planning typically begins with examination of readily available statistics. Quantitative indicators readily highlight gross problems (high turnover, unfilled positions, etc.) and shifts from the norm (by comparison with industry standards, data from other companies, or the company's previous experience).

Turnover is probably the most commonly used measure, indicating possible underlying problems in an organization when it gets too high. But whether 10 percent or 40 percent is the point where turnover is considered "too high" and a signal of problems depends on the comparative norms used. Turnover rates are typically calculated by organizational units, levels, functions, locations, length of service, or other categories to permit useful interpretations.

Staffing ratios, representing the number of employees for a given amount of volume produced, dollar revenues, or net profits earned, provide gross indicators of "proper" staffing. When these measures get out of line, comparatively, management may feel the organization is overstaffed or understaffed. Of course, such ratios may have been built into the forecasting process itself as a control, as well as being an end-result measure (Dahl, 1979). Payroll costs may be used as a substitute for head counts, as a common denominator with other financial indices.

Among other indicators frequently used are the following:

- Number of "qualified backups" for each management position
- Acceptance rates of professional hires
- Cost per hire
- Ratio of internal placements to external hires
- Participation rates in training programs
- Days per employee devoted to training and development
- Cost per participant in given programs

- Length of time before positions are filled
- Occurrence and cost of internal relocations
- Achievement of affirmative action goals and objectives
- Compliance with performance appraisal requirements
- Various indicators of pay adjustments
- Employee attitude measures (shifts)

For operating-level employees, other traditional measures are also applicable such as absenteeism, grievances, safety, and overtime costs.

There is no shortage of quantitative measures in the human resource area. The important consideration is not how to calculate them, but whether they are meaningful indicators of the effectiveness of human resource management and, in turn, human resource planning. Further, most such measures have to do with implementation of programs rather than with the indirect results of the planning itself. Recruitment results may be right on target, but if the target is inappropriate, the measure is not particularly helpful.

Human Resource Accounting

In the 1970s, a number of companies experimented with an innovative way of measuring the impact of human resource actions. They assumed that expenditures for human resource management activities (for example, recruitment, training, transfers) are costs which sometimes generate long-term returns. Hence human resource accounting provided a way to identify, measure, and communicate information about human resources. To some it represented a new way of thinking about people as assets.

Human resource accounting, in essence, means accounting for an organization's employees among its other resources, that is, measuring both the cost and the value of the personnel. It is not necessary to debate whether human resources are assets, as this issue is relevant only to financial reporting and not to the providing of information useful to management. From a taxation viewpoint it is preferable to consider all costs as current (deductible) expenses rather than to capitalize them. Yet people clearly represent capital assets of an organization, providing returns over long periods of time. A management development program, for example, is a current expense, but the benefits are experienced perhaps years later (Blau, 1978; Caplan and Landekich, 1975).

There are two ways to measure costs through human resource accounting: as historical costs or as replacement costs. The historical approach parallels the accepted accounting practice. People are valued on the basis of their actual acquisition cost. This means keeping track of all the costs associated with recruitment, selection, hiring, placement, training and orientation, and on-the-job training. Indirect costs such as trainer's time, lost productivity during training, time of managers spent in interviewing and recruitment, and costs involved in promotion or hiring from within may also be included. The two basic types of historical costs are thus acquisition costs and learning costs, and each type involves both direct and visible expenditures as well as more subtle indirect costs. The historical cost concept calls for tallying of all costs associated with an investment in human resources and then "depreciating" this investment over time. The cost of turnover may thus be more comprehensively measured as including all costs incurred in acquiring and developing employees and not merely the cost of replacing them.

An alternative cost approach examines the replacement costs: People are worth what they cost to replace on the open market. A problem with historical costing is that people may be worth more or less than you actually paid out. The value of an experienced employee may exceed the total costs incurred, as is recognized when a qualified replacement is sought in the open labor market. The replacement cost concept asks, "If all employees were gone tomorrow, what would it cost to replace them at their present level of competence?" This may be three to five times the annual total payroll of a company. But this is a vague estimate and actual replacement costs depend on specific capabilities desired for each position and the availability of talent. There is also the subtle factor of "knowing the organization and how to get things done" that cannot easily be given a replacement value.

Instead of tracking costs, human resource accounting may also follow the economic value approach. This calls for an estimation of the total expected contributions of a person to the value of the organization. In turn this compels an examination of the variables which determine the value of people and the interrelationships among these variables. Such variables may be nonmonetary as well as monetary. Value may be defined as the present value of future services provided either by a given individual or by an organization as a whole. An individual's value may be directly measured by considering both conditional and realizable economic value to be provided over a period of years, or it may be measured more simply by using a surrogate measure such as the present value of future compensation to be paid an individual. What would be the individual's income-producing potential? This question is most easily applied to sales personnel who may have a projected sales volume over a period of years which may be discounted to present value. For most types of jobs such clear future economic returns are not easily identified or measured. The concept, however, has considerable appeal (Flamholtz, 1974).

The value of a group or an organization may be measured by examining the overall results generated (services, profits, etc.). Some companies feel that the value of an individual cannot be measured in isolation. Rather it is the total organization that has value. One technique is the measurement of "unrealized goodwill." The total market value of the firm (or goodwill on the balance sheet) represents the value of various intangible assets, including the potential future value of its people. After the economic value of patents, trademarks, customer relationships, and other items are removed, the remainder would indicate the total value of human resources. This aggregate value may be divided by the total number of employees to result in an individual value estimate. Another approach examines the behavioral complexities of an organization's value, viewing the organization as a system comprising numerous measurable variables. Attitudinal surveys and other diagnostic measures can help determine the relative value of an organization and its overall effectiveness (Flamholtz, 1974; Likert and Bowers, 1969; Rhode and Lawler, 1973; Taylor and Bowers, 1972).

Human resource accounting represents an intriguing concept for measuring the impact of human resource planning in an organization. However, it has been applied in only a few organizations and remains elusive to both accounting and human resource professionals. It works out well in theory, but the practical problems of collecting data and establishing reasonably acceptable measures of costs and values have been insuperable. As management demands for useful information on human resource costs and benefits mount, advances may be made in making human resource accounting techniques operational (McFarland, 1977; Paperman and Martin, 1977; Rhode and Lawler, 1973).

Broader Indicators

One of the frustrations of working in the human resource area is the lack of hard measures of accomplishment. Human resource planning is more a social science than a mathematical science, and its professionals must have a high tolerance for the ambiguities inherent in the field.

Rather than looking at hard measures or statistical comparisons over time, perhaps a more fruitful approach considers the broader indicators of impact on an organization. The cost-effectiveness of human resource planning or of any human resource management activities is a subjective measure by management. Accordingly, the criteria used must come from management, preferably represented in specific objectives and plans of the business, translated into human resource objectives (Machaver, 1977).

The accomplishments in managing human resources are determined in relation to management expectations. Roles, responsibilities, costs, results, and priorities all depend on what management wants accomplished. For this reason, human resource planning approaches vary widely in depth and sophistication among companies and even among divisions within companies. The stage or level of human resource planning practice depends on the needs perceived by management, given the style of management applied and the stage of development of the organization (Walker, 1974).

It is useful, then, to consider the following questions:

- What are our objectives? For what are we responsible?
- What are the expectations of management (and our other "clients" in the corporation)?
- What are the specific indicators of our effective performance in human resource planning?
- What are the priorities by which we are operating?
- How do our accomplishments compare with these criteria?
- What should be our future objectives and criteria?
- How should we change what we are doing in human resource planning? What new tools or systems do we need? What should we stop doing or do differently?

Although subjective, these indicators are pragmatic. They directly address the central issue of determining the impact of human resource planning from a management perspective. Additional specific statistical measures or human resource accounting measures may be used as supplements to such broad judgments, but the evaluation of human resource planning is inescapably subjective and qualitative in nature.

A HUMAN RESOURCE AUDIT

A midwestern manufacturing company had grown rapidly over three decades from a fledgling entrepreneurship. As it grew to become a $1 billion plus revenues company, it expanded and diversified. Its managerial demands increased and specialized staffs evolved in finance, law, research, personnel, and other areas. But the board of directors questioned whether the company was adequately equipped to continue its rapid growth. Did it have the caliber of management, the depth of technical expertise, the capacity to attract and train needed talent? These were raised as critical factors in effectively managing further capital investments.

Accordingly, the president called for a review of management practices and functions in various areas. Data-processing functions were examined and new directions established. A new financial planning and control process was installed with strong functional organization ties across the operating divisions. In the human resource function, the activities were realigned to form a new organizational structure, and several additional professional positions were created to strengthen activities in management development, professional recruitment, and planning.

This is an example of a common circumstance in which an organization undertook a self-examination and charted a new course consistent with the business strategies. It is an excellent circumstance for a human resource audit—a systematic review and assessment of human resource management philosophies, policies, systems, and practices. The organization was keyed to considering innovations and was ready to act in different ways.

Audits may be conducted in various circumstances:

- Felt concern by top management
- An external force compelling a review (parent company, acquirer, committee of the board, government agency, etc.)
- A new officer responsible for human resources
- A significant change in the business impelling reconsideration of human resource management (for example, business downturn, rapid expansion, unionization threat, astounding employee turnover)
- A desire on the part of human resource professionals to advance the company's practices and systems

An audit provides a comprehensive perspective on current practices, resources, and management policies regarding human resource management and identifies opportunities and strategies for redirecting these. Implicit is an assumption that opportunities are being missed by staying with current approaches and that the human resource management process is dynamic and must continually be redirected to be responsive to needs.

Audits need not be exhaustive, but may focus on particular functions such as training and development, benefits, compensation, or information systems. The purpose and the approach remain generally the same, however, regardless of scope.

Approach

The notion of an audit stems from the established practice of accounting audits mandated by SEC regulations and "generally accepted accounting practice." Companies routinely open their doors to auditors to verify the accuracy of their financial information and the reasonableness of their accounting practices. At the same time, inputs are received which guide the improvement of the financial planning and accounting processes.

Human resource audits are not routine, and are, in fact, unusual. While many companies sometimes conduct self-studies involving task forces, surveys, or direct developmental efforts (for example, to install a new forecasting procedure), the notion of an audit is usually reserved for interventions by consultants. In one instance, an internal consulting group (at Citibank) provided an ongoing audit function for operating units within the institution. The focus here was on analyzing the extent to which supervisors complied with established personnel policies and practices, as a basis for determining assistance needed (Sheibar, 1974).

Consultants are used in audits for a variety of reasons, which may or may not be applicable in each instance:

- A desire for impartiality and objectivity.
- The value of gaining experience from other companies.
- The professional (specialized) expertise of the individual consultants.
- The ability of consultants to bypass both "politics" and natural resistance to examination and change.
- The potential leverage and credibility with senior management gained by using a respected external authority.
- The ability of consultants to ask "dumb questions," taking nothing for granted and collecting data that might otherwise be overlooked or unused.
- A willingness by consultants to make judgments regarding needs without risk of prejudice. (Staff managers are sometimes defensive when reviewing their own domains.)

A human resource audit typically involves the following steps:

1   A planning meeting involving key staff persons and senior managers. Here the audit procedure is tailored to address particular issues felt to be important; the data collection and interview plan are developed.

2   Examination of pertinent available information, including personnel data, computer capabilities, managerial and employee manuals, guidebooks, appraisal forms and materials, recruitment materials, communications, and other such material as may be relevant.

3   Interviews with key managers from operating units, key staff divisions, senior executives, and representative employees (certainly optional) to pinpoint issues of concern, present strengths, anticipated needs, and managerial philosophies regarding human resources. The number of interviews is determined in the initial meeting. If a wider survey of employees is desired, the audit is designed as such, an organizational audit or attitude survey.

4   Additional information such as business plans, budgets, appraisal data, and compensation data may be useful in investigating particular issues identified as warranting consideration in planning for future needs.

5   The various inputs are synthesized to present an integrated picture of current activities, priorities, staff resources, and the problems identified. Principal future needs are identified as criteria for assessing human resource priorities, and specific programs/actions are proposed.

6   Normally, the results of the audit are discussed in a series of meetings involving both the managers and the staff professionals. Frequently particular aspects become issues for further, more specialized study (for example, staffing analyses, development of computer information systems, revision of appraisal practices).

Questions to Ask

While an audit necessarily follows a trail of issues developed through the gathering of information, it is helpful to begin with a list of questions. Such a list reflects the initial concerns which gave rise to the audit. The questions are modified as interviews progress and, of course, are rarely asked directly or in sequence. But they serve as a checklist and guide for interviews, ensuring that important points are being covered.

Exhibit 15-1 presents a list of questions adapted from the interview guide used in an electronics company. The questions reflect the kinds of problems felt to be present, but at the same time cover a wide range of topics relating to human resource management practices in the company.

From this particular audit, it was determined that a formalized forecasting and information analysis activity was needed, and steps were taken to establish a function in that area. Also, serious concerns about mobility, particularly across units, led to modifications in job posting and internal search procedures. The personnel staff's role in referring candidates for vacancies increased. Finally, the appraisal process, which the staff had considered "a good system but not well accepted," was adjudged ineffective (in large part due to poor implementation and communication), and it was overhauled.

Using the Results

Human resource professionals typically respond to identified needs. Yet not all needs jump out (like affirmative action commitments). So audits serve the

Exhibit 15-1   Human Resource Audit Interview Questions

Information

What kinds of information do you use regarding human resources?

Payroll?
Basic personnel data?
Turnover?
Hires?
Analyses of training, movement, etc.?
Forecasts?
Cost information?
Other?

Where do you get this information?

Are you satisfied with this information? What additional or different information could you use?

Have you ever asked for a special report? Did you get the information you wanted?
Have you ever had needs for information that were tough to satisfy (inside, outside, legal)?
What do you not know about your people that you would like to know?

Forecasting

How do you go about determining your future personnel requirements?

How much confidence do you place in your estimates?

How do you verify the accuracy (or reasonableness) of estimates made by others for you to use?
How well does the budgeting process work for you in people forecasting?
How far ahead can you forecast needs? Is there a need to forecast further? Should we link our forecasts with long-range strategic plans?
Do you think we will be using new tools and techniques five years from now? What might they be?

Transfers and Promotions

Do you feel our internal staffing practices are systematic enough? Have you experienced any problems in this area?

Is the best person usually selected for a job?

How do you determine choices among candidates?

How well does the job-posting system work?

How much confidence do you have in your appraisal of people?
Are we hiring people too fast? Too slowly? Are we promoting the right proportion of people from within versus recruitment?
Do employees seem to know what they are getting into when considering different jobs? Do they know what their options are?
Some companies have set up workshops for career planning and provided career-planning help. Should we do this?
Would any of your salaried employees feel differently about this?

Exhibit 15-1 Human Resource Audit Interview Questions *(continued)*

Does the personnel department help you identify and select internal candidates? What additional help would you like?

Do you think we will need to change our practices in this aspect in the next few years? How? Why?

Should there be more moves across divisional or functional lines? How can this be effected?

Training and Development

How do you decide who attends certain training programs?

Is there a reasonable level and frequency of participation?

Should we use more internal programs? External programs?

Do you have a good sense of the quality of these programs? How do you know about this?

Do you see major needs for changing our training efforts?

How many days a month (on the average) should managers participate in training or development activities for their own personal development? Are we doing this now?

Management Succession Planning

How do you go about planning for the succession of your key managers? Have you identified your possible successor?

Do you feel you have qualified successors to cover most key positions? Do you have very many high-potential managers who could rise to the top of our organization?

Do you feel we have an adequate definition of our future management requirements—what we are developing people for?

Who has what responsibilities for identifying and developing managers?

In our succession practices, do we move enough people laterally?

Do we face up to performers who are on a plateau in key managerial positions?

Performance Appraisal

How well does our appraisal process work?

Does it fit your unit's situation?

What are the benefits of the process? The drawbacks or problems?

Do your managers know how to conduct appraisals? Do they care?

What happens to the written appraisals? What are they used for?

Do you see our appraisals as being hard-nosed evaluations or as more developmental benchmarks? What are we trying to accomplish?

Do you sense any problems with the timing, forms, or administrative aspects of the process?

Are our ratings consistent across the organization? Have they tended to drift upward? Are they linked with pay?

Do we give adequate attention to individual development plans?

Are the appraisals usually discussed with the employee?

What changes would you like to see in the process?

When were you last appraised? Was it a satisfactory experience?

Compensation

Are our compensation and benefits policies appropriate for our business needs?

Do we have a compensation philosophy as a company?

Exhibit 15-1   Human Resource Audit Interview Questions *(continued)*

Are we rewarding people adequately? Competitively? Equitably?
Are we dealing adequately with compression?
Are our job descriptions reasonably complete and up-to-date? Of what use are they to you?
How flexible is our job evaluation system? Is it fair? Easy to use?
Do you feel you have adequate control over compensation costs?
Can you reward your outstanding performers adequately?
What opportunities do we have to improve our pay practices?

Affirmative Action

Do you have any comments on our affirmative action programs?

How well are they working? Are our goals achievable?

What lessons have we learned about affirmative action?
Any suggestions?

Other Human Resource Functions

Do you have any comments on our other human resource functions?

Employment?
Employee benefits?
Labor relations?
Safety?
Special programs?

Are there activities we are not performing that we should be performing?

Variations in Needs

How do your needs differ from those of other departments? Are yours unique in any way?

What is our most pressing need in human resource management?

Does our company have an overall human resource philosophy? What is it? Is it well communicated?
What would you like to see accomplished from this audit?
Will our philosophy change in the next five years? Will we be equipped to implement it?

The Staff Function

What do you expect from the human resource staff? Are you usually satisfied?

Do they have adequate resources? Or are they overstaffed?

Do they have the proper attitude and approach? Are they appropriately organized? Are they adequately equipped? Are they capable?
If you could make one change in the human resource function or the way it works today, what would it be?

purpose of identifying needs, both needs for doing new things and needs for strengthening or redirecting existing activities.

An audit can provide inputs to the planning and budgeting of a personnel staff as well as guidance to a company's management regarding human resource policies, practices, and philosophies. It is a "shaking up" resulting in a "shaking out" of priorities and requirements.

Ideally, perhaps, such judgments would occur in the normal course of human events. But change is not the norm; managers resist change and cling tenaciously to established ways of managing people. The human resource management process is perhaps the most difficult for management to direct in terms of change because it is also one of the longest established in practice, the most personal in style, and the least definable in terms of critical priorities. Audits provide benchmarks and amass the best available data and insights in the process of reviewing the past and charting the future for human resource practices.

PROSPECTS FOR THE EIGHTIES

In concluding this book, it is timely to consider the major issues that will confront human resource planning during the 1980s. The book represents a turning point in human resource planning practice, by citing 1970s practices as historical (but not necessarily passé). A new decade calls for new thinking; it represents an opportunity for reflection on the past and new forward thinking.

As discussed in Chapter 1, the issues confronting management in human resource planning have shifted from decade to decade. Each period has displayed forces that were largely unanticipated and often failed to generate a widespread response. Times change, needs change, but not every company responds effectively. Effective human resource planning anticipates forces of change and guides management toward actions that will bring the best results for the organization and its individual employees.

The eighties are no exception. Some forecasters have envisioned the decade as the "awkward" eighties, representing no major thrusts but rather a period of stumbling into the 1990s. Others have projected that inevitable energy short-ages, demographic shifts, political upheavals, and economic difficulties (reces-sion and inflation) are virtually upon us now and will intensify in impact in the years immediately ahead. How serious will our difficulties be? What opportuni-ties do these "awkward" or adverse conditions hold for management?

The Environment

Clearly, our work force is aging and new imbalances will be experienced in the years ahead. There will be more older employees, many of whom may wish to continue working, but others who will opt to retire early. There will be a shortage, first, of middle-aged managers, and then of younger workers. These shifts complicate forecasting of staffing needs and also bode change in attitudes and expectations of employees.

The energy crisis, expected to continue unabated, will fuel inflation and, in turn, strain our economic capacity to maintain our historical rates of expansion and international competitiveness. Salaries certainly will not keep pace with inflation; hence the overall standard of living of Americans will likely decline. These conditions will create further strains on staffing levels, organization, cost controls, career management policies and practices, and a plethora of other management actions not necessary back in the "good times."

In response, the sociopolitical environment will shift to reflect public demands for solutions to these massive problems. Egalitarianism, stressed for two decades, will yield to struggles for economic viability and hence increased isolationism and elitism. At the same time, the "have-nots" will press their rights through the courts, under the laws of the previous decades, and create further havoc. Equal employment opportunity and affirmative action pressures will increase, not abate, and new regulatory forces under age discrimination, handicapped, and other legislated protections will increase in force substantially.

This will become a decade of less, not more, creating significant demands on those persons charged with allocating scarce resources, scarce career opportunities, scarce jobs, and scarce oil. Planning will become critically important. Organizations will be compelled to plan and operate far more efficiently to maintain profitability and even modest growth. Certainly expansionist growth will diminish, as economic capacity diminishes and the population's demands level off (also due to aging).

Managing less is more difficult, but in a real sense it is also the greater challenge. Managers have it made when times are booming. To manage under difficult conditions requires extraordinary capabilities. Human resource planning helps equip managers with an essential set of tools heretofore inessential.

Professional Roles

With this new environment, senior management interest in human resource matters will surely continue to mount. The stature and the responsibilities of human resource professionals will increase, paralleling the increased expectations placed upon operating managers for improved human resource practices and results. This is an age of building a lean and hungry organization, and rewards will go to the managers who do this effectively.

At the same time, the skills of human resource planning professionals will deepen and sharpen. In virtually every area outlined in this book, human resource professionals will be called upon for expertise that was considered "state of the art" a decade before. What was once "nice" becomes necessary: information, forecasting, control systems, appraisal systems that work, career management, succession planning, job analysis and classification, career paths, productivity improvement, and so on. Employee relations or personnel professionals will become important contributors to vital business results—both by influencing cost structures and by influencing organizational effectiveness.

Professional roles will change, incorporating these new functions, as discussed in Chapter 3. Human resource management and, more specifically, human resource planning, will become a critical variable in an organization's success. And the measure will not be the fact of installing systems or conducting programs, but rather their impact on identifiable management needs.

Conclusion

This book has examined three major dimensions of human resource planning. Each represents a new thrust of management which implies new demands in the years ahead. Organizations must manage better; practices, systems, and even values must adapt to changing conditions. Human resource planning represents the cutting edge of company management practices in managing a costly and valuable resource—people. The tools described in this book are not particularly complex or difficult to apply. They represent the hope, however, of the future of highly vulnerable business organizations.

Organizations must learn to forecast human resource needs more effectively. More sophisticated analytic techniques, applied to better data, and driven by strategic planning processes, are vital. We must learn to apply the same rigor to human resources as we apply to financial, inventory, and other resources.

Organizations must learn to manage employee performance more effectively. All the systems and practices that bear on performance need to be planned to work in synchronization as a total system: job evaluation, compensation, job definition, appraisal, training, selection, etc. Improved productivity will not result from simple, gimmicky solutions, but only from broad, carefully orchestrated management approaches. Performance of professionals and managers is difficult to manage because it is so complex and ill-defined, yet it is also critical to manage effectively for this very reason.

Finally, organizations must learn to manage careers of their employees more effectively, especially the careers of managers and professionals who have high expectations and constrained opportunities. Dual-career families, changing attitudes toward relocations, lessened intercompany mobility options (due to reduced hiring), and a glut of high-talent, eager professionals make yesterday's career practices obsolete. Companies need defined career options, planned individual career development, and logical succession planning. At the same time individual participation must increase, in a realistic and meaningful way.

Human resource planning is a challenge, and it will be met.

Bibliography

Ackoff, R. L.: *A Concept of Corporate Planning,* John Wiley & Sons, New York, 1970.

Air Force Occupational Measurement Center: *Management Analysis Specialist Career Ladder,* AFSCs 69130, 69150, 69170, and 69190, Lackland Air Force Base, Tex., 1975.

Aldag, R. J., and A. P. Brief: *Task Design and Employee Motivation,* Scott-Foresman & Co., Glenview, Ill., 1979.

Alfred, Theodore M.: "Choice or Checkers in Manpower Management," *Harvard Business Review,* January–February 1967, pp. 157–168.

Allen, Everett: *Pension Planning,* 3d ed., Richard D. Irwin, Homewood, Ill., 1977.

American Friends Service Committee: *Working Loose: A Book about Finding Work,* Random House, New York, 1971.

"Americans Change," *Business Week,* Feb. 20, 1978, pp. 64–71.

Anderson, Donald N.: "Zero-Base Budgeting: How To Get Rid of Corporate Crabgrass," *Management Review,* October 1976, pp. 4–16.

Anderson, Howard J.: *Primer of Equal Employment Opportunity,* Bureau of National Affairs, Washington, 1978.

Ansoff, H. Igor: *Corporate Strategy,* McGraw-Hill, New York, 1965.

Anthony, William P.: "Get To Know Your Employees—The Human Resource Information System," *Personnel Journal,* April 1977, pp. 179–186.

Applebaum, Stephen H., and John B. Millard: "Engineering a Compensation Program To Fit the Individual, Not the Job," *Personnel Journal,* March 1976, pp. 121ff.

Austin, David L.: "Must The Past Be Prologue? Or, Why Can't We Do Things Differently?" *Personnel Journal,* May 1975, pp. 261–265.

Bailyn, L.: "Family Constraints on Women's Work," *Annals of the New York Academy of Science,* vol. 208, 1973, pp. 82–90.

Baker, John K., and Robert H. Schaffer: "Making Staff Consulting More Effective," *Harvard Business Review,* January–February 1969, pp. 62–71.

Bartholomew, D. J.: *Stochastic Models for Social Processes,* 2d ed. John Wiley & Sons, New York, 1973.

————, and A. R. Smith (eds.): *Manpower and Management Science,* English University Press, London, 1970.

Basnight, Thomas, and Benjamin W. Wolkinson: "Evaluating Managerial Performance: Is Your Appraisal System Legal?" *Employee Relations Law Journal,* vol. 3, no. 2, Autumn 1977, pp. 240–255.

Bassett, Glenn A.: "Elements of Manpower Forecasting and Scheduling," *Human Resource Management,* Fall 1973, pp. 35–43.

———— and H. H. Meyer: "Performance Appraisal Based on Self-Review," *Personnel Psychology,* vol. 21, no. 4, 1968, pp. 421–430.

Bates, Marsh W., and Richard G. Vail: "Job Evaluation and Equal Employment Opportunity: A Tool for Compliance—A Weapon for Defense," *Employee Relations Law Journal,* vol. 1, no. 4, 1978, pp. 535–546.

Bednarzik, Robert W., and Deborah P. Klein: "Labor Force Trends: A Synthesis and Analysis," *Monthly Labor Review,* October 1977, pp. 3–15.

Beer, Michael, and Robert A. Ruh: "Employee Growth through Performance Management," *Harvard Business Review,* vol. 54, no. 4, July–August 1976, pp. 59–66.

Belcher, David W.: *Compensation Administration,* Prentice-Hall, Englewood Cliffs, N.J., 1974.

Bell, D. J.: *Planning Corporate Manpower,* Longmans, Harlow, London, 1974.

Bennett, James E.: "What Went Wrong with Manpower Planning?" *Business Quarterly,* Summer 1972, pp. 55–57.

Benson, Ronald G., and Charles R. Klasson: "A Computer Simulation Model for High-Talent Personnel," in E. Burack and J. Walker (eds.), *Manpower Planning and Programming,* Allyn & Bacon, Boston, 1972, pp. 174–187.

Berger, Lance A.: "A Dew Line for Training and Development: The Needs Analysis Survey," *Personnel Administrator,* November 1976, pp. 51–55.

Berkwitt, George S.: "Industrial Relation Is Nowhere," *Dun's Review,* vol. 99, no. 2, February 1972, pp. 58–60.

"The Big Business of Teaching Managers," *Business Week,* July 25, 1977, pp. 106–108.

Blakely, Robert T., III: "Markov Models and Manpower Planning," *Industrial Management Review,* Winter 1970, pp. 39–46.

Blau, Ben Ami: "Understanding Midcareer Stress," *Management Review,* vol. 67, no. 8, August 1978, pp. 57–63.

Blau, Gary: *Human Resource Accounting,* Work in America Institute, Inc., Scarsdale, N.Y., 1978.

Blaxall, Martha, and Barbara B. Reagan: *Women and the Workplace: The Implication of Occupational Segregation,* University of Chicago Press, Chicago, 1976.

Bolles, R. N.: *What Color Is Your Parachute?* Ten Speed Press, Berkley, Calif., 1972.

————: *The Three Boxes of Life,* Ten Speed Press, Berkeley, Calif. 1978.

Bowen, Donald D., and Douglas T. Hall: "Career Planning for Employee Development: A Primer for Managers," *California Management Review,* vol. 20, no. 2, Winter 1977, pp. 23–35.

Bramham, John: *Practical Manpower Planning,* Institute of Personnel Management, London, 1975.

Bray, Douglas W.: "The Assessment Center Method," in Robert L. Craig (ed.), *Training and Development Handbook,* McGraw-Hill, New York, 1976, chap. 16 pp. 1–15.

———, R. J. Campbell, and D. L. Grant: *Formative Years in Business: A Long Term AT&T Study of Managerial Lives,* John Wiley & Sons, New York, 1974.

Bright, James: *Automation and Management,* Harvard University, Division of Research, Cambridge, Mass., 1958.

Bright, William E.: "How One Company Manages Its Human Resources," *Harvard Business Review,* January–February, 1976, pp. 81–93.

Brito v. Zia Company, 478 F. 2d 1200 (1973).

Britton, Donald E.: "Are Job Descriptions Really Necessary?" *Personnel Administrator,* January 1975, pp. 47–49.

Brookmire, David A., and Amy A. Burton: "A Format for Packaging Your Affirmative Action Program," *Personnel Journal,* June 1978, pp. 294–304.

Bryant, Don R., Michael J. Maggard, and Robert P. Taylor: "Manpower Planning Models and Techniques," *Business Horizons,* April 1973, pp. 69–78.

Bucalo, John P., Jr.: "The Assessment Center — A More Specified Approach," *Human Resource Management,* Fall 1974, pp. 2–12.

Bull, Warren: "Compensation Managers: Let's Not Sleepwalk the 70's," *Business Quarterly,* Winter 1973, pp. 23–31.

Burack, Elmer H.: *Strategies for Manpower Planning and Programming,* General Learning Press, Morristown, N.J., 1972.

———: "Why All the Confusion about Career Planning?" *Human Resource Management,* Summer 1977, pp. 21–26.

——— and Thomas G. Gutteridge: "Institutional Manpower Planning: Rhetoric Versus Reality," *California Management Review,* vol. XX, no. 3, Spring 1978, pp. 13–22.

——— and Nicholas Mathys: "Work, Workers and Career Potential: Possibilities for a Common Language," *Personnel Administrator,* vol. 22, no. 4, May 1977, pp. 46–52.

——— and Thomas J. McNichols: *Human Resource Planning: Technology, Policy, Change,* Kent State University, Comparative Administration Research Institute, Kent, Ohio, 1973.

——— and Edwin L. Miller: "The Personnel Function in Transition," *California Management Review,* vol. 18, no. 3, Spring 1976, pp. 32–38.

——— and J. W. Walker (eds.): *Manpower Planning and Programming,* Allyn & Bacon, Boston, 1972.

Burch, E. Earl: "Productivity: Its Meaning and Measurement," *Atlanta Economic Review,* May–June 1974, pp. 43–47.

Burdick, Walton: "A Look at Corporate and Personnel Philosophy," *Personnel Administrator,* July 1976, pp. 21–26.

Burke, Ronald J.: "Characteristics of Effective Performance Appraisal Interviews," *Training and Development Journal,* vol. 24, no. 3, March 1970, pp. 9–12.

"Business Buys the Lie Detector," *Business Week,* Feb. 6, 1979, pp. 100–104.

Bushkin, A., and Samuel I. Schaen: *The Privacy Act of 1974: A Reference Manual for Compliance,* System Development Corporation, McLean, Va., 1976.

Byham, William C.: "Common Selection Problems To Be Overcome," *Personnel Administrator,* vol. 23, no. 8, August 1978, pp. 42–47.

Campbell, John P., Marvin D. Dunnette, R. O. Arvey, and L. W. Hellervik: "The Development and Evaluation of Behaviorally Based Rating Scales," *Journal of Applied Psychology,* vol. 57, no. 1, February 1973, pp. 15–22.

———, ———, Edward E. Lawler III, and Karl E. Weick, Jr.: *Managerial Behavior, Performance and Effectiveness,* McGraw-Hill, New York, 1970.

——— and Robert D. Pritchard: "Motivation Theory in Industrial and Organizational Psychology," in M. D. Dunnette (ed.), *Handbook of Industrial and Organizational Psychology,* Rand McNally, Chicago, 1976, pp. 63–130.

Cannon, James A.: "Introducing Manpower Plans: Problems and Some Possible Strategies," *Personnel Review,* Spring 1973, pp. 28–36.

Caplan, Edwin H., and Stephen Landekich: *Human Resource Accounting: Past, Present and Future,* National Association of Accountants, New York, 1975.

Carey, James F.: "Participative Job Evaluation," *Compensation Review,* vol. 9, no. 4, 1977, pp. 29–38.

Carroll, Stephen, Jr., and Henry Tosi, Jr.: *Management by Objectives,* Macmillan, New York, 1973.

Cash, William H.: "Executive Compensation," *Personnel Administrator,* September 1977, pp. 22–35.

Cawsey, T. F., and Peter Richardson: "Turnover Can Be Managed," *Business Quarterly,* Winter 1975, pp. 57–63.

Ceriello, Vincent R., and Richard B. Frantzreb: "A Human Resource Planning Model," *Human Factors,* vol. 17, no. 1, 1975, pp. 35–41.

Chandler, Alfred: *Strategy and Structure,* M.I.T. Press, Cambridge, Mass. 1962.

Charnes, A., W. W. Cooper, and R. J. Niehaus: *Studies in Manpower Planning,* Navy Office of Civilian Manpower Management, Washington, D.C., July, 1972.

———, ———, ———, and D. Sholtz: "A Model and a Program for Manpower Management and Planning," paper presented at the Joint Engineering Management Conference, Philadelphia, October 1, 1968, Management Sciences Research Report No. 132, Carnegie-Mellon University, Pittsburgh, Pa.

———, ———, ———, and A. Stedig: "Static and Dynamic Assignment Models with Multiple Objectives with Some Remarks on Organization Design," *Management Science,* vol. 15, no. 8, April 1969.

Cheedle, W. Millard, Fred Luthans, and Robert L. Otteman: "A New Breakthrough for Performance Appraisal," *Business Horizons,* August 1976, pp. 66–73.

Christal, Raymond E.: *The United States Airforce Occupational Research Project,* Occupational Research Division, AFSC, Lackland AFB, Tex., January 1974.

Churchill, Neil, and J. Shrank: "Affirmative Action and Guilt-Edged Goals," *Harvard Business Review,* vol. 54, no. 2, 1976, pp. 111–116.

Clough, D. J., C. C. Lewis, and A. L. Oliver (eds.): *Manpower Planning Models,* English Universities Press, London, 1974.

"Companies 'Let the Sunshine In' Salaries," *Industry Week,* Nov. 15, 1976, pp. 70–74.

"Companies Offer Benefits Cafeteria-Style," *Business Week,* Nov. 13, 1978, pp. 116–121.

Company Manpower Planning, Paper No. 1, Department of Employment and Productivity, HMSO, London, 1968.

Connelly, Sheila: "Job Posting," *Personnel Journal,* May 1975, pp. 295–299.

Conner, Richard D., and Robert L. Fjerstad: "Internal Personnel Maintenance Staffing Strategies and Policies," in *ASPA Handbook of Personnel and Industrial Relations, Volume I,* Bureau of National Affairs, Washington, 1974, pp. 204–232.

Cox, D. R.: *Renewal Theory,* Methuen, London, 1962.

Craig, Charles E., and R. Clark Harris: "Total Productivity Measurement at the Firm Level," *Sloan Management Review,* September 1973.

Craig, Robert L.: *Training and Development Handbook,* 2d ed., McGraw-Hill, New York, 1976.

Crites, J. O.: *Vocational Psychology: The Study of Vocational Behavior and Development,* McGraw-Hill, New York, 1969.

Crystal, Graef S.: "The Ten Commandments of Executive Compensation," *Financial Executive,* August 1970.

—— and James W. Walker: "Executive Compensation: The Organizational Interface," *Compensation Review,* Fourth Quarter, 1973, pp. 24–29.

——: *Executive Compensation: Money, Motivation and Imagination,* Amacom, New York, 1978.

Crystal, J., and R. N. Bolles: *Where Do I Go from Here with My Life: The Crystal Life Planning Manual,* Crystal Management Services, McLean, Va., 1974.

Cummings, Larry L., and Donald P. Schwab: *Performance in Organizations: Determinants and Appraisal,* Scott-Foresman, Glenview, Ill., 1973.

Dahl, Henry L.: "Measuring the Human ROI," *Management Review,* January 1979, pp. 44–50.

Dale, Ernest: "Planning and Developing the Company Organization Structure," American Management Association, New York, 1952, p. 36.

Davies, Celia, and Arthur Francis: "There Is More to Performance than Profits or Growth," *Organizational Dynamics,* vol. 3, no. 3, Winter 1975, pp. 51–65.

Davis, Louis E., and Albert B. Cherns: *The Quality of Working Life: Two Volumes,* Free Press, New York, 1975.

—— and James C. Taylor (eds.): *Design of Jobs: Selected Readings,* Penguin Books, Baltimore, 1972.

Davis, Stanley M., et al.: *Matrix,* Organization Development Series, Addison-Wesley Publishing Co., Reading, Mass., 1977.

Dayal, Ishwar: "Role Analysis Techniques in Job Descriptions," *California Management Review,* vol. 11, no. 4, Summer 1969, pp. 47–50.

Decker, Louis R., and Daniel A. Peed: "Affirmative Action for the Handicapped," *Personnel,* May–June 1976, pp. 64–69.

DeCotiis, Thomas A., and Richard A. Morano: "Applying Job Analysis to Training," *Training and Development Journal,* July 1977, pp. 20–24.

Denton, J. C.: *The Position Description Questionnaire,* Psychological Business Research, Cleveland, Ohio, 1975.

Desatnick, Robert L.: *A Concise Guide to Management Development,* AMACOM, New York, 1970.

Digman, Lester A.: "How Well-Managed Organizations Develop Their Executives," *Organization Dynamics,* Autumn 1978, pp. 63–80.

Dipboye, Robert L., Richard D. Arvey, and David E. Terpstra: "Equal Employment and the Interview," *Personnel Journal,* October 1976, pp. 520–523.

Drucker, Peter: *The Practice of Management,* Harper & Row, New York, 1954.

——: *Management: Tasks, Responsibilities, Practices,* Harper and Row, New York, 1974.

——: "What Results Should You Expect? A User's Guide to MBO," *Public Administration Review,* vol. 36, no. 1, January–February 1976, pp. 12–19.

Drui, A. B.: "The Use of Regression Equations to Predict Manpower Requirements," *Management Science,* vol. 9, no. 4, July 1963, pp. 669–677.

Dunham, R. B., R. J. Aldag, and A. P. Brief: "Dimensionality of Task Design as Measured by the Job Diagnostic Survey," *Academy of Management Journal,* vol. 20, no. 2, 1977, pp. 209–233.

Dunlop, J. (ed.): *Automation and Technological Change,* Prentice-Hall, Englewood Cliffs, N.J., 1962.

Dunn, William, and Frederic W. Swierczek: "Planned Organizational Change," *JABS,* vol. 13, no. 2, 1977, pp. 135–157.

Dunnette, Marvin D.: *Personnel Selection and Placement,* Wadsworth, Belmont, Calif., 1966.

——— (ed.): *Work and Nonwork in the Year 2001,* Brooks/Cole Publishing, Monterey, Calif., 1973.

Dyer, Lee: Careers in Organizations: Individual Planning and Organizational Development, New York School of Industrial Relations, 1976.

———, Donald P. Schwab, and John A. Fossum: "Impacts of Pay on Employee Behaviors and Attitudes: An Update," *Personnel Administrator,* January 1978, pp. 51–58.

———, ———, and Roland D. Theriault: "Managerial Perceptions Regarding Salary Increase Criteria," *Personnel Psychology,* vol. 29, 1976, pp. 233–242.

Elbert, Norbert F., and William J. Kehoe: "How to Bridge Fact and Theory in Manpower Planning," *Personnel,* vol. 53, no. 6, November–December 1976, pp. 31–39.

Elbing, Alvan O., Herman Gadon, and R. M. Gordon: "Flexible Working Hours: It's about Time," *Harvard Business Review,* July–August 1974, pp. 9–15.

Elizur, D.: "The Scaling Method of Job Evaluation," *Compensation Review,* vol. 10, no. 3, 1978, pp. 34–46.

Ellig, Bruce R.: "Compensation Management: Its Past and Its Future," *Personnel,* vol. 54, no. 3, 1977, pp. 30–40.

Employee Performance: Evaluation and Control, Survey No. 108, Bureau of National Affairs, Washington, 1975.

English, Jon, and Anthony R. Marchione: "Nine Steps in Management Development," *Business Horizons,* vol. 20, no. 9, June 1977, pp. 88–94.

Erikson, E. H.: *Childhood and Society,* Norton, New York, 1963.

Ettelstein, Morton S.: "Integrating the Manpower Factor into Planning, Programming, Budgeting," *Public Personnel Review,* vol. 31, no. 1, January 1970, pp. 51–54.

Etzioni, Amita: "Opting Out: The Waning of the Work Ethic," *Psychology Today,* July 1977, p. 18.

Ewell, J. M.: "The Effect of Change on Organizations," speech before the Society for the Advancement of Management, 1977.

Ewing, David W.: *Freedom Inside the Organization,* E. P. Dutton, New York, 1978.

Fairfield, Ron P.: *Humanizing the Workplace,* Prometheus Books, Buffalo, N.Y., 1974.

Ferguson, Lawrence L.: "Better Management of Managers' Careers," *Harvard Business Review,* March–April 1966, pp. 139–153.

Fine, Sidney A.: "Functional Job Analysis: An Approach to a Technology for Manpower Planning," *Personnel Journal,* November 1974, pp. 813–818.

———, Ann M. Holt, and Maret F. Hutchinson: *Functional Job Analysis: An Annotated Bibliography,* Methods for Manpower Analysis No. 10, W. E. Upjohn Institute, Kalamazoo, Mich., 1975.

——— and Wretha A. Wiley: *Introduction to Functional Job Analysis,* W. E. Upjohn Institute for Employment Research, Kalamazoo, Mich., 1971.

Finkle, Robert B.: "Managerial Assessment Centers," in M. D. Dunnette (ed.), *Handbook of Industrial and Organizational Psychology,* Rand McNally, Chicago, 1976, pp. 861–888.

———— and William S. Jones: *Assessing Corporate Talent,* John Wiley & Sons, New York, 1970.

Flamholtz, Eric: *Human Resource Accounting,* Dickenson Publishing Company, Encino, Calif., 1974.

Flast, Robert H.: "Taking the Guesswork out of Affirmative Action Planning," *Personnel Journal,* February 1977, pp. 68–71.

Flint, Jerry: "Oversupply of Young Workers Expected To Tighten Jobs Race," *New York Times,* June 25, 1978, pp. 1, 34.

Flowers, Vincent S., and Charles L. Hughes: "Why Employees Stay," *Harvard Business Review,* July–August 1973, pp. 49–60.

Foltman, Felicia F.: *Manpower Information for Effective Management: (Part 2: Skills Inventories and Manpower Planning),* New York State School of Industrial and Labor Relations, Cornell University, Ithaca, N.Y., 1973.

Foster, Kenneth E., and Jill Kanin-Lovers: "Determinants of Organizational Pay Policies," *Compensation Review,* vol. 9, no. 3, 1977, pp. 35–41.

Foulkes, Fred K.: "The Expanding Role of the Personnel Function," *Harvard Business Review,* March–April 1975, pp. 71–84.

———— and Henry M. Morgan: "Organizing and Staffing the Personnel Function," *Harvard Business Review,* May–June 1977, pp. 141–154.

Frantzreb, Richard: "Controlling Turnover," *Manpower Planning,* vol. 1, no. 12, May 1977, p. 1.

Freiburg, Robert: *The Manager's Guide to Equal Employment Opportunity,* Executive Enterprises Publications, New York, 1977.

Freund, Madalyn, and Patricia Somers: "Ethics in College Recruiting: Views from the Front Lines," *PA,* vol. 24, no. 4, April 1979, pp. 30–34.

Friedman, M., and R. H. Rosenman: *Type A Behavior and Your Heart,* Alfred A. Knopf, New York, 1974.

Froehlich, Herbert P., and Dennis A. Hawver: "Compliance Spinoff: Better Personnel Systems," *Personnel,* January–February 1974, pp. 62–68.

Frohman, Alan E., and John P. Kotter: "The Joining Up Process: Issues in Effective Human Resource Development," *Training and Development Journal,* August 1975, pp. 3–7.

Galbraith, Jay: *Organization Design,* Addison-Wesley, Reading, Mass., 1977.

Gascoigne, I. M.: "Manpower Planning at the Enterprise Level," British Journal of Industrial Relations, March 1968, pp. 94–106.

Gatewood, Robert D., and James Ledvinka: "Selection Interviewing and EEO: Mandate for Objectivity," *Personnel Administrator,* May 1976, pp. 15–19.

———— and Lyle F. Schoenfeldt: "Content Validity and EEOC: A Useful Alternative for Selection," *Personnel Journal,* October 1977, pp. 520–525.

Geisler, Edwin B.: *Manpower Planning: An Emerging Staff Function,* American Management Association, New York, 1967.

————: "Organizational Placement of Manpower Planning," *Management of Personnel Quarterly,* Spring 1968, pp. 30–35.

Gerstenberg, Richard C.: "Productivity: Its Meaning for America," *Michigan Business Review,* July 1972, pp. 1–7.

Ghiselli, Edwin E.: *Explorations in Managerial Talent,* Goodyear Publishing Company, Pacific Palisades, Calif., 1971.

Ginzberg, Eli P.: *The Manpower Connection: Education and Work,* Harvard University Press, Cambridge, Mass., 1975.

———: "EEO's Next Frontier: Assignments, Training and Promotion," *Employee Relations Law Journal,* vol. 4, no. 1, Summer 1978, pp. 24–33.

Glaser, B. G. (ed.): *Organizational Careers: A Sourcebook for Theory,* Aldine, Chicago, 1968.

Glaser, Edward M: *Productivity Gains through Work Life Improvement,* Harcourt, Brace & Jovanovich, New York, 1976.

Glueck, William F.: "Personnel: A Diagnostic Approach," Business Publications, Inc., Dallas, 1974.

Goldstein, Irwin I.: *Training: Program Development and Evaluation,* Brooks-Cole, Monterey, Calif., 1974.

Golembiewski, Robert T.: "Mid-Life Transition and Mid-Career Crisis: A Special Case for Individual Development," *Public Administration Review,* vol. 38, no. 3, May–June 1978, pp. 215–222.

Gomez-Meuia, Luis R., Ronald C. Page, and Walter W. Tornow: "Development and Implementation of a Computerized Job Evaluation System," *Personnel Administrator,* February 1979, pp. 46–52.

Gooding, Judson: *The Job Revolution,* Walker & Co., New York, 1972.

———: "Out-placement," *Across the Board,* April 1979, pp. 14–25.

Gordon, Steven R.: "The Impact of Fair Employment Laws on Training," *Training and Development Journal,* vol. 32, no. 11, November 1978, pp. 29–44.

Gordon, T. J., and R. E. LeBleu: "Employee Benefits, 1970–1985," *Harvard Business Review,* January–February 1970, pp. 93–107.

Gould, Sam: "Career Planning in the Organization," *Human Resource Management,* Spring 1978, pp. 8–13.

Graham, Bradley: "Productivity Rate Is Nearing a Standstill," *Washington Post,* Sept. 17, 1978, pp. 16, 24.

Grauer, Robert T.: "An Automated Approach to Affirmative Action," *Personnel,* September–October, 1976, pp. 37–44.

Greene, Charles N.: "The Satisfaction-Performance Controversy," *Business Horizons,* vol. 15, no. 5, 1972, pp. 31–41.

Greene, Robert J.: "DP Career Paths," *Datamation,* January 1975, pp. 47–48.

Grinold, R. C., and K. T. Marshall: *Manpower Planning Models,* North Holland, Inc., New York, 1977.

Grosskopf, Theodore: "Human Resource Planning under Adversity," *Human Resource Planning,* vol. 1, no. 1, Spring 1978, pp. 45–48.

Guion, Robert: *Personnel Testing,* McGraw-Hill, New York, 1965.

———: "Recruiting, Selection and Job Placement," in M. D. Dunnette (ed.), *Handbook of Industrial and Organizational Psychology,* Rand McNally, Chicago, 1976, pp. 777–828.

———: "Content Validity in Moderation," *Personnel Psychology,* vol. 31, no. 3, Summer 1978, pp. 205–213.

Hackman, J. Richard: "Is Job Enrichment Just a Fad?" *Harvard Business Review,* vol. 53, no. 5, September–October 1975, pp. 129–138.

———: "Work Design," in J. Richard Hackman and J. Lloyd Suttle (eds.), *Improving Life at Work,* Goodyear Publications, Santa Monica, Calif., 1977, pp. 96–162.

———: "The Design of Work in the 1980's," *Organizational Dynamics,* Summer 1978, pp. 3–17.

—— and E. E. Lawler: "Employee Reactions to Job Characteristics," *Journal of Applied Psychology,* vol. 55, no. 3, 1971, pp. 259–286.

—— and Greg Oldham: *The Job Diagnostic Survey: An Instrument for the Diagnosis of Jobs and the Evaluation of Job Redesign Projects,* National Technical Information Service, Springfield, Va., 1974.

—— and ——: "Development of the Job Diagnostic Survey," *Journal of Applied Psychology,* vol. 60, 1975, pp. 159–170.

——, ——, Robert Janson, and Kenneth Purdy: "A New Strategy for Job Enrichment," *California Management Review,* vol. 17, no. 4, Summer 1975, pp. 57–71.

Hackman, J. Richard, and J. Lloyd Suttle: *Improving Life at Work,* Goodyear Publishing Co., Santa Monica, Calif., 1977.

Haire, M.: "Approach to an Integrated Personnel Policy," *Industrial Relations,* vol. 7, 1967, pp. 107–117.

——: "Approaches to an Integrated Personnel Policy," *Industrial Relations,* 1968, pp. 107–117.

Hall, Douglas T.: *Careers in Organizations,* Goodyear Publications, Pacific Palisades, Calif., 1976.

—— and Francine S. Hall: "What's New In Career Management," *Organizational Dynamics,* vol. 5, no. 1, Summer 1976, pp. 17–33. (b) Also reprinted in Walker, 1979.

——, ——, and Roy W. Hinton: "Research on Organizational Career Development," *Human Resource Planning,* vol. 1, no. 4, 1978, pp. 203–236.

Hall, Francine S., and Douglas T. Hall: "Dual Careers—How Do Couples and Companies Cope with the Problems?" *Organizational Dynamics,* vol. 6, no. 4, Spring 1978, pp. 57–77.

Hamner, W. Clay: "How To Ruin Motivation with Pay," *Compensation Review,* vol. 7, no. 3, Third Quarter 1975, pp. 17–27.

——: "Worker Motivation Programs: The Importance of Climate, Structure and Performance Consequences," in W. Clay Hamner and Frank L. Schmidt (eds.), *Contemporary Problems in Personnel,* rev. ed., St. Clair, Chicago, 1977, pp. 256–283.

Hastings, Robert E.: "Career Development: Maximizing Options," *Personnel Administrator,* May 1978, pp. 58–62.

Hay Associates: *Survey of Human Resource Practices,* 1975, unpublished.

H.E.W. Task Force: *Work in America,* M.I.T. Press, Cambridge, Mass., 1973.

Hemphill, J. K.: *Dimensions of Executive Positions,* Bureau of Business Research Monograph No. 98, College of Commerce and Administration, Ohio State University, Columbus, 1960.

Henderson, J. A.: "What the Chief Executive Expects of the Personnel Function," *Personnel Administrator,* May 1977, pp. 40–45.

Heneman, and Seltzer: "Manpower Planning and Forecasting in the Firm: An Exploratory Problem?" Office of Manpower Policy, Evaluation and Research, U.S. Dept. of Labor, March 1968.

Higgins, James M.: "A Manager's Guide to the Equal Employment Opportunity Laws," *Personnel Journal,* August 1976.

Hills, Stephen M.: "Organizational Politics and Human Resource Planning," *Human Resource Planning,* vol. 1, no. 1, Spring 1978, pp. 31–38.

Hodges, Wayne L., and Matthew Kelly: *Technological Change and Human Develop-*

ment: An International Conference, NYSSILR, Cornell University, Ithaca, N.Y., 1970.

Hodgson, Richard C., Daniel J. Levinson, and Abraham Zalezhik: *The Executive Role Constellation,* Harvard Business School, Division of Research, Boston, 1965.

Hoffman, Frank O.: "Identity Crisis in the Personnel Function," *Personnel Journal,* March 1978, pp. 126–132.

Holley, William H., and Hubert S. Feild: "Performance Appraisal and the Law," *Labor Law Journal,* vol. 26, no. 7, July 1975, pp. 423–430.

Holmstrom, Linda: *The Two Career Family,* Schenkman, New York, 1973.

Hopkins, W. H.: "Performance Appraisal: Try Action Analysis," *Supervisory Management,* vol. 20, no. 7, July 1975, pp. 10–13.

Howard, Ann: "An Assessment of Assessment Centers," *Academy of Management Journal,* vol. 7, no. 1, 1974, pp. 115–134.

Hrabak, William H.: "An Incentive Plan for Middle Management: A New Approach at International Harvester Company," *Compensation Review,* vol. 10, no. 4, 1978, pp. 26–33.

Hughes, Charles L.: "Help Wanted, Present Employees Please Apply," *Personnel,* July–August, 1974, pp. 36–44.

Human Resource Planning, a quarterly journal published by the Human Resource Planning Society, 1978 (P.O. Box 2553, Grand Central Station, New York, NY 10163).

Husband, T. M.: *Work Analysis and Pay Structure,* McGraw-Hill, Maidenhead, England, 1976.

Idema, Thomas H.: "Systems Career Path Development," *Journal of Systems Management,* vol. 29, no. 4, April 1978, pp. 30–39.

Ingraham, Albert P., and Carl F. Lutz: "Managing Positions—the Key to Effective Organization, Compensation and Productivity," *Human Resource Management,* Summer 1974, pp. 12–21.

Ivancevich, John M., Timothy McMahon, J. William Streidl, and Andrew D. Szilagyi: "Goal Setting: The Tenneco Approach to Personnel Development and Management Effectiveness," *Organization Dynamics,* Winter, 1978, pp. 58–80.

Jablin, Fredric: "The Selection Interview: Contingency Theory and Beyond," *Personnel Administrator,* Spring 1975, pp. 2–9.

Jacobs, Herman S., and Katherine Jilson: *Executive Productivity,* AMACOM, New York, 1974.

Janger, Allen R.: *Personnel Administration: Changing Scope and Organization,* Studies in Personnel Policy No. 203, The National Industrial Conference Board, New York, 1965.

———: *The Personnel Function: Changing Objectives and Organization,* The Conference Board, New York, 1977.

Jaques, E.: *Equitable Payment,* Wiley, New York, 1961.

Jelinek, Mariann: *Career Management,* St. Clair Press, Chicago, 1979.

Jenkins, G. Douglas, Jr., et al.: "Standardized Observations: An Approach to Measuring the Nature of Jobs," *Journal of Applied Psychology,* April 1975, pp. 171–181.

Jennings, Eugene E.: *The Mobile Manager,* McGraw-Hill, New York, 1967.

———: "Mobicentric Man," *Psychology Today,* July 1970, pp. 35–40.

———: *Routes to the Executive Suite,* McGraw-Hill, New York, 1971.

———: "The Supermobile," *Human Resource Management,* Spring 1972, pp. 4–17.

Kahalas, Harvey, and David A. Gray: "A Quantitative Model for Manpower Decision Making," *Omega,* vol. 4, no. 6, 1976, pp. 685–695.

Kalins, Dorothy: *Cutting Loose,* Saturday Review, New York, 1973.

Kase, Stanley R.: "Your Employees: Outplaced, Not Out of Work," *Personnel Administrator,* May 1976, pp. 49–52.

Kearney, William J.: "The Value of Behaviorally Based Performance Appraisals," *Business Horizons,* June 1976, pp. 75–83.

Keil, E. C.: *Performance Appraisal and the Manager,* Lebhar-Friedman Books, New York, 1977.

Kellogg, Marion S.: *Career Management,* American Management Association, New York, 1972.

———: *What To Do about Performance Appraisal,* American Management Association, New York, 1975.

———: "Executive Development," in Dale Yoder and Herbert Heneman (eds.), *Handbook of Personnel and Industrial Relations,* Bureau of National Affairs, Washington, D.C., 1977.

Kendrick, John W., and Daniel Creamer: *Measuring Company Productivity,* The Conference Board, New York, 1975.

Kets de Vries, and F. R. Manfred: "The Mid Career Conundrum," *Organizational Dynamics,* Autumn 1978, pp. 45–62.

Keys, B. A., F. G. Thompson, and M. Heath: *Meeting Managerial Manpower Needs,* Economic Council of Canada, Ottawa, 1971.

Kimmel, Douglas C.: *Adulthood and Aging,* John Wiley & Sons, New York, 1974.

Kmetz, John: "The Personnel Specialist: Consultant or Chief Clerk?" *Journal of Navy Civilian Manpower Management,* vol. 7, no. 1, Spring 1973, pp. 1–4.

Koontz: "Making MBO Effective," *California Management Review,* vol. 20, no. 1, Fall 1977, pp. 5–13.

Korn, Thomas A.: *A Keyed Information Index to the Dictionary of Occupational Titles, Volume I, II and Supplement 1 and 2,* 3d ed., Research and Training Center, Wisconsin University—Stout, Menomonie, 1974.

Koten, John: "Career Guidance: Psychologists Play Bigger Corporate Role in Placing of Personnel," *Wall Street Journal,* July 11, 1978, p. 1.

Kotter, John P.: "Managing the Joining Up Process," *Personnel,* July–August 1972, pp. 46–50.

———: "Power, Dependence and Effective Management," *Harvard Business Review,* vol. 55, no. 4, July–August 1977, pp. 125–136.

———, Victor A. Faux, and Charles C. McArthur: *Self-Assessment and Career Development,* Prentice-Hall, Englewood Cliffs, N.J. 1978.

Kroll, A. M.: *Career Development: Growth and Crisis,* John Wiley and Sons, New York, 1970.

Kronholz, June: "Women at Work: Management Practices Change To Reflect Role of Women Employees," *Wall Street Journal,* Sept. 13, 1978, p. 1.

Kutscher, Ronald E., Jerome A. Mark, and John R. Norsworthy: "The Productivity Slowdown and the Outlook to 1985," *Monthly Labor Review,* vol. 200, no. 5, May 1977, pp. 3–8.

Kwak, N. K., Walter A. Garrett, and Sam Barone: "A Stochastic Model of Demand Forecasting for Technical Manpower Planning," *Management Science,* vol. 23, no. 10, June 1977, pp. 1089–1098.

Lanier, A.: "Selecting and Preparing Personnel for Overseas Transfers," *Personnel Journal,* March 1979, pp. 160–164.

Larson, D. O., B. E. Morre, D. Sholtz, and W. E. Trimble: *A Prototype Test of a Static Multi-Attribute Assignment Model,* OCMM Report No. 15, Department of the Navy, Washington, D.C., October 1973.

Lawler, Edward E., III: *Pay and Organizational Effectiveness: A Psychological View,* McGraw-Hill, New York, 1971.

———: "Participation and Pay," *Compensation Review,* vol. 7, no. 3, Third Quarter 1975, pp. 62–66.

———: "New Approaches to Pay: Innovations that Work," *Personnel,* September–October 1976, pp. 11–23.

———: "Workers Can Set Their Own Wages—Responsibly," *Psychology Today,* February 1977, pp. 109–112. (a)

———: "Reward Systems," in J. Richard Hackman and J. Lloyd Suttle (eds.), *Improving Life at Work,* Goodyear Publishing, Santa Monica, Calif., 1977, pp. 163–226. (b)

Lawrence, John: "Manpower and Personnel Models in Britain," *Personnel Review,* vol. 1, no. 3, Fall 1971, pp. 4–25.

Lawrence, Paul R., Harvey F. Kolodny, and Stanley M. Davis: "The Human Side of Matrix," *Organizational Dynamics,* vol. 6, no. 1, Summer 1977, pp. 43–61.

Lazer, Robert I., and Walter S. Wikstrom: *Appraising Managerial Performance: Current Practices and Future Directions,* The Conference Board, New York, 1977.

Leach, John: "Career Management: Focusing on Human Resources," *Personnel Administrator,* November 1977, pp. 59–63.

Lee, S.: *Goal Programming for Decision Analysis,* Auerbach, Philadelphia, 1972.

Levinson, Daniel J.: *The Seasons of a Man's Life,* Knopf, New York, 1978.

Levinson, Harry: *The Exceptional Executive,* Harvard University Press, Cambridge, Mass., 1968.

———: "Management by Whose Objectives?" *Harvard Business Review,* July–August 1970, pp. 125–134.

———: "Management by Objectives: A Critique," *Training and Development Journal,* April 1972, pp. 3–8.

———: "Don't Choose Your Own Successor," *Harvard Business Review,* November–December 1974, pp. 53–62.

———: "Appraisal of *What* Performance?" *Harvard Business Review,* July–August 1976, pp. 30–36.

Levitan, Sar A., and William B. Johnston: *Work Is Here to Stay, Alas,* Olympus Publishing Company, Salt Lake City, Utah, 1973.

———, Garth L. Mangum, and Ray Marshall: *Human Resources and Labor Markets: Labor and Manpower in the American Economy,* Harper and Row, New York, 1972.

Lewellen, Wilbur G., and Howard P. Lanser: "Executive Pay Preferences," *Harvard Business Review,* September–October 1973, pp. 115–122.

Likert, Rensis, and David G. Bowers: "Organization Theory and Human Resource Accounting," *American Psychologist,* vol. 24, no. 6, 1969, pp. 585–592.

Lilien, Gary L., and Ambar G. Rao: "A Model for Manpower Management," *Management Science,* vol. 21, no. 12, August 1975, pp. 1447–1457.

Ling, Cyril C.: *The Management of Personnel Relations: History and Origins,* Richard D. Irwin, Homewood, Ill., 1965.

Linowes, David F.: "Employee Rights to Privacy and Access to Personnel Records," *Employee Relations Law Journal,* vol. 4, no. 1, Summer 1978, pp. 34–42.

Livingston, J. Sterling: "The Myth of the Well-Educated Manager," *Harvard Business Review,* January–February 1971, pp. 79–89.

———: "Pygmalion in Management," *Harvard Business Review,* vol. 47, 1969, pp. 81–89.

Locke, Edwin A.: "The Nature and Causes of Job Satisfaction," in M. D. Dunnette (ed.), *Handbook of Industrial and Organizational Psychology,* Rand McNally, Chicago, 1976, pp. 1297–1350.

Loomis, Carol J.: "AT&T in the Throes of Equal Employment," *Fortune,* Jan. 15, 1979, pp. 45–57.

Lorange, Peter, and Richard F. Vancil: "How To Design a Strategic Planning System," *Harvard Business Review,* vol. 54, no. 5, September–October 1976, pp. 75–81.

Luthans, Fred: *Contemporary Readings in Organizational Behavior,* 2d ed., McGraw-Hill, New York, 1977.

———: and Robert Kreitner: *Organizational Behavior Modification,* Scott-Foresman, Glenview, Ill., 1975.

———, David Lyman, and Diane L. Lockwood: "An Individual Management Development Approach," *Human Resource Management,* Fall, 1978, pp. 1–5.

MacCrimmon, Kenneth R.: "Improving Decision Making with Manpower Management Systems," *Business Quarterly,* vol. 36, no. 3, 1971, pp. 29–41.

McFarland, Walter B.: *Manpower Cost and Performance Measurement,* National Association of Accountants, New York, 1977.

Machaver, William V.: "Controlling Our Human Resource Systems," in Ruth G. Shaeffer (ed.), *Monitoring the Human Resource System,* The Conference Board, New York, 1977, pp. 30–35.

Mager, Robert F.: *Performance Analysis: You Really Oughta Wanna,* Fearon Publishers, Belmont, Calif., 1970.

———, and Peter Pipe: *Analyzing Performance Problems,* Fearon Publishers, Belmont, Calif., 1970.

Mahler, Walter F., and William F. Wrightnour: *Executive Continuity,* Dow-Jones Irwin, Homewood, Ill., 1973.

Mahoney, Thomas A.: *Compensation and Reward Perspectives,* Richard D. Irwin, Homewood, Ill., 1979.

——— and G. T. Milkovich: "The Internal Labour Market as a Stochastic Process," in D. J. Bartholomew and A. R. Smits (eds.), *Manpower and Management Science,* Lexington Books, Lexington, Mass., 1971, pp. 75–92.

——— and ———: "Computer Simulation: A Training Tool for Manpower Managers," *Personnel Journal,* December 1975, pp. 609–612, 637.

Malabre, Alfred L., Jr.: "Women at Work: As Their Ranks Swell, Women Holding Jobs Reshape U.S. Society," *Wall Street Journal,* Sept. 1, 1978, p. 1.

Managerial Performance Appraisal Programs, Bureau of National Affairs, Survey No. 104, Washington, D.C. 1974.

Mandt, Edward: "Managing the Knowledge Worker of the Future," *Personnel Journal,* March 1978, pp. 138–143.

Manpower Planning: The State of the Art, District of Columbia Government, Washington, D.C., 1973.

Margulies, Newton, and Anthony P. Raia: *Organizational Development: Values, Process and Technology,* McGraw-Hill, New York, 1972.

———— and John Wallace: *Organizational Change,* Scott-Foresman, Glenview, Ill., 1973.

Martin, G. Lowell: "A View of Work toward the Year 2000," *Personnel Journal,* vol. 56, no. 10, October 1977, pp. 502–504.

Martin, Robert A.: "Skills Inventories," *Personnel Journal,* January 1967, pp. 28–83.

Mayo, Clyde C., Dan M. Nance, and Lynn Shigekawa: *Evaluation of the Job Inventory Approach in Analyzing USAF Officer Utilization Fields,* Occupational and Manpower Research Division, Lackland Air Force Base, Tex., June 1976.

McBeath, Gordon: *Productivity through People,* John Wiley & Sons, New York, 1974.

McConkey, Dale: "The Jackass Effect in Management Compensation," *Business Horizons,* June 1974, pp. 81–91.

McCormick, Ernest J.: "A Study of Job Characteristics and Job Dimensions as Based on the Position Analysis Questionnaire," *Journal of Applied Psychology,* August 1972, pp. 347–368.

————: "Job Information: Its Development and Applications," in Dale Yoder and Herbert G. Heneman, Jr. (eds.), *ASPA Handbook of Personnel and Industrial Relations,* vol. 1, Bureau of National Affairs, Washington, 1974, pp. 35–84.

————: "Job and Task Analysis," in M. D. Dunnette (ed.), *Handbook of Industrial and Organizational Psychology,* Rand McNally, New York, 1976, pp. 651–696.

————, P. R. Jeanneret, and R. C. Mecham: *The Development and Background of the Position Analysis Questionnaire (PAQ),* Occupational Research Center, Purdue University, Lafayette, Ind., 1969.

————, ————, and ————: "A Study of the Job Characteristics and Job Dimensions as Based on the Position Analysis Questionnaire (PAQ)," *Journal of Applied Psychology,* Monograph, vol. 56, no. 4, August 1972, pp. 347–368.

McGehee, William: *"Training and Development Theory, Policies and Practices,"* in D. Yoder and H. Heneman (eds.), *ASPA Handbook of Personnel And Industrial Relations,* vol. 5, Bureau of National Affairs, Washington, 1977, pp. 1–30.

McGregor, D.: "An Uneasy Look at the Performance Appraisal," *Harvard Business Review,* May–June 1957, pp. 89–94.

McLaughlin, David: "Roadblocks to Personnel Department Effectiveness," *Personnel Journal,* January 1971.

McNamar, R. T.: "Identifying and Solving Corporate Manpower Problems," in C. Burack and J. Walker (eds.), *Manpower Planning and Programming,* Allyn & Bacon, Boston, 1972.

Mensch, G.: "On the Personnel Assignment Problem," *Omega,* 1973, pp. 353 ff.

Merck, J. W., and K. Hall: *A Markovian Flow Model: The Analysis of Movement in Large Scale Systems,* Rand Corporation, Santa Monica, Calif., 1971.

Merrill, Harwood E. (ed.): *Classics in Management,* American Management Association, New York, 1959.

Meyer, Herbert: "The Pay for Performance Dilemma," *Organizational Dynamics,* Winter 1975, and *Compensation Review,* vol. 7, no. 3, 1975, pp. 55–62.

————: "Personnel Directors Are the New Corporate Heroes," *Fortune,* February 1976, pp. 86–88.

————: "The Annual Performance Review Discussion: Making It Constructive," *Personnel Journal,* vol. 56, no. 10, October 1977, pp. 508–511.

————: "The Headhunters Come upon Golden Days," *Fortune,* Oct. 8, 1978, pp. 100–109.

————, Emmanual Kay, and J. R. P. French, Jr.: "Split Roles in Performance

Appraisal," *Harvard Business Review,* vol. 43, no. 1, January–February 1965, pp. 123–129.

Meyer, Mitchell, and Harland Fox: *Future Trends in Employee Benefits,* A Symposium held in Toronto, Ontario, April 1974, The Conference Board, New York, 1974.

Milkovich, G. T., A. Annoni, and T. Mahoney: "The Use of Delphi Procedures in Manpower Forecasting," *Management Science,* vol. 19, no. 4, December 1972, pp. 381–388.

———— and Thomas A. Mahoney: "Human Resource Planning and PAIR Policy," in D. Yoder and H. Heneman (eds.), *ASPA Handbook of Personnel and Industrial Relations,* vol. 4, Bureau of National Affairs, Washington, 1976, pp. 1–30.

———— and ————: "Human Resource Planning Models: A Perspective," *Human Resource Planning,* vol. 1, no. 1, 1978, pp. 19–30.

Miller, Donald B.: "Career Planning and Management in Organizations," *SAM Advanced Management Journal,* Spring 1978, pp. 33–43.

Miller, Ernest C.: "Setting Supervisors' Pay and Pay Differentials," *Compensation Review,* vol. 10, no. 3, Third Quarter 1978, pp. 13–27. (a)

————: "Supervisory Overtime, Incentive, and Bonus Practices," *Compensation Review,* vol. 10, no. 4, 1978, pp. 12–25. (b)

————: "Top and Middle Management Compensation: Part 2: Incentive Bonus and Merit Increase Plans," *Compensation Review,* vol. 8, no. 4, Fourth Quarter 1976, pp. 33–46.

Miller, James R., III, and Mason Haire: "MANPLAN: A Micro-Simulator for Manpower Planning," *Behavioral Science,* November 1970, pp. 524–531.

Miner, Mary Green, and John B. Miner: *Employee Selection within the Law,* Bureau of National Affairs, Washington, 1978.

Mintzberg, Henry: *The Nature of Managerial Work,* Harper & Row, New York, 1973.

————: "The Manager's Job: Folklore and Fact," *Harvard Business Review,* July–August 1975, pp. 49–61.

————: *Structuring of Organizations,* Prentice-Hall, Englewood Cliffs, N.J., 1979.

Mistretta v. Sandia Corp., 29 U.S.C.A. 621, 1977.

Mobley, William H.: "The Link between MBO and Merit Compensation," *Personnel Journal,* June 1974, pp. 423–427.

Moore, Larry F. (ed.): *Manpower Planning for Canadians,* University of British Columbia, Institute of Industrial Relations, Vancouver, B.C., 1977.

Morsh, J.: "The Analysis of Jobs—Use of the Task Inventory Method of Job Analysis," in E. A. Fleishman (ed.), *Studies in Personnel and Industrial Psychology,* rev. ed., Dorsey Press, Homewood, Ill., 1967, pp. V(2) 11–15.

Moses, Joseph, and William C. Byham (eds.): *Applying the Assessment Center Methods,* Pergamon Press, Elmsford, N.Y., 1977.

Mruk, Edwin S., and Edward J. Giblin: "Compensation as a Management Tool," *Management Review,* May 1977, pp. 50–58.

Muller v. U.S. Steel, 509 F. 2d 923 (10th cir. 1975).

Murg, Gary E., and Marilyn P. Maledon: "Privacy Legislation—Implications for Employers," *Employee Relations Law Journal,* vol. 3, no. 2, Spring 1977, pp. 168–177.

Murphy, Robert H.: "A Personalized Skills Inventory: The North American Rockwell Story," in E. Burack and J. Walker (eds.), *Manpower Planning and Programming,* Allyn and Bacon, Boston, 1972, pp. 206–219.

Murray, Thomas: "Personnel—Fast Track to the Top," *Dun's Review,* April 1975, pp. 74–77.

———: "What Price Management Education," *Dun's Review,* March 1979, pp. 104–106.

Murray, William A.: "Tips on Screening Executives," *Personnel Administrator,* vol. 24, no. 4, April 1979, pp. 1, 39–40, 46–53.

Myers, M. Scott: *Every Employee a Manager,* McGraw-Hill, New York, 1970.

Nadler, David A., and E. E. Lawler, III: "Motivation: A Diagnostic Approach," in J. R. Hackman, E. E. Lawler, and L. Porter (eds.), *Perspectives on Behavior in Organizations,* McGraw-Hill, New York, 1977, pp. 26–38.

National Center for Productivity and Quality of Working Life: *Improving Productivity: A Description of Selected Company Programs, Series 1,* Washington, 1975.

Neuman, John L.: "Make Overhead Cuts That Last," *Harvard Business Review,* May–June 1975, pp. 116–126.

Newsweek: "Too Many U.S. Workers No Longer Give a Damn," Apr. 24, 1972.

Neilson, Eric H.: "The Human Side of Growth," *Organization Dynamics,* Summer 1978, pp. 61–80.

Niehaus, Richard J.: "Computer Assisted Manpower Planning Using Goal Programming," Research Report No. 32, Office of Civilian Personnel, Navy Department, Washington, D.C., 1977.

Nielsen, Gordon L., and Allan R. Young: "Manpower Planning: A Markov Chain Application," *Public Personnel Management,* March–April 1973, pp. 133–143.

Nollen, Stanley D., and Virginia H. Martin: *Alternative Work Strategies, Parts 1 and 2,* AMACOM, New York, 1978.

Nord, Walter R., and Douglas E. Durand: "What's Wrong with the Human Resources Approach to Management?" *Organizational Dynamics,* Winter 1978, pp. 13–25.

Norton, Steven D., David P. Gustafson, and Charles E. Foster: "Assessment for Management Potential: Scale Design and Development, Training Effects and Rater/Ratee Sex Effects," *Academy of Management Journal,* vol. 20, no. 1, 1977, pp. 117–131.

Novick, David: "Long Range Planning through Program Budgeting," *Business Horizons,* vol. 12, no. 1, February 1969, pp. 54–65.

Oates, Wayne Edward: *Confessions of a Workaholic: The Facts about Work Addiction,* Abingdon, Nashville, Tenn., 1972.

Oberg, Winston: "Make Performance Appraisal Relevant," *Harvard Business Review,* January–February, 1972, pp. 61–50.

Odiorne, George S.: *Management by Objectives,* Pitman Publishing Company, New York, 1965.

———: *Training by Objectives,* MacMillan & Co., New York, 1970.

———: "Management by Objectives: Antidote to Future Shock," *Personnel Journal,* April 1974.

———: "MBO in the 1980's: Will It Survive?" *Management Review,* July 1977, pp. 39–42.

Ogilvie, Bruce C., and Albert C. Porter: "Business Careers as Treadmill to Oblivion: The Allure of Cardiovascular Death," *Human Resource Management,* Fall 1974, pp. 14–18.

Oppenheimer, Valerie K.: *The Female Labor Force in the U.S.,* Population Monograph Series, no. 5, Greenwood, Westport, Conn., 1976.

"Organizing and Staffing the Human Resource Function . . . A Personnel Symposium," *Personnel,* January–February 1978, pp. 11–20.

Orth, Charles: "How To Survive the Mid-Life Crisis," *Business Horizons,* vol. 17, no. 4, October 1974, pp. 11–18.

Osipow, Samuel H.: *Theories of Career Development,* 2d ed., Appleton-Century-Crofts, New York, 1973.

Ostrowski, Paul S.: "Prerequisites for Effective Succession Planning," *Manpower Planning Quarterly,* Spring 1968, pp. 10–16.

O'Toole, James: *Work and the Quality of Life: Resource Papers for Work in America,* M.I.T. Press, Cambridge, Mass., 1974.

———: "Work in America and the Great Job Satisfaction Controversy," *Journal of Occupational Medicine,* vol. 16, no. 11, November 1974, pp. 710–715.

Otteman, Robert, and J. Brad Chapman: "A Viable Strategy for Validation: Content Validity," *Personnel Administrator,* November 1977, pp. 17–20.

Paperman, Jacob B., and Desmond D. Martin: "Human Resource Accounting: A Managerial Tool," *Personnel,* vol. 54, no. 2, March–April 1977, pp. 41–50.

Patten, Thomas A., Jr.: *Manpower Planning and Development of Human Resources,* John Wiley & Sons, New York, 1971.

———: *Pay—Employee Compensation and Incentive Plans,* Free Press, New York, 1977.(a)

———: "Pay for Performance or Placation?" *Personnel Administrator,* vol. 22, no. 7, September 1977, pp. 26–29. (b)

———: "Open Communication Systems and Effective Salary Administration," *Human Resource Management,* vol. 17, no. 4, Winter 1978, pp. 5–14.

Pattillo, James W., and Jose G. Secunza: "Mathematical Models: How Helpful Now to the Business World?" *Business Perspectives* vol. 7, no. 4, Summer 1974, pp. 20–25.

Patz, A. L.: "Linear Programming Applied to Manpower Management," *Industrial Management Review,* vol. 11, no. 2, Winter 1970, pp. 31–38.

———: "Performance Appraisal: Useful but Still Resisted," *Harvard Business Review,* vol. 54, no. 3, May–June 1975, pp. 74–89.

Pearson, A. E.: "Sales Power through Planned Careers," *Harvard Business Review,* vol. 44, no. 1, January–February 1966, pp. 105–116.

Perham, John: "New Life for Flexible Compensation," *Dun's Review,* September 1978, pp. 68–70.

"Personnel Widens Its Franchise," *Business Week,* Feb. 26, 1979, pp. 116, 121.

Pettman, Barrie O., and Gerard Tavernier: *Manpower Planning Workbook,* Gower Press, Epping, Essex, England, 1976.

Pierce, Jon L., and Randall B. Dunham: "Task Design: A Literature Review," *Academy of Management Review,* vol. 1, no. 4, October 1976, pp. 83–97.

Pietrofesa, John J., and Howard Splete: *Career Development: Theory and Research,* Grune and Stratton, New York, 1975.

Pinto, Patrick R.: "Your Trainers and the Law," *Training,* October 1978.

——— and James W. Walker: "What Do Training and Development Professionals Really Do?" *Training and Development Journal,* July 1978, pp. 58–64. (a)

——— and ———: *Defining Job Requirements for Employee Selection, Training and Career Development,* unpublished, 1978. (b)

Pirsig, Robert M.: *Zen and the Art of Motorcycle Maintenance,* Morrow and Co., New York, 1974.

Pitts, Robert A.: "Unshackle your 'Careers'," *Harvard Business Review,* vol. 55, no. 3, May–June 1977, pp. 127–136.

Pogrebin, L. C.: *Getting Yours: How To Make the System Work for the Working Woman,* McKay, New York, 1975.

Porter, Lyman W.: "Turning Work into Nonwork: The Rewarding Environment," in M. D. Dunnette (ed.), *Work and Nonwork in the Year 2000,* Brooks-Cole, Monterey, Calif., 1973, pp. 113–133.

———, Edward E. Lawler, and J. Richard Hackman: *Behavior in Organizations,* McGraw-Hill, New York, 1975.

Prather, Richard: "Training: Key to Realistic Performance Appraisals," *Training and Development Journal,* vol. 24, no. 12, December 1970, pp. 4–7.

Price, W. L., and W. G. Piskor: "Goal Programming and Manpower Planning," *Infor,* vol. 10, no. 3, October 1972, pp. 221–231.

Prien, Erich P., Mark A. Jones, and Louise M. Miller: "A Job Related Performance Rating System," *Personnel Administrator,* vol. 22, no. 9, November 1977, special insert.

——— and W. W. Ronan: "Job Analysis: A Review of Research Findings," *Personnel Psychology,* vol. 24, 1971, pp. 371–396.

Privacy Protection Study Commission: *Personal Privacy in an Information Society,* U.S. Government Printing Office, Stock No. 052-003-00395-3, Washington, 1977.

Quarterly Report on the Employment Outlook, Job Absence and Turnover, Bureau of National Affairs, Washington, 1977.

Quindlen, Anna: "Polygraph Tests for Jobs: Truth or Consequences," *New York Times,* Aug. 19, 1977, p. B1.

Rahiya, John: "Privacy Protection and Personnel Administration: Are New Laws Needed?" *Personnel Administrator,* vol. 24, no. 4, April 1979, pp. 19–22.

Raia, Anthony: *Managing by Objectives,* Scott-Foresman, Glenview, Ill., 1974.

Rapaport, R., and R. N. Rapaport: "The Dual Career Family," *Human Relations,* vol. 22, 1969, pp. 3–30.

Reif, William E.: "The Application of Behavior Modification Technology to the Design of Jobs and Organizational Reward Systems," a paper presented at the XXIII TIMS Meeting, Athens, Greece, 1977.

——— and Gerald Bassford: "What MBO Really Is," *Business Horizons,* June 1973.

——— and Robert M. Monczka: "Job Redesign: A Contingency Approach to Implementation," *Personnel,* May–June 1974, pp. 18–31.

Rhine, Shirley H.: *Older Workers and Retirement,* The Conference Board, New York, 1978.

Rhode, John G., and Edward E. Lawler III: "Auditing Change: Human Resource Accounting," in M. D. Dunnette (ed.), *Work and Nonwork in the Year 2001,* Brooks-Cole, Monterey, Calif., 1973, pp. 153–177.

Rice, Berkeley: "Measuring Executive Muscle," *Psychology Today,* December 1978, pp. 95–110.

Rich v. Martin-Marietta, 522 F. 2d at 350.

Rimler, George W., and Guy J. DeGenaro: "Needs Assessment—The Vital Ingredient for Success in Bank Training," *Bank Administration,* March 1978, pp. 36–43.

Risher, Howard: "Job Evaluation: Mystical or Statistical?" *Personnel,* September–October 1978, pp. 23–36.

Ritzer, George, and Harrison M. Trice: *An Occupation in Conflict: A Study of the Personnel Manager,* Cornell University, Ithaca, N.Y., 1969.

Robins, James: "Transfer Payments," *Wall Street Journal,* May 2, 1979, pp. 1, 32.

Rodgers, Frank P.: "Developing Young Managers: An Individualized Program," *Personnel,* November–December 1971, pp. 38–43.

Rogers, Carl: *On Becoming a Person,* Houghton Mifflin Co., New York, 1961.

Roter, Benjamin: "An Integrated Framework for Personnel Utilization and Management," *Personnel Journal,* December 1973, pp. 1031–1039.

Rouleau, Eugene J., and Burton F. Krain: "Using Job Analysis To Design Selection Procedures," *Public Personnel Management,* September–October 1975, pp. 300–304.

Rowland, Kendrith M., and Michael G. Sovereign: "Markov Chain Analysis of Internal Manpower Supply," *Industrial Relations,* October 1969, pp. 88–99.

Ruch, William A., and James C. Hershauer: *Factors Affecting Worker Productivity,* Occasional Paper No. 10, Arizona State University, Bureau of Business and Economic Research, Tempe, 1974.

Rummler, Geary A.: "Human Performance Problems and Their Solutions," *Human Resource Management,* Winter 1972, pp. 2–10.

Runzheimer, Rufus E., Jr.: "U.S. Urban Area Living Cost Data for Compensation Planning," *Compensation Review,* vol. 9, no. 3, 1977, pp. 29–34.

Rush, Harold F. M.: *Job Design for Motivation,* The Conference Board, New York, 1971.

———: *Organization Development: A Reconnaissance,* The Conference Board, New York, 1973.

Salter, Malcolm S.: "Tailor Incentive Compensation to Strategy," *Harvard Business Review,* vol. 51, no. 2, March–April 1973, pp. 94–102.

Sarcini v. Missouri Pacific Railway Co., 431 F. Supp. 389, 393 (1977).

Sayles, Leonard: *Managerial Behavior,* McGraw-Hill, New York, 1964.

———: "Matrix Management: The Structure with a Future," *Organizational Dynamics,* Autumn 1976, pp. 2–18.

Saxon, J. A.: "Promotional Progress Flow Chart," *Journal of Navy Civilian Manpower Management,* vol. 7, no. 4, Winter 1973, pp. 13–17.

Scanlan, B. K.: "Determinants of Job Satisfaction and Productivity," *Personnel Journal,* vol. 55, no. 1, 1976, pp. 12–14.

Schaffer, Robert H.: "Demand Better Results—and Get Them," *Harvard Business Review,* November–December 1974, pp. 91–98.

Schein, Edgar H.: "Organizational Socialization and the Profession of Management," *Sloan Management Review,* Winter 1968, pp. 1–16.

———: *Process Consultation: Its Role in Organization Development,* Addison-Wesley, Reading, Mass., 1969.

———: "How 'Career Anchors' Hold Executives to Their Career Paths," *Personnel,* vol. 52, May–June 1975, pp. 11–24.

———: *Career Dynamics: Matching Individuals and Organizational Needs,* Addison-Wesley, Reading, Mass., 1978.

Schein, Virginia: "Privacy and Personnel: A Time for Action," *Personnel Journal,* December 1976, pp. 604–607.

Scherba, John: "Outplacement: An Established Personnel Function," *Personnel Administrator,* July 1978, pp. 47–55.

Schlei, Barbara Lindemann, and Paul Grossman: *Employment Discrimination Law,* Bureau of National Affairs, Washington, 1976.

Schlesinger, Len: "Performance Improvement: The Missing Component of Appraisal Systems," *Personnel Journal,* June 1976, p. 274.

Schneider, Benjamin: *Staffing Organizations,* Goodyear Publishing, Santa Monica, Calif., 1976.

Schneider, Craig E.: "Content Validity: The Necessity of a Behavioral Job Description," *Personnel Administrator,* February 1976, pp. 38–44.

Schonberger, R. J.: "Inflexible Working Conditions Keep Women 'Unliberated'," *Personnel Journal,* November 1972, p. 834.

Schoonmaker, A. N.: *Executive Career Strategy,* American Management Association, New York, 1971.

Schrader, Albert W.: "Let's Abolish the Annual Performance Review," *Management of Personnel Quarterly,* Fall 1969.

Schreiber, Carol T.: *Changing Places: Women and Men in Non-Traditional Clerical, Craft and Technical Jobs,* Yale University, Department of Administrative Sciences, New Haven, Conn., 1977.

Schwab, Donald P., and Larry L. Cummings: "Theories of Performance and Satisfaction: A Review," *Industrial Relations,* vol. 9, October 1970, pp. 408–430.

———, Herbert G. Heneman III, and T. A. DeCotiis: "Behaviorally Anchored Scales: A Review of the Literature," *Personnel Psychology,* Winter 1975.

Schwartz, Irving R.: "Self Assessment and Career Planning: Matching Individual and Organizational Goals," *Personnel,* January–February 1979, pp. 47–52.

Scott, Richard D.: "Taking Subjectivity out of Performance Appraisal," *Personnel,* vol. 50, no. 4, July–August 1973, pp. 45–49.

Scott, William G.: *Organization Concepts and Analysis,* Dickenson Publishing Co., Belmont, Calif., 1969.

Seamans, Lyman H., Jr.: "What's Lacking in Most Skills Inventories," *Personnel Journal,* March 1978.

Selfridge, Richard J., and Stanley L. Sokolik: "A Comprehensive View of Organization Development," *MSU Business Topics,* Winter 1975, pp. 46–61.

Shaeffer, Ruth: *Staffing Systems: Managerial and Professional Jobs,* The Conference Board, New York, 1972.

———: *Nondiscrimination in Employment: Changing Perspectives, 1963–1972,* The Conference Board, New York, 1973.

———: *Nondiscrimination in Employment, 1973–1975: A Broadening and Deepening National Effort,* The Conference Board, New York, 1975.

Sheehy, Gail: *Passages: Predictable Crises of Adult Life,* Dutton, New York, 1976.

Sheibar, Paul: "Personnel Practices Review: A Personnel Audit Activity," *Personnel Journal,* March 1974, pp. 211–216.

———: "A Simple Selection System Called Jobmatch," *Personnel Journal,* January 1979, pp. 26–29, 53.

Sheppard, Harold L.: "Work and Retirement," in R. H. Binstock and Ethel Shanas (eds.), *Handbook of Aging and the Social Sciences,* Van Nostrand Reinhold, New York, 1977, pp. 286–309.

———: and N. Q. Herrick: *Where Have All the Robots Gone? Worker Dissatisfaction in the '70's,* The Free Press, New York, 1972.

Sherman, Harvey: *It All Depends,* University of Alabama Press, University, 1967.

Short, Larry E.: "Planned Organizational Change," *MSU Business Topics,* Autumn 1973, pp. 53–61.

Sibson, Robert E.: "Executive Pay—Onus on the Bonus," *Nation's Business,* November 1972, pp. 69–73.

Sims, Henry P., Jr, Andrew D. Szilagyi, and Robert T. Keller: "The Measurement of Job

Characteristics," *Academy of Management Journal,* vol. 19, no. 2, June 1976, pp. 195–212.

Sirbu, Marvin A.: "Automating Office Communications: The Policy Dilemmas," *Technology Review,* vol. 81, no. 1, October 1978, pp. 50–57.

Sloan, Stanley, and Alton C. Johnson, "New Context of Personnel Appraisal," *Harvard Business Review,* vol. 46, no. 6, November–December, 1968, pp. 14–31.

Slusher, E. Allen: "A Systems Look at Performance Appraisal," *Personnel Journal,* February 1975, pp. 114–117.

Smith, Arthur B., Jr.: *Employment Discrimination Law: Cases and Materials,* Bobbs Merrill, Indianapolis, 1978.

Smith, A. R.: *Models of Manpower Systems,* English Universities Press, London, 1970.

Smith, Lee: "Equal Opportunity Rules Are Getting Tougher," *Fortune,* June 19, 1978, pp. 152–156. (a)

———: "The EEOC's Bold Foray into Job Evaluation," *Fortune,* Sept. 11, 1978, pp. 58–64. (b)

Smith, P., L. Kendall, and C. Hulin: *The Measurement of Satisfaction in Work and Retirement,* Rand McNally, Chicago, 1969.

Sobkowiak, Roger T.: "Human Resource Planning: A Simulation Model," paper presented at the ORSA/TIMS Conference, Miami, Fl., 1976.

Sokolik, Stanley L.: "Reorganize the Personnel Department?" *California Management Review,* vol. 11, no. 3, Spring 1969, pp 43–51.

Souerwine, Andrew: *Career Strategies: Planning for Personal Growth,* AMACOM, New York, 1978.

Spencer, Hollister: "Task Definition and Exposition: The Catalyst in the Matching Process," *Personnel Journal,* June 1974, pp. 428–434.

Spirn, Steven, and Lanny Solomon: "A Key Element in EDP Personnel Management: Functional Job Analysis," *Personnel Journal,* November 1976, pp. 552–567.

Steers, Richard, and Lyman Porter: *Motivation and Work Behavior,* McGraw-Hill, New York, 1978.

Stein, Carroll I.: "Objective Management Systems: Two to Five Years after Implementation," *Personnel Journal,* October 1975, pp. 525–528, 549 ff.

Steiner, George A. (ed.): *Managerial Long-Range Planning,* Macmillan & Co., New York, 1969.

Steiner, Jerome: "What Price Success?" *Harvard Business Review,* March–April 1972, pp. 69–74.

Stewart, Rosemary: "To Understand the Manager's Job: Consider Demands, Constraints, Choices," *Organizational Dynamics,* 1977, pp. 22–32.

———: *Managers and Their Jobs,* Macmillan, New York, 1967.

———: *Contrasts in Management,* McGraw-Hill, New York, 1976.

Stone, C. Harold, and Floyd L. Ruch: "Selection, Interviewing and Testing," in D. Yoder and H. Heneman (eds.), *ASPA Handbook of Personnel and Industrial Relations,* vol. 1, Bureau of National Affairs, Washington, 1974, pp. 118–135.

Strauss, George: "Organization Development," in R. Dubin (ed.), *Handbook of Work, Organization and Society,* Rand McNally, Chicago, 1976, pp. 617–686.

———: "Managerial Practices," in J. R. Hackman and J. L. Suttle (eds.), *Improving Life at Work,* Goodyear Publishing, Santa Monica, Calif., 1977, pp. 1–29.

Super, D. E.: *The Psychology of Careers,* Harper and Row, New York, 1957.

Sutermeister, Robert A.: *People and Productivity,* 3d ed., McGraw-Hill, New York, 1976.

Suttle, J. Lloyd: "Improving Life at Work: Problems and Prospects," in J. R. Hackman and J. L. Suttle (eds.), *Improving Life at Work,* Goodyear Publishers, Santa Monica, Calif., 1977, pp. 1–29.

Taylor, James C., and David G. Bowers: *Survey of Organizations,* University of Michigan, Ann Arbor, 1972.

Taylor, James D.: "The Human Side of Work: The Socio-Technical Approach to Work Systems Design," *Personnel Review,* Summer 1975, pp. 17–22.

Tetz, Frank: "System for Managing Human Resources," *Journal of Systems Management,* October 1974.

Theodore, A. (ed.): *The Professional Woman,* Schenkman Publishing, Cambridge, Mass., 1971.

Thomsen, David J.: "Keeping Track of Managers in a Large Corporation," *Personnel,* vol. 53, no. 6, November–December 1976, pp. 23–27.

———: "Eliminating Pay Discrimination Caused by Job Evaluation," *Personnel,* vol. 55, no. 5, September–October 1978, pp. 11–22.

Thompson, P. H., and G. W. Dalton: "Performance Appraisal: Managers Beware," *Harvard Business Review,* vol. 48, no. 1, January–February 1970, pp. 149–157.

Tiger, Lionel: "Is This Trip Necessary: The Heavy Human Costs of Moving Executives Around," *Fortune,* September 1974, pp. 139–144.

"The Tightening Squeeze on White Collar Pay," *Business Week,* Sept. 12, 1977, pp. 82–94.

Tornow, Walter W., and Patrick R. Pinto: "The Development of a Managerial Job Taxonomy: A System for Describing, Classifying and Evaluating Executive Positions," *Journal of Applied Psychology,* vol. 61, no. 4, 1976, pp. 410–418.

Towers, Perrin, Forster & Crosby, Inc.: *Corporate Manpower Planning: A Survey of 220 Organizations,* New York, 1971.

———: *Top 100 Compensation Study 1978,* New York, 1979.

Travin, Richard: "Manpower Bank and Reward Systems for Professionals," *Personnel,* July–August 1973, pp. 19–29.

Trice, Harrison, and George Ritzer: "The Personnel Manager and His Self Image," *Personnel Administrator,* vol. 38, no. 1, 1972, pp. 46–51.

Tuckett, Peter J. F.: *Military Manpower Planning: A Responsive Approach,* Naval Postgraduate School, Monterey, Calif., December 1974.

Tullis, Richard B.: "Manpower Planning Today, Management Power Tomorrow," *The President's Forum,* Spring 1969.

Turner, A. N., and Paul R. Lawrence: *Industrial Jobs and the Worker,* Harvard University, Boston, 1965.

U.S. Civil Service Commission: *From Slogan to Reality: The Severely Handicapped in Federal Service,* Bureau of Recruiting and Examining, Manpower Source Division, Office of Public Policy Employment Programs, Washington, 1973.

———: *Planning Your Staffing Needs,* U.S. Civil Service Commission, Bureau of Policies and Standards, Washington, 1977.

U.S. Department of Labor, Manpower Administration: *Handbook for Analyzing Jobs,* U.S. Government Printing Office, Washington, 1972.

Uyterhoeven, Hugo E. R.: "General Managers in the Middle," *Harvard Business Review,* March–April 1972, pp. 75–85.

Van Maanen, J. (ed.): *Organizational Careers: Some New Perspectives,* John Wiley & Sons, New York, 1977.

———: "People Processing: Strategies of Organizational Socialization," *Organizational Dynamics,* Summer 1978, pp. 19–36.

—— and Edgar H. Schein: *Improving the Quality of Worklife: Career Development,* U.S. Department of Labor, Monograph Series on Strategies for Improving the Quality of Worklife, Washington, 1975.

Vetter, E. W.: *Manpower Planning for High Talent Personnel,* Bureau of Industrial Relations, University of Michigan, Ann Arbor, 1967.

Vroom, Victor H.: *Work and Motivation,* John Wiley & Sons, New York, 1964.

—— and K. R. MacCrimmon: "Towards a Stochastic Model of Management Careers," *Administrative Science Quarterly,* vol. 13, no. 1, June 1968, pp. 26–46.

Wade v. Mississippi Cooperative Extension Service, 373 F. Supp. 126, 1974.

Walker, James W.: "Forecasting Manpower Needs," *Harvard Business Review,* March–April 1969, pp. 152–175.

——: "Problems in Managing Manpower Change: Some Obstacles to Overcome," *Business Horizons,* February 1970, pp. 63–68.

——: "Manpower Planning: An Integrated Approach," *Management of Personnel Quarterly,* vol. 16, no. 1, Spring 1970, pp. 38–42.

——: "Individual Career Planning: Managerial Help for Subordinates," *Business Horizons,* vol. 16, no. 1, February 1973, pp. 65–72.

——: "Evaluating the Practical Effectiveness of Human Resource Planning Applications," *Human Resource Management,* vol. 13, no. 1, Spring 1974, pp. 19–27.

——: "Human Resource Planning: Managerial Concerns and Practices," *Business Horizons,* June 1976, pp. 55–59.

——: "Let's Get Realistic about Career Paths," *Human Resource Management,* Fall 1976, pp. 2–7.

——: *A Methodology for Planning and Reviewing Bank Officer Staffing Requirements,* a paper presented at the sixth annual meeting, Northeastern Region, American Institute for Decision Sciences, Albany, N.Y., 1977 (a).

——: "Personal and Career Development," in D. Yoder and H. G. Heneman, Jr. (eds.), *ASPA Handbook of Personnel and Industrial Relations,* vol. 5, Bureau of National Affairs, Washington, 1977, pp. 57–64. (b)

—— (ed.): *The Challenge of Human Resource Planning,* Human Resource Planning Society, New York, 1979.

—— and Thomas G. Gutteridge: *Career Planning Practices,* AMACOM, New York, 1979.

—— and Harriet L. Lazer: *The End of Mandatory Retirement: Implications for Management,* John Wiley & Sons, New York, 1978.

—— and Michael N. Wolfe: "Patterns in Human Resource Planning Practices," *Human Resource Planning,* vol. 1, no. 4, 1978, pp. 189–198.

Walters, Roy W.: *Job Enrichment for Results: Strategies for Successful Implementation,* Addison-Wesley Publishing Co., Reading, Mass., 1975.

Walton, Richard: "Improving the Quality of Worklife," *Harvard Business Review,* May–June, 1974, pp. 12ff.

Wangler, Lawrence A.: "The Intensification of the Personnel Role," *Personnel Journal,* vol. 58, no. 2, February 1979, pp. 111–120.

Wanous, John P.: "Tell It Like It Is at Realistic Job Previews," *Personnel,* 1975, pp. 52–60.

——: "Realistic Job Previews: Can a Procedure To Reduce Turnover Also Influence the Relationship between Abilities and Performance?" *Personnel Psychology,* vol. 31, no. 3, Summer 1978, pp. 249–258.

——: *Organizational Entry: Recruitment, Selection and Socialization of Newcomers,* Addison-Wesley, Reading, Mass., 1979.

Weber, Arnold R.: "The Bonus Babies," *Wall Street Journal,* May 15, 1978, p. 17.

Weber, W. L.: "Manpower Planning in Hierarchical Organizations: A Computer Simulation Approach," *Management Science,* vol. 18, no. 8, November 1971, pp. 119–144.

———— and E. Hofman: "Quantitative Techniques for Bridging the Decision Gap in Manpower Planning," in Larry Moore (ed.), *Manpower Planning for Canadians,* University of British Columbia, Institute of Industrial Relations, Vancouver, B.C., 1975, pp. 277–281.

Wedderburn, D.: *Co-ordinated Technical and Manpower Planning for Change,* OECD, Paris, 1967.

————: *Enterprise Planning for Change: Co-ordination of Manpower and Technical Planning,* OECD, Paris, 1968.

Weeks, David A.: *Compensating Employees: Lessons of the 1970's,* Report No. 707, The Conference Board Reports, New York, 1976.

Weihrich, Heinz, and Jack Mendleson: *Management: An MBO Approach,* Kendall-Hunt, Dubuque, Iowa, 1978.

Wendt, George R.: "Should Courts Write Your Job Descriptions?" *Personnel Journal,* September 1976, pp. 447–450.

Wernimont, Paul F.: "Recruitment Policies and Practices," in D. Yoder and H. Heneman (eds.), *ASPA Handbook of Personnel and Industrial Relations,* vol. 1, Bureau of National Affairs, Washington, 1974, pp. 86–114.

Werther, William B., Jr.: "Flexible Compensation Evaluated," *California Management Review,* vol. 19, no. 1, Fall 1976, pp. 40–46.

Westin, Alan, and Michael A. Baker: *Data Banks in a Free Society,* Quadrangle, New York, 1978.

"What Is the Personnel Manager's Job?" *Personnel Journal,* August 1973, pp. 735–736.

What Makes an Executive? Columbia University Press, New York, 1955.

Whisler, T. L., and S. F. Harper (eds.): *Performance Appraisal Research and Practice,* Holt, Rinehart and Winston, New York, 1965.

White, Ben H.: "Problems of Industrial Organizations in Manpower Planning and Forecasting," in E. Burack and J. Walker (eds.), *Manpower Planning and Programming,* Allyn and Bacon, Boston, 1972, pp. 63–76.

White, Harrison: *Chains of Opportunity: System Models of Mobility in Organizations,* Harvard University Press, Cambridge, Mass., 1970. (a)

————: "Matching Vacancies and Mobility," *Journal of Political Economy,* vol. 78, no. 1, January–February 1970, pp. 97–105. (b)

White, Todd: "Increasing Your Effectiveness as a Training and Development Professional," *Training and Development Journal,* May 1979, pp. 3–12.

Wikstrom, Walter S.: "Charting Management Manpower Plans," *Management Record,* July–August 1961, pp. 8–14.

————: *Developing Managerial Competence: Changing Concepts and Emerging Practices,* The Conference Board, New York, 1964.

————: *Manpower Planning: Evolving Systems,* The Conference Board, New York, 1971.

Wilson, Michael: *Job Analysis for Human Resource Management: A Review of Selected Research and Development,* Manpower Research Monograph No. 36, U.S. Department of Labor, Washington, February 1974.

Wirtz, Willard: *The Boundless Resource,* The New Republic Book Company, Washington, 1975.

Woodman, Richard W., and John J. Sherwood: "A Comprehensive Look at Job Design," *Personnel Journal,* August 1977, pp. 384–418.

Wooton, Leland, and Jim L. Tarter: "The Productivity Audit: A Key Tool for Executives," *MSU Business Topics,* Spring 1976, pp. 31–41.

Wortman, Max S., and Joann Sperling: *Defining the Manager's Job,* 2d ed., AMACOM, New York, 1975.

Yoder, Dale: *Personnel Principles and Policies,* Prentice-Hall, Englewood Cliffs, N.J., 1952.

Young, Mary E.: *The Role of Women in the Workforce (A Bibliography with Abstracts),* National Technical Information Service, Springfield, Va., February 1976.

Younger, Jonathan C.: "Response to Carey's Participative Job Evaluation Article," *Compensation Review,* vol. 10, no. 3, Third Quarter 1978, pp. 47–50.

Zaleznik, Abraham: "Managers and Leaders: Are They Different?" *Harvard Business Review,* vol. 55, no. 3, May–June 1977, pp. 67–78.

Indexes

Name Index

Subject Index